Understanding Violence and Victimization

FIFTH EDITION

Robert J. Meadows
California Lutheran University

Prentice Hall
Upper Saddle River, New Jersey
Columbus, Ohio

Library of Congress Cataloging-in-Publication Data

Meadows, Robert J.
    Understanding violence and victimization/Robert J. Meadows.—5th ed.
        p.   cm.
Includes bibliographical references and index.
ISBN-13: 978-0-13-515464-9 (alk. paper)
ISBN-10: 0-13-515464-2 (alk. paper)
    1. Victims of crimes.   2. Violent crimes.   3. Violence.   I. Title.
HV6250.25.M43 2010
362.88—dc22

2008049589

Editor in Chief: Vernon Anthony
Acquisitions Editor: Tim Peyton
Editorial Assistant: Alicia Kelly
Production Coordination: Shiji Sashi
Project Manager: Renata Butera
Operations Supervisor: Renata Butera
Art Director: Jayne Conte
Cover Designer: Bruce Kenselaar
Cover art/image/photo[s]: Getty Images, Inc.
Director of Marketing: David Gesell
Marketing Manager: Adam Klosa
Marketing Coordinator: Alicia Dysert

Photo credits appear on same page as image.

This book was set in 11/13, Palatino by Integra and was printed and bound by Bind-Rite, Robbinsville/
Command Web. The cover was printed by Bind-Rite, Robbinsville/Command Web.

Pearson Education Ltd., London
Pearson Education Singapore Pte. Ltd
Pearson Education Canada, Inc.
Pearson Education—Japan
Pearson Education Australia PTY, Limited

Pearson Education North Asia Ltd., Hong Kong
Pearson Educación de Mexico, S.A. de C.V.
Pearson Education Malaysia Pte. Ltd.
Pearson Education Upper Saddle River,
    New Jersey

Prentice Hall
is an imprint of

www.pearsonhighered.com

10 9 8 7 6 5 4 3
ISBN-13: 978-0-13-515464-9
ISBN-10:   0-13-515464-2

Contents

Preface   ix

1 Measuring and Understanding Violence   1

Learning Objectives   1

Introduction   1

The Fear of Violent Crime   2

Fear and Effect of Violent Crime   3

Crime Data   5

Sources of Data on Victimization   5

The Uniform Crime Reports (UCR)   5 • The National Crime
Victimization Survey (NCVS)   9

Statistics on Violent Crime   10   *Understanding Violence*   12
The Individual Influences   15   *The Familial Influences*   21
The Community influences   24

SUMMARY   26   KEY TERMS AND CONCEPTS   27   DISCUSSION QUESTIONS   27
WEB SOURCES   27   RECOMMENDED READINGS   27   REFERENCES   28

2 Victimization Theory   31

Learning Objectives   31

Introduction   31

Impact of Victimization   32

Culture of Victimization   38   Review of Early Victimization Theory   40
Hentig's Victim Classification   40   Mendelshon's Typology   42   Sellin and
Wolfgang's Typology of Victimization   43

Modern Victimization Theories   44

Cultural Trappings   44   Victim Precipitation Theory   45   Spatial
Relations   48   The New Technology   51

SUMMARY   53   KEY TERMS AND CONCEPTS   54   DISCUSSION QUESTIONS AND
LEARNING ACTIVITIES   54   WEB SOURCES   55   RECOMMENDED READINGS   55
REFERENCES   55

3   Victims of Intimate Violence   58

Learning Objectives   58

Introduction   58

The Stalking Problem   59

Anti-Stalking Legislation   64   Federal Law on Stalking   67
The Psychological and Social Consequences of Stalking   67

Intimate Partner Violence   68

Extended Victims of Partner Violence   71   Explaining Partner
Violence   73   Recognizing a Potentially Abusive Partner   76

The Law and Domestic Violence   78

Developments in the States   79   The Federal Crime Control Act
and Domestic Violence   86

Elder Abuse and Neglect   87

Nursing Home Negligence   89

Child Abuse and Neglect   91

Child Victims of Sexual Exploitation   95

Victims of Rape and Sexual Violence   96

Marital Rape   97   Date Rape and Dating Violence   98   Impact
of Rape and Dating Violence   102   Responding to Victims of Rape
and Sexual Assault   102

SUMMARY   103   KEY TERMS AND CONCEPTS   103   DISCUSSION QUESTIONS AND
LEARNING ACTIVITIES   104   WEB SOURCES   104   RECOMMENDED READINGS   104
REFERENCES   105

4   Stranger Violence and Victimization   110

Learning Objectives   110

Introduction   110

Robbery   111

Home Invasion Robbery   112   Carjacking   115

Murders and Assaults by Strangers   118

Spontaneous Murders   118   Directed Targets   124

Bias and Hate-Motivated Crimes   127

Hate and Bias Crime Legislation   131

SUMMARY   131   KEY TERMS AND CONCEPTS   132   DISCUSSION QUESTIONS AND
LEARNING ACTIVITIES   132   WEB SOURCES   132   RECOMMENDED READINGS   133
REFERENCES   133

5   Workplace Violence and Harassment   135

Learning Objectives   135

Introduction   135

Overview of Violence in the Workplace   136

Categorization of Workplace Violence   141

Sources of Workplace Violence   142

Warning Signs of Violence   144

Bullying in the Workplace   157

Employer Liability for Workplace Victimization   159

Sexual Harassment and Legal Liability   163

Reducing the Violence Threat: The Targeted Human Resource
Approach   166

SUMMARY   170   KEY TERMS AND CONCEPTS   170   DISCUSSION QUESTIONS AND
LEARNING ACTIVITIES   170   WEB SOURCES   171   RECOMMENDED READINGS   171
REFERENCES   172

6   School Violence and Victimization   174

Learning Objectives   174

Introduction   174

Research on School Crime and Violence   175

Teachers at Risk   183

Explaining School Violence   184

Early Warning Signs of Violent Behavior   189

Bullying   189   Understanding School Violence   190

Responding to School Violence   193

SUMMARY   198   KEY TERMS AND CONCEPTS   199   DISCUSSION QUESTIONS AND
LEARNING ACTIVITIES   199   WEB SOURCES   199   RECOMMENDED READINGS   200
REFERENCES   200

7   Criminal Justice Injustice   **203**

Learning Objectives   203

Introduction   203

Sources of Injustice   204

The Police   204
    Remedies for Police Injustice   207

Prosecution and the Judicial Process   208

Crime Legislation and Injustice   216

Corrections   221

SUMMARY   224   KEY TERMS AND CONCEPTS   224   DISCUSSION QUESTIONS AND
LEARNING ACTIVITIES   224   WEB SOURCES   225   RECOMMENDED READINGS   225
REFERENCES   225

8   The Violence of Terrorism   **227**

Learning Objectives   227

Introduction   227

Domestic and International Terrorism   228
    Domestic Terrorism   228   International Terrorism   233

The Violence and Victims of Terrorism   237
    Motives of Violence   239
        Secular Motivations   240 • Nonsecular Motivations   240
    Violence Dissemination   241   Suicide Terrorism   242

Weapons of Mass Destruction   243
    *Biological and Chemical Weapons   243   Nuclear or Radiological
    Terrorism   244   Cyber Terrorism   245*

Combating Terrorism   246
    Homeland Security   246

The USA Patriot Act   247

SUMMARY 248   KEY TERMS AND CONCEPTS 248   DISCUSSION QUESTIONS AND
LEARNING ACTIVITIES 248   WEB SOURCES 249   RECOMMENDED READINGS 249
REFERENCES 250

9   Responding to Criminal Victimization   253

Learning Objectives   253

Introduction   253

Proactive Responses   254

   Community Violence Prevention Strategies   254

      Rebuilding the Village   254 • Providing Access to Health
      Care   255 • Improving Bonding, Attachment, and Connectedness
      Dynamics   255 • Improving Self-Esteem   255 • Increasing Social
      Skills   256 • Reestablishing the Adult Protective Shield   256 •
      Minimizing the Residual Effects of Trauma   256 • Law and
      Prevention   257

   Personal Defense Measures and the Gun Debate   257   *Security
   Measures*   260   *Opportunity Reduction Strategies*   264

      Defensible Space Theory   264 • Crime Prevention Through
      Environmental Design   266 • Situational Crime Prevention   271

Reactive Responses to Victimization   271

   Victim Rights and Compensation Programs   275   *Legislation to
   Protect Victims*   283

Sexual Offender Notification Laws   286

   Sexually Violent Predator Act   286   *Anti-Gang Legislation*   287
   Crime Control Legislation in 2000 and Beyond   288   *Victim Advocacy
   Groups*   291   *Civil Justice for Victims*   294

SUMMARY 297   KEY TERMS AND CONCEPTS 298   DISCUSSION QUESTIONS AND
LEARNING ACTIVITIES 298   WEB SOURCES 299   RECOMMENDED READINGS 299
REFERENCES 300   FURTHER READINGS 303

Appendix A: Major Sources of Victimization Data and Information   305

Appendix B: Resource Guide   308

Index   311

Preface

Violence and the resulting victimization have a serious impact on individuals and society. It is difficult to predict when or where they will occur. In writing this book, I have been interested in exploring selected types of violence, particularly the types that capture media and public attention because of their seriousness, callousness, and, in some cases, randomness. Therefore, I choose not to write about nonviolent victimization, such as property crimes and frauds. It is not my intention to downplay the importance of these crimes, but to focus more on the crimes of violence that we fear most.

This book combines theories on violence, victimization with applied responses to victimization. It is written for the person studying victimization and violence, as well as for those employed in crime prevention and victim service programs. My purpose is to discuss offender-victim relationships, provide data, and explore situational factors and responses to victims. Also discussed are some precursors of violence such as stalking and harassment. Throughout the book are case studies called *Focuses* that enhance points and can be used to generate discussion. A constant theme in this book is that the experience of violence, whether at home, in the community, or as the result of personal assault or abuse, has a devastating effect. Many criminals who commit violence on others have mental disease, abusive or dysfunctional backgrounds, leading to targeting others for personal gain, thrill, recognition, or hate. Sometimes violence perpetrated by these predators is planned, committed in the course of completing other crimes, or simply a random act.

Other forms of violence such as terrorism are the result of political or religious convictions.

New to this edition is a chapter on understanding violence. In this chapter (Chapter 1), some causes of violence as well as data on violent crime measures and the fear violence causes in others are presented. Chapter 2 addresses theory of victimization. It introduces criminal victimization, discussing how and why some people are victimized. Chapter 3 covers intimate victimizations, such as domestic violence, child abuse, elder abuse, rape, dating violence, and stalking. My intent in this chapter is to address legal and social issues of intimate violence, as well as preventive measures. Chapter 4 addresses stranger violence. Two of the most prevalent types of stranger violence are murder and robbery. The chapter focuses on the situations in which people become victims of violence by strangers and what can be done to prevent these occurrences. There is also a discussion of serial killers, their motives, and their victims. Chapter 5 focuses on workplace violence and harassment. These are important topics because of the stresses of the work environment and attacks on coworkers by disgruntled employees or by third parties. Research conducted on the sources of and responses to workplace violence is covered. The purpose is to offer suggestions on what can be done to reduce the potential for violence.

Chapter 6 addresses school violence and victimization. Because of recent acts of violence on our nation's campuses, I felt compelled to discuss some possible explanations and responses. After all, schools are microcosms of society, as are some workplaces and communities. Chapter 7 discusses how the criminal justice system, through its decision-making capacities, causes victimization, either intentionally or inadvertently. Why is it that the police overstep their authority, or why are some persons convicted of crimes they never committed? Are laws designed to address violent crime being applied fairly? Chapter 8 discusses terrorism. The threat of terrorism and the random violence it produces instill new fears in American citizens. Presented in this chapter are motives, strategies, and types of terrorism. In Chapter 9, selective proactive and reactive crime response measures are addressed. The chapter concludes with a presentation of measures to aid victims through victim compensation programs and laws. In some instances, victims seek relief from the courts in the form of personal damages from property owners. Victims criminally assaulted at work or on private property, for instance, may have a civil case against a property owner or manager. Thus, litigation has an impact on organizational business policy and operations.

I would like to offer a disclaimer. Throughout the book, I refer to a number of legal cases and crime response procedures. They are offered as a general guide. I recognize that laws, statistics, and procedures may change or may not apply in some situations. By the time this edition is published, new laws or amendments to existing ones may be instituted. To address this problem, I have included an appendix (Appendix A) with information on retrieving current information relative to victimization. The reader is also advised to consult with local law enforcement or other authorities for information on changes or new programs relevant to victimology.

ACKNOWLEDGMENTS

I want to thank my family for their patience and understanding. Special thanks to Robin Baliszewski and Frank Schmalleger for inspiring me to write in the first place. I wish to express my appreciation to the Prentice Hall staff, especially Sarah Holle, and others for working with me on the preparation of this book. I especially want to thank California Lutheran University students Tiffany Holzer and Shannon Quigley for assisting in the research for this fifth edition. Without their dedication and hard work, numerous updates and expanded sections would not have been possible. I thank former California Lutheran University students Brittany Bartold, Shantee Ravare, Precious Moyo, Stephen Seper, Sirrel Maldonado II, Jennifer Weir, Claire Gordon, and Pat Engle, faculty secretary, for assisting with word processing. I also thank the following reviewers who offered advice in preparing this edition: Thompson Ryan, Utica; Debra Johnson, Lindenwood University; Tom Gilligan, Remington College; Betty Walker, Remington College–Mobie Campus, Susan Craig, University of Central Florida.

ABOUT THE AUTHOR

Robert J. Meadows is Professor and Chair of Criminal Justice at California Lutheran University. Dr. Meadows' research and teaching interests include legal issues in criminal justice, security, violence and victimization, and delinquency. He authored a book on Saudi Arabian justice and a parent's guide for coping with difficult teenagers. He is also a coauthor of *Evil Minds: Understanding and Responding to Violent Predators*. Dr. Meadows is a member of the Academy of Criminal Justice Sciences and the American Society of Industrial Security.

1

Measuring and Understanding Violence

LEARNING OBJECTIVES

After studying this chapter, you will:

- Be able to explain the meaning of violent crime
- Learn about reported and unreported crime
- Understand the impact of violent crime
- Learn about the fear of crime
- Become familiar with some general reasons for violent behavior
- Understand the dynamics of violence

INTRODUCTION

> *Many causes of violence concern issues of morality, love, fear, anger, jealousy, injustice, and many other emotions. The majority of cases of violence occur because of anger. Anger is an emotional state that varies in intensity from mild irritation to intense fury and rage.*
>
> —American Psychological Association

Interpersonal violence is committed every day in our homes, schools, businesses, and on the streets. These nonsanctioned acts such as murder, assault, and robbery are committed for profit, revenge, jealousy, political or religious motives (terrorists), or simply for pleasure. There is no shortage of motives in explaining violence, and there certainly is an ample supply of candidates seeking to impose violence on others for whatever reason. A number of factors, such as dysfunctional families and communities, drug addiction, mental illness, learning disabilities, or other conditions, cause violent crime.

On the other hand, violent offenders are not always disenfranchised street criminals or predatory gang members. Numerous examples exist of violent criminals reared in so-called stable middle-class families, with no criminal history, and who have achieved high social status. Education and social status are no barriers to violence.

Consider the physician who kills his ex-wife to avoid expensive alimony payments; the stockbroker who kills his entire family and himself to save them embarrassment from poor investments; or, the wealthy, privileged, high school students who kill a classmate just to experience the thrill of killing. This chapter begins with a discussion on the fear of crime, followed by an overview of crime data, and concludes with some general explanations of criminal violence in American society.

THE FEAR OF VIOLENT CRIME

> *We look forward to a world founded upon four essential freedoms. First is the freedom of speech and expression. The second is freedom of every person to worship God in his own way. The third is freedom from want. . . . The fourth is freedom from fear.*
>
> —Franklin D. Roosevelt

During the early morning hours of April 16, 2007, a disgruntled mentally distraught Virginia Tech student entered a dormitory and class room and killed 32 fellow students, faculty, and staff and left about 30 others injured in the deadliest shooting rampage in the nation's history. The shooter carried a 9 mm semiautomatic and a .22 caliber handgun. He later committed suicide. On a cold February night, handyman Cary Stayner, with a gun and rope, knocked on the door of Room 509 at the Cedar Lodge Motel near Yosemite National Park. Inside were three tourists, a mother and her 15-year-old daughter and a young family friend. According to the offender's own admissions, he entered the cabin room, strangled and sexually assaulted two of the women at the scene, and savagely murdered all three.

The victims were removed from the cabin and burned beyond recognition. Six months later, on July 14, his rage continued: he murdered and decapitated Joie Armstrong, a 26-year-old environmental educator assigned to the park. After his arrest, the quiet loner admitted that he held a hatred for women, a hatred he had felt since he was 7 years old. In 2005 and 2006, a string of freeway shootings in Los Angeles engendered fear and panic for many freeway commuters. Several commuters were killed while driving in their cars in apparently unrelated and unsolved attacks. In at least three cases, the shooters were in other cars. Although so-called road rage is blamed for some of the shootings, other shootings are believed to be by snipers.

The murdered victims in each of the preceding situations had no warning and in some cases did not know the killers. Who would expect this type of violence in a national park, on a highway, or on a college campus? We constantly read about gang and youth violence, racial and hate crimes, terrorism, and domestic violence, including child and elder abuse. As a nation, we rank first of all developed nations in the world in the number of homicides. The recent surge of school shootings, although rare, is not restricted to crime-ridden schools but also occurs in middle-class communities. And, we will never forget the sniper shootings in the Washington, D.C., area and the calculated attacks of September 11, 2001, when Islamic extremists killed thousands of innocent people. In addressing violent criminal acts, we need to understand the definition of violent crime. Violent crime for the purposes of this book is those acts committed against another in violation of a prescribed law. Examples of these offenses are murder, sexual assault, robbery, weapons crimes, or crimes involving bodily harm.

Fear and Effect of Violent Crime

In many communities, the right to be free from fear has been replaced by the knowledge that most of us will be victims of violence at some time in our lives, or at least direct witnesses. The fear of violence results from past victimizations, media accounts of violent crime, and interactions with people who are knowledgeable about or have witnessed crime.

A *Los Angeles Times* poll asked Americans whether their fear of crime was based on what they read or heard from the media or what they had personally experienced. Sixty-five percent of the respondents reported that the media were responsible for their perceptions; 21 percent reported personal experiences (Russell, 1995) were responsible. Of 119 black Atlantic City residents aged 65 years and over, 76 percent considered their neighborhoods to be "bad," and only 24 percent felt that their neighborhoods were safe. Fifty-one percent knew someone who had been victimized during the last year, and 27 percent had been victims of crime during that period (Joseph, 1997).

In 2003, 60 percent of Gallup Poll respondents reported that they believed there was more crime than a year ago (Bureau of Justice Statistics, 2003). In the poll, 54 percent of blacks and 47 percent of whites worried frequently or occasionally about their home being burglarized when they are not there. In addition, 43 percent of males and 55 percent of females avoided going to certain places or neighborhoods they might otherwise want to go because of their fear of crime (Bureau of Justice Statistics, 2003).

It is common to find acts of violence, such as gang attacks and robberies, reported in the news. These reports fuel the notion that crime is pervasive and thus ignite fears in the public. Part of the reason for increased fear is the expansion of the middle-aged population. As a group, they are more likely to own a gun, install burglar alarms or special locks, and practice security procedures (Russell, 1995). Thus, older citizens are concerned about their families' safety, a concern that is driven by media reports of violent crime. Research on victimization indicates that women are more fearful of crime than men, as are the elderly, the poor, and minorities (Parker, McMorris, and Smith, 1993). Those who are more fearful tend to be more likely to carry self-protection devices or participate in self-defense classes. However, many people who are fearful of violent crime really have no reason to be. Yet perceptions are powerful indicators of behavior. Studies have concluded that residents who witnessed what they thought were drug and gang behaviors were more likely to believe that all types of criminal and disorderly activity were present. In other words, residents who saw such activity believed crime, as well as moral decay, was higher in their community. These perceptions also affected their feelings of personal safety (Crank, Giacomazzi, and Heck, 2003).

Although studies have found that women and the elderly report higher levels of fear of crime than do men and younger people, these two groups are much less likely to be victimized by crime. Those who are most fearful actually report the fewest victimizations. The concept of who is fearful and who should be fearful of victimization is referred to as the **fear–victimization paradox**.

The effects of crime have had consequences on mental health and sociability, such as depression and anxiety resulting from living in a high crime area. According to an English study by Stafford, Chandola, and Marmot (2007), longitudinal data from 2002 to 2004 of more than 10,000 London civil servants aged 35–55 years revealed the negative effects of crime. The study found that the fear of crime was associated with "poorer mental health, reduced physical functioning and lower quality of life". Participants reporting greater fear were more likely to suffer from depression than those reporting lower fear of crime. Those fearful exercised less and participated in fewer social activities. The study concluded that fear of crime may be a "barrier to participation in health-promoting physical and social activities" (Strafford, Chandola, and Marmot, 2007). But what are the reasons for violence and how does one become violent? We will examine some reasons for violence.

CRIME DATA

Sources of Data on Victimization

Information on violent and nonviolent crime is available from two major sources: the Federal Bureau of Investigation's *Uniform Crime Reports (UCR)* and the Bureau of Justice Statistics' *National Crime Victimization Survey (NCVS)*, both published by the Department of Justice.

The focus of this discussion is on the *UCR* and *NCVS*. Additional sources are listed in Appendix A.

The Uniform Crime Reports (UCR).   Begun in 1930 and published annually, the *Uniform Crime Reports (UCR)* includes offenses reported to law enforcement agencies at the city, county, and state levels. State universities and colleges are required to report in the *UCR* offenses committed on their campuses. The purpose of the *UCR* is to enable law enforcement agencies to exchange information about reported crime and to assist in future crime planning and control.

The *UCR* is a nationwide reporting program, a cooperative effort of more than 16,000 city, county, and state law enforcement agencies voluntarily reporting data on crime and arrests. Indexed crimes are categorized as property and personal offenses and include murder, forcible rape, arson, burglary, robbery, larceny-theft, motor vehicle theft, and aggravated assault.

The *UCR* is valuable to law enforcement, but it has some limitations. First, it details only reported crime. Thus, the so-called **dark figure of crime**, or unreported crime, is not included. Second, the *UCR* primarily concerns arrests and offender demographics; it does not include information on victims. It is also subject to manipulation of information, or false reporting, by an agency. That is, some law enforcement agencies alter reports to reduce the negative image that may accompany high crime activity in their communities (McCleary, Nienstedt, and Erven, 1982). There has been some sharp criticism in recent years of the *UCR* reporting process. Criminal justice experts warn that crime statistics are unreliable (Sherman, 1998). For example, the FBI dropped Philadelphia from its national crime-reporting program because of egregious errors in crime reporting. The city had to draw its crime figures from the *UCR* system for 1996, 1997, and at least the first half of 1998 because of underreporting and general sloppiness. The problems resulted when the police failed to take written reports of all crimes, downgraded reports to less serious offenses, or failed to take these reports very seriously (Butterfield, 1998). These errors in one city raise questions as to the validity of the decrease in violent crime rates reported in other jurisdictions in recent years.

As mentioned, dark figure of crime exists because some people are reluctant to report crimes of violence to authorities because they fear retaliation, embarrassment, or view the offenses as a private matter (Table 1–1). Also, a number of victims may be crime participants who will not report their victimization for fear of arrest. Encounters with prostitutes or drug dealers may result in victimization of the client (robbery, assault, etc.), making it less likely that that person will file an official report. In addition, coconspirators, such as drug dealers, robbers, and other criminal types, who disagree over the division of their illegal profits may victimize one another.

The decision to report a crime is a calculated one, often based on the seriousness of the offense, the probability of financial redress, the perception that the criminal justice system will take action to aid the victim, the degree of the victim's participation in the crime, the degree to which the victim is embarrassed by the crime, and the fear of personal harm if the crime is reported. The *UCR* does provide data on the nature and extent of reported crime rates in a given community. Without these reports, police are at a disadvantage in their efforts to control crime. Crime rates relate the incidence of crime to the population. The **determination of crime rates** uses the following formula:

$$\text{Crime rate} = \left(\frac{\text{Number of reported crimes}}{\text{Population of a city}} \right) \times \text{Rate}$$

To determine the rate of robbery in a city with a population of less than 100,000, for example, the total number of reported robberies for a given year is divided by the population of the city or jurisdiction, which is then multiplied by 10,000. If the city's population is more than 100,000, multiply by 100,000. To compare the crime rate of two cities, one with a population of more than 100,000 and the other less than 100,000 (e.g., 50,000), 10,000 is used. Likewise, when comparing two cities with populations of, for example, 25,000 and 6,000, multiply by 1,000.

The crime rate within a city can be determined by using the same formula. Many cities are divided into geographical reporting districts

TABLE 1–1 PERCENTAGE OF REASONS FOR NOT REPORTING VICTIMIZATIONS TO THE POLICE, BY TYPE OF CRIME

Type of crime	Number of reasons for not reporting	Total (%)	Reported to another official (%)	Private or personal matter (%)	Object recovered; offender unsuccessful (%)	Not important enough (%)	Insurance would not cover (%)
All personal crimes	3,447,480	100.0	13.0	19.8	20.1	6.4	0.1
Crimes of violence	3,271,670	100.0	13.2	20.3	20.1	6.4	0.1*
Completed violence	828,580	100.0	11.4	15.7	11.9	3.8*	0.0*
Attempted/ threatened violence	2,443,100	100.0	13.8	21.9	22.8	7.3	0.1*
Rape/Sexual assault[a]	142,410	100.0	18.2*	22.0*	3.7*	0.0*	0.0*
Robbery	392,510	100.0	2.3*	13.3	21.1	0.0*	0.0*
Completed/property taken	229,230	100.0	1.4*	9.8*	18.5	0.0*	0.0*
With injury	60,390	100.0	0.0*	0.0*	11.3*	0.0*	0.0*
Without injury	168,840	100.0	1.9*	13.4*	21.1*	0.0*	0.0*
Attempted to take property	163,280	100.0	3.6*	18.2*	24.8	0.0*	0.0*
With injury	38,960	100.0	7.7*	27.5*	9.7*	0.0*	0.0*
Without injury	124,320	100.0	2.3*	16.3*	29.6	0.0*	0.0*
Assault	2,736,760	100.0	14.5	21.3	20.8	7.6	0.1*
Aggravated	497,490	100.0	7.6	23.9	24.9	7.2	0.0*
Simple	2,239,270	100.0	16.1	20.7	19.9	7.7	0.1*
Purse snatching/ Pocket picking	175,810	100.0	9.6*	10.6*	21.6	6.8*	0.0*

TABLE 1–1 (continued)

Type of crime	Number of reasons for not reporting	Total (%)	Percentage of reasons for not reporting				
			Reported to another official (%)	Private or personal matter (%)	Object recovered; offender unsuccessful (%)	Not important enough (%)	Insurance would not cover (%)
All property crimes	14,073,950	100.0	8.6	5.1	26.7	3.9	3.0
Household burglary	2,023,280	100.0	4.2	4.2	20.2	5.5	4.5
Completed	1,710,040	100.0	3.9	5.0	18.2	3.8	4.9
Forcible entry	381,430	100.0	2.7*	4.1*	9.5*	2.3*	6.6*
Untawful entry without force	1,328,610	100.0	4.3	5.3	20.7	4.3	4.4
Attempted forcible entry	313,240	100.0	5.8*	0.0*	31.5	14.5	2.9*
Motor vehicle theft	211,600	100.0	1.3*	9.5*	31.2	0.0*	6.6*
Completed	81,870	100.0	0.0*	20.0*	5.3*	0.0*	6.8*
Attempted	129,730	100.0	2.2*	2.9*	46.9	0.0*	4.6*
Theft	11,839,070	100.0	9.5	5.2	27.8	3.7	2.7
Completed	11,455,860	100.0	9.7	5.2	27.3	3.7	2.7
Attempted	383,210	100.0	4.9*	3.4*	42.6	5.7*	2.8*

Note: Detail may not add to total shown because of rounding.
Some respondents may have cited more than one reason for not reporting victimizations to the police.
*Estimate is based on about 10 or fewer sample cases.
[a]Includes verbal threats of rape and threats of sexual assault.

Source: Bureau of Justice Statistics, 2006. Washington D.C.: U.S. Department of Justice.

or areas, and the police record reported crime in each district or area. A researcher can determine the crime rate of a specific area of a city versus another by using population and crime data. The type of crime and the crime rate of each district or area vary by such factors as population density and socioeconomic status.

The *UCR* publishes crime rates according to region, month, race, sex, and other variables. For example, the *UCR* provides data on murder and nonnegligent manslaughter, which it defines as the willful killing of one human being by another. Clearance rates—the number of crimes the police clear by arrest—are also reported. Clearance rates are higher for personal crimes (e.g., murder) than they are for property crimes (e.g., burglary). Obviously, clearance rates are driven by the chance of detection, crime scene evidence, witness and victim information, and so forth.

The National Crime Victimization Survey (NCVS).   The *National Crime Victimization Survey (NCVS)* is another source of victimization data. The *NCVS*, begun in 1972 to complement the *UCR*, recognizes incidents not reported to the police and includes a detailed report of crime incidents, victims involved, and trends affecting victims. Unlike the *UCR*, which collects data on the crime, the *NCVS* seeks detailed information on the victim. It tracks the crimes of rape, robbery, assault, burglary, personal and household larceny, and motor vehicle theft; it does not track murder, kidnapping, so-called victimless crimes, or commercial robbery and burglary.

Perhaps the most important contribution of the *NCVS* is its data about the dark figure of crime, those crimes not reported to the police. Data published by the *NCVS* are gathered from household surveys conducted by trained U.S. Census Bureau interviewers. The *NCVS* reports the following information:

- Crime records
- Profiles of crime victims
- Methods that victims of violent crime use to protect themselves
- The relationship of the victim to the offender
- The amount of crime that occurs in schools
- The extent to which weapons are involved in crimes
- Data concerning whether crimes are reported to the police

Not all crimes are reported. The data for rape as reported by the *UCR* and the *NCVS* are quite different, suggesting that for various reasons many rapes are not reported. The most common reason given by victims of violent crime (including rape) for not reporting a crime was that it was a private or personal matter. Nonreporting is also attributed to fear of reprisal, embarrassment, or the belief that the victim may not be believed.

Statistics on Violent Crime

Between 1976 and 2005, blacks, although 13 percent of the population, committed more than 52 percent of the nation's homicides . . . Ninety-four percent of black homicide victims had a black as their murderer.

Source: Bureau of Justice Statistics 2007

The above figure is frightening and raises the question as to why this is occurring. Some possible explanations are discussed later, but suffice to say there are a number of reasons in explaining violence, as well as those who commit violence. Violent crime is more likely to occur in lower socioeconomic environments such as inner cities. In these communities, unemployed youth or street gangs are more likely to exist and there is less social cohesion and community support. There is also a competition for space and jobs as new ethnic groups immigrate into these communities. Violence can be directed toward an individual or group or take place between groups competing for community resources.

Violent crime is composed of four offenses: murder and nonnegligent manslaughter, forcible rape, robbery, and aggravated assault. Violent crimes are defined and tracked by the *UCR* system. According to figures released by the Department of Justice, there was an increase of about 1.3 percent in violent offenses from 2006 to 2007. The rise was in robberies and homicides. The increase follows a 2.3 percent increase in 2005, which was the first significant increase in violent crime in 15 years. The data indicates that the increase was concentrated in medium-size cities, including the District of Columbia. The rise is attributed to an increase in the juvenile population, growing numbers of released prison inmates, and gang problems. The extent of violent crime is often regional.

The South was the most violent region in the United States in 2006, and South Carolina led the nation with 765 violent crimes per 100,000 people. That's down from 767 per 100,000 in 2005. But only the District of Columbia had a higher violent crime rate, with 1,508 violent crimes per 100,000 people.

In addition to tracking and compiling violent crime statistics, the FBI assists local agencies in apprehending violent offenders by operating the Violent Criminal Apprehension Program (VICAP). **VICAP** is a nationwide data center designed to collect, collate, and analyze information about crimes of violence—specifically murder. VICAP examines the following types of cases:

- Solved or unsolved homicides or attempted homicides, especially those that involve an abduction; that are apparently random, motiveless, or sexually oriented; or that are known or suspected to be part of a series
- Missing persons, especially when the circumstances indicate a strong possibility of foul play and the victim is still missing
- Unidentified dead bodies when the manner of death is known or suspected to be homicide

VICAP assists law enforcement agencies by coordinating a multiagency investigative force. Multiagency cooperation becomes especially important when the suspect or suspects have traveled between states and across jurisdictions. Especially valuable is the coordination of activities, such as obtaining search warrants, interviewing, and testing.

In most violent crimes, murder rates differ based on victim characteristics, but the relationship between victim characteristics and incidence of homicide tends to remain the same as in past years. Some demographic characteristics of homicide are presented here (Bureau of Justice Statistics, 2007):

Gender. Males were most often the victims and the perpetrators of homicides: They were 10 times more likely than females were to commit murder, and male and female offenders were more likely to target male rather than female victims. As for arrests for violent crimes in 2006 by gender, 76.3 percent of all persons arrested were male, and 82.2 percent of persons arrested for violent crime were male.

Race. Blacks were six times more likely to be homicide victims and seven times more likely than whites to commit homicides. Most murders are intraracial.

Age, race, and gender. In the late 1980s and early 1990s, there were large increases in the rates of both homicide offenses and victimization among young black males before there were declines and stabilization in both measures. Young adults (aged 18–24) continue to have the highest offending rates in each racial and gender group. Although much lower than the offending rates experienced in the late 1980s and early 1990s, rates for black and white males aged 18–24 remain higher in 2002 than in the mid-1980s.

What are some of the reasons for violence? Arguments involving drug or alcohol usage were often the predominant circumstance leading to murder. About 1 million violent crimes in which victims perceived the offender to have been drinking at the time of the offense occurred in 2005 (Figure 1–1). Homicides are most often committed with guns, especially handguns. In 2006, over 50 percent of homicides were committed with handguns, 16 percent with other guns, 13 percent with knives, 5 percent with blunt objects, and 16 percent with other weapons.

As for murder victims, 43 percent were related to or acquainted with their assailants; 14 percent of victims were murdered by strangers, while 43 percent of victims had an unknown relationship to their murderer in 2002. As depicted in Figure 1–1 from 1975 to 2005, arguments precipitate many murders (Bureau of Justice Statistics, 2007).

Understanding Violence

Crime statistics provide us with demographic factors associated with violence, but the underlying reasons are not included. There is no shortage of theories explaining the causes of human violence. However, it is not the intention of this book to critically examine all theories of violence, nor to advance any one theory or cause over another. Suffice to say, violence is often situational and difficult to predict or plan against it. Most theories addressing violence are grouped into trait theories: biological, psychological, sociological, economic, and so forth (see generally: Ferrell, 2004; Ferri, 2003; Robbins, Monahan, and Silver, 2003; Williams, 2004; Wilson, 1985). In general, unsanctioned violence is the result a number of personal and social

FIGURE 1–1   MURDER CIRCUMSTANCES, 1975–2005

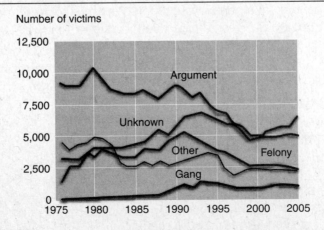

factors including mental illness, childhood abuse and neglect, brain injuries, retaliation (e.g., street gang warfare), drug use, jealousy, twisted political or religious beliefs, and so forth. Others take the approach that antisocial behavior results from a series of evolutionary stages. In other words, people become violent through a process called violentization, which involves four stages: brutalization and subjugation, belligerency, violent coaching, and criminal activity (virulency). First, this person is a victim of violence and feels powerless to avoid it. Then the victim is taught how and when to become violent and to profit from it. Then he acts on that. If a person from a violent environment does not become violent, it is because some part of the process is missing (Athens, 1992).

Violent acts may be reactionary or planned or committed in the further-ance of other crimes such as robbery, or may be committed to advance a partic-ular cause (terrorism) or to conceal the commission of other crimes. Some turn to violence because of sudden changes in lifestyle (e.g., divorce, sudden loss of employment, etc.), thrill, or the need for instant gratification. And, we cannot ignore the fact that the infliction of violence in some cases is a matter of rational choice (Earls and Reiss, 1994). Despite the seductions or other influences of crime, crime is rewarding and if the probability of getting away with crime outweighs the chances of apprehension, then crime may be the choice.

For the purposes of this discussion, the study of violence encom-passes a three-level social-ecological model. This model (Figure 1–2) is modified from research by Dahlberg and Krug (2002).[1] The model

FIGURE 1–2   INFLUENCES OF VIOLENCE

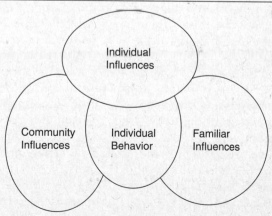

___

[1]The model originally included individual, relationship, community, and societal levels. However, the last two were combined for this discussion.

considers the interplay between **individual**, **familial**, and **community influences** experienced by a person. The three influences overlap, but the individual and familial influences are viewed as the most prominent contributors. According to the office of Juvenile Justice Programs (Loeber, 2003), the most important risk factors for delinquency and violence stem from individual and family influences, which include genetics and the child's environment. This is not to dismiss community influences; however, having quality individual characteristics and positive familial relationships will compensate for harmful community influences. This chapter focuses on individual violence as opposed to political or religious violence (terrorism), which is addressed in Chapter 8. A case study of a violent person is addressed in Focus 1–1 and 1–2.

Focus 1–1   Explaining Violence: Aileen Wuornos

Aileen Wuornos was born in 1959. Her mother married her father when she was 15 and had two children. Wournos' parents divorced within two years of the troubled marriage, before Aileen was born. Her biological father was a convicted child molester and sociopath who was strangled in prison in 1969. Her mother was unwilling to care for her children, resulting in Aileen and her brother being adopted by their maternal grandparents. Her grandmother drank heavily and was strict with the children; her grandfather physically and sexually abused Aileen as a child. Reportedly, she was often whipped with a belt by her grandfather. Her grandparents raised her and her brother with their own children. They did not reveal that they were, in fact, the children's grandparents. At the age of 12, Aileen and her brother discovered that their grandparents were not their biological parents. When they discovered their true parentage, they became more incorrigible. Aileen claimed to have had sex with multiple partners, including her own brother, at a young age. Aileen became pregnant at the age of 14. The father was unknown. Upon giving birth, the baby was put up for adoption; she was banished from her grandparents' home and disowned by the small community in which she lived. Aileen subsequently dropped out of school, left the area, and took up hitchhiking and prostitution. In 1974, she was jailed for drunk driving and firing a pistol from a moving vehicle. In 1976, Wuornos hitchhiked to Florida, where she met a 76-year-old yacht club president. They married that same year. However, Wuornos continually involved herself in confrontations at their local bar and was eventually sent to jail for assault. She also hit her elderly husband with his own cane, leading him to get a restraining order against her. She returned to prostitution and eventually murdered seven men she met while hitchhiking and soliciting truck drivers at truck stops. In 1992, Aileen was executed for the murders in Florida.

FOCUS 1–2 Explaining Violence: Gary Gilmore

Gary Gilmore murdered two young men in cold blood and refused to appeal his death sentence. He was executed in Utah in 1977. His background was violent. He was one of five children who lived dysfunctional lives. One died as an infant, one of complications from being viciously stabbed, and one by execution, and the other living brother simply wandered away. Gilmore's father, Frank, was a con man, a gypsy, an alcoholic, a brutal autocrat, and an abusive husband and father. The family moved around a lot. His father had married at least half a dozen times and had families scattered in many places. He was of no use for his children. He often disappeared without explanation for long stretches of time. His father drank heavily and vented his considerable rage on his wife Bessie, often physically assaulting her in front of the children. Shortly after Gary was born, Frank decided that Gary was not his son, but the progeny of a son of his from a previous marriage whom Bessie knew. It seemed a way for him to detach from his son the way his own father had detached from him. There was little chance that Frank would feel much affection for this boy. When Frank's sons got older, he began to whip them with a belt, much more severely than usual.

The boys soon learned that no matter what they said or did, their father simply wanted to brutalize them, all the while insisting that they love him. Their mother would not protect them. In fact, she let them know that the ideal family was childless. Eventually Gilmore's mother beat her children as she was being beaten. Gary reacted with a rebellious streak. He acted out in school, tested his courage by running in front of trains, exploited and violated friends, hung out with an antisocial crowd of boys, and engaged in petty crimes, such as burglary, auto theft, and substance abuse. This landed him in reform school, where he became more sophisticated in the criminal attitude. By the age of 16, Gary was in jail.

The Individual Influences

> *Literally speaking, bad brains lead to bad behavior. . . .One of the reasons why we have repeatedly failed to stop crime is because we have systematically ignored the biological and genetic contributions to crime causation.*

—Adrain Raine

After watching the 2008 New York Giants super bowl victory over the New England Patriots, I began thinking about the athletic accomplishments of quarterback Eli Manning and his brother Payton Manning of the Indianapolis Colts. Their father, Archie Manning, was an NFL quarterback for the New Orleans Saints for many years. Is the success of the Manning brothers a matter of luck, environment, or genes? Maybe a little of each, but their success in football could not have happened if they were 5'7"unable to throw a football more than 20 yards, and lacked the ability to remember and successfully execute dozens of plays. What we inherit has an effect on who we are or what we become. As for violent behavior, are such persons the product of their biological makeup as well? We cannot discount the argument that biology or genetics plays a role in behavior, including violent behavior.

The individual influence identifies biological and personal traits that increase the likelihood of becoming a perpetrator of violence. Behavioral genetic research has shown that genes influence individual differences in a wide range of human behaviors—cognition, academic achievement, personality and temperament (including such traits as aggression and hostility), psychopathology, and even vocational interests and social attitudes (Plomin, DeFries, and McClearn, 1989). More specifically, violent behavior and heritable factors have been implicated in the research (Moffitt, 2005). In other words, the way we behave may be related to the way we are wired. This is not to say that some are born violent and doomed to become sociopathic murderers, but there may be a tendency for some to be more aggressive and thus less likely to control emotions absent some type of positive interventions.

By analogy, medical studies have indicated certain diseases such as cystic fibrosis, sickle cell anemia, and diabetes have genetic links. Generally, if a parent has the condition, it is possible that an offspring may develop the disease later in life. As for mental illnesses, there is evidence that certain mental conditions such as chronic depression and so-called bipolar disorders are present in families and may be transmitted especially if both parents have the same illness (Zandi, 2002). A history of antisocial personality disorder in a parent is the strongest predictor of persistence of conduct disorder from childhood into adolescence, and researchers have recognized that genetic factors contribute to conduct problems in children. In support of this position, studies have indicated that conduct disorder is significantly heritable, with estimates ranging from 27 percent to 78 percent (Scourfield, 2004).

Other conditions such as attention deficit/hyperactivity disorder (**ADHD**) have heritable links, with experts suggesting that ADHD has a strong genetic basis and is more common among people who have a close relative with the disorder. Current research is focusing on investigating genes and the brain chemical dopamine. In other words, people with ADHD seem to have lower levels of dopamine in the brain, which influences risk-taking behavior, leading to unacceptable social behavior and crime (Martin, 2007).

Untreated, children with ADHD, and other related mental disorders, are likely to experience problems at school and difficulties getting along with parents and teachers, resulting in low self-esteem and rejection.

As these children become adults, they may experience low employment, poor academic achievement, high rates of automobile accidents, family difficulties, antisocial behavior, and mood problems (Waschbusch et al., 2002). It is not surprising that ADHD is remarkably high among prison inmates. A study of 82 male prisoners convicted of murder, sexual offenses, and other violent acts also found a high prevalence of reading disability and personality disorders among prisoners associated with ADHD. Eighty-six percent of the prisoners qualified for a diagnosis of personality disorder, with a significant relationship seen between ADHD and personality disorders (Rasmussen, Almvik, and Levander, 2001).

Studies on twins and adopted children raised apart from the biological parents lend credence to the argument that individual differences in violent/antisocial behavior are heritable (Rhee and Waldman, 2002). The twin studies have been utilized to investigate the heritability of certain disorders such as oppositional defiant disorder. Several twin studies have found significant genetic influences in oppositional defiant disorder symptoms, with heritability estimates ranging from 14 percent to 65 percent (Coolidge, 2000).

As for adoptees, research has looked at the rate of criminal behavior in young adoptees whose birth mother was a criminal. Studies found that almost 50 percent of the adoptees whose mother had a criminal record had a record of criminal behavior themselves by age 18. In the control group, only 5 percent of adoptees had criminal records by age 18 if their birth mother was not a criminal (DiLalla, 1991). In another study of 199 male adoptees, it was discovered that 85.7 percent of males with a criminal or minor offences record had a birth father with a criminal record. They further noted that young male adoptees without a criminal record had a criminal father 31.1 percent of the time (Burke, 2001). While other factors may account for their crimes, there may be some biological connections.

Further research on parental influences comes from studies on parents' alcoholism and its effects on their children. It is well recognized that alcohol abuse is often present in violent criminal behavior, posing the argument that there is an indirect connection between biological factors and later criminal behavior. The risk for developing alcoholism is familial, with males having the greatest risk if one of the parents has an alcohol abuse problem (Crabbe, 2002). Accordingly, individuals whose mothers drink three or more glasses of alcohol at any one occasion in early pregnancy have an increased risk of developing drinking disorders by 21 years of age (JAMA and Archives Journals, 2006). Children of alcoholics are approximately four times as likely to become alcoholics as are children of nonalcoholics, even when the children of alcoholics are separated from their biological parents at birth and raised by nonalcoholic parents. Interestingly, children of nonalcoholic parents have a low rate of alcoholism, even when adopted by alcoholic parents. And, there is a 25–50 percent lifetime risk of alcoholism among sons and brothers of severely alcoholic men (Lappalainen et al., 1998).

As with alcohol, cigarette smoking during pregnancy has its risks. Studies have consistently reported that mothers who smoked more than half a pack of cigarettes daily during pregnancy were significantly more likely to have a child with conduct disorder than mothers who did not smoke during pregnancy. It is reported that the association was statistically significant when controlling for socioeconomic status, maternal age, parental antisocial personality, substance abuse during pregnancy, and maladaptive parenting (Wakschlag et al., 1997). Thus, cigarette smoking during pregnancy appears to be a robust independent risk factor for conduct disorder in male offspring.

One particular gene receiving attention is the monoamine oxidase A (MAOA) gene. Some research suggests that this gene has been linked to violent behavior. The **MAOA gene** breaks down key neurotransmitters, or message-carrying chemicals, linked with mood, aggression, and pleasure. In one study, all men belonging to a family in the Netherlands harboring this mutation were arsonists and rapists. And, in animal studies, mice without the MAOA gene have been found to be more aggressive than those with the gene. In other words, low expression of the MAOA gene is linked to violent tendencies. Research on the gene has been reported in the literature. Using magnetic resonance imaging (MRI) and DNA analysis, 142 healthy men and women, who had no history of violence, were shown pictures of angry and fearful faces.

Researchers found (Lei, 2006) the following:

- Those with low expression of MAOA were more impulsive.
- People with low expression of MAOA had different brain size and activity.
- Activities of those parts of the brain in males with low-expression of MAOA differed more greatly than their female counterparts.

The research on the MAOA gene suggests that people who are genetically predisposed to violence have a different brain structure to others, but this is not to suggest they are born to commit violence, because aggressive behavior and violence can also be the product of early childhood abuse. This is also not to say that genes predict specific behavior or violence, but certain genetic variations may be responsible for individual differences in neurocognitive functioning, which if untreated may predispose a person to violent behavior. In other words, abuse along with the low expression of the MAOA gene may lead to violent behavior.

Other biological factors attributed to violence are exposure to toxins such as lead poisoning, prescription drugs, and brain injuries due to birth traumas and other injuries, and even low cholesterol. Some argue that exposure to lead may be one of the most significant causes of violent crime in young people. According to one study, between 18 percent and 38 percent of all delinquency in a Pennsylvania youth facility could be due to lead poisoning. Recent studies have shown a strong relationship between sales of leaded gasoline and rates of violent crime. According to the U.S. Environmental Protection Agency, lead is found in deteriorating paint and dust, and in contaminated air, drinking water, food, and soil. Today, much of that lead is found in the drinking water of many American cities (Needleman, 2005).

Research is focusing on the influences of prescription drugs, along with other drugs, illegal or otherwise, as a cause of violence. The reason for prescribing such drugs is a mental condition such as manic depression or bipolar disorder. Many senseless acts of violence where prescription drugs were allegedly involved include the Columbine school shootings in 1999, where it was revealed that one of the shooters, Eric Harris, was taking Luvox. Another school shooter, Kip Kinkel, in 1998 was prescribed Prozac. The U.S. FDA warns that antidepressants can cause suicidal ideation, mania, and psychosis. And, the manufacturers of one antidepressant, Effexor, now warn that the drug can cause violent acts. Another study revealed the antidepressant Paxil raises the risk of violence. Other antidepressant drugs like Prozac, Celexa, and Zoloft most likely pose the same risk of violence (Healy, Herxheimer, Menkes, 2006). These drugs may not necessarily be a direct cause, but may a contributor due to incorrect dosages and combinations.

Accordingly, those who fail to take properly prescribed medications may be at risk for later violence. In the wake of the 2008 shooting and suicide on the campus of Northern Illinois University in which five students were killed, the shooter, a graduate student named Steven Kazmierczak, reportedly had obsessive-compulsive tendencies and had stopped taking Prozac three weeks before the shooting. Experts warn that taking certain medications or the wrong type, as well as stopping a medication, may be linked to violence (Tanner, 2008).

According to the National Institute on Drug Abuse (NIDA), high doses of anabolic steroids may increase irritability and aggression. Some steroid abusers report that they have committed aggressive acts, such as physical fighting or armed robbery, theft, vandalism, or burglary. Abusers who have committed aggressive acts or property crimes generally report that they engage in these behaviors more often when they take steroids than when they are drug free (NIDA, 2006). While there is some evidence that medications are a factor in violence, more research is needed to confirm this hypothesis. However, the effects of medications on individual behavior cannot be ignored, especially with individuals who may harbor other risk factors.

Considering brain injuries, aggression following head trauma is often attributed to a loss of behavioral self-control. Injury to the brain, specifically the prefrontal cortex region, harms the ability to plan and reason. Thus, many individuals who exhibit aggression after brain injury are assumed to lack regulatory control over their behavior (Wood, Liossi, and Wood, 2005). Brain injuries can be caused by such factors as childhood physical abuse, sports injuries, accidents, infections, or birth injuries. One study found that brain injury led to increased acts of domestic violence and other violent crimes (Wood, Liossi, and Wood, 2005). The risk of violence is accentuated with a low IQ, lower socioeconomic status, being male, or a prior victim of abuse. In other words, these predisposing factors contribute to the negative effects of brain injury. Those with lower intellectual functioning resulting from an injury are more prone to develop aggressive behavior because of difficulty in learning pro-social interpersonal skills which are often required in gaining meaningful employment, education, or maintaining healthy social relationships.

One of the most prolific researchers on the topic of brain injury and violence is Adrian Raine (Raine, 1997). Raine argues that violent behavior is often related to brain trauma and maternal rejection. In a study of murderers, he used positron emission tomography (PET) to scan the brains of 41 murderers who had pleaded not guilty by reason of insanity. He found significant metabolic abnormalities in as many as six areas of the brain, several of which suffered damage during gestation or birth. Raine provides evidence that damage to the six brain regions resulted from such traumas as vigorous baby shaking, fetal alcohol syndrome, and eclampsia (an advanced stage of toxemia in pregnancy).

When these injuries are combined with maternal rejection, the chances of later violence were greatly increased. In a study of murderers, neuropsychological testing revealed abnormalities in all subjects. It was reported that there was a confirmed history of profound and enduring physical abuse in 26 of these 31 cases. The authors concluded that prolonged and severe physical abuse likely interacts with neurological brain dysfunction and contributes to violent behavior (Blake, Pincus, and Buckner, 1995). Having a brain injury, along with being unwanted by a parent, particularly the mother, is a recipe for raising an angry and violent child. This is not to say that all persons experiencing these conditions grow into killers, but without positive socialization or treatment the chances of such behavior increase.

According to some research, low cholesterol is a risk factor for violent death and violent behavior in both animals and human studies.

In reviewing data from 32 different studies, it was concluded that low or lowered cholesterol levels were associated with violence (Golomb, 1998). These observational studies "consistently showed increased violent death and violent behaviors in persons with low cholesterol levels." In one meta-analysis study, it was revealed that there were 50 percent more violent deaths in men with cholesterol levels less than 160 mg/dl than in men with higher cholesterol levels. And, some randomized experiments showed an excess of violent deaths in healthy men randomly assigned to receive cholesterol-lowering therapies (Golomb, 1998). Caution must be made regarding these findings because other variables may be operating to cause violent behavior, yet there is some suggestion that high cholesterol may be good.

The Familial Influences

The professional literature of criminology is surprisingly consistent on the real root causes of violent crime: the breakdown of the family. The sequence has its deepest roots in the absence of stable marriage.

—Patrick F. Fagan

The familial level includes factors that increase violent behavior because of risks associated with dysfunctional relationships among family members, including fatherless homes, abuse, and so forth. Positive familial relationships, particularly at young age, are crucial in developing pro-social values and act as a shield against violent behavior. As discussed, some offenders have inherent biological risks which the family (or lack thereof) is unable or unwilling to address.

Escapes from these plights are often accomplished through gang violence, substance abuse, transient lifestyles, or other antisocial activities. In short, how one is raised and the type of early socialization and community influences experienced have something to do with future behavior. To better explain this level of violence, a discussion on the role of the family is presented. This is an important area to address because many violent offenders were once angry young men, spawned in dysfunctional homes without positive role models.

Consider the following facts:

- The rise in violent crime parallels the rise in families abandoned by fathers.
- High-crime neighborhoods are characterized by high concentrations of families abandoned by fathers.

- State-by-state analysis by Heritage scholars indicates that a 10 percent increase in the percentage of children living in single-parent homes leads typically to a 17 percent increase in juvenile crime.
- The rate of violent teenage crime corresponds with the number of families abandoned by fathers.
- The type of aggression and hostility demonstrated by a future criminal often is foreshadowed in unusual aggressiveness as early as age five or six.
- The future criminal tends to be an individual rejected by other children as early as the first grade, who goes on to form his own group of friends, often the future delinquent gang. (Fagan, 1995)

Figures released by the Department of Justice of inmates incarcerated in our nation's prisons indicate 31 percent of jail inmates had grown up with a parent or guardian who abused alcohol or drugs. About 12 percent had lived in a foster home or institution, and 46 percent had a family member who had been incarcerated. More than 50 percent of the women in jail said they had been physically or sexually abused in the past, compared to more than 10 percent of the men. This data suggests that unstable homes, especially during the formative years, have an effect on one's self-worth and values. Accordingly, children who grow up in violent homes have much higher risks of becoming drug or alcohol abusers or being involved in abusive relationships, as a batterer or a victim. Men and women who were physically punished as youth are more likely to abuse their partners or spouses (Straus, 1991). And, the highest predictors of involvement in crime and delinquency are being hit once or more per week at 11 years of age and having a mother, at that age, with strong beliefs in, and a commitment to, corporal punishment (Newson and Newson, 1990). Clearly, the effects of child abuse and neglect may create an angry person who may target others, including family members, for violence.

Prisons are populated primarily by men who were abandoned or rejected by their fathers. Ninety-five percent of those on death row hated their fathers.

Bill Glass, Prison counselor

The research on the role of the family in causing or shielding against violence is consistent. The best predictor of violence in adulthood is violent behavior in childhood. Families can and often do provide the security and love necessary to "protect" children—even high-risk children—from becoming violent (Wave trust, 1995). Many youth are involved in violent crimes such as gang violence, with a large portion of these offenses committed by unemployed minority youth who are arrested and sentenced to prison. Is this the result of failed social programs, racism, or other injustices? While there are social inequalities, the lack of family structure is often cited as the key variable.

A 1988 study of 11,000 individuals found that "the percentage of single-parent households with children between the ages of 12 and 20 is significantly associated with rates of violent crime and burglary." The same study makes it clear that the popular assumption that there is an association between race and crime is false. In other words, illegitimacy, not race or other social injustices, is the major factor for violence in some communities. The absence of marriage and the failure to form and maintain intact families explain the incidence of crime among whites as well as blacks (Fagan, 1996).

Included in this level is social learning theory (Sutherland, 1924; Tarde, 1912), which has been around for many years. In other words, learning pro-social or antisocial behaviors is a function of imitation. Imitation includes modeling behavior expressed by significant others and learning values and actions from others. If a child witnesses violence in the home on a regular basis (domestic abuse, etc.) he or she may feel that violence is an acceptable way to gain compliance from others because it achieves results. In other words, pro-social behavior, as well as antisocial behavior, is a learned process. And, the more constant or intense the learning experiences, the more they will translate into a pattern of behavior.

Divorced- and single-parent homes are inevitable in today's society. Separation occurs in nearly half of all American marriages, currently separating 45 million fathers from their children and depriving these children of the safety and security of a two-parent family. Certainty not all family breakups cause children to become violent. A number of other variables can overcome these changes, such as income level of the parents, extended-family support, and so forth. However, for many the effects can be disastrous. This well-documented social trend is evidenced in the following statistics (Young, 2005).

- Nearly 70 percent of black youths don't live with their father.
- Forty percent of those same black youths have not seen their father in at least a year, and 50 percent have never visited their father's home.
- Children not in contact with their father are five times more likely to live in poverty and twice as likely to commit crime, drop out of school, and abuse drugs and alcohol.

- Girls who grew up without a father are more likely to become pregnant during their teenage years.
- The majority of violent criminals were raised without their fathers, according to numerous studies.

Data suggests that some children turn to violence, substance abuse, or other antisocial behaviors to compensate for their broken or poor family environments and upbringing. And those reared without fathers are especially prone to criminal behavior if other undesirable conditions exist. In these settings without fathers, there is more likely to be poverty and problems with supervision. This is not to suggest that all so-called stable families with fathers are a shield against criminal behavior; however, a quality attentive family or stable two-parent home can insulate a person from negative community influences and help shield against poverty and violence.

The Community Influences

Structural characteristics of neighborhoods shape the level of social control in the neighborhood . . . . neighborhoods where poverty is high, people are divided by ethnic and racial differences, and where few people live in the neighborhood for any length of time, neighbors' abilities to establish relationships, work together, promote institutions and control crime are diminished.

—Ruth A. Triplett and Randy R. Gainey

Community violence is a complex term encompassing riots, gang wars, and so forth. In explaining violence from this perspective, we know that most street criminals are disproportionately poor, unemployed, or at the poverty level. In addition, violence results from overcrowded and deplorable living conditions, because many view such conditions as traps (Siegel, 2006). For offenders, violence is a way to lash out at society or privileged others who are perceived as the cause of their troubles. To truly understand the influence of environment, consider the violence occurring in the underdeveloped poverty-stricken nations in Africa, Central America, and the Middle East, where violence is often an expression of hopelessness and inequality. Social deterioration and lack of opportunity may create a sense of despair, causing reactionary violence against anyone, especially those who are living better.

At this level, we find decaying communities frequented by street criminals and gangs and with an abundance of liquor establishments and other unruly places. A community wrought with high crime, street drug dealing, prostitution, and gang activity sends a message that disorder and violence are tolerated, and in fact may be encouraged. The community chaos and violent crime occurring in Iraq and other Third World nations undergoing change are examples. Until social order is firmly established, violent acts and senseless bombings are likely to continue.

The community influences on crime, violence, and victimization have strong research support (Sampson, 1993, 2004). Consider a youth with poor family support who may also have a biological risk for aggressive behavior growing up in a disorderly community. In other words, joining a gang or participating in a criminal enterprise is a way to satisfy family needs (belonging and recognition) and to cope with a community in disarray.

In studying the causes of inner-city race riots, for example, it has been found that urban unrest is rooted in a multitude of political, economic, and social factors including lack of affordable housing, urban renewal projects, economic inequality, and rapid demographic change (Herman, 1999). Simply stated, close-knit communities are more likely to identify strangers, report deviants to their parents, and pass warnings along; but high rates of residential mobility and high-rise housing disrupt the ability to establish and maintain social ties. Unstable communities often lack the organization and political connections to obtain resources for fighting crime and offering young people an alternative to deviant behavior.

One study found that exposure to community violence was a strong indicator of future violence (Wake Forest University Baptist Medical Center, 2000). And in another study, researchers asked 722 Georgia middle school 11- and 12-year-olds, living in or around decaying public housing, how many times they had been exposed to or had been a victim of violence in their communities. In the study, violence was defined as participating in five different types of violent activities, including participating in a physical fight which resulted in seeking medical attention, attacking someone with a weapon, using a weapon to force or get money or things from someone, carrying a concealed firearm, and carrying another weapon such as a razor or knife. Only 1.4 percent of the students had not witnessed or been the victim of any violence, and 54.1 percent of all students reported witnessing or being the victim of between 1 and 15 acts of violence (Waldman, 2002).

According to a University of Washington study on domestic violence, a number of personal factors, including disorganized neighborhoods where attitudes toward drug sales and violence were favorable, increased a person's likelihood of committing domestic violence. Individuals who have a history of antisocial behavior may be more likely to find a partner in these lower socioeconomic neighborhoods, where having a partner who used or sold drugs, had a history of violence toward others, had an arrest record, or was unemployed was prevalent (University of Washington, 2007).

A disorderly community promotes violence because there are many opportunities for criminal behavior. And these communities are also the gathering place for many who lead dysfunctional or violent lives. In some cases, the police are less likely to patrol these areas aggressively or respond to complaints as quickly as in the higher socioeconomic bedroom communities. Furthermore, community violence gives rise to subsets of associated violence that impact schools and other institutions. Youth who live in fear of violence, witness violent acts, or actually become victims of violence suffer an array of consequences ranging from personal injury and debilitating anxiety that interrupt the learning process to a pattern of absence and truancy that can lead to dropping out of school and delinquency. Such disassociation restricts individual options and limits the development of academic and life skills. Constant exposure to violence also creates a type of desensitization which can lead one to believe that violence is a normal part of life. People who are surrounded by violence may reach a point where they no longer notice violent events and may even embrace it.

SUMMARY

There are multiple reasons in explaining interpersonal violence. In examining violent people, it is important to examine their personal characteristics, family backgrounds, and socioeconomic status. How a child is raised and where he or she is raised are factors to consider in explaining violent behavior. We cannot ignore the role of biology in violence. Violent people may have a predisposition toward violence due to their genetic makeup. In other words, genetic and structural brain variations increase the risk of violent behavior. However, a combination of other risk factors such as deficiencies in the early mother–child relationship, abuse in childhood, parental neglect and inconsistent parenting, a breakup or loss in the family, parental criminality, poverty, and long-term unemployment increase the risk of violence. It is often argued that the violence depicted in media, availability of guns, and other cultural deviances are the real causes of violence. These influences are minimal as they act as facilitators rather than causes. We need to examine the person and his or her environment to assess the root causes of individual violence. To ban guns or to censure the media is as counterproductive as outlawing alcohol and automobiles since both are often associated with or are contributors to violence.

KEY TERMS AND CONCEPTS

ADHD
Aileen Wuornos
Community influences
Dark figure of crime
Determination of crime rates
Familial influences
Fear–victimization paradox
Gary Gilmore

Individual influences
MAOA gene
National Crime Victimization Survey (NCVS)
Terrorism
Uniform Crime Reports (UCR)
VICAP (Violent Criminal Apprehension Program)

DISCUSSION QUESTIONS

1. Explain why only some violent crimes are reported to police. What factors determine whether a crime is reported? Are reporting rates different for personal and property crimes? If so, why?
2. Why are some people more fearful of crime than others? Do you believe that the media promote fear? Explain.
3. Develop an argument that genetics is a powerful factor in predicting behavior.
4. Discuss why some individuals raised in violent dysfunctional families or communities do not become violent.
5. Research a case study of a violent offender and determine the effect of individual, familial, and community levels in his or her violent behavior?
6. Is there a relationship between the media and violence?
7. Are certain mental conditions attributed to violence more prevalent in men or women?

WEB SOURCES

Bureau of Justice Statistics. *The Sourcebook of Criminal Justice Statistics Online*: 30th Edition. www.albany.edu/sourcebook/
Bureau of Justice Statistics. www.ojp.usdoj.gov/bjs/
Federal Bureau of Investigation. www.fbi.gov

RECOMMENDED READINGS

Callanan, Valerie J. 2004. *Feeding the Fear of Crime: Crime-Related Media and Support for Three Strikes (Criminal Justice: Recent Scholarship).* El Paso, Texas: LFB Scholarly Publishing.
Conklin, John E. 2002. *Why Crime Rates Fell.* Boston: Allyn and Bacon.

Ditton, Jason and Stephen Farall, eds. 2000. *The Fear of Crime (The International Library of Criminology, Criminal Justice and Penology)*. Brookfield, VT: Ashgate.

Sampson, Robert J. and Stephen W. Raudenbush. 2004. Seeing Disorder: Neighborhood Stigma and the Social Construction of "Broken Windows". *Social Psychology Quarterly* 67:319–342.

REFERENCES

Athens, L. 1992. *The Creation of Dangerous Violent Criminals*. Chicago, IL: University of Illinois Press.

Blake, P.Y., J.H. Pincus, and C. Buckner. 1995. Neurologic Abnormalities in Murderers. *Neurology* 45(9):1641–1647.

Bureau of Justice Statistics. 2003. *The National Crime Victimization Survey*. Washington, D.C.: U.S. Department of Justice.

Bureau of Justice Statistics. 2007. *Reported Crime in the United States*. Washington, D.C.: U.S. Department of Justice.

Burke, R.H. 2001. *An Introduction to Criminology Theory*. London, England: Willan Publishing.

Butterfield, Fox. 1998. As Crime Falls, Pressure Rises to Alter Data. *New York Times*, August 3, 1998.

Coolidge, Frederick. 2000. Heritability and the Comorbidity of Attention Deficit Hyperactivity Disorder with Behavioral Disorders and Executive Function Deficits: A Preliminary Investigation. *Developmental Neuropsychology* 17:273.

Crabbe, J.C. 2002. Alcohol and Genetics: New Models. *American Journal of Medical Genetics (Neuropsychiatric Genetics)* 114:969–974.

Crank, John P., Andrew Giacomazzi, and Cary Heck. 2003. Fear of Crime in a Nonurban Setting. *Journal of Criminal Justice* 31(3):249–263.

Dahlberg, L.L. and Krug, E.G. 2002. Violence–a Global Public Health Problem. In *World Report on Violence and Health*, eds Krug, E., Dahlberg, L.L., Mercy, J.A., Zwi, A.B., and Lozano, R., 1–56. Geneva, Switzerland: World Health Organization.

DiLalla, L.F. 1991. Biological and Genetic Contributors to Violence—Widom's Untold Tale. *Psychological Bulletin* 109(1):125–129.

Earls, Felton and Albert Reiss. 1994. *Breaking the Cycle: Predicting and Preventing Crime* Washington, D.C.: National Institute of Justice.

Fagan, Patrick. 1995. *The Real Root Causes of Violent Crime: The Breakdown of Marriage, Family, and Community*. Washington, D.C.: The Heritage Foundation.

Fagan, Patrick F. 1996. Disintegration of the Family Is the Real Root Cause of Violent Crime. *USA Today* (Society for the Advancement of Education). May 1996.

Ferrell, J. 2004. Boredom, Crime and Criminology. *Theoretical Criminology*, Special Edition. London: Sage Publications.

Ferri, E. 2003. The Causes of Criminal Behaviour In *Criminological Perspectives: Essential Readings*, eds Muncie, J., McLaughlin, M., and Hughes, G. Thousand Oaks, CA: Sage Publications.

Healy, D., Herxheimer, A., and Menkes, D.B. 2006. Antidepressants and Violence: Problems at the Interface of Medicine and Law. *PLoS Medicine* 3(9):e372.

Herman, Max A. 1999. Fighting in the Streets: Ethnic Succession and Urban Unrest in 20th Century America. Doctoral Dissertation, University of Arizona. Available from University Microfilms.

JAMA and Archives Journals. September 5, 2006. Drinking During Pregnancy Linked to Offspring's Risk of Alcohol Disorders in Early Adulthood. *Science Daily*. Retrieved on January 18, 2008 http://www.sciencedaily.com/releases/2006/09/060904160530.htm

Joseph, Janice. 1997. Fear of Crime Among Black Elderly. *Journal of Black Studies* 27:698.

Lappalainen, Jaakko, Jeffrey C. Long, Monica Eggert, Norio Ozaki, Robert W. Robin, Gerald L. Brown, Hannu Naukkarinen, Matti Virkkunen, Markku Linnoila, and David Goold-man. November 1998. Linkage of Antisocial Alcoholism to the Serotonin 5-HT1B Receptor Gene in 2 Populations. *Archives of General Psychiatry* 55:989–994.

Lei, Hsien Hsien. 2006. MAOA Gene Linked To Violent Behavior. *Genetics and Health*. Retrieved ABC news online: http://www.abc.net.au/news/newsitems/200603/s1597238.htm

Loeber, Rolf. 2003. *Child Delinquency: Early Intervention and Prevention, OJJDP.* Washington, D.C.: U.S. Department of Justice.

Martin, Ben. 2007. *Causes of Attention Deficit disorder (ADHD).* Psych Central, Retrieved on January 18, 2008, http://psychcentral.com/disorders/adhd/adhd_causes.htm

McCleary, R., B. C. Nienstedt, and J. M. Erven. 1982. Uniform Crime Reports as Organization Outcomes: Three Time Series Experiments. *Social Problems* 29:361.

Moffitt, T.E. 2005. The new look of behavioral genetics in developmental psychopathology: Gene-environment interplay in antisocial behavior. *Psychological Bulletin* 131:533–554.

Needleman, Herbert L. 2005. Lead in the Environment Causes Violent Crime, Reports University of Pittsburgh Researcher. *Science Daily*. Retrieved on January 21, 2008, http://www.sciencedaily.com /releases/2005/02/050223145108.htm

Newson, J., and Newson, E. 1990. *The Extent of Physical Punishment in the U.K.* London: Approach.

Parker, Keith D., Barbara J. McMorris, and Earl Smith. 1993. Fear of Crime and Likelihood of Victimization. *Journal of Social Psychology* 133:5.

Plomin, R., J.C. DeFries, and G.E. McClearn. 1989. *Behavior Genetics: A Primer*, 2nd ed. San Francisco: W.H. Freeman.

Raine, Adrian. University of Southern California. 1997, September 13. Research Links Brain Damage & Violent Crime—USC Studies Point to Underlying Causes of Violent Crime in Young Offenders. *Science Daily*. Retrieved on January 18, 2008, http://www.sciencedaily.com/releases/1997/09/970913073401.htm

Rasmussen, Kirsten, Roger Almvik, and Sten Levander. 2001. Attention Deficit Hyperactivity Disorder, Reading Disability, and Personality Disorders in a Prison Population. *Journal of the American Academy of Psychiatry and the Law* 29:186–193.

Rhee, S.H., and Waldman, I.D. 2002. Genetic and environmental influences on antisocial behavior: A meta-analysis of twin and adoption studies. *Psychological Bulletin* 128:490–529.

Robbins, P.C., Monahan, J., and Silver, E. 2003. Mental Disorder Violence and Gender. *Law and Human Behavior* 27(6):561–571.

Russell, Ron. 1995. Insecurity About Crime Runs Deep, Even in Utopia. *Los Angeles Times*, October 14, 1.

Sampson, Robert J. 1993. The Community Context of Violent Crime. In *Sociology and the Public Agenda*, ed.William Julius Wilson, 267–274. Newbury Park, CA: Sage Publications.

Sampson, Robert J. 2004. Neighborhood and Community: Collective Efficacy and Community Safety. *New Economy* 11:106–113.

Sherman, Lawrence W. 1998. Needed: Better Ways to Count Crooks. *Wall Street Journal.* August.

Siegel, Larry. 2006. *Criminology.* Belmont, CA: Thomson/Wadsworth.

Sutherland, Edwin H. 1924. *Principles of Criminology.* Chicago: University of Chicago Press.

Scourfield, Jane. 2004. Conduct Problems in Children and Adolescents: A Twin Study. *Archives of General Psychiatry* 61:489.

Stafford, Mia, Chandola, Tarani, and Marmot, Michael. 2007 Association Between Fear of Crime and Mental Health and Physical Functioning. *American Journal of Public Health* 97(11):2076–2081.

Straus, M.A. 1991. Discipline and Deviance: Physical Punishment of Children and Violence and Other Crime in Adulthood. *Social Problems* 38:133–154.

Tanner, Lindsey. 2008. Experts Say Stopping Medication May Lead to Violence. *Ventura Star.* February 20, A5.

Tarde, Gabriel. 1912. *Penal Philosophy.* Boston: Little Brown.

The National Institute on Drug Abuse (NIDA). 2006. *Research Report Series—Anabolic Steroid Abuse.* U.S. Department of Health and Human Services., Washington, D.C., September 14.

University of Washington. 2007, June 26. Teenage Violence Linked to Later Domestic Violence. *Science Daily.* Retrieved on February 28, 2008 http://www.sciencedaily.com/releases/2007/06/070625111433.htm

Wake Forest University Baptist Medical Center. 2000, November 9. Violence is a Learned Behavior, Say Researchers at Wake Forest University. *Science Daily.* Retrieved on January 28, 2008 http://www.sciencedaily.com/releases/2000/11/001106061128.htm

Wakschlag Lauren, S. et al. 1997. Smoking During Pregnancy Increases Conduct Disorders. *Archives General Psychiatry* 54:670–676.

Wave Trust. 1995. *Summary of the 1995 Report of the Commission on Children and Violence,* Convened by the Gulbenkian Foundation in the UK, Wave Trust, Inc. Retrieved on January 20, 2008 http://www.wavetrust.org/Preventing_Violence/Children_and_violence.htm

Waschbusch, Daniel, William E. Pelham, J. Richard Jennings and Andrew Greiner, 2002. Reactive Aggression in Boys with Disruptive Behavior Disorders: Behavior, Physiology, and Affect. *Journal of Abnormal Child Psychology* 4:234.

Williams, K. 2004. *Textbook on Criminology.* Oxford: Oxford University Press.

Wilson, J.Q. 1985. *Thinking About Crime.* London: Vintage.

Wood, R.L., Liossi, C., and Wood, L. 2005. The Impact of Head Injury Neurobehavioral Sequelae on Personal Relationships: Preliminary Findings. *Brain Injuries* 19:10, 845–853.

Young, Yolanda. 2005. Poor choices create "Baby Mamas". *USA Today.* Retrieved on January 22, 2008 http://www.usatoday.com/news/opinion/2005–03–03-baby-mamas_x.htm

Zandi, John and Johns Hopkins Medical Institutions. 2002, January 14. Discovery that Common Mood Disorders Are Inherited Together May Reveal Genetic Underpinnings. *Science Daily.* Retrieved on January 18, 2008 http://www.sciencedaily.com/releases/2002/01/020110074124.htm

2

Victimization Theory

LEARNING OBJECTIVES

After studying this chapter, you will:

- Understand the difference between criminology and victimology.
- Become familiar with the early theorists on victimology.
- Understand recent theories on victimization.
- Understand why some crimes are not officially reported.

INTRODUCTION

One of the most neglected subjects in the study of crime is its victims.

—The President's Commission on Law Enforcement
and the Administration of Justice, 1967

The terrorist attacks on September 11, 2001, and the deadly sniper attacks in the Washington, DC, area in 2002 awakened Americans to our vulnerability to violent crime. At any given time, dedicated criminals may victimize anyone, without warning or without clear motive. **Victimology** is the study of crime victims and their relationship to offenders and the criminal justice system. Victimology is unlike criminology, which focuses on the dynamics of victimization; criminology concerns the etiology of crime and criminal behavior. Victimology attempts to address questions of how crime victims have been exploited, abused, neglected, harmed, and oppressed in public and private (workplace) settings.

It is equally interested in how victims can be assisted, served, and educated about crime and violence. Victimologists are concerned with the demographics of victimization, particularly age, race, sex, location, and other situational factors. Researchers have always been interested in why some people are victimized more than others or why some are more fearful than others. The problems associated with being a crime victim are not restricted to physical injury resulting from violent acts perpetrated by strangers or intimates. Victims of crime experience economic losses, such as medical expenses and lost wages. The average cost of crime for a rape victim, for example, may exceed $50,000 when medical and other costs are included. Victims may also believe that they are responsible for their victimization; thus, there is a degree of stress, anxiety, and blame associated with victimization referred to as post-traumatic stress disorder. This chapter reviews the impact of victimization and theories and explanations on victimization.

IMPACT OF VICTIMIZATION

The impact of criminal victimization imposes economic and emotional costs on the victim and society. The costs are both tangible and intangible. Individuals victimized lose time from work or may require extensive medical treatment or therapy. It is estimated that the direct intangible costs to crime victims annually are $105 billion in medical expenses, lost earnings, and public program costs related to victim assistance (National Institute of Justice, 1996). Almost $4.1 billion a year is spent on direct medical and mental health care services in the United States as a result of intimate partner violence (Centers for Disease Control and Prevention, 2003).

The major impact on victims of violence is emotional or *intangible losses*. Such losses include long-term problems, such as pain and suffering and reduced quality of life.

It is difficult to measure the amount of pain and anguish a victim experiences. In some cases, his or her life may never be the same. Although these losses are more difficult to quantify, economists use various measures, such as educational level, income, family size, and so forth, to place monetary value on one's life.

The direct tangible costs to crime victims are estimated to be $105 billion annually in medical expenses, lost earnings, and public program costs related to victim assistance. Pain, suffering, and reduced quality of life increase the cost to $450 billion annually (National Institute of Justice, 1996).

As indicated in Table 2–1, the financial and emotional costs of crime to the victim are enormous. The highest losses are for crimes of violence (rape and sexual assault, etc.). In other words, the cost of victimization includes the extent of injury, type of crime, and the psychological reactions that victims often experience after a violent crime. These psychological aspects are discussed in the next section.

TABLE 2–1 LOSSES PER CRIMINAL VICTIMIZATION

Type of crime	All crimes				Crimes involving loss of $1 or more			Crimes involving loss-no monetary value specified
	Gross loss (in millions of dollars)	Total crimes	Mean dollar loss	Median dollar loss	Total crimes	Mean dollar loss	Median dollar loss	Total crimes
All crimes	17,014	23,440,72	726	100	16,708,451	1,018	140	2,131,460
Personal crimes	1,390	5,400,790	257	80	1,019,830	1,363	200	500,120
Crimes of violence	1,356	5,173,720	262	80	802,300	1,690	250	493,840
Rape/Sexual assault	26	191,670	136	500	31,010*	843	500	25,570*
Rape/Attempted rape	25	130,140	194	500	28,270*	891	500	25,570*
Rape	13	69,370	183	500	21,630*	588	500	21,940*
Attempted rape[a]	12	60,770	205	500	6,640*	1,876	5,000	3,630*
Sexual assault[b]	1	61,530	16	350	2,740*	350	350	0*
Robbery	494	624,850	791	120	384,070	1,286	200	76,580
Assault	836	4,357,190	192	50	387,230	2,158	250	391,690
Purse snatching	9	46,810	191	110	43,550	205	110	0*
Pocket picking	26	180,260	142	62	173,980	148	62	6,280*
Property crimes	15,623	18,039,930	866	100	15,688,620	996	135	1,631,340
Household burglary	5,086	3,456,220	1,471	250	2,738,510	1,857	300	371,280
Motor vehicle theft	5,237	978,120	5,354	2,500	817,700	6,404	3,000	105,150
Theft	5,301	13,605,590	390	90	12,132,410	437	100	1,154,910
Gender								
Male	10,070	12,471,070	807	100	8,897,180	1,132	150	1,014,310
Female	6,943	10,969,650	633	100	7,811,270	889	125	1,117,150
Race								
White only	12,522	19,215,840	652	100	13,799,21	907	125	1,663,410
Black only	2,917	2,952,750	988	115	2,049,900	1,423	195	355,720
Other race only[c]	1,168	812,250	1,437	150	592,480	1,971	200	52,220
Two or more races[d]	407	459,880	886	100	266,860	1,526	175	60,110

Ethnicity								
Hispanic	3,024	3,429,570	882	150	2,458,900	1,230	199	322,650
Non-Hispanic	13,937	19,947,070	699	100	14,206,030	981	125	1,803,990
Age								
12–15	16	777,930	20	10	98,360	162	50	68,990
16–19	191	1,148,580	166	75	535,240	357	100	85,060
20–24	1,575	2,652,740	594	156	1,647,960	956	200	192,730
25–34	3,289	4,467,040	736	115	3,232,590	1,018	150	377,760
35–49	6,629	8,057,430	823	100	6,284,440	1,055	125	710,940
50–64	4,038	4,553,230	887	100	3,555,500	1,136	100	400,560
65 and over	1,275	1,783,770	715	60	1,354,370	941	112	295,420
Income								
Less than $7,500	649	1,364,740	476	100	933,660	695	145	155,650
$7,500–$14,999	1,115	1,916,880	582	100	1,423,390	783	130	165,190
$15,000–$24,999	1,997	2,684,390	744	100	1,818,840	1,098	150	271,440
$25,000–$34,999	1,219	2,540,350	480	100	1,827,680	667	130	244,670
$35,000–$49,999	1,659	2,977,820	557	100	2,125,280	781	100	242,820
$50,000–$74,999	2,560	3,197,830	801	100	2,237,010	1,145	125	280,430
$75,000 or more	4,199	4,595,520	914	100	3,382,090	1,242	140	378,130

*Estimate is based on about 10 or fewer sample cases.

aIncludes verbal threats of rape.

bIncludes threats.

cIncludes American Indian, Eskimo, Asian Pacific Islander if only one of these races is given.

dIncludes all persons of any race, indicating two or more races.

Source: Bureau of Justice Statistics, 2006. *Criminal Victimization in the United States.* Washington, DC: U.S. Department of Justice.

Who is responsible for paying for the cost of crime? Most costs of victimization are covered by insurance carriers. The government pays millions annually to emergency services for victims (victim compensation programs). State compensation programs paid crime victims and their families $455 million in benefits in the federal fiscal year 2003. Since 1997, payments from state compensation programs increased 82.5 percent (National Association of Crime Victim Compensation Boards, 2004). In short, taxpayers and insurance companies cover the tangible costs for some crimes; in some cases, however, victims of violent crimes occurring on private property attempt to recover losses through lawsuits.

Emotional reactions of victimization vary depending on the age, life experiences, and emotional strength of the victim. But in many cases the reaction to the violence is **post-traumatic stress disorder (PTSD)**. According to the PTSD Alliance (2004), the estimated risks of developing PTSD after the following traumatic events are: rape, 49 percent; severe beating or physical assault, 31 percent; other sexual assault, 23.7 percent; shooting or stabbing, 15.4 percent; sudden unexpected death of a family member or loved one, 14.3 percent; and witness to a murder or assault, 7.3 percent.

This disorder affects hundreds of thousands of people who have been exposed to violent events, such as rape, domestic violence, and child abuse. The mental health costs, which include disorders resulting from violence, are costly. In the United States, tangible costs associated with the trauma from intimate partner violence were approximately $4.1 billion (Centers for Disease Control and Prevention, 2003).

The *Diagnostic and Statistical Manual of Mental Disorders* (American Psychological Association, 1994) states that PTSD occurs when a person has been exposed to an extreme traumatic stressor in which both of the following are present:

1. The person directly experienced an event or events that involved actual or threatened death or serious injury, or other threat to one's physical integrity; or the person witnessed an event or events that involved death, injury, or a threat to the physical integrity of another person; or the person learned about unexpected or violent death, serious harm, or threat of death or injury experienced by a family member or other close associate.

2. The person's response to the event or events involves intense fear, helplessness, or horror.

The symptoms of PTSD may initially appear to be part of a normal response to a traumatic experience. Sometimes the disorder does not surface until months or even years later. PTSD was once thought to be a disorder restricted to war veterans involved in heavy combat, but researchers now know that it can result from many types of trauma, particularly those that include a threat to life. A study about lifetime criminal victimization experience, crime reporting, and the psychological effect of crime victimization found that 28 percent of all crime victims subsequently developed crime-related PTSD and 7.5 percent of all crime victims still suffered from PTSD at the time of the assessment (Kilpatrick et al., 1987). Findings from a South Carolina study (Kilpatrick, Tidwell, and Saunders, 1988) indicate that PTSD rates for victims and families who had high exposure to the criminal justice system were even greater, with 51 percent of these crime victims having developed crime-related PTSD and 24 percent still suffering from PTSD at the time of assessment. Results of this study also indicate that of all the victims surveyed, direct victims of sexual assault and aggravated assault and family members of homicide victims were the most likely groups to develop crime-related PTSD. In some cases, the symptoms of PTSD disappear with time, but in others they persist for many years.

Not all people who experience trauma require treatment; some recover with the help of family or friends. Many need professional help, however, to recover successfully from the psychological damage that can result from experiencing, witnessing, or being involved in an overwhelmingly traumatic event. Thus, people, especially children, who witness a violent act can suffer PTSD.

Many witnesses near the explosion of the federal building in Oklahoma City in 1995 suffered from illnesses and PTSD. In a study of survivors, it was reported that many suffered from illnesses that included chronic depression and drug and alcohol abuse. However, most survivors suffered from PTSD that included flashbacks, nightmares, sleep disorders, and angry outbursts (*Los Angeles Times*, 1999). The horror of the September 11 terrorist attacks will undoubtedly scar many lives for years to come. Traumatic occurrences, such as sexual or physical abuse or loss of a parent, have a profound impact on the lives of children. They may develop learning disabilities and problems with attention and memory in addition to PTSD symptoms. They may become anxious or clingy and may abuse themselves or others as a result. Children of abuse may become tomorrow's abusers.

Psychologist recognize three categories of PTSD symptoms: intrusive, avoidance, and hyperarousal. People suffering from PTSD often have an episode in which the traumatic event "intrudes" into their current life. This can happen in sudden, vivid memories that are accompanied by painful emotions. Sometimes the trauma is reexperienced, at times in nightmares.

In young children, distressing dreams of the traumatic event may evolve into generalized nightmares of monsters, of rescuing others, or of threats to themselves or others. At times, the reexperience comes as a sudden, painful onslaught of emotions—grief that brings tears, fear, or anger—that seem to have no cause. Individuals say these emotional experiences occur repeatedly, much like memories or dreams about the traumatic event.

Another category of symptoms involve what are called *avoidance phenomena*. People experiencing these symptoms often avoid close emotional ties with family, colleagues, and friends, thus affecting their relationships. These people feel numb, have diminished emotions, and can complete only routine, mechanical activities. When reexperiencing symptoms occur, people seem to spend their energies suppressing the flood of associated emotions. They are often incapable of mustering the necessary energy to respond appropriately to their environment; people who suffer from PTSD frequently say they cannot feel emotions, especially toward those with whom they are closest. As the avoidance continues, sufferers seem to be bored, cold, or preoccupied. Family members often feel rebuffed by them because they show no affection and act mechanically. In other words, emotional numbness and diminished interest in significant activities occur. This avoidance is especially apparent in children. People with PTSD also avoid situations that remind them of the traumatic event because their symptoms may worsen. For example, people who survived a beating from a youth gang might experience symptoms of PTSD when they see groups of young people. Over time, persons with PTSD can become so fearful of particular situations that their daily lives are ruled by their attempts to avoid these situations; these people can become prisoners in their own homes.

Those who suffer with hyperarousal symptoms of PTSD act as if they are continually threatened by the trauma that caused their illness. They may become irritable, have trouble concentrating or remembering current information, and develop insomnia. Because of their chronic hyperarousal, many people with PTSD have poor work records and poor relationships with their family and friends.

There are other types of trauma experienced by crime victims. Women who have been battered over the years suffer from what has been identified as **battered-women's syndrome**. This syndrome is being used frequently as a legal defense for committing a crime. In the California case of *People v. Humphrey* (Supreme Court of California Ct. App, 5 F020267, 1996), the court ruled that evidence of spousal battering may be entered as a defense. In that case the court stated:

> *Battered Women's Syndrome seeks to describe and explain common reactions of women to that experience. Thus, you may consider the evidence concerning the syndrome and its effects only for the limited purpose of showing, if it does show, that the defendant's reactions, as demonstrated by the evidence, are not inconsistent with her having been physically abused or the beliefs, perceptions, or behavior of victims of domestic violence.*

A related condition confronted by rape victims is known as **rape trauma syndrome**. The syndrome has two phases: acute and reorganization. During the acute phase, the survivor experiences a complete disruption of her life, resulting from the violence she experienced. The victim may display a number of emotional responses, including crying, shouting, swearing, or laughing inappropriately. In general, the survivor responds initially to the assault with shock and disbelief. Following the acute stage is the reorganization stage. During this stage, survivors reorganize themselves and their life. Basically, with the help of family and friends, they learn to cope again.

The effects of violence on one's physical health can be disastrous. For instance, researchers at the Harvard School of Public Health (HSPH) found a strong association between domestic violence and asthma. The study raises questions about the role of stress in the development of this common respiratory condition. The study examined a nationally representative database of 92,000 households in India, where domestic violence is highly prevalent. Women who had experienced domestic violence in the past year had a 37 percent increased risk of asthma. For women who had not experienced domestic violence themselves, but lived in a household where a woman had been beaten in the past year, there was a 21 percent increased risk of asthma than for women who did not live in such households. In addition, living in a household where a woman experienced domestic violence also increased the risk of reported asthma in children and adult men. The possible link between domestic violence and asthma may be explained by the fact that exposure to violence may affect the immune system and cause inflammation, which have a role in asthma development (Harvard School of Public Health, 2007).

Victimization impacts victims' families, social relations, employers in many ways. In other words, victimization not only primarily or directly affects the victim, but secondarily affects the family, and affects the community or society at large in a tertiary manner. However, are some claims of victimization real or simply a way to blame others?

Culture of Victimization

There is no question that much of violent victimization is real with many victims who suffer lifelong consequences. However, are some capitalizing on victimization or are some persons truly victims? Consider the following case: In Pennsylvania, a robber named Dickson had just finished robbing a house he had entered by way of the garage. He was not able to get the garage door to go up since the automatic door opener was malfunctioning. He couldn't reenter the house because the door connecting the house and garage locked when he pulled it shut. The family was on vacation, and Mr. Dickson found himself locked in the garage for eight days. He subsisted on a case of Pepsi he found, and a large bag of dry dog food. He sued the homeowner's insurance, claiming the situation caused him undue mental anguish. The jury agreed awarding a verdict of $500,000. The decision no doubt included pain and suffering including PTSD.

Sykes (1992) argues that we have become a nation of victims, where everyone is competing for the status of a victim. The constant cry for empathy and justice by the victim industry reduces our capacity to deal with genuine victims, such as children who are molested, women who are raped, and immigrants who are assaulted, etc. Add to the mix that there is evidence of false accusations of victimization. In a study of a small metropolitan community, 45 consecutive, disposed, false rape allegations covering a 9-year period were studied. These false rape allegations constitute 41 percent of the total forcible rape cases ($n = 109$) reported during this period. These false allegations appear to serve three major functions for the complainants: providing an alibi, seeking revenge, and obtaining sympathy and attention (Kanin, 1994). These complaints often reflect impulsive and desperate efforts to cope with personal and social stress situations, as in the case of the Duke University Lacrosse team and the false accusations of rape against several team members.

Some argue that we are creating a victim culture, where criminal behavior or bad choices are passed on to others. And in the process, certain professionals such as lawyers and psychotherapists are profiting (Zur, 1994). The victim culture interferes with helping those who truly need and deserve assistance. Anxiety disorder, the so-called borderline personality disorder, and PTSD are becoming popular (Zur, 1994). Many ask why so many patients within a few years have been labeled as traumatized. And, one must wonder why in an age where technology, medicine, environmental concerns, and diet have reached new peaks, Americans feel a heightened sense of vulnerability and are buying into the new psychiatric diagnosis (Zur, 1994). Increasingly, Americans are told that they are traumatized, victimized, and are in need of a psychotherapist or personal injury attorney. Those who do not feel victimized may be labeled as being in denial. In other words, if you do not feel you're a victim we'll convince you that you are.

In a book by Dineen (1996), the author writes how the victim industry has been fueled by psychotherapists and outlines the direct economic and professional benefits that psychotherapists derive from perpetuating the idea of victimology. She discusses how therapists need patients, so they create disorders such as PTSD and other behavioral conditions with which to label prospective customers. Many lawyers also pursue questionable personal injury cases, knowing that a certain percentage may settle out of court. It is not this writer's position to demean psychology or the legal profession, but questions need to be raised about the real meaning of a victim. In the following discussions on victimization theory, there is some enlightenment on the causes of victimization.

Review of Early Victimization Theory

Early scholarly work on victimization dates back to the 1940s. However, because of its lack of theoretical grounding, the study of victimization has not become a recognized academic discipline. One of the first researchers to address victimization was Hans von Hentig. His early work examined the relationship between offenders and their victims. Hentig hypothesized that the victim shapes the criminal and the crime. (See the section titled "Hentig's Victim Classification" that follows for more information.) In other words, he searched for and found a reciprocity that exists between the criminal and the victim, or "the killer and the killed" (Hentig, 1948).

In addition to Hentig's early work, Mendelshon (1963), who claims to have originated the study of victimology, studied rape victims and their relationships with their offenders. According to Mendelshon's theory, some victims may unintentionally invite their own victimization, depending on the degree of relationship with the offender. Mendelshon developed a number of typologies describing the degree of culpability between victims and offenders.

Hentig's Victim Classification

Hentig's classification of victims is more comprehensive than Mendelshon's typology. Mendelshon explains victimization through **situational victimization factors**; Hentig uses **personal factors associated with victimization**, such as social, psychological, or biological characteristics, to explain victimization. His victim typology, which laid the foundation for further work on the subject, incorporates the following 12 categories of victims (Hentig, 1948: 404–438).

The first category includes the *young*, who are prone to victimization because of their immaturity and vulnerability. Hentig believed that children are usually victims of violent crimes and sexual offenses rather than of property offenses (although adults use children in the commission of crimes against property).

The second category includes *females*. Hentig argued that younger women are vulnerable to murder and sexual assault, and older women are prone to property crimes (e.g., fraud). Because a woman has less physical strength than a man and because men commit most violent crimes, women are more likely to suffer at the hands of a male aggressor. The aggressor is usually known to the victim (a former spouse or an acquaintance).

The *elderly* are the third category. They are likely to be victims of property crimes. They are less likely to fend off attackers because of their weaker physical state and possible decreased mental alertness, making them prime targets for scam artists and predatory offenders.

The fourth category includes victims who are *mentally defective*. Clearly, those in this category are susceptible to victimization. This is one of the largest groups because it includes alcoholics, drug addicts, and those who suffer from various mental handicaps. Hentig found that alcohol plays a role in victimization, especially when both victims and offenders are intoxicated.

The fifth category includes *immigrants*, who are vulnerable because of their lack of familiarity with their new culture, rejection by the dominant population, and deprived economic status. Many immigrants are marginally employed or otherwise near poverty, forcing them to reside in communities where crime is prevalent or to become involved in crime. A recent extension of this theory is the enslavement of illegal aliens for the purpose of working in sweatshops. A study of the garment industry in California revealed that most of the 69 manufacturers studied were breaking labor laws. They employed children as young as 13 years of age, many of whom worked up to 16-hour days. Fire exit doors were locked, and workers were forced to live on the premises (Silverstein, 1994). A blatant example of immigrant victims occurred in El Monte, California. On August 2, 1995, state and federal agents raided a garment manufacturer suspected of worker abuse. What they found was worse than what they expected. The workers, illegal Thai immigrants, were forced to live in the factory and were not allowed to leave the premises. Thai guards kept the workers from escaping, and barbed wire was strung around the compound. Food and other necessities were brought to the workers, the cost of which was deducted from their wages. Workers were paid less than $2 an hour and were required to repay the costs of their travel from Thailand, which amounted to $5,000. They were afraid to escape because of their immigrant status, but one worker who did leave prompted the investigation (White, 1995).

Further evidence of this problem is the transporting of immigrants by "coyotes," who charge a fee to smuggle illegal immigrants into the United States. Coyotes prey on people from developing countries who have few economic opportunities and are desperate to improve their socioeconomic status. The immigrant's safety and well-being during the long trip are often compromised because of the inhumane conditions. In 2003, a trailer bound for Houston carrying 74 undocumented immigrants was abandoned and 19 people in it died from lack of oxygen (Parks, 2005).

The sixth category includes *minorities*. Their plight is similar to that of immigrants. They are often forced to live where crime flourishes, subjecting them to victimization by members of their own group or street gangs, as well as a lack of opportunities in the dominant culture.

The *dull normals* are in the seventh category. Hentig views this group as born victims. Because of their diminished intellectual status—which has a biological cause—swindlers and other criminal types easily victimize them. The low IQ of members of this group prevents them from understanding or recognizing the deception.

The eighth category includes the *depressed,* those who suffer from a psychological problem. Depressed people are likely victims because of their apathetic state of mind. A depressed person is generally a submissive person, frequently weak in both mental and physical strength, gullible, and easily swayed. Many homeless people are of this type, as well as persons under the influence of alcohol or other drugs.

The ninth category includes the *acquisitive.* An acquisitive person is one who is greedy and desires financial gain and thus is likely to be targeted by gamblers or other confident people. Poor people struggle to survive, and the rich seek to increase their wealth. In either case, they can fall victim to criminal types, such as frauds and cheats, if they have an acquisitive attitude.

The *lonesome and heartbroken* represent the tenth category. Those who seek and desire companionship and intimate relationships are likely to succumb to victimization. In their relentless search for true friendship or love, they lower their defenses or ignore undesirable traits in their partners. These types may believe that it is better to be abused than to be alone. And some abused spouses may refuse to leave because of the undesirable consequences of being alone or the belief that they have nowhere to go.

The eleventh category includes those referred to as *tormentors*, such as alcoholic or psychotic fathers who abuse and assault their families over a long period of time and who may finally be killed by a family member. This type of person becomes a victim because he or she creates the situation by being an abuser.

The twelfth category includes the *blocked, exempted, and fighting victims.* They become victims because of situations they have created, but generally less violence is involved than when tormentors are involved. For example, a person who is blackmailed because of his or her previous involvement in criminal activity becomes a victim of extortion and is afraid to contact the police because of his or her record.

Mendelshon's Typology

Mendelshon's first type is the *innocent victim.* Innocent victims are unconscious of and unaware of their potential for victimization. Young children fall into this category. Other victims just happen to be in the wrong place at the wrong time. For example, in the well-publicized O. J. Simpson case, Ronald Goldman, who was slain along with Nicole Brown Simpson, was an innocent victim. It is assumed that Nicole was the intended target, but because Goldman was also at the scene, he became a victim of consequence.

The next five types of victimization in Mendelshon's typology are commonly categorized as *victim-precipitated crimes*, or *victimization*, in which the victim somehow contributes to his or her own injury. The second type is the *victim with minor guilt*. Examples of this type are victims who frequent high-crime areas, associate with deviant types, or are customers of prostitutes who then become victims. The *victim as guilty as the offender* is the third type. In this situation, victim and offender engage in criminal activity (e.g., robbery), after which one partner victimizes or robs the other. The fourth type is called the *victim is more guilty than the offender*. Here, a victim provokes or attacks another, but the defending person injures the provoking person. The final type, the *most guilty victim*, occurs when a person is killed by another in self-defense. The victim initiating the confrontation becomes a guilty victim, as well as a dead one.

Sellin and Wolfgang's Typology of Victimization

Sellin and Wolfgang (1964) offer a victim typology that addresses situations rather than relationships. Their five categories are primary victimization, secondary victimization, tertiary victimization, mutual victimization, and no victimization.

Primary victimization refers to personalized or individual victimization such as when an individual or group selects a specific person to target for victimization. Victims of hate crimes or domestic violence are examples. Victims of *secondary victimizations* are impersonal targets of the offender. When a corporation or business sells faulty products to the public or church officials embezzle the offerings of a church congregation, the public or church member are secondary victims. The evangelist Jim Bakker engaged in this type of victimization, and the victims of corporate scandals, such as former employees of the Enron Corporation who lost their life savings, are other examples. *Tertiary victimization* involves the public or society as a victim. Crimes committed by the government, as opposed to businesses, are included in this category, such as when public officials embezzle funds or defraud the public. An elected official who takes pleasure trips and writes them off as business expenses is cheating the public. Victims may not recognize their victimization unless the government intervenes. *Mutual victimization* refers to when offenders become victims, as when two people engage in a criminal activity and then one becomes the victim of the other: the prostitute robs her customer or the drug dealer shoots the buyer.

The final category identified by Sellin and Wolfgang is called *no victimization*, which includes situations in which victimization is difficult to define. So-called victimless crimes are often mentioned in this category. It is difficult to define victimization in situations such as those when consenting adults engage in prostitution, an illegal activity, in a private home. Another example is pseudomasochism whereby two consenting adults agree to participate in sexual activities that cause bodily injury.

Modern Victimization Theories

Modern theories of victimization are basically revised versions of earlier perspectives. As with the older theories, they address victimization through associations, behaviors, culture, spatial relationships, victim lifestyle, and situations.

Cultural Trappings

Cultural trappings and victimization can be linked. Violence and resulting victimization is a product of structural arrangements in our culture conducive to violence (Galtung, 1996). Culture consists of a totality of values, norms, attitudes, beliefs, race and gender relations, child-rearing practices, governance, and other practices of a society. Social relations, the media, the entertainment industry, and other forms of commercial enterprise influence the culture. When cultural messages are flawed, however, violence and victimization are possible outcomes. When a culture allows the dehumanization of certain people or groups, as in violent video games or R-rated films, violence may be the result.

A pathetic or weak cultural base can lead to *structural violence,* or the acting out of an individual or group incorporated into formal legal and economic exchanges. In other words, those who are poor or disenfranchised may turn to violence against property as a means to an end or to produce a feeling of recognition. Many of the inner-city racial riots of the 1960s and 1970s were the result of expressive disillusionment with systemic inequality. The malicious burning and looting were the result of perceived inequality by many.

Individual acts of direct violence, such as those committed by gangs, street thugs, and hate killers, are often grounded in cultural causes or fostered in environments that permit the perpetuation of violence. Because children continue to come from dysfunctional families that promote negative cultural values, where survival and recognition are based on gratifying personal needs, little else can be expected. As children grow and are exposed to violence at home, in the community, in the media, or at school, some will express anger and turn into bold, violent predators. Community predators victimize many, which results in the victims retaliating by bullying, which leads to more violent acts. This is not to suggest that everyone raised or exposed to these negative influences will become violent criminals, but many will commit crimes and justify their behavior by the fact that society has cheated them. Thus, robbery, rape, and murder are get-even measures or means to exhibit power and control over others.

In regards to victimization, many of these offenders are streetwise and recognize that the average person is not crime conscious, making that person an easy target. In other words, victimization will occur as social and economic differences increase between those who have much and those who have little, particularly when both coexist in the same communities.

Victim Precipitation Theory

According to the **victim precipitation theory**, victimizations result from a number of precipitating factors one of which is the victim's behavior, including lifestyle interactions in situations in which deviance and criminality flourish. Simply put, one who undertakes a crime risk activity or participates in a deviant act, however temporarily, takes a chance of becoming either a victim or an offender. The culture or physical environment and one's social standing may not make a difference in victim-precipitated events. Victim precipitation can be active or passive, depending on the role or behavior of the victim.

Active precipitation refers to situations in which victims provoke violent encounters or use words to cause a physical confrontation with another. The victim in a gang-related retaliatory killing or participants in a barroom brawl are examples of **active victims**. Research studies of homicide offenders and their victims have consistently identified precipitating factors to the crime. Comparisons of data of murder victims in large cities with those of victims in small communities find similarities such as previous relationships between the victim and offender and similar socioeconomic backgrounds (Hewitt, 1988).

Victimologists generally agree that the offender's behavior in homicides is directly related to the type of victim selected. In other words, victims of homicide and their offenders are often partners in crime—in some way victims contribute to their own deaths. The use of drugs also contributes to victimization and violence. That is, drug usage increases the chance of violence initiated by or against the person.

The evidence indicates that drug users are more likely than nonusers to commit crimes, that arrestees frequently were under the influence of a drug at the time they committed their offense, and that drugs generate violence.

—Drug Policy Information Clearinghouse, 1999.

Studies on the relationship between drugs and violent crime have consistently indicated high rates of homicide and suicide that often involve firearms. Deaths from illicit drug use or overdose also contribute to the high victimization rates (Mokdad et al., 2004). Based on incarceration rates in federal and states prisons, many inmates committed murders, robberies, and assaults while under the influence of drugs or in the pursuit of additional drugs (U.S. Department of Health and Human Services, 1999).

As for domestic disputes, many fatalities result from victim retaliation. And in many of these cases, drugs were often used by the perpetrator. In these situations, the abused spouse or partner may fight back, provoking more anger in the abuser and resulting in the death of the victim.

This is not to suggest that the victim is responsible, but that the victim's response incited the offender. Family members are still the primary targets of murders, which often result from abusive, violent, or dysfunctional family situations.

Passive precipitation occurs when a victim unknowingly provokes a confrontation with another. Unsuspecting lovers who are assaulted by their partner's estranged spouse are considered **passive victims**, especially if the suitor had no knowledge of the spouse. People victimized because of their religious beliefs, sexual orientation, or racial background are considered to be passive victims. These victims of hate crimes often are unaware of the intended aggression directed toward them, as evidenced by the victims of the bombing of the Oklahoma City Federal Building in 1995 and the thousands killed on September 11, 2001. The government was the target, and the victims were unaware of the intended aggression.

The concept of victim precipitation involves controversial issues. In cases of rape, for example, it has been suggested that some female rape victims contribute to their victimization by their actions and behavior (Amir, 1971). Although this position seems preposterous, evidence indicates that rape defendants have been acquitted because the jury accepted the argument that the victim "asked for it." In a celebrated Florida case, the clothing worn by a rape victim, which was described as a lace miniskirt with no underclothing, was successfully offered as evidence, contributing to the acquittal of the defendant (*Boston Globe*, 1989).

Evidence indicates that some people become crime victims because of their lifestyle or associations. Those who frequent areas prone to high crime activity or hang out with deviant types are more prone to victimization than those who choose safer environments or associate with more stable people. Researchers have suggested that when offenders come together in social encounters prompted by excessive alcohol use, uncontrolled rage, mental instability, depression, or frustration over socioeconomic status, a violent offense is likely to occur. In these situations, either party can be victim or offender. These situations are magnified when cultural differences or competition for employment, housing, or social recognition are factors (Hindelang, Gottfredson, and Garofalo, 1978; Lashley, 1989; Wolfgang, 1967).

The homeless are often passive victims of predatory crime. To be homeless is to be placeless, where life consists of attempts to survive in places that offer little protection from predators. Homeless people are dropouts, often with no relationships with relatives or significant others. Their mental state, anonymity, and lack of resources make them vulnerable to predatory offenders and other deviant types (Fitzpatrick, Lagory, and Ritchey, 1993). In addition, some homeless men and women are depressed or mentally unsound, making them easy targets. Predators recognize that some homeless people have disabilities and so are more likely to receive financial support. The homeless, whose ranks include juveniles and other disenfranchised people seeking security in the streets, free from the authorities, are not likely to report their victimization. Also, to survive, some homeless persons resort to criminal activity, such as prostitution, theft, or selling drugs. As a result, they are not likely to be reported as missing by family or friends. These victims are part of an anonymous subculture of violence and deviance.

Prostitutes are at a high risk of victimization. Photo by John Maher/Stock Boston.

Spatial Relations

Good fences make good neighbors.

—Robert Frost

Spatial relations and victimization can be intimately connected. The spatial relations of the community provide an opportunity for victimization. Both criminals and victims often live in physical proximity to one another, coexisting in socially disorganized, high-crime communities (Fagan, Piper, and Cheng, 1987). This is not to suggest that victims encourage crime but that their normal activities make them targets for the motivated criminal (Garofalo, 1987: 234–240). Unfortunately, many people are unable to afford the luxury of gated communities or the strong fences needed to deter predators.

Research conducted by Sherman, Gartin, and Buerger (1989) revealed that some communities are considered dangerous places or have crime "hot spots" requiring a continuous police presence. The probability of victimization is high for those living in or frequenting areas that have drug houses or so-called nuisance bars. These communities commonly have a number of deteriorated buildings, low-rent apartments, abandoned vehicles, liquor establishments, large gatherings of unemployed young people, graffiti, overt prostitution, and drug dealing. In other words, the physical environment, along with the type of people in the area, sets the stage for crime and victimization. Many law-abiding citizens living in these areas are victimized simply because they are in contact with criminal types.

The disenfranchised lifestyles of transients make them easy targets for criminals.
Photo by Robert J. Meadows

More recent research on spatial relations theory and crime victimization is known as the *spatial syntax theory* (Hillier and Shu,1999). Space syntax is a system for analyzing the connectivity of street patterns and its relationship to factors like pedestrian activity and crime. It defines connectivity in multiple ways, the most common being the number of corners one must turn to get from one place to another. Space syntax also measures connectivity with visibility, or how much of a street is visible from any other streets or intersections. The safest locations are on well-connected streets with plenty of foot traffic and many highly visible dwellings. An analysis of crime in London found the more residences on a street, the lower the crime rate. As the researchers concluded, "There is safety in numbers!" (Hillier, 2004). In other words, research indicates that the layout of street design, building placement, and building size are correlated with crime and other social conditions (Baran, Smith, and Toker, 2006; Nubani and Wineman, 2005). Spatial syntax components may be used as potential correlates of crime or any other social phenomenon.

Related to space theory, is the **broken windows theory** (Kelling and Coles, 1996; Wilson and Kelling, 1982). As a community deteriorates, crime increases. Factors contributing to such decline are nonenforcement of building codes and overlooking of minor criminal conduct, such as public drinking. Other evidence suggests that high-crime communities in decay appear to have very high concentrations of locations selling alcohol, further influencing incivilities and disorder (Roncek and Maier, 1991).

A vandalized, run-down area is a signal to the potential offender that the neighborhood lacks stability and protection. As Newman (1972) proposes with his **defensible space theory**, people are more likely to defend themselves from crime if they live in conditions conducive to reporting. Communities with clearly defined territories, natural surveillance, and an image of protection are less likely to be frequented by undesirable types and are more likely to resist the presence of criminals. The defensible space theory suggests that criminals victimize others if the chance that they will be detected is low. Thus, detection and victimization are related to the physical environment in which incidents occur.

Another collateral theory on spatial relationships and victimization is the **routine activities theory** proposed by Cohen and Felson (1989). They argue that the motivation to commit crime and the number of offenders are constant. According to this theory, victimization has three requirements. The first is the availability of suitable targets (such as homes with valuable goods or vulnerable people, especially females and elderly citizens living alone). As addressed in Focus 2–1, students and young adults, especially females engaged in partying and other festive activities, run a high risk of victimization because they are suitable targets for sexual predators and

Focus 2–1   Disappearance in Aruba

On May 30, 2005, high school student Natalee Holloway was reported missing during her trip to the island of Aruba. Like many tourists, students often travel to the island for excitement and escape. In this case, Holloway had just graduated from high school and traveled to Aruba with friends to celebrate. Like many teens, Holloway and her friends engaged in risky behaviors (partying, excessive drinking, etc.) away from normal protections or guardians. In places such as Aruba, violent crime is uncommon and there is an expectation of safety. Holloway appears to be the victim of foul play or some tragic accident because her body was not recovered, and she was last seen in the presence of several young men whom she met on the island. As of this writing, a Dutch student who reportedly was with Holloway on the evening she disappeared was questioned. Holloway reportedly was a very trusting but naïve girl, which may have contributed to her disappearance.

date rapists (Schwartz and Pitts, 1995). Cohen and Felson suggest that some people are prone to victimization through their social interactions or living conditions, prompting others to take advantage of them.

The second requirement for victimization to occur is the absence of capable guardians. People living alone, especially senior citizens, are vulnerable because they lack someone to defend them against intruders. The lack of adequate police or security protection also contributes to victimization. For example, single parents with a number of children may have less money to use to protect themselves against intruders, especially in communities with high crime rates; may have few security measures in place; or live in an area with slow law enforcement response (Maxfield, 1987).

The third requirement for victimization to occur is the presence of motivated offenders. Motivated offenders are more likely to victimize when a suitable target and an absence of capable guardians exist. Gang members may be motivated to burglarize or commit assault when opportunities are provided and the probability of anyone reporting their activities is low.

Studies suggest that homes that are well guarded (such as those in guarded gated communities) are less likely to be burglarized (Maume, 1989). The message is that victimization is less likely to occur when measures are taken to reduce criminal opportunity and when the chances of detection are high. Criminal offenders will very likely attempt to flee to avoid detection or arrest. Operating under the premise that most rational offenders prefer escape to apprehension and detection, one can argue that the use of strategies to reduce the opportunity for victimization is highly desirable. Unfortunately, many citizens are without resources to control or secure their environments or to leave communities to avoid victimization.

New Technology

Our reliance on and appetite for technology, which is pleasurable, informative, and indeed necessary, is quickly becoming a new area of victimization. There are those who exploit the benefits of technology to victimize the young, immature, or naïve. Others use computers to sabotage or to inflict terror, referred to as cyber terrorism.

A **cyber crime** is a criminal offense that has been devised or made possible by computer technology or is a traditional crime that has been transformed by the use of computers. Distinct types of computer-related crimes lead to victimization. The major crimes that include violence are the following:

- Criminal threats
- Stalking (cyber stalking)
- Threatening or annoying electronic mails
- Distribution of child pornography
- Luring and enticement
- Computer hacking

The perception of cyberspace lowers people's inhibitions, encouraging them to say things they might not say when they are face to face with another person. People are anonymous online (no one really knows with whom they are interacting) and are far away from each other physically. Anonymity and physical distance mean that people online are protected from the immediate consequences of their actions. This impersonal connection has a desensitizing effect on the cyberspace bandit.

Computer bulletin boards and chat services can be dangerous, especially for children who then have ready access to sexually explicit material. Most cyber victims are, in fact, children or teenagers. Predators contact them over the Internet and try to entice them into engaging in sexual acts. Cyber criminals also use the Internet for the production, manufacture, and distribution of child pornography. In response to this threat, the FBI initiated an undercover operation code-named **Innocent Images National Initiative** to target offenders who use computers to receive or disseminate child pornography and lure minors into illicit sexual relationships (see Focus 2–2).

The FBI reported that between fiscal year 1996 and fiscal year 2003, the Innocent Images National Initiative recorded more than 9,000 new cases, more than 2,000 indictments and arrests, and more than 2,500 convictions. And, under federal law, The Communications Act of 1934

Focus 2–2   A Case of Online Luring

In 2002, a 15-year-old girl disappeared from her home. Her parents reported that she was on the Internet frequently and may have become the victim of Internet enticement. The local police requested FBI assistance. Several days after the report, the FBI received a telephone call from an anonymous individual who stated he was online in a chat room with the topic of sadomasochism. The caller said a person in the chat room was bragging and sending real-time photographs of a young female he identified as his sex slave, who he was allegedly molesting and torturing. The FBI determined the girl in the photographs was the 15-year-old reported missing. The Internet Protocol (IP) address of the perpetrator was retrieved and the Internet service provider was subpoenaed to obtain the identity and address of the subject. When the subject's home was identified, the FBI and local police convened at the location, made forcible entry, and recovered the victim. The victim was found restrained to a bedpost with a dog collar around her neck and a chain with two padlocks. She was clothed only in thong underwear and had visible bruises. The kidnapper was arrested and prosecuted (Federal Bureau of Investigation (FBI), 2005).

---

criminalizes anonymous harassment by a telecommunications device. Congress recently amended the law to criminalize anonymous harassment via the Internet.

Troubled or rebellious teens seeking emancipation from parental authority can be especially susceptible to Internet predators. The risk of victimization is particularly great for emotionally vulnerable youth dealing with issues of sexual identity. In 1999, Dr. David Finkelhor conducted a research survey on Internet victimization of youth (Finkelhor, Mitchell, and Wolak, 2000). The report contains the following statistical highlights:

- One in five youth were approached sexually or received a solicitation over the Internet in the last year.
- One in 33 youth received an aggressive sexual solicitation in the last year; that is, a predator asked the young person to meet in person, called on the phone, and/or sent correspondence, money, or gifts through the mail.
- One in four youth had an unwanted exposure in the last year to pictures of naked people or people having sex.
- Only a fraction of all episodes was reported to authorities such as the police, an Internet service provider, or a hotline.

More evidence of potential abuses was reported in a study of online usage of more than 1,200 teenage girls between the ages of 13 and 18 years (Roban, 2002). It was revealed that many entered certain chat rooms without their parents' knowledge. More than 80 percent of the girls reported that they make their own online decisions regarding whom to chat with. Although girls may act older than their years, many are still naïve and vulnerable and are swayed by online contacts who express caring and emotional sentiments toward them. This type of emotional vulnerability attracts predators and others seeking so-called cyber sex. Whereas cyber romances are rare, face-to-face interactions between young girls and online contacts do occur, which reveals that common sense does not always prevail.

In an unusual case of online harassment and cyber bullying resulting in the suicide of a 13-year-old female, in 2006, a neighborhood mother, her 18-year-old employee, and her 13-year-old daughter are accused of creating a fake Internet profile of a teenage boy that was used to send harassing messages to the teen. In 2008, charges were against the women. Although many of the respondents reported that their parents set specific ground rules for using the Internet, nearly 45 percent admitted breaking these rules at least once. When confronted with pornography or sexual harassment online, fewer than 7 percent reported it to their parents.

SUMMARY

This chapter provides an overview of the impact of victimization and some significant theories on victimology. The theories presented are not intended to explain all types of victimization because there are exceptions and some types overlap. Also, some cases of victimization do not fit neatly into any of the typologies presented. Yet, violent victimization can occur in any community, regardless of its socioeconomic makeup or the availability of capable guardians.

Although theories are open to criticism and sometimes appear to state the obvious, they suggest that victimization is associated with lifestyle, behavior, and personal characteristics of the individual. By understanding how and why people are victimized and the factors associated with victimization, the development of systemic prevention and response strategies is possible. The literature is replete with studies on crime and the categorization of criminal types, but a need exists to examine the victims of crime and the events that led to the victimization. People should be educated in ways to avoid becoming victims. Later chapters examine specific types of victimizations and review approaches and strategies to control the chances of becoming a victim of violence.

Key Terms and Concepts

Active precipitation
Active victim
Battered-women's syndrome
Broken windows theory
Cultural trappings and
　victimization
Cyber crime
Defensible space theory
Innocent Images National Initiative
Passive precipitation
Passive victim

Personal factors associated with
　victimization
Post-traumatic stress
　disorder (PTSD)
Rape trauma syndrome
Routine activities theory
Situational victimization factors
Spatial relations and victimization
Terrorism
Victimology
Victim precipitation theory

Discussion Questions and Learning Activities

1. Compare, contrast, and critique the routine activities theory.
2. Write a paper taking the position that some crime victims are responsible for their victimization. What theories or examples would you provide to support this position?
3. Identify and explain the five victim categories offered by Sellin and Wolfgang.
4. Consult local newspapers or other news sources and find examples of the routine activities, lifestyle, proximity, and victim precipitation theories. Report your findings to the class.
5. Visit a police department and interview officers who patrol high-crime areas. Ask them to relate, from their experiences, how some people become crime victims.
6. Do a content analysis of victimization in the media. That is, watch a film or television show about crime and violence, and list the extent and type of victimizations depicted. How often are women victimized? Children? Are any of the victimization theories presented in the film or television program?
7. Research court decisions from your jurisdiction or interview a defense attorney and find out how often the defense of battered-women's syndrome is used. Has PTSD been used successfully in any cases?
8. Do you agree that technology is becoming a medium of victimization? How?
9. Which victimization theories would apply in the Holloway case (Focus 2–1)? Can you find other examples where someone has disappeared and was never found? Discuss the events of the case.
10. Explain the culture of victimization discussed on page 38. Do you feel that victimization in some instances is misrepresented or overstated? Why?

WEB SOURCES

Bureau of Justice Statistics. *The Sourcebook of Criminal Justice Statistics Online*: 30th Edition. www.albany.edu/sourcebook/

Bureau of Justice Statistics. www.ojp.usdoj.gov/bjs/

Federal Bureau of Investigation. www.fbi.gov

RECOMMENDED READINGS

Clarke, Ronald V., ed. 2004. *Routine Activity and Rational Choice (Advances in Criminological Theory)*. Somerset, NJ: Transaction Publishers.

Goodey, Jo. 2004. *Victims and Victimology*. Longman Criminology Series. White Plains, NY: Pearson Longman.

Haining, Robert. 2003. *Spatial Data Analysis: Theory and Practice*. Cambridge, MA: Cambridge University Press.

REFERENCES

American Psychological Association. 1994. *Diagnostic and Statistical Manual of Mental Disorders*, 4th ed. Washington, DC: American Psychological Association.

Amir, Menachin. 1971. *Patterns in Forcible Rape*. Chicago: University of Chicago Press.

Baran, P. K., Smith, W. R., and Toker, W. 2006. *Conflict Between Space and Crime: Exploring the Relationship Between Spatial Configuration and Crime Location*. Paper Presented at EDRA37, Atlanta, May 3–7. Retrieved on February 5, 2008 http://www2.chass.ncsu.edu/garson/pa765/routine.htm

Boston Globe. 1989. Jury Stirs Furor by Citing Dress in Rape Acquittal. October 6, 12.

Bureau of Justice Statistics. 2004. *Homicide Trends in the United States: 2002 Update*. Washington, DC: U.S. Department of Justice. www.ojp.usdoj.gov/bjs/homicide/homtrnd.htm (accessed June 2004).

Centers for Disease Control and Prevention (CDC). 2003. *Costs of Intimate Partner Violence Against Women in the United States*. Atlanta, GA: U.S. Department of Health and Human Services.

Cohen, Lawrence, and Marcus Felson. 1989. Social Change and Crime Rate Trends: A Routine Activities Approach. *American Sociological Review* 44:88–100.

Dineen, T. 1996. *Manufacturing Victims: What the Psychology Industry is Doing to People*. Westmount, Canada: Robert Davies Multimedia Publishing.

Fagan, Jeffrey, Elizabeth Piper, and Yu-Teh Cheng. 1987. Contributions of Victimizations to Delinquency in Inner Cities. *Journal of Criminal Law and Criminology* 78:286–300.

Federal Bureau of Investigation. 2005. *Uniform Crime Reports: Crime in the United States, 2003*. Washington, DC: U.S. Department of Justice.

Finkelhor, David, Kimberly J. Mitchell, and Janis Wolak. 2000. *Online Victimization: A Report on the Nation's Youth*. Arlington, VA: National Center for Missing and Exploited Children.

Fitzpatrick, Kevin M., Mark E. Lagory, and Ferris J. Ritchey. 1993. Criminal Victimization Among the Homeless. *Justice Quarterly* 10(3): 353–368.

Galtung, J. 1996. *Peace by Peaceful Means: Peace and Conflict, Development and Civilization.* London: Sage Publications.

Garofalo, James. 1987. Reassessing the Lifestyle Model of Criminal Victimization. In *Positive Criminology*, ed. Michael Gottfredson and Travis Hirschi, 234–240. Newbury Park, CA: Sage Publications.

Harvard School of Public Health. May 2, 2007. Domestic Violence and Asthma Linked, According to Study. *ScienceDaily.* Retrieved February 28, 2008 http://www.science daily. com/releases/2007/05/070501115040.htm

Hentig, Hans von. 1948. *The Criminal and His Victim: Studies in the Sociobiology of Crime.* New Haven: Yale University Press.

Hewitt, J. D. 1988. The Victim–Offender Relationship in Homicide Cases 1960–1984. *Journal of Criminal Justice* 16:27–28.

Hillier, Bill. 2004. Can Streets be Made Safe? *Urban Design International* 9(1):31–45.

Hillier, Bill, and Shu, Simon C.F. 1999. *Do Burglars Understand Defensible Space? New Evidence on the Relation Between Crime and Space.* Space Syntax website, 1999.

Hindelang, Michael, Michael R. Gottfredson, and James Garofalo. 1978. *Victims of Personal Crime: An Empirical Foundation for a Theory of Personal Victimization.* Cambridge, MA: Ballinger Press.

Kanin, Eugene J. 1994. False Rape Allegations. *Archives of Sexual Behavior* 23(1):81(12) Plenum Publishing Corporation.

Kelling, George L., and Catherine M. Coles. 1996. *Fixing Broken Windows: Restoring Order and Reducing Crime in Our Communities.* New York: Free Press.

Kilpatrick, Dean, Benjamin Saunders, Lois Veronen, Connie Best, and Judith Von. 1987. Criminal Victimization: Lifetime Prevalence, Reporting to Police, and Psychological Impact. *Crime and Delinquency* 33(October): 479–489.

Kilpatrick, Dean, Ritchie Tidwell, and Benjamin Saunders. 1988. *Counseling Victims of Violent Crimes, Final Report.* Charleston, SC: Crime Victims Research and Treatment Center, MUSC.

Lashley, James R. 1989. Drinking Routines/Lifestyles and Predatory Victimization: A Causal Analysis. *Justice Quarterly* 6:4.

Los Angeles Times. 1999. Oklahoma City Bombing Survivors Still Show Mental Toll. May 26, A-23.

Maume, David. 1989. Inequality and Metropolitan Rape Rates: A Routine Activities Approach. *Justice Quarterly* 6:255–260.

Maxfield, Michael. 1987. Household Composition, Routine Activity, and Victimization. *Journal of Quantitative Criminology* 3: 301–320.

Mendelshon, B. 1963. The Origin of the Doctrine of Victimology. *Excerpta Criminologica* 3:30.

Mokdad, Ali H., James S. Marks, Donna F. Stroup, and Julie L. Gerberding. 2004. Actual Causes of Death in the United States, 2000. *Journal of the American Medical Association* 291(10):1242.

National Association of Crime Victim Compensation Boards. 2004. *National Victim Center: National Crime Victims' Resource Center.* Washington, DC: U.S. Department of Justice. www.nacvcb.org/index.html (accessed June 2005).

National Institute of Justice. 1996. *Victim Costs and Consequences: A New Look.* 1996 Washington, DC: National Institute of Justice.

Newman, Oscar. 1972. *Defensible Space Crime: Crime Prevention Through Environmental Design.* New York: Macmillan.

Nubani, L., and Wineman, J. 2005. The Role of Space Syntax in Identifying the Relationship Between Space and Crime. In Akkelies van Nes, ed. *Proceedings of the Fifth Space Syntax Symposium.* New York, NY: Techne Press.

Parks, Yvonne. 2005. The Victimization of Smuggled Immigrants. *Houston Catholic Worker.* XXV (May–June).

People v. Humphrey. 13 Cal. 4th 1073 (1996)

PTSD Alliance. 2004. *Post Traumatic Stress Disorder Fact Sheet.* Sidran Institute. www.sidran.org (accessed September 24, 2004).

Rohan, Whitney. 2002. *Girl Scout Research Institute: Girls and the New Media Girl Net Effect.* New York, N.Y.: Scouts of the USA, 420 Fifth Avenue,. www.girlscoutsofscc.org/pdf/Publications/net_effect.pdf (accessed July 2004).

Roncek, Dennis, and P. A. Maier. 1991. Bars, Blocks and Crime Revisited: Linking the Theory of Routine Activities to the Empiricism of Hot Spots. *Criminology* 29:725–753.

Schwartz, Martin D., and Victoria L. Pitts. 1995. Exploring a Feminist Routine Activities Approach to Explaining Sexual Assault. *Justice Quarterly* 12:166–175.

Sellin, Thorsten, and Marvin E. Wolfgang. 1964. *The Measurement of Delinquency.* New York: Wiley.

Sherman, L., P. R. Gartin, and M. E. Buerger. 1989. Hot Spots of Predatory Crime: Routine Activities and the Criminology of Place. *Criminology* 27:288–290.

Silverstein, Stuart. 1994. Survey of Garment Industry Finds Rampant Labor Abuse. *Los Angeles Times.* April 15, A-1.

Sykes, C. J. 1992. *A Nation of Victims: The Decay of the American Character.* New York: St. Martin's Press.

U.S. Department of Health and Human Services. 1999. *National Household Survey on Drug Abuse: Main Findings 1997.* Washington, DC: SAMHSA, Office of Applied Studies.

National Institute of Justice. 1996. *Victim Costs and Consequences: A New Look.* 1996 Washington, DC: National Institute of Justice.

White, George. 1995. Workers Held in Near Slavery, Officials Say. *Los Angeles Times.* August 3, Part A.

Wilson, James Q., and George Kelling. 1982. Broken Windows: The Police and Neighborhood Safety. *Atlantic Monthly* 249:29–38.

Wolfgang, Marvin E. 1967. Victim-Precipitated Criminal Homicide. In *Studies in Homicide,* ed. Marvin E. Wolfgang. New York: Harper & Row.

Zur, Ofer. 1994. *Psychology of Victimhood: Reflections on a Culture of Victims & How Psychotherapy Fuels the Victim Industry.* Sonoma, CA: Zur Institute)

3

Victims of Intimate Violence

LEARNING OBJECTIVES

After studying this chapter, you will:

- Be familiar with stalking laws.
- Understand the victimization associated with stalking.
- Understand the situations leading to violence between intimates.
- Understand the laws relating to domestic violence.
- Understand the laws dealing with acquaintance or date rape.
- Learn how the criminal justice system responds to violence between intimates.
- Understand the circumstances leading to intimate violence and dating violence.

INTRODUCTION

Intimate violence includes murder, rape, robbery, or assault committed by spouses, ex-spouses, boyfriends, girlfriends, or other acquaintances of the victim, as well as stalking behaviors, which are often a prelude to violence. Both males and females commit such crimes and are victims; however, women and children are more likely to be targets.

Victims of intimate violence may be physically injured or threatened with injury unless they comply with the demands of the offender. They are often targets of jealous or possessive acquaintances, ex-spouses, or admirers unknown to the victim. This chapter explores the dynamics of intimate violence, including violence to spouses, significant others, dates, elders, and children.

THE STALKING PROBLEM

We are going to slice her up like meat on a bone and feed her to the dogs.

—Letter written to actress Catherine Zeta-Jones by her convicted stalker

When examining the dynamics of intimate violence, there is a need to study **stalking** behavior. Stalking is often a prelude to violence, perpetrated either by former partners, acquaintances, or strangers. Data released by the National Center for Victims of Crime (2000, M Street NW, Suite 480 Washington, DC 20036) indicate that 81 percent of women who were stalked by a current or former husband or cohabiting partner were also physically assaulted and 31 percent were also sexually assaulted by that partner. Seventy-seven percent of female victims were stalked by someone they knew, whereas 64 percent of male victims were stalked by someone they knew. Victims of stalking include both people presently in imminent danger and those with danger continually pending but not at immediate risk of harm. On college campuses, students stalking other students is an emerging problem, which often goes unreported. National studies show an alarming number of college women have been the victim of a stalker, and the majority said it wasn't by a stranger. Most victims said they were threatened by an obsessive boyfriend or ex-boyfriend. Although stalking has been practiced for some time, the conduct first captured public attention as a result of the 1989 murder of actress Rebecca Schaeffer, co-star of the TV series *My Sister Sam*, by a deranged, obsessed fan. In 2007, celebrity Sandra Bullock and her husband were stalked by an obsessive female fan. In 2008, a former psychiatric patient was indicted for writing to Uma Thurman threatening to kill himself if he saw the actress with another man. He was accused of stalking Thurman for the past 2 years.

Women are not, however, the only victims of stalkers. The National Institute of Justice's *National Violence against Women Survey* estimates that more than one in four of the nation's 1.4 million annual stalking victims are men. And despite the impression given by the movie *Fatal Attraction*, 90 percent of the men stalked are targets of other men. Experts say the motive can be romantic jealousy, with gay men being the most likely victims of male-on-male stalking (National Center for Victims of Crime, 2000). But the stalking of men often is linked to the high-profile positions that the targets, often entertainers, politicians, and other well-known figures, hold in society.

In 1998, without invitation, Margaret M. Ray entered talk show host David Letterman's New Canaan, Connecticut, home while he was away. She and her son slept in his bed, watched television, and drove around in his Porsche. She was eventually caught at a tollbooth without any money, claiming to be his wife. Another notable example of stalking is when Jonathan Norman, a bodybuilder, made verbal threats and unwanted visits to film producer Steven Spielberg. The obsessed, angry stalker was upset over Spielberg's rejection of his film script. Spielberg said, "The threat was very real to me. . . . No one before has come into my life in a way to do me harm or my family harm. . . . I really felt—and I still to this day feel—I am prey to this individual." Spielberg learned of Norman's plan to rape him while he and his family were in Ireland filming a movie. Norman was finally arrested after he made two attempts to invade Spielberg's Pacific Palisades palazzo in 1997. Norman was subsequently convicted and sent to prison (Willing, 1998).

Another trend in stalking is facilitated by electronic media. As discussed in Chapter 1, victimization through cyber crimes is very real. About 20 percent of the 600 cases reviewed by the Los Angeles district attorney's Stalking and Threat Assessment Team in 1997 involved some form of e-mail or electronic communication. An extreme case from Los Angeles involved a woman who was victimized via the Internet by a former boyfriend, who allegedly placed personal ads on the Internet in her name that made it appear she was seeking to fulfill fantasies of being raped. It was reported that on six occasions men came to the woman's home in response to the ads before investigators solved what became the first crime to be prosecuted under California's cyberstalking statute (Miller and Maharaj, 1999b). Under the statute, passed in 1998, an offender can be charged with stalking, computer fraud, and solicitation of sexual assault. The law also updates California's anti-stalking laws to include threats by e-mail, pagers, and other forms of electronic communication.

> If you've read much about serial killers, they go through what they call different phases. In the trolling stage, basically, you're looking for a victim at that time. . . . You can be trolling for months or years, but once you lock in on a certain person, you become a stalker.
>
> —Dennis Rader, serial murderer

Stalking is not restricted to the famous, however. Ex-spouses, coworkers, acquaintances, and strangers also stalk. As indicated in the preceding quote by Dennis Rader, dubbed the BTK killer, who killed 10 people in the Wichita, Kansas, area between 1974 and 1991, the stalker might even be your respected neighbor. Rader was married with two children and served as a Boy Scout leader and president of his local church council. He also stalked and killed women to fulfill sexual fantasies.

Like most of Rader's victims, women are especially prone to stalking. However, former spouses or acquaintances stalk most victims. It is estimated that intimate partners stalk more than 1 million women and 371,000 men each year (Tjaden and Thoennes, 2000). In response to the stalking problem, all states have passed laws that seek to prevent stalking and punish those who engage in it. California passed the first anti-stalking law in 1991. Since then, all 50 states have passed similar laws (National Institute of Justice, 1993:12–13).

What are the motives of stalkers, and why do they become so obsessed with particular people? Zona, Palarea, and Lane (1998) provide a comprehensive interpersonal typology based on the relationship between the victim and the offender. The researchers gathered data from law enforcement agencies and classified stalkers into the following four categories:

Simple obsession. The victim and the perpetrator have had a prior relationship. This stalker category is considered the largest and probably the most threatening to the victim. The motivation behind these stalkers may be coercion to reenter a failed relationship or revenge by making the life of the former partner miserable. The use of fear tactics and harassment is typical of this category. Common examples are former spouses who stalk because of jealousy and anger, as in the case of Nicole Simpson who, with Ronald Goldman, was allegedly murdered by estranged husband O. J. Simpson in 1996.

Love obsession. This type is the obsessed fan or celebrity stalker, such as the stalkers of David Letterman and Steven Spielberg. Generally, no prior relationship exists between the victim and the stalker. The victims are usually known through the media or Internet. Unfortunately, a large number of these stalkers may be suffering from a mental disorder, such as schizophrenia, making it difficult to predict what they will do.

Erotomanic. **Erotomania** is a love obsession with an unwilling or unaware target. Much of the information on stalking resulted from the psychiatric study of erotomania and psychological studies on sexual harassment (see the case of Laura Black in Chapter 5) (Meloy, 1998). These cases differ from the simple and love obsession groups because the stalker falsely believes that the victim is in love with him or her. Many perpetrators are female, with the majority of victims being older males of higher social status. There are even examples of students stalking their teachers under the delusion that the teacher is in love with them.

False victimization syndrome. In this group, the stalker may accuse the victim of stalking to foster sympathy and support from those around the stalker. The majority of these perpetrators are female, and their motive seems to be attention. They may also falsely accuse another of harassment or crimes such as rape.

Whatever the motives, stalking generally involves any one of the following behaviors:

- Watching or following someone
- Making threatening or harassing phone calls or hang-ups
- Sending hate mail
- Making verbal threats to the intended victim or a family member
- Vandalizing personal property
- Making drive-bys
- Sending unwanted love notes, flowers, gifts, and so on

Stalking behavior may also fall into other categories. Some stalkers with no violent motive simply want to follow a target and have no personal contact. Their intent is to experience the other person's activities. Others, such as Dennis Rader and other serial killers and sex offenders, may stalk a target with the express purpose of committing murder or sexual violence.

Stalking may begin with a chance encounter and then escalate into a violent attack. Focus 3–1 illustrates how innocently stalking can begin and how it can become a nightmare for the victim. This is a true story about a stalker and how the victim managed to deal with the situation.

Focus 3–1   Shannon's Story

Shannon worked as waitress. She was 21, had a son, and recently broke up with the father of her baby. Later she met Tom, one of the customers at the restaurant where she worked. They began dating.

About three weeks into the relationship, Tom asked to marry her. Shocked and flattered, she asked him to give it some time. But a few days later something happened that really unnerved her. They were out driving when Tom saw his ex-girlfriend. He stated that he had an injunction against her for breaking the windows in his house and slashing his tires. Shannon became suspicious and had him checked out with a friend who was a police officer. It was found that Tom had a record for criminal mischief and grand theft. He'd been in jail for assaulting a police officer and had charges of lewd and lascivious acts with children.

(Continued)

(*Continued*)

Shannon broke off the relationship, but Tom continued to come to the restaurant for hours and stare at her. One night Shannon found a note on her windshield of her car. The note threatened her that she would be harmed unless she would meet with him soon. Shannon drove to his place and told him she never wanted to see him again and to quit coming to the restaurant. Tom hit her in the face. Terrified, Shannon drove away and called the police. When the police arrived at Tom's, he said that Shannon had struck him. No arrest was made. The next day Tom left a threatening note on her car and called and threatened to kill her. About a week later Shannon went to pick up her son at day care. The gas gauge showed empty, even though it was recently filled up. Apparently someone had loosened the gas hose. Then the calls started at work. Tom would say, "I'll get even with you. I'll make you hurt like you hurt me." Similar messages were left on her home answering machine. Over the next 3 months, the terrifying events escalated, starting with a friend's car being rammed one night by Tom. Shannon was the fourth woman who said that Rick had done something like this. Tom was later arrested.

Generally, former husbands are stalkers and their motives can be violent. The data in Table 3–1 indicate a number of motives for stalking ex-spouses, including frightening, provoking arguments, or shouting or

TABLE 3–1   PERCENTAGE OF EX-HUSBANDS WHO ENGAGED IN EMOTIONALLY ABUSIVE OR CONTROLLING BEHAVIOR, BY STALKING

Types of Controlling Behavior	Ex-Husbands Who Stalked (%) ($N = 166$)
Couldn't see things from her point of view	87.7
Jealous or possessive	83.7
Tried to provoke arguments	90.3
Tried to limit her contact with family and friends	77.1
Insisted on knowing where she was at all times	80.7
Made her feel inadequate	85.5
Shouted or swore at her	88.0
Frightened her	92.2
Prevented her from knowing or having access to family income	59.6
Prevented her from working outside the home	30.7
Insisted on changing residences without her consent	33.9

Note: Based on responses for first ex-husbands only.
Source: Office of Justice Programs. 1998. *Stalking and Domestic Violence in America: The Third Annual Report to Congress under the Violence Against Women Act.* Washington, DC: U.S. Department of Justice.

swearing at her. Also, evidence shows that husbands or partners who stalk their former partners are four times more likely than husbands or partners in the general population to physically assault their targets, and they are six times more likely than husbands and partners in the general population to sexually assault their targets. These data suggest that anyone associated with the target or known by the stalker (particularly a male friend or confidante) may be victimized as well.

Anti-Stalking Legislation

Prior to the passage of anti-stalking legislation, victims were generally told that nothing could be done unless the stalker tried to harm them physically. Currently, the primary intent of **anti-stalking legislation** is to stop those stalkers who threaten and harass before they commit violent acts.

As of 1999, all 50 states, the District of Columbia, and the federal government enacted laws making stalking a crime. The laws vary in defining the specific behaviors outlawed and the penalties of violation. In brief, the 50 states' laws treat stalking as a felony offense; however, many states do not necessarily make a first stalking offense a felony, unless there is an associated offense such as a weapons violation (Miller and Nugent, 2002).

The protections against stalking usually involve court orders, often termed stay-away, protection, or **restraining orders**, which are issued to prohibit contact between a victim and another person (stalker or ex-spouse). These orders typically prohibit a defendant from communicating with the victim and from entering his or her residence, property, school, or place of employment. The orders can also prohibit an alleged stalker from visiting a place frequented by the victim or from coming within a certain distance of the victim or the victim's family members. The orders must specify, however, where the defendant cannot go (e.g., a specific club or office).

In most states, law enforcement officials can make warrantless arrests based on probable cause if they believe that a person has violated an order. In many jurisdictions, violating the order is a misdemeanor and may result in civil or criminal contempt charges against the defendant. In some states, such as California, the police can obtain emergency orders from a magistrate during nonbusiness hours, until more formal orders are available.

The U.S. Supreme Court ruled in **United States v. Dixon** (1993) that the police can enforce protection orders through criminal contempt proceedings, in addition to bringing subsequent charges based on the same conduct. This ruling prohibits the use of the constitutional claim of double jeopardy. Thus, criminal prosecution of a defendant who violates a protective order does not bar a subsequent prosecution for stalking if the incident involving the violation of the protective order is considered stalking behavior.

States typically define stalking as willfully, maliciously, and repeatedly harassing and following others. Three states include lying in wait in the definition. Other states prohibit nonconsensual communication and unwelcome surveillance. The primary elements of stalking statutes are threatening behavior and the criminal intent of the stalker. Determining when legal action can be taken to enforce anti-stalking laws is a problem for the states. Fourteen states require that the offender make a threat against the victim. Stalking generally requires that the offender engage in a specific course of conduct, which is a series of acts over a period of time.

California has been in the forefront of the movement to criminalize stalking and has one of the most detailed laws against stalking, a model for many other states. Key portions of the California code are reproduced here. Under *California Penal Code,* § 646.9., stalking is defined as follows:

(a) Any person who willfully, maliciously, and repeatedly follows or harasses another person and who makes a credible threat with the intent to place that person in reasonable fear for his or her safety, or the safety of his or her immediate family, is guilty of the crime of stalking, punishable by imprisonment in a county jail for not more than one year or by a fine of not more than one thousand dollars ($1,000), or by both fine and imprisonment, or by imprisonment in the state prison years. . . . For the purposes of the section, "harasses" means a knowing and willful course of conduct directed at a specific person that seriously alarms, annoys, torments, or terrorizes the person, and that serves no legitimate purpose.

This course of conduct must be such as would cause a reasonable person to suffer substantial emotional distress, and must actually cause substantial emotional distress to the person. . . . "Course of conduct" means a pattern of conduct composed of a series of acts over a period of time, however short, evidencing a continuity of purpose. . . . "Credible threat" means a verbal or written threat or a threat implied by a pattern of conduct or a combination of verbal or written statements and conduct made with the intent to place the person that is the target of the threat in reasonable fear for his or her safety or the safety of his or her family and made with the apparent ability to carry out the threat so as to cause the person who is the target of the threat to reasonably fear for his or her safety or the safety of his or her family. It is not necessary to prove that the defendant had the intent to actually carry out the threat.

The California code, like many state codes, takes stalking behavior very seriously, as evidenced, for example, by the length of restraining orders. However, there is concern that some of the state laws may face constitutional challenges because of the language of the statutes. The three critical problems with existing anti-stalking laws are vagueness, over inclusiveness (trying to restrict conduct that may be protected), and under inclusiveness (excluding some types of conduct that are actually stalking behavior) (Faulker and

Hsiao, 1994). Terms such as *harass, annoy,* and *alarm* may suffer from vagueness, raising First and Fourteenth Amendment questions.

The frequent use of restraining orders has prompted discussion on enforcing these court orders, particularly in domestic violence or stalking situations. In other words, questions may arise regarding the liability of law enforcement officials in enforcing restraining orders. The U.S. Supreme Court addressed this question in 2005. In the case, a woman contacted the police because her ex-husband failed to return her three children after a custody visitation. Because she had a restraining order against her former spouse, she requested that the police arrest him. The police refused because they did not have enough information and suggested she wait. Her estranged spouse later killed the children. The victim sued the police for failure to enforce a court order, claiming that the police had a constitutional obligation to protect her and her children.

In a 7-2 decision, the Supreme Court ruled that the police cannot be sued on how they enforce a restraining order. In other words, the police are allowed some discretion in how or when to enforce such orders (*Town of Castle Rock, Colorado v. Gonzales*, 2005).

A victory for stalking victims came in a court decision from New Hampshire, which may have legal implications in other states. The case involved a private investigative agency obtaining personal information about a target for a stalker. The court ruled that if a "private investigator discloses information that creates a foreseeable risk of criminal misconduct against a person whose information was disclosed, the investigator owes a duty to exercise reasonable care to avoid subjecting the person to an unreasonable risk of harm" (*Remsburg v. Docusearch*, 2003). As discussed in Focus 3–2, a stalker obtains information from an investigative agency, which results in the death of another.

Focus 3–2   Third-Party Liability in Stalking

In 1999, New Hampshire resident Liam Youens shot and killed Amy Lynn Boyer, a young woman he had been stalking for several years. Youens had been obsessed with Boyer since high school and had created a Web site featuring information about Boyer and a detailed description of how he was stalking her and planning to kill her. Youens hired an online private detective service to obtain personal information, including Boyer's social security number and place of employment. The service acquired her employment information through trickery, and then sold that information to Youens. Youens then located Boyer's workplace, murdered Boyer as she left work, and then killed himself.

(Continued)

(Continued)

The victim's parents filed a civil lawsuit against the investigative service for wrongful death, invasion of privacy, and various other laws. The New Hampshire Supreme Court concluded that the service could be held responsible under several different legal theories. The court held that if a private investigator's disclosure of information, including a social security number, creates a foreseeable risk of criminal misconduct against the person whose information was disclosed, the investigator has a duty to exercise reasonable care to avoid subjecting the person to an unreasonable risk of harm. After the court ruled that the investigative agency could be held liable for having sold the victim's personal information, the company entered into a financial settlement with the victim's family. The suit set a precedent that third parties may be held liable for injuries that would not have been suffered but for their negligence.

Source: Helen Remsburg, Administratrix of the Estate of Amy Lynn Boyer, v. Docusearch, Inc., 149 N.H. 148 (N.H. 2003)

Federal Law on Stalking

A stalker can be punished under federal, as well as state, law. The federal code on stalking (18 United States Code § 875(c) [1999]) reads as follows:

> Whoever transmits in interstate or foreign commerce any communication containing any threat to kidnap any person or any threat to injure the person of another, shall be fined under this title or imprisoned not more than five years, or both.

The law is based on intent, and, therefore, intent to injure must be proved for a conviction. This law was tested in the case of *Baker v. United States* (1995) in which a young male student from the University of Michigan posted a story that described how he intended to torture, rape, and murder a female classmate. Baker was charged with five counts of transmitting by e-mail threats to injure or kidnap another and was convicted (*Baker v. United States*, 1995). In other words, federal jurisdiction in stalking cases usually arises from the Interstate Stalking Act of 1996. The law makes it a federal offense to cross state lines with the intent to place another person in fear of death or serious bodily injury or with the intent to use the mail or any other method of communicating across state lines for that purpose.

The Psychological and Social Consequences of Stalking

As with any victimization, stalking has a definite mental health impact. About one-third of the women (30 percent) and a fifth of the men (20 percent) said they sought psychological counseling as a result of stalking victimization.

In addition, stalking victims were significantly more likely than nonstalking victims to be very concerned about their personal safety and about being stalked, to carry something on their person to defend themselves, and to think personal safety for men and women had gotten worse in recent years. More than a quarter (26 percent) of the stalking victims said the victimization caused them to lose time from work. Although the survey did not query victims about why they lost time from work, it can be assumed they missed work for a variety of reasons—to attend court hearings, to meet with a psychologist or other mental health professional, to avoid contact with the assailant, and to consult with an attorney. When asked how many days of work they lost, 7 percent of these victims said they never returned to work. On average, however, victims who lost time from work and then returned to work missed 11 days. Stalking victims were asked whether they took any measures (other than reporting their victimization to the police or obtaining a protective order) to protect themselves from the stalker. Fifty-six percent of the women and 51 percent of the men reported taking some type of self-protective measure, such as carrying a weapon or altering their lifestyles and movements (Office of Justice Programs, 1998).

The threat of stalking and its effects have been studied in other countries. Pathe and Mullen (1997) conducted research on stalking in Australia. Their 1997 survey of 100 stalking victims found that stalking resulted in significant activity changes for victims, including the following:

- Major lifestyle changes or modification of daily activity for 94 percent of victims
- Curtailment of social activities for 70 percent of victims
- Decrease or cessation of work or school attendance for 50 percent of victims (as a result of either absenteeism or stalker invasion of work or school site)
- Relocation of residence for 40 percent of victims
- Change of workplace or school for 34 percent of victims

INTIMATE PARTNER VIOLENCE

Among women killed by a partner they have separated from, 88 percent had been stalked prior to being killed. . . . Although most stalkers do not kill their victims, most mate-killing men do stalk their victims. Stalking is one danger sign that women should not ignore.

—Dr. David Buss, an evolutionary psychologist

In recent years, the term *domestic violence* is being replaced by a more encompassing term—*intimate partner violence,* or *IPV.* **IPV** is defined as actual or threatened physical or sexual violence or psychological/emotional abuse by a spouse, ex-spouse, boyfriend/girlfriend, ex-boyfriend/ex-girlfriend, or date. Some common terms that are used to describe intimate partner violence are *domestic abuse, spouse abuse, domestic violence, courtship violence, battering, marital rape,* and *date rape.*

As discussed earlier, women are particularly prone to stalking and other violent partner victimization. Data suggest that certain socioeconomic groups are more prone to violence. Black and Hispanic females who are young and live in the inner city are highly victimized, as are poor single women with low education levels. Young women and those below the poverty line are disproportionately affected by IPV (Heise and Garcia-Moreno, 2002).

"The strongest risk factor for intimate partner homicide is an abuser's lack of employment: unemployment increases the risk of intimate partner homicide fourfold" (*American Journal of Public Health*, 2003). Although disenfranchisement and low economic standing are more strongly associated with IPV, intimate partner violence occurs across all population groups, irrespective of social, economic, religious, or cultural characteristics. Many women murdered by their intimate partner had visited an emergency department within 2 years of the homicide. More shocking data reveal that nearly 25 percent of women have been raped and/or physically assaulted by an intimate partner at some point in their lives, and more than 40 percent of the women who experience partner rapes and physical assaults sustain a physical injury (Tjaden and Thoennes, 2000). While the reasons for IPV are many, some research indicate a relationship between early child maltreatment and later adult violence. Gender differences also exist in linking child maltreatment, youth violence, and IPV. For instance, the link between IPV perpetration and child maltreatment in the forms of physical abuse and neglect was stronger in females. The link between child sexual abuse and future IPV perpetration was significant for males but not for females (Elsevier Health Sciences, 2007).

Through history, the abuse of a wife by her husband not only was socially acceptable but was often government sanctioned. In medieval times, a husband was able to discipline his wife by corporal punishment, and even as late as the 19th century in England, husbands were not punished for murdering their wives. The United States, following English law, in the 19th century, allowed a husband to physically discipline his wife without subjecting himself to prosecution for assault and battery. Thus evolved the colloquial expression "rule of thumb," whereby a husband could beat his wife with "a stick no thicker than his thumb." It was not until the 20th century that U.S. courts began to uphold laws that criminalized wife beating.

In IPV, the violent behavior of the batterer has often been explained by the characteristics of the victim, in other words, by what makes the victim susceptible to abuse or why some people are targeted for abuse. These questions place a certain amount of blame on the victim. It is, however, better to focus on the characteristics of the abuser. Male batterers, although they exhibit many different personality types, do share some common characteristics. Many batterers show a higher level of dependence on their wives than nonbattering men. Their dependence conflicts with fear of intimacy and loss of control. Batterers also exhibit higher levels of suspicion and paranoia, according to the Minnesota Multiphasic Personality Inventory (Vaselle Augenstein and Ehrlich, 1993). Batterers often will isolate their wives and are jealous of any interactions with other men, which create suspicions of infidelity. In addition, batterers have been observed to have an excessive need for control in the relationship. High levels of hostility, depression, and anxiety have also been noted. Batterers tend to deny responsibility for their actions, blaming the victim for provoking them, or they ignore the violent incident altogether (Vaselle-Augenstein and Ehrlich, 1993).

Many victims of IPV do not report their attacks. More than 18 percent of the women who were attacked by an intimate partner did not report the attack, compared with only 3 percent of those attacked by strangers. As expected, divorced and separated women have a higher rate of victimization than do married women (Pagelow, 1988). Although many of these victimizations result from disputes over child custody, alimony, or the terms of the separation, the violence is damaging and often repetitive. About one in five females victimized by a spouse or ex-spouse reported to the *National Crime Victimization Survey* (*NCVS*) that she had been a victim of three or more assaults in the previous 6 months.

Men are also victims of domestic abuse although they are even less likely to report it than women are. One longitudinal study reported that 31 percent of men and 44 percent of women admitted using aggression against their partner in the year before their marriage. Eighteen months after they were married, 27 percent of the men and 36 percent of the women reported being violent with their partner (O'Leary et al., 1989). In an early study conducted by Steinmetz (1977), the percentage of wives who used physical violence against their husbands is higher than the percentage of husbands who commit physically violent acts against their wives. Steinmetz also concluded that women were as likely as men to initiate the violence. Although men generally have a physical advantage over women, women are more likely to use weapons (McLeod, 1984).

Further evidence of violence by women was revealed in a more recent study. In an Oregon youth study of more than 200 young men, ages 17 to 27 years, and their romantic partners, new research indicates that "young women were more likely to initiate physical aggression than young men," and "young men were injured as well as young women and were sometimes afraid of their partners" (Peterson, 2003). This is not to suggest that women are more culpable, but that a woman can be just as capable of violence as a man.

Studies of spousal homicide also reveal that "black husbands were at greater risk of spousal homicide victimization than black wives or white spouses of either sex" (Mercy and Saltzman, 1989).

The notion that women are violent is hard for many to believe. The opposite perception is prevalent, despite the fact that women are more likely to commit child abuse and child murder than are men. The increased violence by women may be attributed to the fact that women generally have more access to children, but data indicate that the propensity for this type of violence is not gender neutral.

Many disenfranchised people, such as homeless women, come from violent situations. In a study of 777 homeless parents (the majority of whom were mothers) in 10 U.S. cities, 22 percent said they had left their last place of residence because of domestic violence (Owen et al., 1998). In addition, officials in 46 percent of cities surveyed by the U.S. Conference of Mayors (1998) identified domestic violence as a primary cause of homelessness. State and local studies also demonstrate the impact of domestic violence on homelessness.

In Minnesota, the most common reason women enter a shelter is domestic violence. Approximately one in five women (19 percent) surveyed indicated that one of the main reasons for leaving housing was to flee abuse; 24 percent of women surveyed were homeless, at least in part, because of a previous abuse experience (Owen et al., 1998). In Missouri, 18 percent of the sheltered homeless population are victims of domestic violence (DeSimone, 1998). A 1995 survey of homeless adults in Michigan found that "physical abuse/being afraid of someone" was most frequently cited as the main cause of homelessness (Douglas, 1995b).

Extended Victims of Partner Violence

Early exposure to abuse vastly increases children's risk of violent behavior toward others or themselves later on. . . . Boys who see their mothers beaten are far more likely to be abusive adults.

—Bessel van der Kolk, MD, Boston University School of Medicine

Early experiences with abuse and violence may have consequences in later life. Victims of abusive situations may visit physicians for isolated injuries, multiple emotional complaints, chemical dependency, depression, and other problems. Abuse also puts children at higher risk of later medical problems, including HIV infection, heart disease, and diabetes. Abused children may try to compensate for their emotional state through self-mutilation, anorexia, overeating, or abuse of drugs. Abused children are 18 times more likely to commit suicide than those who were not abused (van der Kolk, 1998). In a study conducted by Clarke et al. (1999), it was found that large numbers of intravenous drug users, both men and women, who victimized family members or sexual partners also had experienced childhood abuse, including witnessing violence at home. Silvern et al. (1995) revealed further evidence of this problem in a study of 550 undergraduate students. The study found that witnessing violence as a child was associated with adult reports of depression, trauma-related symptoms, and low self-esteem among women and trauma-related symptoms among men.

Research has shown that children exposed to domestic violence suffer a variety of psychological consequences from witnessing the violence or its effects, which may make them vulnerable to victimization as a juvenile or later as an adult (Edleson, 1999). Consequences of witnessing domestic violence may be traumatic stress and anxiety. Individuals suffering from post-traumatic stress disorder (PTSD) or other emotional disorders have been shown to be at higher risk for revictimization (Arata, 1999) by intimate partners or others. This vulnerability may result from forms of coping behaviors that youth adopt to deal with their anxiety, which include using drugs, using alcohol, participating in risky behaviors to gain attention, or engaging in promiscuous sexual behavior. The vulnerability or fatalistic perception may result from the youth's belief that he or she is doomed to a life of misery and is unable to control his or her destiny.

These children perform significantly below their peers in such areas as school performance, organized sports, and social activities (Kolbo, 1996). Children's exposure to adult domestic violence may further generate attitudes justifying their own use of violence. In other words, children who witness IPV are at greater risk of developing psychiatric disorders, developmental problems, low self-esteem, and experiencing school failure and violence against others (National Clearinghouse on Child Abuse and Neglect, 2003).

Spaccarelli, Coatsworth, and Bowden (1995) suggest that among a sample of 213 adolescent boys incarcerated for violent crimes, "those who had been exposed to family violence believed more than others that acting aggressively enhances one's reputation or self-image." Simply stated, being abused and watching Dad beat Mom repeatedly and brutally affect later development. These studies add credence to the notion that early learning experiences, whether positive or negative, impact later life and values. In other words, there is a transfer of oppression from being a victim to being an offender.

Explaining Partner Violence

A variety of methods is used by the batterer to intimidate or harm the victim. A number of factors are proposed to contribute to family/intimate violence. According to Gelles (1993:31–47), the amount of time spent together (cabin fever), conflicting interests, tensions in family interactions, age and generational differences, finances, and lack of privacy are among the factors that contribute to violence between intimates. Some of the methods used by batterers parallel the distorted tactics of stalkers, such as instilling fear, making threats, and so forth. The following classifications are generally used to explain the types of spousal battering (Brown, Dubau, and Merritt McKeon, 1997):

Psychological abuse. The batterer tries to frighten the victim by intimidation, threatening harm or harm to others, threatening death, harassing, killing pets, and destroying property.

Emotional abuse. The batterer undermines the victim's sense of self-worth by constant criticism, belittling, name calling, using the silent treatment, subverting the parent–child relationship, making and breaking promises, and so forth.

Economic abuse. This abuse includes making, or trying to make, a person financially dependent—for instance, by maintaining control over both parties' income, withholding money or access to money, keeping the victim from outside activities such as school or employment, harassing the victim at work, and requiring the victim to justify all money spent.

Sexual abuse. Sexual abuse is coerced (unconsenting) sexual contact—for instance, rape and beating of the sexual parts of the body, as well as forced bestiality, prostitution, unprotected sex, fondling, sodomy, forced sex with others, or use of pornography. Sexual abuse may also include undermining a person's sexuality with insults and unfounded accusations of infidelity. Rape in marriage is illegal, yet it happens all too often.

Physical abuse. Hurting or trying to hurt someone—for instance, grabbing, pinching, shoving, slapping, hitting, hair pulling, biting, arm twisting, kicking, punching, hitting with objects, stabbing, and shooting—is abuse. Other kinds of physical abuse include withholding access to resources necessary to maintain health, for example, medications, medical care, a wheelchair, food or fluids, sleep, or hygienic assistance. An abuser may also force the victim to use alcohol or drugs.

Legal abuse. The abuser may force the victim to engage in a vicious custody battle or an expensive court case. The abuser may give the victim less than deserved by law and may drag out the proceedings. The abuser may refuse to pay court-ordered support or alimony or to turn over assets. Although this may sound like a typical divorce, this type of legal abuse continues a pattern of abuse established in the marriage.

Another factor contributing to violence is substance abuse. Overindulgence in alcohol or drugs is often the symptom of other emotional problems. For example, feelings of inadequacy prompted by unemployment or underemployment may cause a spouse to vent frustration in undesirable ways. The person may abuse substances or become involved in deviant lifestyles. The victim spouse or children are perceived by the abuser as obstacles or liabilities. If the victim spouse is employed or pursuing an education, the abuser's jealousy, fueled by drugs or alcohol, may become abuse. In other words, the abuser, who is usually a male in this situation, feels a sense of loss because of his inability to succeed, and he feels threatened by his spouse's ability or desire to succeed. The abuser displaces toward his wife his anger at others that results from his own situation. Thus, a **cycle of violence** is associated with domestic violence.

The cycle begins with tension building in the abuser as a result of frustration, stress, and, generally, low self-esteem. It changes into anger or fear and then rage, resulting in an attack on his partner. The final phase is the honeymoon, in which the abuser feels remorse and guilt. There is often a repeat of the assaults, causing another cycle of violence to occur. See Figure 3–1.

Mary's story (Focus 3–3) points out the horror of being victimized by a controlling, overdominant partner. Although Mary suffered a great deal of pain, she is lucky. She was able to leave the relationship before it got worse. Many partners fail to leave abusive relationships as quickly; instead, they remain targets of continued and often increasing violent abuse.

So why don't women in abusive relationships simply leave? Eventually, most battered spouses do leave the relationship. However, leaving an abusive relationship is not as easy as it may seem. Many victims are without

FIGURE 3–1 CYCLE OF VIOLENCE

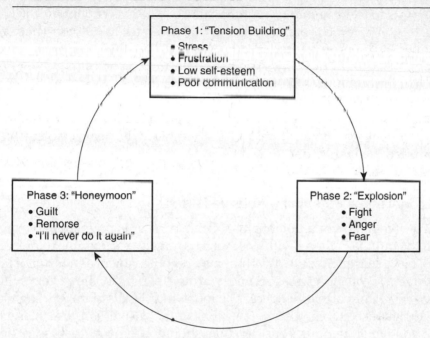

much support, either financial or emotional. Thus, women in these situations confront two major obstacles—fear and finances: fear for their safety and that of their children and lack of money to support themselves and their families.

Focus 3–3 Mary's Story

I left my ex-husband about 12 years ago, and many emotional scars still remain. At the time I was in counseling, and although I knew I would have to deal with the remnants of abuse from time to time, I honestly believed the worst was past me. I have been writing up many specific incidents, hoping to find what is causing this current level of pain. There are many similar incidents, starting with a beating, and then following a beating he often wanted sex, to show how sorry he was. I tried saying no a few times but soon learned that meant another beating. So I learned to allow him to have sex, and that is exactly what it was. Many times I remember crying while he was having sex with me, which he either didn't notice or didn't care. Shortly before I left I remember one night going to bed and pretending to be asleep, hoping he would leave me alone. Well, I don't know if he knew I was awake and wanted to teach me a lesson, or if he just wanted more power; however, he pulled a gun up on the bed and made sure I was awake. Then he laughed, told me it was to protect us, and then told me he wanted sex. Needless to say, we had sex.

The most dangerous time in the life of a battered woman is when she attempts to leave her abuser. Threatened by the loss of control, the batterer is likely to become more violent and may even try to kill her. There are not enough shelters to protect all the women and their children who need them. Despite stronger laws against domestic violence and greater willingness of the authorities to enforce these laws, the risk to an abused woman's life is enormous. Even when a batterer is served with an order of protection, he may stalk and harass the woman and taunt her with threats of further violence. More than half the women who leave violent men are hounded, badgered, and forced to return.

Recognizing a Potentially Abusive Partner

Early recognition of a potentially abusive partner is preferable to experiencing the trauma of living with one. Yet, it is not always possible to predict who will be violent and when. A partner may become violent as a result of lifestyle changes or other stresses. Some warning signs do, however, suggest a propensity for partner violence. The following signals of impending violence in a relationship are posed as questions. If the answer is "yes" to any one of the following, serious consideration should be given to terminating the relationship or to seeking counseling (Mount Auburn Hospital Prevention and Training Center, 1995):

1. Is this person jealous or possessive, will not let you have friends, or will not accept breaking off the relationship?
2. Does this person try to control you by giving orders, being bossy, insisting on making all the decisions, and not taking your opinions seriously?
3. Are you fearful about how this person will react to things you say or do? Does this person threaten or scare you?
4. Does this person have a history of violence? Fighting with others? Losing his or her temper frequently? Bragging about mistreating others?
5. Does this person pressure you for sex, even though you say no? Does the person make statements such as, "If you really loved me, you would . . . "?
6. Does this person abuse drugs or alcohol?
7. Does this person have a history of bad relationships and/or poor employment?
8. Has this person pushed, choked, kicked, or physically abused you?
9. Does this person blame you when you are mistreated? Does this person tell you that you caused it or that it is your own fault?

Obviously, spousal battering can endanger lives. Batterers who have killed or seriously injured their partners often display the following traits or behaviors. To evaluate whether an assailant is likely to kill his or her partner, other family members, and/or himself or herself, consider the following behaviors:

1. *Threats of homicide or suicide.* The batterer who has threatened to kill himself, his partner, the children, or her relatives must be considered dangerous. A person living with someone like this should take immediate steps to leave the situation.

2. *Fantasies of homicide or suicide.* The more the batterer has developed a fantasy about who, how, when, and/or where to kill, the more dangerous he may be. The batterer who has previously acted out part of a homicide or suicide fantasy—buying a weapon or other instrument likely to cause injury—may be considering violence.

3. *Weapons.* A person who threatens another with a weapon, especially when a weapon such as a handgun is available in the home, may act on his threats. Access to weapons increases the potential for lethal assault. A person who shows a fascination with weapons and who may play with or display them in inappropriate ways is potentially dangerous.

4. *Obsessiveness about partner or family.* A person who is obsessive about her partner, who either idolizes him and believes that she cannot live without him or is entitled to him because he is her husband, is likely to be dangerous. This type of batterer assumes a possessive role that often turns violent.

5. *Pet abuse.* Batterers who kill or torture animals, especially those owned by a partner, are likely to kill or maim a loved one. These behaviors have been exhibited by many serial killers as children (e.g., Jeffrey Dahmer) and are good indications of a lack of respect for life.

6. *Rage.* When the batterer believes that his partner is about to leave him, a certain life-endangering rage may erupt. This behavior is central to understanding the potential for violence in a partner. Naturally, if drug use, alcohol consumption, and depression are also factors, the potential for violence increases. A partner who knows or senses that the batterer is likely to be violent should leave secretly or at least not announce her intentions. A victim of abuse can seek assistance from community domestic violence shelters, local law enforcement, or the battered-women's hotline. Some victims may

seek shelter in a safe house. The locations of these houses are kept confidential, and in many states, it is a crime to disclose the location of a safe house without authorization of the shelter.

Risk factors for IPV exist at every level of society and may include the following socioeconomic conditions (Heise and Garcia-Moreno, 2002):

- Marital conflict
- Marital instability
- Male dominance in the family
- Poor family functioning

A number of personal indications or warning signs suggest future violence by an intimate partner. The dynamics of a relationship, as well as socioeconomic factors, may also predict violence. Unfortunately, many victims of IPV will not report their injuries or will remain in an abusive relationship out of fear or ignorance.

THE LAW AND DOMESTIC VIOLENCE

Until the 1970s, the police and justice system tended to overlook domestic violence victims. As a result, victims have filed lawsuits claiming their right to due process and equal protection from violence under the law. The landmark case on police failure to protect victims of domestic violence is *Thurman v. City of Torrington* (1984). The case brought attention to the need for the police to take domestic violence calls seriously. In this case, the police failed to arrest an abuser after receiving repeated calls for help from the victim. The victim was told that the police would respond quickly, but they did not, and she was brutally beaten. The suit alleged that the police denied due process and equal protection of the law to the victim. The jury found for the victim and awarded her $2.3 million in compensation.

In response to the increasing incidence of domestic violence, a number of states have passed legislation making it easier for the police to arrest abusers. These laws are referred to as **mandatory arrest laws**. The catalyst for this movement was a Minneapolis domestic violence study (Sherman and Berk, 1984). The study used an experimental design to prove that arrest was better in deterring future violence than were traditional methods of mediation and separation of parties. Although the research on arrest as a deterrent to repeat violence contains mixed conclusions, mandatory arrest laws are still widely popular laws.

Developments in the States

The legislative intent of many states is to define domestic violence as a clear and present danger to the well-being of citizens. In a number of states, the concept of *vertical prosecution* is used on abusers. According to this concept, a specially trained deputy district attorney handles a domestic violence case from filing to completion, which improves the chances of convicting the abuser. In addition, the police often follow the policy of preferred arrest or taking into custody abusers who have inflicted physical harm on their partners. By 1983, 27 states had expanded police arrests in domestic violence cases (Lerman, Landis, and Goldwcig, 1983).

In 1986, six states passed laws requiring arrest with probable cause (Ferraro, 1989:61) if the victim has signs of physical injury. In other words, the police are mandated to arrest the abuser even if the victim recants or somehow attempts to make excuses for the abuse. In many jurisdictions, the police can arrest abusers who have violated protection orders. Currently, protection or restraining orders can be issued in most states, and a number of states mandate an arrest if the orders are violated (Finn and Colson, 1990). Another feature of domestic violence legislation requires doctors, nurses, and other health practitioners to report suspected battering to the police. In 1994, California became the first state to require licensed health practitioners to notify the police as soon as possible and to file a written report with authorities within 72 hours detailing the injuries to the victim.

Some states have a "must arrest" approach for domestice violence, while other states adopted a less-restrictive "pro-arrest" policy. In California, for example, when a "must arrest" policy was first adopted at the beginning of the 1990s, officers were required to arrest anyone they had probable cause to suspect of engaging in criminal violence, including women. However, a 1998 study of arrests in Los Angeles revealed the effects of the "must arrest" law: Whereas the number of arrested men doubled, the number of arrested women quadrupled with the implementation of mandatory arrest (Simon and Kristen, 2008). In response, the state implemented the current "pro-arrest" policy, and men were again arrested in higher percentages.

Although questions as to whether the law helps or hurts victims have been raised, a failure to report can result in a possible jail term or fine. This law parallels those laws requiring educators and health practitioners to report suspected child abuse. Thus, as with preferred arrest policy, the law is designed to limit the victim's discretion of reporting. The mandatory arrest policy in cases of domestic violence has serious disadvantages. Arrest and pretrial detention can traumatize law-abiding citizens. Focus 3–4 is the account of a college student who was arrested under the mandatory arrest policy.

**Focus 3–4   Lost Inside the System: A Student's Real-Life
Experience Behind Bars**

On a warm, fall Sunday evening last year, I found myself on the wrong side of the
justice system. Earlier that evening, I had had a disagreement on the phone with my
estranged husband about my daughter's Thanksgiving vacation. His uncooperative
behavior frustrated me, and I lost my temper because he slammed the phone down
on me. I decided to drive over to his house and confront him, but once I arrived he
came out and ordered me to leave, since he had company. I tried to explain that
I needed to talk, but he refused to listen and turned his back to walk away. I wanted
to get his attention, so I grabbed his shirt, which ripped as he tried to pull away from
me, and I accidentally scratched him. He became extremely enraged and pushed me
so hard that I flew across the driveway. Someone inside his house called 911 because
of the commotion, and, as a result, a patrol car was sent out to investigate. A local
sheriff interviewed both of us but decided to arrest me, since he felt sorry for my
husband because he had a slight scratch. I, on the other hand, had several scratches
and a swollen wrist but nevertheless was handcuffed, escorted to the sheriff's car,
and driven to the Lost Hills Sheriff's Station. I was never even read my rights.

I was placed in custody and put in a holding cell with a metal bench and a pay
telephone. Above the phone was the phone number for the bail bond office. Once the
handcuffs were finally removed, I was allowed to use the telephone, but the deputies
had taken my purse, which contained my calling card. A female deputy on duty was
kind enough to open my wallet and find the calling card so I could make several
calls. I woke my girlfriend and her husband and asked for advice and consolation,
but we realized that I would be spending the rest of that evening at the station. I kept
wondering about the bail bond phone number. What would I need one for, I innocently wondered. It was now nearing 2 A.M., and after fingerprinting and photo-
graphing, I was told that the arresting officer insisted on taking me to Westlake
Hospital for emergency treatment for my swollen wrist. I replied that I was fine and
that it wouldn't be necessary. I didn't want to risk any more embarrassment by being
seen at the hospital, where I had recently done volunteer work. The officer said that
I had no choice and he was taking me whether I liked it or not. As he started to handcuff me, he saw me wince in pain. I was escorted to the patrol car and placed in the
back seat. It was then that he decided that he would uncuff my left wrist and cuff me
to the screen that separates the officer from the prisoner. He let me know that he was
doing me a favor but also warned me that he would cuff me again if I gave him
reason. He asked me what I did for a living, and I replied that I was a criminal justice
student at California Lutheran University. As he realized the irony of the situation,
he explained that he decided to arrest me and not my husband because I had gone
over to my husband's home. Therefore, I was in the wrong. Furthermore, he said,
once we arrived at the hospital, I could refuse treatment, which is exactly what I did.
I didn't want to make matters worse. I was also worried about my husband's
reputation, since he is a doctor. We drove back in silence to the station but were more

(Continued)

(*Continued*)

at ease with one another. I was taken to a cell and given a plastic pillow and blanket. I slept very little that evening.

The next morning I was taken from the cell back to the holding area. The deputies told me to call my friend back and that my husband had called. I called my friend back, and she told me that I was being transferred to Sybil Brand Institute for Women in Los Angeles since there were no female deputies assigned to duty that day at the Lost Hills Station. I was being charged with a felony and being held on $50,000 bail.

I couldn't speak; I was so terrified. I had read many books about "real" criminals (female) spending time at this institution. My friends and even my husband tried to get the $50,000 cash, but since it was Monday morning, our small community bank was unable to get enough money in time and soon the bus would come to pick up the prisoners to transport them downtown. My husband came to the station, but they wouldn't let me see him. However, as we spoke on the phone, he explained the charges and that he had already hired a criminal defense attorney to help me. He also told me to call the bail bond number. I dialed the number repeatedly only to get a busy signal for the next 10 minutes—another sign that it was a Monday morning. Finally, I spoke to an operator who wrote down all of my information and said that he would try to find me once I was "inside the system." Meanwhile, the deputies brought me a breakfast tray, but I couldn't eat. My attorney, who had just arrived, encouraged me to eat because this food was better than what I would see at the jail I was being sent to. He told me I would probably be out later in the day and not to have eye contact with any of the other prisoners. This really frightened me more, and I wanted to die. He gave me his business card and asked me if I wanted him to represent me. Of course I did.

Once again I was handcuffed and placed in a prison van with my hands chained to a mesh panel in front of me. A young guy, who was being transferred with me, issued a few words of reassurance and soon we were on our way to the "real jail," stopping at other city jails to pick up more prisoners. I had no idea what was going to happen to me. You cannot even imagine it until you come face to face with the "criminal justice system."

Once the van stopped, I was told to come forward and a deputy uncuffed me and presented me to my new incarcerators. I didn't even know where I was but later found out that it was a women's holding cell at the Central Men's Jail. There was a stainless steel toilet, which was continually being used, and a sink in the front of a large room filled with women prisoners awaiting transfer to various jails. Eventually, my name was called, and along with about a half dozen others, I was handcuffed, chained, and put aboard a bus that would take us to Sybil Brand Institute for Women. It was at this point that I lost my identity.

At Sybil Brand I was photographed and fingerprinted again, and I waited in a holding cell with my box lunch until my name was called. I was told to open my mouth, lift my tongue, pull my ears forward and pick up my hair from my neck. They gave me a wristlet with a number on it—my new identity. I was told to take off

(*Continued*)

(*Continued*)

my street clothes, but I could keep my own underwear, socks, and shoes, and put on the assigned "prison blue" dress, complete with a ripped seam from under my arm to my thigh. I picked up my blanket, sheet, towel, nightshirt, and toiletry articles and waited with the others. I noticed there were no clocks in the building and since I had already relinquished my watch along with my other personal items, I began to wonder how much longer I would have to stay here. My attorney's business cards were also taken away and put in a brown paper bag along with my other belongings. I was then taken to my new "home."

My bunk assignment was 43J; apparently, J stands for top bunk. Another incoming inmate told me I was lucky to have a top bunk. A Mexican woman took me under her wing, and she showed me her bunk, telling me that if I had trouble from anyone to come and see her. I didn't even know her name, but I memorized her bunk. I finally found my bunk in the far corner of the large dormitory-like room. The deputy's glass cage was ten rows of bunks in front of me and five rows to my right. I wasn't certain who my "friends" were. I noticed a Mexican woman with red hair staring at me. I became very aware of my vulnerability, and all I wanted to do was get out of there. In order to get to the shower or toilets, which were all out in the open, I would have to walk through 50 women without being singled out. I felt like banging my head on the wall, and I began to feel very claustrophobic in this room filled with 135 other women.

Moreover, to add to my fears, I noticed many lesbian couples hanging around the toilet area. They were very open about their relationships. I also noticed that toilet paper was a hot commodity because the African American women used it to wrap around their heads. I soon realized that if I needed to find a bathroom, I should find one with paper already in it; otherwise, I would have to ask someone for it. Several of the women had ripped their bedding and used it to wrap around their heads. Pretty soon, the female deputies turned on their microphones, telling all of them to take that "crap" off their heads. Evidently, it was not a part of the jail uniform, and furthermore, they had destroyed county property by tearing sheets.

The television was blaring in the background, and most of the African American women were watching *Oprah*. There was definitely a group of the women who commandeered that television. Many of the women slept, while others were either fixing each other's hair or, like me, simply lying on the bed with their eyes wide open, too afraid to sleep. I finally gained the courage to use the bathroom, but I had to walk between rows of bunks, and to my horror, I noticed two African American women sprawled in the aisle in my direct path. I decided that I would either have to step over them or find another way around. I decided against the former, since another woman had just tried to step over them, without saying excuse me, and ended up with a mouthful from both of them. I decided to avoid the entire situation and find a different route. However, once I came back, I realized that my towel was missing. I was cautioned to hide everything under my 1½-inch thick mattress in the future. Needless to say, I followed that advice for the rest of my stay.

(*Continued*)

(*Continued*)

When dinner rolled around, I silently marched with everyone else along the inmate walkway, but once I entered the cafeteria, I fought back the nausea (I actually gagged) and noticed a few others do the same because of the smell of the food. As I sat there in silence, I realized that it didn't take long for the others to covet my food, first my milk and cake and finally my entire meal. I was thankful, though, that they had taken it, for I didn't want to risk getting into trouble with the deputies for not eating. Once we filed back to the "room," I noticed the clock in the deputies' glass sanctuary and saw that it was only 4:45 P.M.

Several hours later, I noticed a scurry of women heading toward the middle of the room. I found out that the phones had been turned on, and, feeling very brave, I hurried along to one of the shortest of the three lines and wondered how I would remember my MCI calling card number. After standing silently in that line for over 2 hours, I learned an awful lot. Most of the women were calling home, their kids, their boyfriends, their parents, their friends, and in that order. There is no limit to the number of calls you can make, just as long as they are collect. I hoped only that I could remember my friend's phone number and that her children wouldn't answer the phone and refuse my collect call. I was exhausted over the whole ordeal and ended up calling my husband. I couldn't breathe and thought that I was going to go crazy if I didn't get out of there soon. He told me that even though the bail bondsman had tried to find me in the jail, he was unable to do so. He also told me that there was a possibility that I might have to spend the night because I was going to be arraigned in the morning in Malibu.

What had I done to deserve this? I couldn't believe that any of this was happening to me. I was surrounded by real criminals, drug addicts, prostitutes, and probation violators. They were even plotting their next "score" as soon as they were to be released. I began to cry hysterically, but nothing my husband said could reassure me. He wasn't there; I was. Whispering to him how frightened I was to spend a night in there, he finally told me the truth. My new attorney had already spoken to the district attorney, and she would be willing to drop the felony charge to a misdemeanor if I spent one night in the county jail. Then we would not have to relinquish the $5,000 bond that we had to put up to get me out that day. The DA thought that it would look more favorable to the judge the following day if I came before her having spent the night in jail and still dressed in my "prison blues," as my husband so knowingly termed it.

He had become an expert on the criminal justice system in the short time that I was incarcerated. I also became an expert on the system, and quickly learned what "bed check" meant. Shut up, sit up on your bunk, do not lie down, and hold out your wrist for the male deputy to check. Also, I found that it was advantageous to memorize my ID number printed on my wristlet. Several of the women, though, found it very difficult to follow these simple rules and, as a result, more male deputies came in to "shape us up." Still sitting up, we endured an extra half hour of arguments from two or three inmates who were repeatedly warned to be quiet. Eventually, they were removed to an area of isolation as punishment. The rest of us were lectured about shutting up and getting our "asses" on our bunks, not in them.

(*Continued*)

(Continued)

Sometime around midnight the lights were dimmed and a flurry of activity on the lesbian couples' bunks became apparent. I was unable to breathe, let alone close my eyes. I envisioned the redheaded Mexican woman coming to my bunk but, thankfully, it never happened. The lights were eventually turned up around 4 A.M. and the P.A. system blared out the name of everyone being arraigned later that day.

My name was one of the last ones to be called, and I was thankful that the night was over and I would have "my day in court." I was unable to eat breakfast again, and I soon realized that I had not showered in two days. The girl in the bunk below lent me a towel and as I squeezed the soap from its paper tube, I prayed that I wouldn't get athlete's foot from the shower area. Anxiously, I brushed my teeth, put on my "prison blues" and tried to feel human again. It was hard to believe that I hadn't seen daylight in over a day. There are no windows in the women's dorm. I walked along the yellow lines to the holding cell, where I waited quietly to get on the bus that would take me to "freedom." I wondered why we had to leave so early, since the hearings wouldn't start until much later in the morning; it wasn't even 6 A.M. I later found out that the bus stops at several other jails to take prisoners to various courthouses. I was heading to the Malibu Courthouse.

I was handcuffed and chained to six other women. Our first stop was somewhere in West Los Angeles. We waited quietly on the bus while other prisoners who were also handcuffed and chained struggled to get on the bus. It was quite the procedure. We made several stops, but the memorable one was Santa Monica Courthouse, where six of us were removed from the bus and marched through the Santa Monica Jail. We were ushered into a "bathroom" with the standard jailhouse decor, a stainless steel toilet and sink. There was also a low stainless steel bench, which four of us could sit on comfortably, but the other three were told to sit on the floor or stand. None of us knew what was happening, but Sondra, my "handcuff partner," and I both gasped when the deputy, without saying a word, slammed the stainless steel door shut. There was no window, and it was stifling. We spent more than 2 hours in that bathroom; I had never felt so claustrophobic.

It was almost noon when we arrived at the Malibu Courthouse and were ushered into a holding cell. We were finally uncuffed and given a "box lunch." I knew that I had to eat but couldn't face the turkey bologna sandwich that I had been seeing these past few days. I was grateful to get juice instead of milk, which I don't drink. If you wanted a sip of water, you had to use your hands as a "scoop" in the sink.

As I waited for my case to come up, I noticed that a pay phone was turned on. I called my husband to see if there was anything new about the situation. He said the judge had a very busy morning hearing other cases and my attorney was nowhere to be found, but that all cases had to be heard before 2 P.M. that day in order for them to get us back to the jail so we could be released that evening. Finally, at 1:45 P.M., my name was called. I was recuffed behind my back and marched into the courtroom where I saw my girlfriend and her husband waiting to give me support, but alas, no husband. I was embarrassed for them to see me like this but grateful for their love.

(Continued)

(Continued)

We could communicate only through my attorney, and he had to get Kleenex from my friends so he could wipe my tears. Unable to stand up before the judge, since I was considered a physical threat, I remained seated, with my hands cuffed behind my back. I barely knew my attorney, but I had to rely on him to speak for me, even though in reality he knew very little about the case. The judge listened, asked him a few questions, and the DA agreed with them that I had suffered enough indignation and should be released that day on my own recognizance. I was elated but somewhat skeptical about my release. My attorney made verbal arrangements with my friends for me to call them upon my release once all the paperwork was completed. He thought that it could be as late as 9 or 10 P.M.

We boarded the jail bus once again and as it drove down Pacific Coast Highway, I gazed longingly at the ocean that I had seen thousands of times before, but it looked better now. I thought of the roses on the judge's desk, and the roses in my own yard and realized how much we take these things for granted.

Once again, the bus stopped at several facilities to pick up more prisoners, but this time, to our surprise and fear, we were now picking up male prisoners. We were sitting in the front of the bus, which meant that they would walk right past us. I was on the outside of the seat and my new friend, Sondra, was next to the window. The men disgusted me as they spoke about us as though we weren't there. They talked very explicitly and graphically about what they would like to do to us. Sondra and I realized that most of those comments were aimed at us. Our next stop was even worse since the driver and his partner got off the bus, left the air conditioning on, and went in the jail for over an hour. Not only were the men continually sexually harassing us, but we were freezing cold and couldn't do a thing about it. Finally, the driver and his partner returned with new male prisoners. This time, they made the women get off the bus before they put the men on.

It was late once we finally got downtown to Men's Central Jail, and it was very dark outside. The women were taken off first and placed in a holding cell for another hour with a roomful of other women. By the time they got us back to the jail, it was past 8 P.M. We were taken to a large empty room and told to pick up our dresses so they could search us for contraband. It was humiliating. Then they shuttled us right to the dining room to eat so the employees could clean up and leave for the night. I couldn't think about anything except going home.

I returned to my bunk, sat up, and waited as several names were called for release that evening, but mine was not one of them. Finally, around 11:30 P.M., my name was called, and I gathered my bedding and gladly gave a large African-American lady my clean nightdress. However, once the deputy saw me with my bedding, she told me to take it back since I was being sent down to the medical doctor for a TB test, of all things.

I was so distressed I slept very little that evening too. All I could do was pray. It was my deceased mother's birthday, and I was grateful that she didn't have to see me in this condition.

(Continued)

(Continued)

The next morning they started calling off releases. I was too nervous to sit on my bunk again, so I stood with my friend, Sondra, and waited by the deputy's sanctuary where the names were posted. Pretty soon Sondra was called, as well as many of the others who came in with me or who had been in court yesterday, but not me. My girlfriend had been waiting outside since 8:30 A.M. Lunchtime came and went, but again, I couldn't even think about food. Finally, around 1:30 P.M., they announced the last call of releases for the day. Finally, my name was among them. As I left, the female deputy asked, "What could you have possibly done to be here?" I replied, "Spousal battery," and her response was "Oh, come on."

Release is not a speedy process in the correction system. There is no such thing as hurrying up to get you out. Disappointments greet you each time you think they are ready to come and get you out of the glass holding cell. They are usually heading somewhere else. No one comes to tell you anything. Instead, you wait until they are good and ready to release you.

At 4:45 P.M., my name was called and I was issued a brown bag containing my personal belongings and allowed to present a receipt to pick up my clothing. I never felt so happy to be in street clothes. After another 10 minutes of final fingerprinting and matching I.D. numbers, I was out of there. As I placed my finger, for a matching print, in the gate to freedom, I saw my girlfriend running toward me.

Six months have passed since this event, and I appeared in court this morning before the same judge, dressed quite differently from the first time she saw me. She congratulated me on my therapy (part of my release) as she read the letter from my therapist. On June 3, 1996, I will have all this erased from my record, providing, of course, that I do not harass or molest my ex-husband during this time. This, I assure you, will never happen.

The Federal Crime Control Act and Domestic Violence

The federal government has not been silent on domestic violence and stalking. The Federal Violent Crime Control and Law Enforcement Act, which went into effect in 1994, is the most comprehensive crime bill in the history of the country. It provides for stringent penalties for criminal violations and provides funds for grant programs addressing personal violence. It specifically addresses domestic violence crimes; it prohibits firearms sales to and possession by persons subject to family violence restraining orders. The act also addresses interstate domestic violence and authorized $1 million in 1995 for a domestic violence hotline and $325 million for battered-women's shelters administered by the Department of Health and Human Resources. Clearly, this act and similar ones passed by states indicate that government is taking seriously the threat of domestic violence.

The federal law on domestic violence is found in the United States Code (18 United States Code § 2261 [2006], also known as the Interstate Domestic Violence Law). The statute reads as follows:

> If a person travels across a State line or enters or leaves Indian country with the intent to injure, harass, or intimidate that person's spouse or intimate partner, and who, in the course of or as a result of such travel, intentionally commits a crime of violence and thereby causes bodily injury to such spouse or intimate partner, shall be punished as provided in subsection. . . . And a person who causes a spouse or intimate partner to cross a State line or to enter or leave Indian country by force, coercion, duress, or fraud and, in the course or as a result of that conduct, intentionally commits a crime of violence and thereby causes bodily injury to the person's spouse or intimate partner, shall be punished.

Under the Federal Interstate Stalking Punishment and Prevention Act of 1996, a new rider was enacted permitting protective orders issued in one state to be enforceable in all states, and it provides stiff penalties for interstate stalking offenders.

The first person convicted under the federal domestic violence law was sentenced on September 1, 1995. Christopher Bailey of West Virginia was convicted of kidnapping. He received the maximum 20-year sentence for violating the law and a life sentence for kidnapping. Bailey was convicted of beating his wife and driving for 6 days across West Virginia and Kentucky with her in the trunk of his car (*Los Angeles Times*, 1995).

ELDER ABUSE AND NEGLECT

The evidence of violence and mistreatment of senior citizens by relatives, acquaintances, and institutions is increasing. According to the best available estimates, between 1 and 2 million Americans aged 65 years or older have been injured, exploited, or otherwise mistreated by someone on whom they depended for care or protection (National Research Council Panel to Review Risk and Prevalance of Elder Abuse and Neglect, 2003).

Since 1977, special attention has been paid to elder abuse and neglect. A report on the problem estimated that more than 1 million older Americans are physically or emotionally abused by relatives or loved ones (Douglas, 1995a).

A University of Iowa study based on 1999 data found 190,005 domestic elder abuse reports from 17 states; 242,430 domestic elder abuse investigations from 47 states; and 102,879 substantiations from 35 states. Significantly higher investigation rates were found for states that require mandatory reporting and tracking of reports (Jogerst et al., 2003).

As with other types of intimate abuse, there is no one explanation for elder abuse and neglect. Elder abuse is a complex problem that can emerge from several different causes and often has roots in multiple factors. These factors include family situations, caregiver issues, and cultural issues. Family situations that can contribute to elder abuse include discord in the family created by the older person's presence, a history and pattern of violent interactions within the family, social isolation or the stresses on one or more family members who care for the older adult, and lack of knowledge or caregiving skills.

In some instances, elder abuse is simply a continuation of abuse that has been occurring in the family over many years. If a woman has been abused during a lengthy marriage, she is not likely to report abuse when she is very old and in poor health. Also, the burdens of paying for health care for an aging parent or living in overcrowded quarters can lead to stress that can trigger elder abuse. Such a situation can be especially difficult when the adult child has no financial resources other than those of the aging parent.

Elder abuse, as with other forms of intimate abuse, may take many forms. It can include financial abuse, physical abuse, emotional abuse, and neglect. As with child abuse or spousal abuse, elder abuse happens everywhere—in poor, middle-class, and upper-income households. It is a problem that has no demographic or ethnic boundaries. Because family members or close friends are often the culprits of financial, physical, and emotional abuse, this abuse is often difficult to discover and to accept. Elder abuse may also be defined as either passive or active neglect. In *passive neglect* the primary caregiver, perhaps a son or daughter, for some reason is unable to provide the required care. For example, middle-class people who cannot afford expensive nursing homes often attempt to care for elderly relatives at home, but the care is inadequate. Focus 3–5 discusses a case of passive neglect. *Active neglect* involves a conscious attempt to inflict injury or emotional stress on the older person. It includes deliberate withdrawal of health services, food, or other necessities. Focus 3–6 discusses a case of active neglect.

The relative weakness of older people makes them targets for abuse. Of course, as with other intimate victimizations, physical, psychological, sexual, and emotional abuse are also prevalent. In the cases discussed in Focus 3–5 and Focus 3–6, the primary caregivers were either unprepared, unable, or unwilling to provide the necessary care. The case of active neglect involved an attempt to cash in a life insurance policy. Both cases include a lack of sincere concern for the well-being of an elderly dependent

---

Focus 3–5   A Case of Passive Neglect

Mr. and Mrs. A. retired from their jobs 5 years after coping with the deaths of her parents and his father. The surviving parent, Mr. A.'s mother, a severe diabetic, was living with them. The senior Mrs. A. had suffered three strokes before the couple retired. Three months after their retirement, she suffered a fourth stroke that left her completely dependent on others for feeding, hygiene, and all personal care. Although mentally alert, the elder Mrs. A. could not speak and was unable to write. She became very depressed and lost interest in food. Five months after his mother's fourth stroke, Mr. A. died of a stroke. Mrs. A. Jr. vowed to continue caring for her mother-in-law. During the next 3 years, Mrs. A. Jr., who was 67 years old, became depressed, unkempt, and isolated from formerly close friends and relatives. When her oldest daughter visited, 3 years to the day after her father's death, she found the elder Mrs. A. crying in her bed in her own body wastes with spoiled food and insects throughout the bedroom. The younger Mrs. A. explained that she could no longer care for her mother-in-law. The elder Mrs. A. was taken to a local nursing home.

---

relative. Victimization of the elderly by intimates will increase in the future because many people are living longer. The primary caregivers, usually middle class, will have financial and/or emotional difficulty in providing the necessary care, especially for elders who are ill or incapacitated.

Nursing Home Negligence

In addition to elder abuse in private homes, there is growing evidence of abuse in nursing homes and other care institutions. The number of nursing home negligence cases is increasing. A federal study conducted by the General Accounting Office found that nearly one out of three California nursing homes had been cited for "serious or potentially life-threatening care problems" (California Nursing Homes, 1998). The Senate Special Committee

---

Focus 3–6   A Case of Active Neglect

Walter had lived with his 52-year-old son, Milan, since his 73rd birthday and the sale of his farm. Walter and Milan agreed to pool their funds and incomes and live together. Walter required several medications daily but had no health insurance. After 4 years, Milan convinced his father that he no longer needed medications and suggested that his father buy a substantial life insurance policy. Walter's health further deteriorated, and he was hospitalized. After his discharge, his son refused to take him to his medical appointments or give him his medications. Walter's health got worse, and he was admitted to a Veterans hospital.

on Aging requested the study in response to allegations that in 1993 3,113 California nursing home residents died from malnutrition, dehydration, and other conditions resulting from substandard care. In 2003, state Long-Term Care Ombudsman programs nationally investigated 20,673 complaints of abuse, gross neglect, and exploitation on behalf of nursing home board and care residents. Among seven types of abuse categories, physical abuse was the most common type reported (National Ombudsman Reporting System, 2003).

Researchers are continuing to exam deaths and injuries of elderly residents in long-term care facilities to identify potential markers of abuse. One example is a study by Erik Lindbloom, MD, of the University of Missouri-Columbia. The study examined coroners' reports of elderly nursing home residents in Arkansas over a 1-year period. The study revealed the folowing several markers indicating potential injuriy or death to nursing home patients (Lindbloom et al., 2005).

1. **Physical condition/quality of care.** Specific markers include documented but untreated injuries; undocumented injuries and fractures; multiple, untreated, and/or undocumented pressure sores; medical orders not followed; poor oral care, poor hygiene, and lack of cleanliness of residents; malnourished residents who have no documentation for low weight; bruising on nonambulatory residents; bruising in unusual locations; statements from family concerning adequacy of care; and observations about the level of care for residents with nonattentive family members.

2. **Facility characteristics.** Specific markers include unchanged linens; strong odors (urine, feces); trash cans that have not been emptied; food issues (unclean cafeteria); and documented problems in the past.

3. **Inconsistencies.** Specific markers include inconsistencies between the medical records, statements made by staff members, and/or observations of investigators; inconsistencies in statements among groups interviewed; and inconsistencies between the reported time of death and the condition of the body.

4. **Staff behaviors.** Specific markers include staff members who follow an investigator too closely; lack of knowledge and/or concern about a resident; unintended or purposeful, verbal or nonverbal evasiveness; and a facility's unwillingness to release medical records.

Nursing home abuse can be physical, emotional, or simply the result of negligent care by an understaffed or poorly trained staff. The following case is an example of pure neglect in the care and treatment of an elder. After suffering a stroke, a 77-year-old man was sent from the hospital to a skilled care facility for rehabilitation. Within a week, the man was transferred back to a hospital, suffering from severe dehydration. Records indicated he was suffering from early signs of pressure sores. Ten days later, while visiting her father at the nursing home, his daughter noticed that his catheter bag remained empty for several hours, and she told the nurses something was wrong. At the family's insistence, the man was sent to the emergency room where they found he had a kidney infection, other urinary problems, and elevated blood sugar. They also noted a small broken area of skin and early pressure sores on both heels. Nine days later, he was readmitted to the same nursing home for the third time. His condition worsened, yet the staff would not inform the man's wife. When she asked to see his feet, the staff refused. When she finally saw his feet, she was shocked. The sores had gotten worse, they were open with dead tissue, a bad odor, discharge, and exposed bones. After many attempts to treat him at a hospital, the doctors had to amputate both legs below the knee. A $1 million settlement was awarded for negligent care.

Whether victimization through nursing home abuse is intentional or the result of neglect, criminal or civil liability can result. Residents of nursing homes have rights and protections under the law. In other words, they have the right to be treated with dignity and respect and to have their privacy and personal worth protected. Patients and their families must be informed about their medical care and have the right to make their own decisions regarding their money and services. In 1987, Congress passed the Nursing Home Reform Act, which requires each state to issue regulations to protect the rights of nursing home residents. In 1992, Congress passed the Vulnerable Elder Rights Protection Program (42 U.S.C. § 3058), which promoted advocacy efforts through ombudsmen offices; abuse, neglect, and exploitation prevention programs; and legal assistance on behalf of older Americans. The law also offers federal funding incentives, which make it possible for states to develop and maintain programs designed to assist the elderly. In many respects, state elder abuse laws are similar to legislation designed to address the problems of child abuse and neglect.

CHILD ABUSE AND NEGLECT

In 1874, residents of a New York apartment building reported that a woman was abusing her stepchild in one of the apartments. A nurse found a young child named Mary Ellen Wilson chained to her bed with signs that she had been beaten. The child was eventually placed in an orphanage (Gelles and Cornell, 1990). This was the first reported case of child abuse.

The terms *abuse* and *neglect* are sometimes used interchangeably to describe maltreatment of children. Neglect is similar to passive abuse with elders; it refers to withholding food, shelter, clothing, love, and so forth. Abuse, on the other hand, is an overt form of physical mistreatment; it involves inflicting physical harm on the child. Figure 3–2 includes data related to child abuse.

Each state provides its own definitions of child abuse and neglect. Some states define child abuse and neglect as a single concept, whereas others provide separate definitions for physical abuse, neglect, sexual abuse, and/or emotional abuse. Many states define abuse in terms of harm or threatened harm to a child's health or welfare. All states, however, include sexual abuse in their definitions. Neglect is frequently defined in terms of deprivation of adequate food, clothing, shelter, or medical care. Several states distinguish between failure to provide based on the financial inability to do so and failure to provide for no apparent financial reason. The latter constitutes neglect.

It is reported that each week, child protective services (CPS) agencies throughout the United States receive more than 50,000 reports of suspected child abuse or neglect. In 2002, 2.6 million reports concerning the welfare of approximately 4.5 million children were made. And, in approximately two-thirds (67 percent) of these cases, the information provided in the report was sufficient to prompt an assessment or investigation. As a result, 896,000

FIGURE 3–2   VICTIMIZATION RATES BY MALTREATMENT TYPE, 2000-2003

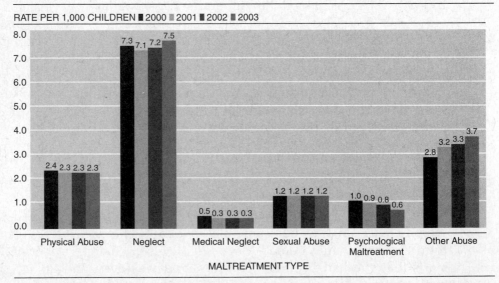

Source: Children's Bureau. Administration for Children and Families. Washington, DC. www.ACF.dhhs.gov/. Retrieved August 2004.

children were found to have been victims of abuse or neglect—an average of more than 2,450 children per day (National Clearinghouse on Child Abuse and Neglect, 2003).

According to data from the American Medical Association, the number of young children killed by their parents or caregivers is underreported by nearly 60 percent. Caregivers commit 85 percent of the homicides of children 10 years of age and younger; strangers are the killers only 3 percent of the time (Coleman, 1999).

As previously discussed, child abuse and neglect have grave consequences on the emotional development of children. Some recent findings on the impact of child abuse are as follows (Windom and Maxwell, 2001):

- Being abused or neglected as a child increases the likelihood of arrest as a juvenile by 59 percent, as an adult by 28 percent, and for a violent crime by 30 percent.

- Maltreated children are younger at the time of their first arrest, commit nearly twice as many offenses, and are arrested more frequently.

- Physically abused and neglected (versus sexually abused) children are the most likely to be arrested later for a violent crime.

- In contrast to earlier research findings, the new results indicate that abused and neglected females are also at increased risk of arrest for violence as juveniles and adults.

- White abused and neglected children are no more likely to be arrested for a violent crime than their nonabused and nonneglected white counterparts. In contrast, black abused and neglected children in this sample showed significantly increased rates of violent arrests compared with black children who were not maltreated.

Child victims of sexual abuse experience post-traumatic symptoms, including depression and aversion to sex. Children who experience long-term, severe abuse are likely to leave home, become criminals, or become victims of crime. The resulting low self-esteem and betrayal make the abused child vulnerable to a variety of behavioral problems that can lead to criminality (Browne and Finkelhor, 1986). For example, 95 percent of teenage prostitutes were sexually abused at some time (Goldston, Turnquist, and Knutson, 1989). Research indicates that abused children who wet the bed, sadistically abuse animals, or set fires are candidates for becoming violent adult criminals (Simon, 1996). People who were sexually victimized during childhood are at higher risk of arrest for committing crimes as adults, including sex crimes, than are people who did not suffer sexual or physical abuse or neglect during childhood (Windom, 1995). The fact that victims become offenders is referred to as the cycle of violence. There is some truth to the adage that violence begets violence and the view that frequent exposure to violence influences later behavior.

A number of behavioral symptoms indicate that children are being or have been abused, including the following:

- Aversion to a relative, neighbor, or baby-sitter
- Change in eating patterns
- Sudden lack of interest or achievement in school
- Sudden desire for privacy or marked separation from family activity
- Trouble sleeping, having nightmares, or wetting the bed
- Irritation of the genital areas
- Signs of increased anxiety or immature behavior

These signs may indicate the need to investigate the cause. If abuse is occurring or has occurred, immediate response is needed. Those in service occupations who come in contact with children, such as nurses and teachers, are often in the best position to recognize abuse. In 2002, more than one-half (57 percent) of all reports made to CPS agencies came from professionals, such as teachers, medical personnel, and law enforcement officers, who came in contact with the child (National Clearinghouse on Child Abuse and Neglect, 2003).

All states require certain professionals and institutions to report suspected child abuse, including health care providers and facilities of all types, mental health care providers of all types, teachers and other school personnel, social workers, day care providers, and law enforcement personnel. Many states also require film developers to report pictures depicting illegal activity involving children. Depending upon the state, failure to report suspected child abuse can result in criminal or civil liability.

A substantial number of states impose a legal duty on any person who knows of, or strongly suspects, child abuse to report it to authorities. Typically, the law requires an immediate report by telephone or some other means, followed by a written report within a few days. Most states give immunity from lawsuits for any person who makes such a report in good faith and frequently keep the identification of the reporter confidential. Such confidentiality usually does not prevent the reporter from being identified, however, in any legal proceedings that result from the investigation of the initial report. Time limits have been imposed in some states for the initiation and completion of the investigation of any abuse or neglect report. In some states, the person who initially made the report of child abuse is entitled to a copy of the resulting investigative report.

Child Victims of Sexual Exploitation

Related to abuse and neglect is commercial sexual exploitation of children (CSEC). While most child abuse and neglect occurs at the familial level, there is growing evidence that children are often victimized for profit. The government has not been silent on addressing child exploitation. In 1996, the U.S. Congress established the Exploited Child Division within the National Center for Missing & Exploited Children (NCMEC). The Exploited Child Division serves as a resource center for the public, parents, law enforcement, and others about the issues surrounding the sexual exploitation of children.

More recently, attention to the problem of exploitation was drawn by a study published by the National Institute of Justice which revealed that CSEC takes place at three levels: local exploitation by one or a few individuals, small regional networks involving multiple adults and children, and large national or international sex crime networks where children are traded and sold as commodities (Albanese, 2007). Some of the key findings of the study are:

- About half of the exploitation occurs at the local level by one or several adults.
- Approximately 25 percent occurs through citywide or small regional networks.
- Another 15 percent occurs through well-financed, large regional or national networks, with adults recruiting, indoctrinating, and moving children.
- About 10 percent is international, which normally involves trafficking children for the pornography or sex tourism industry (Albanese, 2007).

It is estimated between 10 and 15 percent of children living on the streets in the United States are trafficked for sexual purposes. This figure includes U.S. residents and children from other countries. Many victims are lured from poorer countries such as Mexico, Argentina, and India with the promise of jobs and cash advances for their parents (Estes and Weiner, 2002).

The backgrounds of children who are victims of commercial sexual exploitation follow a similar pattern as those of other abused children.

Most suffered from prior abuse by an adult caretaker or friend, and a high percentage of victims of pornography were victimized while living at home. Their parents received money for exploiting their children. The home environments of these children create low self-esteem and poor social or job skills. As a result, a number of these children run away from home or frequent such hangouts as bus stations, arcades, and malls. Children become prime targets for pimps or other exploiters, who prey upon the child's emotional and financial dependency. Once they become dependant on the exploiters, it is difficult to leave, because they are often threatened with harm (Estes and Weiner, 2002).

VICTIMS OF RAPE AND SEXUAL VIOLENCE

> *During the past three decades, women have become more likely to report rapes and attempted rapes—particularly those involving known assailants—to police. Reporting by others, such as friends and family members, has also risen.*
>
> —Laura Taylor Freelance writer

Rape and other sexually violent acts performed without a person's consent or knowledge are serious crimes. They can occur among strangers or intimates of all ages, races, and social classes. The definition of rape includes forced vaginal, oral, and anal sex. One survey found that one in six U.S. women and one in thirty-three U.S. men have experienced an attempted or completed rape as a child or adult. Specifically, 18 percent of surveyed women and 3 percent of surveyed men said they experienced a completed or attempted rape at some time in their life (Tjaden and Thoennes, 2000). These findings are similar to findings from the *National Health and Social Life Survey*, which found that 22 percent of surveyed women and 2 percent of surveyed men had been "forced to do something sexual" at some time in their lifetime.

According to the Federal Bureau of Investigation, the rate of reported rape offenses in the year 2006 was slightly down from that of 2005. The data in Table 3–2 depict the rate changes between 2005 and 2006.

TABLE 3–2   FORCIBLE RAPE

Year	Number of Offenses	Rate per 100,000 Female Inhabitants
2005	93,934	62.5
2006	92,455	60.9
Percent Change	−2.0	−1.6

Source: FBI. 2007. *Uniform Crime Reports.* Washington, DC: Department of Justice.

The following information indicates the seriousness of the rape problem in the United States:

- Convicted rape and sexual assault offenders serving time in state prisons report that two-thirds of their victims were under the age of 18 years, and 58 percent of those—or nearly four in ten imprisoned violent sex offenders—said their victims were aged 12 years or younger.
- In 90 percent of the rapes of children younger than 12 years old, the child knew the offender, according to police-recorded incident data.
- Among victims 18–29 years old, two-thirds had a prior relationship with the rapist.

Definitions of forcible rape vary greatly—from sexual intercourse accomplished without the consent of the individual to the more encompassing definition by the *National Crime Victimization Survey* that describes forcible rape as forced sexual intercourse, including both psychological coercion and physical force. Forced sexual intercourse means vaginal, anal, or oral penetration by the offender(s), and this category also includes incidents where the penetration is from a foreign object, such as a bottle. Males may be victims of either heterosexual or homosexual rape. In most states, actions such as administering drugs or alcohol to a victim to coerce sex and having intercourse with an unconscious or mentally defective victim are considered rape. Following is a discussion of the various types of rape offenses where the victim and the offender are known to each other.

Marital Rape

Marital rape is a type of intimate violence, or is an extension of domestic violence (Johnson and Sigler, 1997:22). In "battering rapes," women experience both physical and sexual violence in the relationship (Finkelhor and Yllo, 1985). Women who are raped and battered by their partners experience the violence in various ways. In other words, some are battered during the sexual violence, or the rape may follow a physically violent episode where the husband wants to "make up" and coerces his wife to have sex against her will (Bergen, 1996; Finkelhor and Yllo, 1985).

Historically, husbands have had unlimited power over and sexual access to their wives. Rape statutes excluded the wife as a rape victim, but in recent years many states have revised their statutes to recognize marital rape. Marital rape is a crime in all 50 states. In 17 states and the District of Columbia, no exemptions from rape prosecution are granted to husbands. However, in 33 states, and in some circumstances, some exemptions from rape prosecution are still given to husbands. For example, when his wife is most vulnerable (e.g., she is mentally or physically impaired, unconscious, asleep) and is legally unable to consent, a husband is exempt from prosecution in many of these 33 states (Bergen, 1996; Russell, 1990).

In those jurisdictions in which statutes do not specify spousal rape, the courts have interpreted the laws to include spousal rape. In *Warren v. State* (1985), the Georgia Supreme Court held that when a woman says, "I do," it does not mean "I always will." The court upheld the conviction of a man accused of raping and sodomizing his wife. Marital rape cases are, however, difficult to prosecute. Important points to remember are that victims of these crimes have legal recourse and that intimacy and prior relations do not prohibit prosecution.

Date Rape and Dating Violence

Traditionally, rape has been used to describe the act of a stranger threatening to kill or injure a woman unless she has intercourse with him. Many sexual assaults, however, occur between victims and offenders who know each other. These rapes—commonly referred to as **date rape**—occur in the context of familiarity and trust, as opposed to random violent encounters between strangers.

These sexual assaults are reaching crisis proportions, with most date rapes occuring on college campuses. The coed lifestyle and active social environment can lead to nonconsensual sexual encounters. Studies on college campuses have indicated that date rape is increasing. More than half of a representative sample of more than 1,000 female students at a large urban university had experienced some form of unwanted sex. The study revealed that 12 percent of these acts were perpetrated by casual dates and 43 percent by steady dating partners (Abbey et al., 1996). A different study of 703 college students revealed that date rape tends to occur when the date was unplanned or the woman had been picked up in a social setting (Johnson, 1995).

Many women raped by men they know do not think of themselves as rape victims (although they were violated and there was at least verbal aggression) and are reluctant to report the act for fear that their own behavior will be scrutinized by others (Bownes, 1991). Many of the victims of date rape had been drinking or otherwise involved in some type of festivity when the rape occurred, but these elements are not invitations to sexual activity. Yet risky lifestyles and alcohol or drug usage increase the chances of victimization.

The use of drugs to incapacitate victims is also blamed in a number of date rapes. Referred to as **date rape drugs**, the drugs produce prolonged sedation, a feeling of well-being, and short-term memory loss. A number of drugs on the market have no particular color, smell, or taste and are easily added to flavored drinks without the victim's knowledge. At least three date rape drugs are commonly used:

- Gamma hydroxybutyric acid (GHB)
- Rohypnol (flunitrazepam)
- Ketamine (ketamine hydrochloride)

One such drug, Rohypnol, which is prescribed for insomnia and as a preoperative anesthetic, has been a factor in numerous date rape cases. Dates have allegedly slipped Rohypnol into their companion's drinks, rendering the person unconscious. Afterward, these women realize that they have been sexually assaulted. The Drug Enforcement Administration reports that it has recorded more than 2,400 criminal cases involving this drug (Sheridan, 1996).

Rohypnol has become increasingly popular, however, among teens and young adults, who take it for the euphoric, drunklike high it can provide. Focus 3–7 provides more information on these drugs. Prosecuting for rape someone who knows the victim and may even have a history of intimacy with her is difficult. Without some physical evidence suggesting violence, the fact that two consenting adults are involved in a sexual relationship makes it difficult to determine that an alleged rape has occurred. Focus 3–8 reports on one young woman's experience.

Focus 3–7 Rohypnol and GHB

Rohypnol and GHB are predominantly central nervous system depressants. Because they are often colorless, tasteless, and odorless, they can be added to beverages and ingested unknowingly. These substances emerged a few years ago as "drug-assisted assault" drugs. Because of concern about their abuse, Congress passed the "Drug-Induced Rape Prevention and Punishment Act of 1996" in October 1996. This legislation increased federal penalties for use of any controlled substance to aid in sexual assault. Rohypnol, a trade name for flunitrazepam, belongs to a class of drugs known as benzodiazepines. Rohypnol can incapacitate victims and prevent them from resisting sexual assault. It can produce "anterograde amnesia," which means individuals may not remember events they experienced while under the effects of the drug. Also, Rohypnol may be lethal when mixed with alcohol and/or other depressants. Rohypnol is not approved for use in the United States, and its importation is banned. Illicit abuse of Rohypnol started appearing in the United States in the early 1990s, where it became

(Continued)

(*Continued*)

known as "rophies," "roofies," "roach," and "rope." Since about 1990, GHB (gamma hydroxybutyrate) has been abused in the United States for its euphoric, sedative, and anabolic (body-building) effects. It is a central nervous system depressant that was widely available over-the-counter in health food stores during the 1980s and until 1992. Combining abuse of GHB with other drugs such as alcohol can result in nausea and breathing difficulties. According to the 2005 Monitoring the Future (MTF) survey, NIDA's annual survey of drug use among the nation's high school students, 0.7 percent of 8th-graders, 0.5 percent of 10th-graders, and 1.2 percent of 12th-graders reported annual use of Rohypnol. Annual use of GHB among 8th-graders and 10th-graders remained relatively stable from 2004 to 2005, but 12th-graders reported a significant decrease according to MTF findings. In 2005, 0.5 percent of 8th-graders, 0.8 percent of 10th-graders, and 1.1 percent of 12th-graders reported annual use. Hospital emergency department (ED) episodes involving GHB were estimated at 990 for the third and fourth quarters of 2003. Males made up the majority of patients involved in these mentions (52 percent), as did whites (86 percent). The two age categories with the highest number of mentions were the 18–20 age group and the 35–44 age group, each estimated at 28 percent of total mentions.

Source: The National Institute on Drug Abuse (NIDA) U.S. Department of Health & Human Services—200 Independence Avenue, S.W.—Washington, DC 2008.

Focus 3–8   Sue's Story

Sue had known Gary for about 3 years. He was Tony's best friend, and she had dated Tony for almost a year. Sue and Tony were having difficulties, and she and Gary had gotten together casually a few times to discuss her feelings for Tony. These were casual get-togethers. Recently, Sue invited Gary over to her apartment for dinner. She explained that her roommate was out of town and it would be nice for them to talk alone. While Sue fixed dinner, they chatted, drank wine, and teased each other in their normal way. However, the conversation turned serious when Gary told Sue that he would like to date her. Sue listened and then responded by saying that she was flattered but confused. She still cared for Tony, yet she really enjoyed being with Gary. She wanted some time to think about whether she really wanted to get involved with him. Sue then took Gary's hand and led him to the living room couch.

They sat close together on the couch and continued their conversation. Gary told Sue he understood her confusion and would wait. Sue gave Gary a kiss on the cheek and a hug. As they started to get up, Gary told Sue that he knew she would change her mind if she would let him show her how much he cared for her. He gently pulled Sue back on the couch and started to kiss her. She initially responded but pulled her head back and again told him that she was confused. Sue explained that

(*Continued*)

(Continued)

she was not interested in having any type of physical relationship. Gary tried to kiss her again and she pulled away and tried to get off the couch.

Gary started yelling, saying that he thought she had been leading him on in the past and was leading him on now. He called her a tease. She kept explaining that she wasn't interested in a physical relationship. Gary became angry and threatened to sabotage any efforts to mend her relationship with Tony. Gary then pushed Sue back on the couch, pinned her arms down, removed her clothes, and proceeded to have intercourse with her. She asked him "not to do this," but Gary told her it was his way of showing her how much he cared for her. Afterward, Gary dressed and told Sue he really liked her and hoped to see her again.

Was Sue raped or merely a victim of bad judgment? Can or should the offender be prosecuted? Without her full consent, it is reasonable to conclude that she was the victim of an unlawful sexual act. A review of the California law on rape discussed earlier indicates that a rape did occur, but proving it is difficult. For example, the law has no provision to exclude evidence that the parties knew each other or had a prior relationship. Thus, Sue's case would be difficult to prosecute because of what the jury might think about Sue's relations with Gary. In a Pennsylvania case, ***Commonwealth v. Berkowitz***, a defendant's conviction was reversed based on evidence that the victim consented to his initial advances. The defendant and victim were in a dating relationship when the defendant allegedly used no force other than penetration to commit the act, although the victim repeatedly and continually said no. The court was not persuaded that the sexual act was without the victim's consent (*Commonwealth v. Berkowitz*, 1992).

Dating violence may be defined as the perpetration or threat of an act of violence by at least one member of an unmarried couple on the other member within the context of dating or courtship (Sugerman and Hotaling, 1989). This violence encompasses any form of sexual assault, physical violence, and verbal or emotional abuse. The average prevalence rate for nonsexual dating violence is 22 percent among male and female high school students and 32 percent among college students. Females are more likely than males to be victims of dating violence (Sugarman and Hotaling, 1989).

Research has indicated that women traumatized by dating violence have certain characteristics. Young women aged 12 to 18 years who are victims of violence are more likely than older women to report that their offenders were acquaintances, friends, or intimate partners (Bachman and Saltzman, 1995). The likelihood of becoming a victim of dating violence is associated with having female peers who have been sexually victimized (Gwartney-Gibbs, Stockard, and Bohmer, 1987), lower church attendance

(Makepeace, 1987), a greater number of past dating partners (Gray and Foshee, 1997), the acceptance of dating violence (Gray and Foshee, 1997), and personally having experienced a previous sexual assault (Ageton, 1983).

Impact of Rape and Dating Violence

Many victims of sexual assault develop a type of post-traumatic stress syndrome that has been referred to as rape trauma syndrome. Symptoms can include fear, helplessness, shock, disbelief, guilt, humiliation, embarrassment, anger, self-blame, flashbacks of the rape, avoidance of previously pleasurable activities, avoidance of the place or circumstance in which the rape occurred, depression, sexual dysfunction, insomnia, and impaired memory.

Medical problems resulting from rape can include acute injury, risk of acquiring sexually transmissible diseases, risk of pregnancy, and lingering medical complaints. A cross-sectional study of medical patients found that women who had been raped rated themselves as significantly less healthy, visited a physician nearly twice as often, and incurred medical costs over twice as high as women who had not experienced any criminal victimization. The level of violence experienced during the assault was found to be a powerful predictor of future use of medical services.

Sexual assault affects the family and friends of the victim, as well. Following sexual assault, victims often pull away from intimate relationships or, alternatively, become regressively fearful, clinging, and needy. Victims of rape often manifest long-term symptoms, such as chronic headaches, fatigue, sleep disturbance, recurrent nausea, decreased appetite, eating disorders, menstrual pain, sexual dysfunction, and suicide attempts.

In a longitudinal study, sexual assault was found to increase the odds of substance abuse (Kilpatrick et al., 1997). The adult pregnancy rate associated with rape is increasing based on the U.S. Census reports, suggesting that there may be 32,100 rape-related pregnancies annually among American women over the age of 18 years (Homes et al., 1996).

Responding to Victims of Rape and Sexual Assault

After a rape occurs, the threat exists of contracting acquired immune deficiency syndrome (AIDS) or other sexually transmitted diseases. Most states have enacted laws on the testing of criminal offenders and their victims for infection and transmission of the human immunodeficiency virus (HIV), which causes AIDS.

Such laws were passed in response to the recognized dangers of the transmission of HIV/AIDS during sexual assault or abuse and other crimes when an exchange of bodily fluids takes place. The laws were also the result of a new understanding of the added trauma a sexual assault victim endures when faced with the very real possibility of having contracted a deadly disease. The laws primarily require the testing of alleged and convicted sex offenders for HIV/AIDS and the disclosure of the results of the offenders' tests to the victims. In about half of the states, the victim must request that the offender be tested. In some states, the victim petitions directly; in others, the prosecutor files a petition at the request of the victim. Under many of the laws requiring testing, there must be a showing of significant exposure of the victim to the bodily fluids of the offender. Most of the laws mandating the testing of offenders before conviction require a finding of probable cause that the defendant committed the offense and that the circumstances of the offense resulted in significant exposure of the victim to the semen or other bodily fluids of the offender, placing the victim at risk of transmission of HIV/AIDS. Even when a state does not have a law specifically relating to the testing of sex offenders, it may have a law that permits any person to seek a court order for disclosure of another person's confidential HIV/AIDS information when the individual can demonstrate a compelling need for access to the information (National Center for Victims of Crime, 2005).

Summary

Many of the abuses discussed in this chapter, such as child abuse, elder abuse, and IPV, are similar in certain terms. The abuse may be emotional, physical, or sexual. Intimate violence is common and is precipitated by a number of factors, including strained relationships, frustrations in caregiving, family tensions, substance abuse, and so forth. Several behaviors indicate impending intimate or family violence, such as stalking, making unwelcome sexual advances, and harassment. People displaying uncontrolled anger or jealousy in the early stages of a relationship may become physically abusive of their partner in the future. It is important that victims seek help immediately when they experience an abusive relationship.

Key Terms and Concepts

Anti-stalking legislation	IPV (intimate partner violence)
Baker v. United States	Mandatory arrest laws
Commonwealth v. Berkowitz	Restraining order
Cycle of violence	Stalking
Date rape	*Thurman v. City of Torrington*
Date rape drugs	*United States v. Dixon*
Erotomania	*Warren v. State*

DISCUSSION QUESTIONS AND LEARNING ACTIVITIES

1. Explain how a person can be charged with stalking. What constitutes the offense?
2. What problems exist in prosecuting someone for date rape?
3. Does your state have a mandatory arrest policy for domestic violence? Interview a police officer or judge to get his or her views on the policy. If such a policy exists, is it effective in deterring repeat offenses? If your state doesn't have such a policy, do you think it should? Explain.
4. Read Focus 3–4. Based on what you read, do you agree with the decision to arrest? In what other ways was the woman victimized as she moved through the system?
5. Discuss the warning signs of an abusive relationship.
6. Make up a questionnaire guaranteeing anonymity, and survey employees or students on whether they have been victims of spousal abuse, stalking, or acquaintance rape. Make sure you define what each means.
7. Explain the process a victim of stalking would go through in your community to get a restraining/protection order. Interview a police officer or district attorney.
8. Why does domestic violence occur?
9. Identify the services available in your community for victims of spousal abuse and rape.
10. Identify the behavioral and legal responses to stalking.
11. What common factors are associated with child abuse, spousal abuse, and elder abuse?
12. Describe the effects of the drug Rohypnol or any other so-called date rape drug. Are you aware of any cases of their use?

WEB SOURCES

Los Angeles County District Attorney's Office—Crimes of Violence. http://da.co.la.ca.us/violentcrimes.htm

The National Center for Victims of Crime. www.ncvc.org/ncvc/main.aspx?dbID=dash_Home

National Criminal Justice Reference Service (NCJRS): Victims of Crime—Additional Resources. www.ncjrs.org/victwww.html#general

RECOMMENDED READINGS

Berry, Dawn Bradley. 2000. *The Domestic Violence Sourcebook*, 3rd ed. New York, NY: McGraw-Hill.

Boon, Julian, and Lorraine Sheridan, eds. 2002. *Stalking and Psychosexual Obsession: Psychological Perspectives for Prevention, Policing and Treatment*. Wiley Series in Psychology of Crime, Policing and Law. New York: Wiley.

Delaplane, David, and Anne Delaplane. 2004. *Victim of Child Abuse; Domestic Violence, Elderly Abuse; Rape, Robbery, Assault; and Violent Death: A Manual for Clergy and Congregations,* 4th ed. Boston, MA: Diane.

Flowers, R. Barri. 2000. *Sex Crimes, Predators, Perpetrators, Prostitutes, and Victims: An Examination of Sexual Criminality and Victimization.* Cincinnati, OH: Charles C. Thomas.

Haley, James, ed. 2003. *Date Rape.* At Issue Series. Chicago, IL: Greenhaven Press.

Hines, Denise A., and Kathleen Malley-Morrison. 2004. *Family Violence in the United States: Defining, Understanding, and Combating Abuse.* Thousand Oaks, CA: Sage Publications

REFERENCES

Abbey, A., L. T. Ross, D. McDuffie, and P. McAuslan. 1996. Alcohol and Dating Risk Factors for Sexual Assault among College Women. *Psychology of Women Quarterly* 20(1):147–169.

Ageton, S. 1983. *Sexual Assault Among Adolescents.* Lexington, MA: Heath Publishing Co.

Albanese, Jay. 2007. *Commercial Exploitation of Children: What Do We Know and What Do We Do About It?* Washington, DC: National Institute of Justice.

Estes, Richard, and Neil Weiner. 2002. *The Commercial Sexual Exploitation of Children in the U.S., Canada, and Mexico.* Philadelphia, PA: University of Pennsylvania, School of Social work, Center for the Study of youth Policy.

American Journal of Public Health. July 2003, 93: 1098–1103. Washington, DC.

Arrest Policies for Domestic Violence Allegations, retrieved from: http://dontmakehermad.com/research/arrestpolicies/index.html May 8, 2008.

Arata, C. M. 1999. Sexual Re-victimization and PTSD: An Exploratory Study. *Journal of Child Sexual Abuse* 8(1):49–65.

Bachman, R., and L. E. Saltzman. 1995. *Violence Against Women: Estimates from the Redesigned Survey.* Washington, DC: Bureau of Justice Statistics, U.S. Department of Justice.

Baker v. United States. 1995. Criminal Case No. 95-80106. Eastern Michigan: United States District Court.

Bergen, R. K. 1996. *Wife Rape: Understanding the Response of Survivors and Service Providers.* Thousand Oaks, CA: Sage Publications.

Bownes, Ian T. 1991. A Comparison of Stranger and Acquaintance Assaults. *Medical Science Law* 31:102.

Brown, Lou, Francois Dubau, and J. D. Merritt McKeon. 1997. *Stop Domestic Violence: An Action Plan for Saving Lives.* New York: St. Martin's Griffin.

Browne, Angela, and David Finkelhor. 1986. Impact of Child Sexual Abuse: A Review of the Research. *Psychological Bulletin* 113:114–126.

California Nursing Homes: Federal and State Oversight Inadequate to Protect Residents in Homes with Serious Care Violations. 1998. G.A.O. (T-HEHS98–219) (July 28). Washington, DC: Government Accounting Office.

Clarke, Jennifer, Michael D. Stein, Mindy Sobota, Margaret Marisi, and Lucy Hanna. 1999. Physical Aggression by Persons with a History of Childhood Abuse. *Archives of Internal Medicine* 159:1920–1924.

Coleman, Brenda. 1999. Child Abuse Deaths Go Unreported. *Los Angles Times,* Associated Press, 66–68.

Commonwealth v. Berkowitz. 1992. 602 A.2d 1338 (Pa. Super).

DeSimone, Peter. 1998. *Homelessness in Missouri: Eye of the Storm?* Jefferson City: Missouri Association for Social Welfare.

Douglas, Richard L. 1995a. *Domestic Mistreatment of the Elderly.* New York: American Association of Retired Persons.

Douglas, Richard. 1995b. *The State of Homelessness in Michigan: A Research Study.* East Lansing: Michigan Interagency Committee on Homelessness. Available at no cost from the committee, Michigan State Housing Development Authority, P.O. Box 30044, Lansing, MI 48909; 517-373-6026.

Edleson, J. L. 1999. Children's Witnessing of Adult Domestic Violence. *Journal of Interpersonal Violence* 14(8):839–870.

Elsevier Health Sciences. 2007, September 27. Victims of Child Maltreatment More Likely to Perpetrate Youth Violence, Intimate Partner Violence. *ScienceDaily.* Retrieved February 28, 2008, from http://www.sciencedaily.com/releases/2007/09/070925090242.htm

Faulker, Robert P., and Douglas H. Hsiao. 1994. And Where You Go I'll Follow: The Constitutionality of Antistalking Laws and Proposed Model Legislation. *Harvard Law Review* 31:467.

Ferraro, Kathleen J. 1989. Policing Women Battering. *Social Problems* 35:61–74.

Finkelhor, D., and Yllo, K. 1985. *License to Rape: Sexual Abuse of Wives.* New York: Holt, Rinehart & Winston.

Finn, Peter, and Sarah Colson. 1990. *Civil Protection Orders: Legislation, Current Court Practice, and Enforcement.* Washington, DC: U.S. Department of Justice.

Gelles, Richard. 1993. *Through a Sociological Lens: Social Structure and Family Violence, Current Controversies on Family Violence.* Newbury Park, CA: Sage Publications.

Gelles, Richard, and Claire Cornell. 1990. *Intimate Violence in Families,* 2nd ed. Thousand Oaks, CA: Sage Publications.

Goldston, David, Dawn C. Turnquist, and John F. Knutson. 1989. Presenting Problems of Sexually Abused Girls Receiving Psychiatric Services. *Journal of Abnormal Psychology* 98:366–375.

Gray, H. M., and V. Foshee. 1997. Adolescent Dating Violence: Differences between One-sided and Mutually Violent Profiles. *Journal of Interpersonal Violence* 12(1):126–141.

Gwartney-Gibbs, P. A., J. Stockard, and S. Bohmer. 1987. Learning Courtship Aggression: The Influence of Parents, Peers, and Personal Experiences. *Family Relations* 36:276–282.

Heise, L., and C. Garcia-Moreno. 2002. *Violence by Intimate Partners. World Report on Violence and Health.* Geneva: World Health Organization.

Homes, M. M., H. S. Resnick, D. G. Kilpatrick, and C. L. Best. 1996. Rape-related Pregnancy: Estimates and Descriptive Characteristics from a National Sample of Women. *American Journal of Obstetrics and Gynecology* 175(2):320–324.

Jogerst, Gerald J. et al. 2003. Domestic Elder Abuse and the Law. *American Journal of Public Health* 93(12):2131–2136.

Johnson, I., and R. Sigler. 1997. *Forced Sexual Intercourse in Intimate Relationships.* Brookfield, VT: Dartmouth/Ashgate.

Johnson, Kim. 1995. Attributions About Date Rape: Impact of Clothing, Sex, Money Spent, Date Type, and Perceived Similarity. *Family and Consumer Research Journal* 23:3.

Kilpatrick, D. G., R. Acierno, H. S. Resnick, B. E. Saunders, and C. L. Best. 1997. A 2-Year Longitudinal Analysis of the Relationships between Violent Assault and Substance Use in Women. *Journal of Consulting and Clinical Psychology* 65(5):834–847.

Kolbo, J. R. 1996. Risk and Resilience among Children Exposed to Family Violence. *Violence and Victims* 11:113–128.

Lerman, Lisa G., Leslie Landis, and Sharon Goldweig. 1983. State Legislation on Domestic Violence. In *Abuse of Women: Legislation, Reporting, and Prevention*, ed. J. J. Costa. Lexington, MA: Heath.

Lindbloom, E., J. Brandt, C. Hawes, C. Phillips, D. Zimmerman, J. Robinson, B. Bowers, and P. McFeeley. 2005. *The Role of Forensic Science in Identification of Mistreatment Deaths in Long-Term Care Facilities.* Washington, DC: Final report submitted to the National Institute of Justice, April 2005.

Los Angeles Times. 1995. Man Convicted under Domestic Violence Act Given Life Term. September 2, A-2.

Makepeace, J. M. 1987. Social Factors and Victim–Offender Differences in Courtship Violence. *Family Relations* 36:87–91.

McLeod, J. 1984. Female Violence. *Justice Quarterly* 2:223–238.

Meloy, J. R., ed. 1998. *The Psychology of Stalking: Clinical and Forensic Perspectives.* San Diego, CA: Academic Press.

Mercy, J. A., and L. E. Saltzman. 1989. Fatal Violence among Spouses in the United States, 1976–1985. *American Journal of Public Health* 79:5.

Miller, Greg, and Davan Maharaj. 1999b. Internet: Mother's Account of Daughter's Ordeal Points Up the Unique Problems Such Web Crimes Present for Law Enforcement. *Los Angeles Times*, January 23, C-1, home edition.

Miller, Neal, and Hugh Nugent. 2002. *Stalking Laws and Implementation Practices: A National Review for Policymakers and Practitioners (Full Report).* Minneapolis: Institute for Law and Justice, Minnesota Center Against Violence and Abuse (MINCAVA).

Mount Auburn Hospital Prevention and Training Center. 1995. *The Dating Violence Intervention Project.* Cambridge, MA: Mount Auburn Hospital Prevention and Training Center.

National Center for Victims of Crime. 2000. http://www.ncvc.org

National Center for Victims of Crime. 2005. www.ncvc.org/ncvc/Main.aspx (accessed June 2005).

National Clearinghouse on Child Abuse and Neglect. 2003. *Recognizing Child Abuse and Neglect: Signs and Symptoms.* Washington, DC: National Clearinghouse on Child Abuse and Neglect.

National Institute of Justice. 1993. *Anti-Stalking Laws.* Washington, DC: U.S. Department of Justice.

National Ombudsman Reporting System. 2003. *Data Tables.* Washington, DC: U.S. Administration on Aging.

National Research Council Panel to Review Risk and Prevalence of Elder Abuse and Neglect. 2003. *Elder Mistreatment: Abuse, Neglect and Exploitation in an Aging America.* Washington, DC: National Research Council Panel to Review Risk and Prevalence of Elder Abuse and Neglect.

Office of Justice Programs. 1998. *Stalking and Domestic Violence in America: The Third Annual Report to Congress under the Violence against Women Act.* Washington, DC: U.S. Department of Justice.

O'Leary, Daniel K., et al. 1989. Prevalence and Stability of Physical Aggression between Spouses: A Longitudinal Analysis. *Journal of Consulting and Clinical Psychology* 57(2):263–268.

Owen, Greg, et al. 1998. *Minnesota Statewide Survey of Persons Without Permanent Shelter; Volume I: Adults and Their Children.* St. Paul, MN: Wilder Research Center.

Pagelow, M. 1988. Marital Rape. In *Handbook of Family Violence*, eds. V. Van Hasselth, R. Morrison, A. Bellack, and M. Hereen. New York: Plenum Press.

Pathe, Michele, and Paul Mullen. 1997. The Impact of Stalkers on Their Victims. *British Journal of Psychiatry* 170:12, 13.

Peterson, Karen. 2003. Studies Shatter Myth About Abuse. *USA Today,* June 22, A-I.

Remsburg v. Docusearch, Inc., 816 A.2d 1001 (2003).

Russell, D. E. H. 1990. *Rape in Marriage.* New York: Macmillan.

Sheridan, Mary Beth. 1996. Rohypnol. *Los Angeles Times,* July 5, A-1.

Sherman, Lawrence, and R. A. Berk. 1984. The Specific Deterrent Effects of Arrest for Domestic Assault. *American Sociological Review* 49:261–272.

Silvern, L., J. Karyl, L. Waelde, W. F. Hodges, J. Starek, E. Heidt, and K. Min. 1995. Retrospective Reports of Parental Partner Abuse: Relationships to Depression, Trauma Symptoms and Self-Esteem among College Students. *Journal of Family Violence* 10:177–202.

Simon, R. 1996. Bad Men Do What Good Men Dream. Washington: American Psychiatric Press. www.appi.org/appi. html; simonb.html.

Simon, Leonore, and Kristen, Zgoba. 2008. "The Effects of State Mandatory Arrest Policies on Actual Domestic Violence Arrests." *Paper presented at the annual meeting of the American Society of Criminology (ASC).* Los Angeles Convention Center, Los Angeles, CA, October 31.

Spaccarelli, S., J. D. Coatsworth, and B. S. Bowden. 1995. Exposure to Serious Family Violence among Incarcerated Boys: Its Association with Violent Offending and Potential Mediating Variables. *Violence and Victims* 10:163–182.

Steinmetz, Suzanne K. 1977. The Battered Husband Syndrome. *Victimology* 2:177.

Sugarman, D. B., and G. T. Hotaling. 1989. Dating Violence: Prevalence, Context and Risk Markers. In *Violence in Dating Relationships*, eds. M. A. Pirog-Good and J. E. Stets. New York: Praeger.

Thurman v. City of Torrington, 595 F. Supp. 1521 (D.Conn., 1984).

Tjaden, P., and N. Thoennes. 2000. *Extent, Nature, and Consequences of Intimate Partner Violence: Findings from the National Violence against Women Survey (research report).* Washington, DC: U.S. Department of Justice.

Town of Castle Rock, Colorado v. Gonzales (United States Supreme Court, Case No. 04-278, June 27, 2005).

U.S. Conference of Mayors. 1998. *A Status Report on Hunger and Homelessness in America's Cities: 1998.* Washington, DC: U.S. Conference of Mayors. Available for $15 from U.S. Conference of Mayors, 1620 Eye St. NW, 4th Floor, Washington, DC 20006-4005; 202-293-7330.

United States. v. Dixon, 113 S.Ct. 2849 (1993).

van der Kolk, Bessel. 1998. *American Journal of Preventive Medicine* 14:245–258.

Vaselle-Augenstein, Renata, and Annette Ehrlich. 1993. Male Batterers: Evidence for Psychopathology. In *Intimate Violence: Interdisciplinary Perspectives*, ed. Emilio Viano. Washington, DC: Hemisphere Publishing.

Warren v. State, 336 S.E. 2nd. 221 (1985).

Willing, Richard. 1998. Men Stalking Men: Stalkers Often Gravitate Toward Positions of Power. *USA Today,* June 17, 38.

Windom, Kathy Spatz. 1995. *Victims of Childhood Sexual Abuse—Later Criminal Consequences.* Washington, DC: National Institute of Justice.

Windom, Kathy S., and Michael G. Maxwell. 2001. *An Update on the "Cycle of Violence."* Washington, DC: National Institute of Justice.

Zona, M. A., R. E. Palarea, and J. C. Lane. 1998. Psychiatric Diagnosis and the Offender–Victim Typology Stalking. In *The Psychology of Stalking: Clinical and Forensic Perspectives,* ed. J. R. Meloy. San Diego, CA: Academic Press.

4

Stranger Violence and Victimization

LEARNING OBJECTIVES

After studying this chapter, you will:

- Understand the victimization associated with robbery and carjacking.
- Learn about the dynamics of homicides committed by strangers.
- Become familiar with the paradigm of spontaneous victimization.
- Learn the motives and victim choices of serial killers.
- Understand the dynamics of hate and bias crimes.
- Learn the settings in which violent crimes occur.
- Understand why strangers victimize some people.

INTRODUCTION

Random stranger-on-stranger violence is unpredictable and can occur anywhere. Consider the events of December 5, 2007, when 19-year-old Robert A. Hawkins, a high school dropout with a criminal past, walked into a shopping mall in Omaha, Nebraska, with a semiautomatic rifle and killed eight people including himself. Victimization on the roadway is also a threat. A total of 36 shootings were reported on the Los Angeles freeways in 2005. Victims varied, including a 20-year-old college student who was gunned down in heavy midday traffic just south of downtown Los Angeles. On the same highway, a father of two was shot. A 32-year-old man was fatally shot on a freeway east of Los Angeles. As noted by a veteran police detective, "There are no links between victims, suspects, time or motive . . . other than driving on the freeway" (Edds, 2005).

Violent crime has occurred in society for many years, but the nature of such crimes is changing. Being victim to stranger-on-stranger or nonacquaintance violence, such as carjacking, gang violence, robbery, and murder, and random acts of violence such as so-called road rage is a constant threat. Although it is recognized that relatives or acquaintances of the victim commit most violent offenses, an increasing number of crimes are committed by strangers. In other words, automatic teller machines, fast-food restaurants, and shopping malls have become places where predators take advantage of victims. Communities with transient populations or ones that have significant numbers of disenfranchised or troubled youth report high victimization rates. Simply staring or looking at someone could be an invitation to violence in such places. Predators target innocent and naïve citizens simply because these people possess whatever the predators want or need. Visiting an ATM, walking through a deserted parking lot, driving an expensive car, inadvertently cutting off someone in traffic, or wearing expensive clothing or jewelry are simple acts that can lead to serious injury, sexual assault, or death. According to the Bureau of Justice Statistics (2003b), more than 40 percent of all victims of violent crime in 2000 identified the offenders as strangers. More specifically, more than 40 percent of the victims of sexual assault and victims of simple assault reported not knowing the offender.

ROBBERY

> *Robbery ranks among the most serious and feared criminal offenses because it involves both threatened or actual violence and a loss of property to the victim. It also occurs more frequently than either rape or homicide.*
>
> —Steve Schlisinge, Bureau of Justice Statistics

Robbery is generally defined as feloniously taking property from a person or in the immediate presence of a person by means of force or threat of force. The use of a weapon is not required to commit a robbery. In some communities, it is not uncommon to hear of residents carrying extra amounts of money to give to muggers, in the event they are robbed.

According to figures released by the FBI (Federal Bureau of Investigation, 2004), more than 400,000 robberies were reported nationwide in 2006, translating to a rate of 142.2 robberies per 100,000 population. As discussed in Chapter 1, the *National Crime Victimization Survey* (*NCVS*) reports an even higher number of robberies (and other crimes) than does the official *Uniform*

Crime Reports (*UCR*). According to the *UCR*, of all major crimes, robbery victims had the lowest percentage (28 percent) of victims having known the offender. Most victims were robbed while shopping or traveling. And almost 50 percent of the robberies occurred less than five miles from the victim's home. More than half of the offenses were robberies on streets and highways involving strangers with firearms. (See Table 4–1.)

Poor families with annual incomes of less than $10,500 are frequently robbed. The higher the income and educational level, the less likely a person is to be a robbery victim, suggesting that lifestyle or living conditions are associated with robbery victimization.

The circumstances under which a victim is robbed may vary. The aggressor may enter the victim's home, accost him or her on the street in or out of view of others, or, occasionally, rob a victim in a commercial establishment, a park, or on public transportation. The most common robbery locations are streets and highways, followed by commercial establishments such as nightclubs. Bank ATM robberies also pose a threat. Most ATM robberies occur at night between 7 P.M. and midnight, while the machine only produces 10 percent of the daily transactions. Between 7 P.M. and 4 A.M., the ATMs process only 11 percent of the total daily transactions but suffer 60 percent of the crime. Bank ATM robbers are generally males under 25 years of age and many of them work alone. ATM robbers usually position themselves nearby and wait for a person to approach and withdraw cash. Many ATM robbery victims are ladies and many are alone when attacked.

As indicated in Table 4–1, many robberies occur in residences and on the streets, suggesting that robbers are becoming more desperate due to increased security in businesses. Two examples of bold stranger-on-stranger robberies are home invasion robberies and carjacking.

Home Invasion Robbery

Home invasion robberies frequently target residents unknown to the invaders, but whose lifestyle or habits they may know. The targets are usually senior citizens and women living alone and are usually of the same racial/ethnic group as the invader. In many cases, the invaders know that the victim has cash or other valuables and is not likely to offer much resistance. Invaders plan their attacks well in advance by following a target home from work or shopping or surveying the residence for a period of time (Hurley, 1995). In Los Angeles in 1994, a series of home robberies occurred when thieves answered computer bulletin board and classified ads, masquerading as potential respondents (Williams, 1996).

Home invaders rely on stealth and surprise. Although some burglars or petty thieves prefer anonymity, home invaders prefer open confrontation.

TABLE 4–1 ROBBERY, PERCENT DISTRIBUTION WITHIN REGION, 2005

Region	Total[1]	Street/ highway	Commercial house	Gas or service station	Convenience store	Residence	Bank	Miscellaneous
Total	**100.0**	**42.3**	**14.6**	**2.8**	**5.9**	**14.9**	**2.2**	**17.2**
Northeast	100.0	55.9	9.9	2.8	6.2	10.1	2.9	12.2
Midwest	100.0	44.4	13.3	4.4	4.7	13.4	2.7	17.1
South	100.0	36.0	14.4	2.5	6.7	20.6	1.6	18.2
West	100.0	44.5	17.6	2.5	5.2	9.7	2.4	18.1

[1]Because of rounding, the percentages may not add to 100.0.

Source: Federal Bureau of Investigation, 2005. *Uniform Crime Reports.* Washington, DC: U.S. Department of Justice.

Once a residence is targeted, the entry is direct, relying on sheer force, false pretenses, or various forms of impersonation to gain entry. After entry, one of the robbers forcefully controls the victim while another ransacks the house or, in some cases, sexually assaults or kills the victim.

In a 1995 study of 198 home invasion robberies in Atlanta, Kellerman et al. (1995) found one-half were forced entries occurring between midnight and 6 A.M. The intruder carried a gun in 17 percent of the cases, and in 20 percent of the cases at least one resident was injured. Victims who resisted the attackers were more likely to be injured than those who did not. Home invaders prefer residences where detection is difficult. Thus, apartments or other similar units are attractive because of the ease in which strangers can move about (Kellerman et al., 1995).

Home invasions are attractive to criminals for several reasons. First, they do not have to worry about home alarm devices because they often invade when someone is home. Second, they can avoid suspicion by parking their vehicles in front of the home or in the driveway as if they belong there. They may enter through an open garage door. Finally, invaders can leave their victims bound and gagged, allowing time for their escape.

Another factor explaining the popularity of home invasions is the increased security used by businesses. As banks and convenience stores increase their security by using cameras and other measures to prevent burglary, criminals are turning to residential opportunities. Robbers understand that residents, for the most part, are not as security-conscious as businesses.

One factor leading to home invasions is the need to seek cash and valuable items to support drug habits. Gangs in Asian communities know that Asian families often keep cash and valuables at home. They also know that fear and cultural differences may deter Asians from reporting victimization to the police. In Los Angeles County, Asian gang members often cruise neighborhoods looking for signs of Asian occupants, such as a Chinese good luck symbol hanging over the door or shoes left on the front porch. Typically, the gangs strike during the day, when usually only elderly persons or mothers with young children are home. Home invaders use a number of tactics to enter homes and steal property. The following are some examples (Williams, 1996):

- An elderly couple opened their front door to a man claiming to be from the local gas company. He and two other offenders forced their way into the home. They made the couple lie on the floor and forced the husband to reveal the location of the cash and jewelry by telling him that his wife would be killed if he did not cooperate.
- Four armed offenders joined a party through an unlocked door. They forced the victims to lie on the floor while they gathered cash and jewelry.

- Two young men knocked on a woman's door to say that they had struck her parked car. They pushed their way into her home, ransacked it, and sexually assaulted her.

- An apartment manager was showing a unit in her building to a potential renter when a man with a gun pushed the pair inside. The robber demanded money and then forced the manager to unlock her apartment, from which he took money and valuables.

Even the famous have been victimized by home invasion robberies. In January 1996, actor Harry Dean Stanton was tied up and injured in a home invasion robbery. Two men forced their way into his home and ransacked the premises. They stole Stanton's car but were arrested after a tracking device in the car was activated. The robbers eventually crashed when chased by the police (*Los Angeles Times*, 1996b).

Carjacking

Another contemporary form of robbery by strangers is carjacking. **Carjacking** is the theft or attempted theft of a motor vehicle by force or threat of force. In response to this crime, Congress passed a law in 1992 that made it a federal crime to steal any vehicle "transported, shipped, or received in interstate commerce" while possessing a firearm during the commission of the offense (18 United States Code, § 2119). In 1993, the Federal Bureau of Investigation (FBI) devoted 13 agents and spent $1.5 million to investigate approximately 290 carjackings nationwide (Scheb, 1996). Carjacking, however, is primarily a local crime problem, requiring local authorities to increase crime prevention efforts to deal with the crimes and the victims. The Bureau of Justice Statistics reports the following demographic factors on carjackings (Bureau of Justice Statistics, 2003b):

- Men were more often victimized than were women; blacks more than whites; and Hispanics more than non-Hispanics.

- Households with annual incomes of $50,000 or more had lower rates of carjacking than those earning less than $50,000.

- Carjacking victimization rates were highest in urban areas, followed by suburban and then rural areas. Ninety-three percent of carjackings occurred in cities or suburbs.

- A weapon was used in 74 percent of carjacking victimizations. Firearms were used in 45 percent of carjackings, knives in 11 percent, and other weapons in 18 percent.

- The victim resisted the offender in two-thirds the number of carjackings. Twenty-four percent of victims used confrontational resistance (threatening or attacking the offender or chasing or trying to capture the offender).

- Approximately 32 percent of victims of completed carjackings and approximately 17 percent of victims of attempted carjackings were injured. Serious injuries, such as gunshot or knife wounds, broken bones, or internal injuries, occurred in approximately 9 percent of the cases.

- The victims were hospitalized in approximately 1 percent of carjackings. Approximately 14 percent of victims were treated in hospital emergency departments and then released. Another 6 percent of cases involved victims who were treated elsewhere, such as in a doctor's office or at the crime scene.

- Multiple carjackers committed approximately 56 percent of the total number of carjackings.

- Males committed 93 percent of carjacking incidents, whereas groups involving both males and females committed 3 percent. Women committed about 3 percent of carjackings.

- Carjacking victims identified 56 percent of the offenders as black, 21 percent as white, and 16 percent as members of other races, such as Asians or American Indians. In 6 percent of carjackings, the victim(s) reported multiple offenders.

- Sixty-eight percent of carjacking incidents occurred at night (6 P.M. to 6 A.M.).

- Forty-four percent of carjacking incidents occurred in an open area, such as on the street (other than immediately adjacent to the victim's own home or that of a friend or neighbor) or near public transportation (such as a bus, subway, train station, or airport), and 24 percent occurred in parking lots or garages or near commercial places such as stores, gas stations, office buildings, restaurants/bars, or other facilities.

- Approximately 63 percent of carjacking incidents occurred within five miles of the victim's home, including the 17 percent that occurred at or near the home. Four percent occurred more than 50 miles from the victim's home.

Another strategy is to use a procedure called "bump and rob" in which carjackers target a vehicle (often an expensive car) or person (usually a lone female) and cause a minor collision. Once stopped, the victim's car is taken by one of the criminal parties; in the worst case, the victim is kidnapped, robbed, assaulted, or killed (National Crime Prevention Council, 1997).

A content analysis of 28 news articles involving carjackings (reported by the *Los Angeles Times* in an 18-month period from 1995 to 1996) revealed additional information, including the time of attack, the victim's sex and age, the location of the carjacking, the extent of victimization, and the offender's characteristics, such as age and sex. The analysis revealed that most carjackers are a different race than the victim. The offenders' ages ranged from 15 to 45 years, although most offenders were teenagers or in their early twenties. Most victims were lone females carjacked from a parking lot or street by a lone male offender. Some victims were approached at an intersection, a freeway off-ramp, a drive-through of a fast-food restaurant, and, in one case, the driveway of the victim's home. In one case, the offenders used the bump-and-rob tactic. With some exceptions, the carjackers carried a handgun. In a majority of the cases, the victim was battered or sexually assaulted. In eight of the cases, the victim was murdered or seriously wounded, and in six cases the victim was able to escape. Most of the attacks occurred during evening hours near the victim's home. In all cases, the victim and offenders were strangers. It appears victims' vulnerability and the type of car they were driving made them targets. A frightening fact is that many offenders are armed teenagers who show no remorse for their crimes.

In response to the carjacking threat, Louisiana passed the Shoot the Carjacker Law. The law makes killing a potential or actual carjacker a justifiable homicide (Carjacking Law Takes Effect, 1997). In other words, if a driver believes that he or she is about to be carjacked, the driver may use deadly force. The information in Focus 4–1 indicates the callousness of a carjacker toward a victim and why laws like the Louisiana law are passed.

Focus 4–1   A Case of Carjacking

Before she was smothered by a teenage carjacker, Kathleen Weinstein used a miniature cassette player to secretly record herself pleading for her life. "Don't you understand what kind of trouble you are going to get in? Don't you think they're going to find you?" Weinstein asked the boy who abducted her at gunpoint from a shopping plaza. Although it didn't save her life, the dramatic 24-minute recording helped authorities identify the suspect, a 17-year-old. On the tape, Mrs. Weinstein valiantly and persistently used every skill and power she had to convince her attacker to simply take her car but not her life. . . . Weinstein offered her attacker help and advice during their conversation and promised not to tell anyone if he just took her car and left her alone . . . but in the end, the youth suffocated Weinstein with her coat and other pieces of clothing . . . her body was found in a wooded area with the cassette in one of her pockets. The youth admitted that he was looking for a car like the one driven by Mrs. Weinstein, a 1995 Toyota Camry.

Source: Victim Made Tape of Her Pleas with Killer. 1996. *Los Angeles Times*, March 20, A-15.

MURDERS AND ASSAULTS BY STRANGERS

*The most frequently cited reason for not carrying through on the homicidal fantasies
was the fear of getting caught and spending their life behind bars. Many of us owe
our lives to the fact that murder is so costly to commit in the modern world.*

—Dr. David Buss, evolutionary psychologist

Whereas most murders are committed by acquaintances, many are committed by persons unknown to the victim. As suggested by the preceding
quote, more murders would be committed if it were not for the punishment. Early research on homicide by Wolfgang (1958) resulted in dividing
the offense into two categories. The first is referred to as *primary homicide*,
or homicides committed against nonstrangers or acquaintances. These
include homicides resulting from domestic violence. The other is *stranger*,
or *secondary*, *homicide*, the focus of this discussion. The leading circumstances surrounding stranger homicide include the commission of a felony
(robbery), arguments, juvenile gang killings, and drug dealing. All major
factors involved in homicide as reported by the *Uniform Crime Reports* for
2005 are presented in Table 4–2.

Some victims facilitate their victimization through their behavior and
lifestyle choices. Thus, people who visit places known for crime or who
undertake risky activities (e.g., hitchhiking, using or selling drugs, and
prostitution) invite anonymous victimization. Strangers kill most victims
during the commission of a violent crime (Federal Bureau of Investigation,
2004). The media is replete with examples of people murdered or seriously
assaulted by a stranger. For purposes of discussion, stranger-on-stranger
murders are divided into two broad categories: spontaneous murders and
targeted murders.

Spontaneous Murders

On May 23, 2001, Patrick Gott walked into the New Orleans airport armed
with a shotgun. He opened fire, killing one woman and wounding several
bystanders. Gott told investigators that he was a practicing Muslim and
fired the gun because he was angry that people had ridiculed the turban he
was wearing. In April 2001, 50,000 to 80,000 motorcycle enthusiasts arrived
in Laughlin, Nevada, a town of 8,000 located 80 miles southeast of Las
Vegas, for an annual festival. Unfortunately, a gunfight broke out between
rival gangs in a casino and left 3 men dead and 15 wounded.

Encounters between strangers resulting in murder, such as these two
examples, are called **spontaneous murder** and are a major threat to society

(Luckenbill, 1997). These encounters often result from arguments, threats made over trivial events such as a dispute over a parking space, a negative comment about a tattoo, or, as in the New Orleans case, one's attire. Another example is so-called road rage, where one driver may kill another because of a challenge over a lane change or other traffic infraction. In any case, uncontrolled anger combined with a personal intrusion can result in deadly violence.

In some situations, one or both parties are drinking or using other drugs. The victims of these types of homicides are threatened more frequently with firearms than they are with other kinds of weapons. If no firearm is available, it is not uncommon for one of the combatants to obtain a firearm and return to settle the score (Lundesgaarde, 1997).

In places where alcohol is served and potentially unruly people are jammed together, there can be explosive encounters and assaults, as evidenced by the violence in the Laughlin casino. In other words, liquor, testosterone, overcrowding, and seething attitudes are conducive to violence. Any negative encounter can escalate into physical confrontations, resulting in serious injury or death to one of the parties or innocent bystanders. Focus 4–2 presents the case of the victim of a bar shooting.

A paradigm of the spontaneous victim assault process is presented in Table 4–3. The paradigm indicates that the triggering event, such as an accidental bumping or an unwelcome remark, sets the situation in motion. Touching or invasion of space is perceived as serious by one of the parties. An argument or challenge to the intrusion occurs and escalates to the point of violence. In Focus 4–3, we see family dysfunction, mental issues, and school failures may have contributed to their problems. As a means of retaliation, they chose vulnerable strangers.

FOCUS 4–2   A Bar Shooting

The victim, a former employee of the bar, arrived at the bar at about 8:30 P.M. The bar attracted a rough crowd, and no security officers were on the premises. The bar employed four females at the time of the incident. An argument resulting in a pushing and shoving match broke out between two men over a woman. The owner of the bar (a woman) did not intervene; however, the victim broke up the fight. Near the end of the evening, another fight broke out between the same two men. One of the men left and returned with a gun, shooting the victim and four other patrons who were not involved in the fracas. The offender fled the scene and was never apprehended or identified.

Source: California Jury Verdicts, Case No. 647 927, 1993.

TABLE 4–2 MURDER CIRCUMSTANCES BY STRANGERS AND OTHERS, 2005

Circumstances	Total murder victims	Husband	Wife	Mother	Father	Son	Daughter	Brother	Sister
Total	14,860	135	594	123	118	245	190	100	21
Felony type total:	2,161	1	12	13	15	6	12	7	1
Rape	44	0	0	0	0	0	0	0	0
Robbery	921	0	1	4	6	0	0	2	0
Burglary	88	0	2	0	2	0	0	0	0
Larceny-theft	12	0	0	0	0	0	0	0	0
Motor vehicle theft	31	0	0	1	0	0	0	0	0
Arson	37	0	1	1	1	0	5	1	0
Prostitution and commercialized vice	13	0	0	0	0	0	0	0	0
Other sex offenses	9	0	0	0	1	0	0	0	0
Narcotic drug laws	589	0	0	0	1	1	1	2	0
Gambling	2	0	0	0	0	0	0	0	0
Other—not specified	415	1	8	7	4	5	6	2	1
Suspected felony type	44	0	0	0	0	0	1	0	0
Other than felony type total:	7,044	114	493	87	85	204	147	83	16
Romantic triangle	117	0	7	0	0	0	0	1	0
Child killed by babysitter	26	0	0	0	0	0	0	0	0
Brawl due to influence of alcohol	120	0	2	1	1	3	0	2	0
Brawl due to influence of narcotics	97	1	1	1	1	3	2	0	0
Argument over money or property	211	0	3	4	3	0	0	4	1
Other arguments	3,692	90	325	46	59	43	20	64	7
Gangland and killings	96	0	0	0	0	0	0	0	0
Juvenile gang killings	754	0	0	0	0	0	0	0	0
Institutional killings	12	0	0	0	0	0	0	0	0
Sniper attack	2	0	0	0	0	0	0	0	0
Other—not specified	1,917	23	155	35	21	155	125	12	8
Unknown	5,611	20	89	23	18	35	30	10	4

Relationship is that of victim to offender.

Note: The relationship categories of husband and wife include both common-law and ex-spouses. The categories of mother, father, sister, brother, son, and daughter include stepparents, stepchildren, and stepsiblings. The category of acquaintance includes homosexual relationships and the composite category of other known to victim.

Source: Adapted from Federal Bureau of Investigation. 2006. *Uniform Crime Reports*, Washington, DC: U.S. Department of Justice.

Other family	Acquaintance	Friend	Boyfriend	Girlfriend	Neighbor	Employee	Employer	Stranger	Unknown
297	3,210	324	152	461	86	4	6	2,070	6,724
25	516	45	3	9	23	0	2	573	898
3	9	1	0	1	2	0	0	11	17
5	152	16	2	1	3	0	0	363	366
3	19	2	0	3	3	0	0	31	23
1	1	0	0	0	1	0	0	5	4
1	7	0	0	1	1	0	0	10	10
1	11	3	0	0	3	0	0	1	9
0	7	0	0	0	0	0	0	1	5
0	5	0	0	0	1	0	0	2	0
2	233	17	1	0	3	0	1	63	264
0	0	0	0	0	0	0	0	0	2
9	72	6	0	3	6	0	1	86	198
0	7	2	0	0	0	0	0	5	29
221	2,080	225	133	378	51	2	2	1,083	1,640
1	71	3	1	8	1	0	0	14	10
1	25	0	0	0	0	0	0	0	0
4	46	14	4	0	0	0	1	27	15
1	41	5	0	3	1	0	0	16	21
8	111	12	0	2	7	2	0	29	25
128	1,214	132	109	288	30	0	1	498	643
1	33	0	0	0	0	0	0	19	43
1	136	3	0	0	0	0	0	208	406
0	9	0	0	0	0	0	0	1	2
0	2	0	0	0	0	0	0	0	0
81	392	56	19	77	12	0	0	271	475
51	607	52	16	74	12	2	2	409	4,157

TABLE 4–3 PARADIGM OF SPONTANEOUS VICTIMIZATION

Situational Factors	Contributing Factors
Triggering event? Intrusion/insult	Anonymity Alcohol usage Peer pressure
Argument? Challenge to intrusion/insult	Availability of weapons Unruly atmosphere
Escalation? Attempt to save face/show off	Lack of security/control Community disorder
Assault? Victim injury or death	Public invitation Previous life experience or stress

If a community is located in a high-crime area, the chances of stranger victimization increase. High-crime areas often have a high density of establishments serving liquor and other trouble spots. Research in several cities shows increased risk of violent crimes on blocks where taverns are located. In Milwaukee, for example, 12 percent of all homicides in the 1980s were connected to certain bars (Sherman, Schmidt, and Velke, 1992). Thus, when

---

Focus 4–3   Murder partners: Lawrence Bittaker and Roy Norris

Lawrence Bittaker and Roy Norris were products of dysfunctional homes. They were both sociopathic individuals who dropped out of school and acquired a long criminal history of violence against women. Norris was dishonorably discharged from the Navy. They met in prison and soon learned that they shared near-identical fantasies of domination, rape, and torture of young women. They talked about driving around in a specially equipped van selecting victims to see how long each victim could be kept alive and screaming. Andrea Hall was one such victim who was 18 when she was picked up hitchhiking in Southern California by Bittaker and Norris. Unknown to her, Norris was hiding in the back of the van. After she entered the van, Norris lunged from hiding and threw her to the floor screaming. Norris bound her wrists and ankles and covered her mouth with tape.

They drove to a deserted road and repeatedly raped her. When both of them were tired, Bittaker loaded his Polaroid camera, dragged Hall from the van, and sent Norris on a beer run, down the mountain to a small roadside convenience store. When Norris returned, he found Bittaker alone, smiling over photos of Andrea Hall, her face contorted by fear. Bittaker told Norris that he had stabbed Hall twice with an ice pick, once in each ear, but he had to strangle her when she refused to die. When the murder was finished, Bittaker said he had pitched her off a cliff. Bittaker and Norris were subsequently caught and convicted of murdering five girls in 1978. They are on California death row.

an argument erupts and there is no management intervention or effort to defuse the encounter, the situation is ripe for a physical confrontation. Innocent parties are victimized by their proximity to the situation.

Although rare, another type of spontaneous violence is the freeway murder or assault. Such incidents can be triggered when two strangers compete for the same space or traffic lane. Shaking fists or making other nonverbal gestures escalates the event. The anonymity of the highway and the privacy of a car can be stimulants for further actions. There have been a number of news accounts of drivers shot for cutting off another driver on a freeway. In many cities, experts blame traffic gridlock for road rage and random shootings of drivers (Fiore, 1997; *Los Angeles Times*, 1996a). The relative anonymity and ease of escape add to the temptation to victimize.

Gang-related murders and assaults are also stranger victimizations. Although a number of victims of gang violence are rival gang members targeted for victimization, an increasing number of their murder victims have no association with gangs. These victims are simply in the wrong place at the wrong time. Therefore, those who live in gang areas, associate with gang members, and encounter gangs by accident are at risk of victimization.

A study of Los Angeles gang violence between 1979 and 1994 revealed that about one-third of the gang-related homicide victims had no gang involvement (Hutson, Anglin, and Pratts, 1994). Other studies suggest that most victims of gang drive-by shootings are unknown by the gang; they were victims of mistaken identity (Maxson and Klein, 1995).

Felony murders are also considered to be spontaneous. A first-degree felony murder occurs when a stranger is robbed or carjacked and dies in the process. It is immaterial whether the offender intended to kill the victim. A study by Erickson and Stenseth (1996) focused on violence committed during a robbery. The study polled 310 prisoners in 20 state prisons convicted of armed robbery. Most had committed convenience store or street robberies against strangers. Forty percent of the robbers had lived within two miles of the crime location, and 60 percent reported committing the robbery with a partner. The 1995 survey indicated that the victim's resistance determined the likelihood of violence against the victim. Most robbers stated that victims who resist, make sudden moves, or try to stop the robbery risk injury. The robbers generally agreed that victims should cooperate—give up the money; not talk, stare, or make sudden moves; and keep their hands in sight of the robber. Older inmates reported that younger robbers are more likely to use violence against their victims, in part because robberies were hastily planned.

The chance of being killed in a robbery is greater if the robber has a gun. Focus 4–4 presents one case involving robbery–murder in which subsequent investigations led to the arrest of two teenagers. The apparent motive was

---

Focus 4–4   Stranger Attack

No one knew who John Doe was when he was taken from a South Carolina swamp. He had a bullet wound in his chest and no identification. Only two days later, after a car was found about 60 miles away, did clues start coming together. . . . Chicago Bulls' fans and friends went numb when they learned that John Doe was James Jordan, 57, the father of megastar Michael Jordan. The senior Jordan disappeared after attending the North Carolina funeral. His car was found on a wooded back road, stripped of its tires, stereo system, and license plates.

---

robbery. But the question remains as to why the murder was committed. Murder is often the follow-up to robbery. The initial criminal intention is to rob, but concern about detection or reprisal inspires the offender to kill. In these situations, because many offenders are ex-offenders fearful of returning to prison, the murder is often a spontaneous afterthought.

Directed Targets

Some criminals target their victims because of specific characteristics, such as sex, age, race, or religion. Some pursue others for the thrill or the need for excitement, and a number of others kill for profit. Serial killing or murders resulting from hate or bias are **targeted murders**.

    Serial Killers. Despite media accounts and films, **serial killers** are relatively rare. But they are offenders who draw a great deal of attention because of their motives and brutal methods. Serial killers often seek unknown victims because there is less chance of apprehension. They also seek undocumented residents or people in some way involved in criminal activity, such as prostitutes or runaways. These victims also are not likely to be reported missing because of their transient or secretive lifestyles, and the police are less able to investigate as thoroughly as they can with more stable, franchised victims (Jenkins, 1993).

    Robert Hansen, a notorious serial killer from Alaska, killed approximately 20 women between 1971 and 1983 (Linedecker, 1988). The victims came to Alaska to seek their fortune and to conceal their identities. And unfortunately, they were less likely to be reported missing, making them desirable targets for someone like Hansen. The anonymity and thrill derived from seeking unsuspecting strangers are attractive to many serial killers (Leyton, 1986). Since the 1888 killings attributed to Jack the Ripper, who targeted prostitutes, streetwalkers remain at high risk for victimization by serial killers.

Serial killers carefully select and stalk unwary victims. After surveying the area of the planned assault many times, working out details, and taking precautions, they strike at the right moment. John Wayne Gacy, convicted of killing 33 teenage boys, lured his victims into his home. Serial killer Ted Bundy frequented college communities seeking coeds, and Jeffrey Dahmer invited young homosexual boys to his apartment and then killed and cannibalized them. Anthony Buono and Kenneth Bianchi, known as the Hillside Stranglers, terrorized the Los Angeles area in the late 1970s, as did Lawrence Bittaker and Roy Norris discussed earlier. The victims were similar in one respect—they were all strangers who were lured or forcibly kidnapped from public areas.

Common characteristics of serial killers have been identified in the literature (Hickey, 2006; Simon, 1995). They generally are white males between 20 and 39 years of age. They have a psychopathic personality, a hedonistic outlook on life, and a pronounced lack of conscience. The backgrounds of serial killers are consistent in behaviors. Many display early signs of behavioral problems in terms of fire setting, animal abuse, and constant bed-wetting. Impulsive behavior leading to outbursts of violence is characteristic of these predators. Many are the product of dysfunctional homes or are victims of physical and sexual abuse. They learn at an early age that pain and suffering are means to an end.

Some of these killers, however, possess an unusually high degree of intelligence. Ted Bundy, for example, attended law school. Michael Ross, who had a high IQ, achieved a college education, and lived a relatively normal childhood, was convicted of killing six women in Connecticut and New York. Ross also raped and sexually violated all of his victims, demonstrating sexual sadism. He specifically targeted Caucasian women between 17 and 20 years of age. Edmund Kemper, who murdered his mother and grandparents and eight women, had an extremely high IQ; he would drive around seeking hitchhikers and other vulnerable women.

Dennis Rader, discussed in Focus 4–5, preyed on women in his community because of his so-called sexual fantasies. He confessed to killing 10 people over several years. Serial killers have a striking preference for fantasy over reality; their sadistic and murderous fantasies usually begin approximately 10–15 years before their first murder. As with killers such as Rader, the fantasies eventually become so overwhelming that the killer finally acts them out.

Many serial killers impersonate figures of authority, perhaps to gain the power and prestige that they lack. They often are attracted to law enforcement and may work as security guards or impersonate police officers to exploit position and status in search of potential victims. When he was

---

Focus 4–5   Dennis Rader: The BTK killer

Dennis Rader was born in 1945 and grew up in Wichita with three brothers, all of whom graduated from Heights High School in Wichita. Rader served in the Air Force in Vietnam from 1965 to 1969. After discharge, he worked for a grocery store and then as an assembler at the Coleman camping gear firm. Rader later secured employment with a security company and the U.S. Census Bureau, going door to door collecting information. While working in both positions, Rader had access to many area residents' homes. Rader was married and the father of two children. He attended Wichita State University and graduated with a degree in Administration of Justice. In later years, he worked as a code enforcement officer. In his free time, Rader lead a Cub Scouts group and was active in his church. Many referred to him as the kind of guy who wasn't very noticeable, one who never really stood out from others. However, by his own confession he was responsible for killing and torturing 10 people to fulfill a sexual fantasy. He described his victims as projects that he would stalk before killing.

---

apprehended, serial killer Kenneth Bianchi was employed as a security officer and had applied to work for the Los Angeles Police Department.

With some exceptions, typical victims of serial killers are the homeless, prostitutes of either sex, the elderly, hitchhikers, and unaccompanied children and women (Ginsburg, 1993; Hickey, 2002). The victims of at least 10 of the 52 cases of serial killings reported since 1971 were prostitutes, especially streetwalkers. As noted in Chapter 1, they are easy targets, and the police are less likely to investigate their disappearance, suggesting that social rank or standing are factors in investigations. Young women and children who are alone or can be isolated are at greatest risk of victimization (Hickey, 2002).

Serial killers who are child sex offenders use a number of lures to attract their child victims, such as telling the child that he or she should be in a beauty contest but needs to go with the offender to have photographs taken first (Wooden, 1994). Serial offenders often target children because of their vulnerability and naiveté. Although most child abductors are acquainted with the victim, the abduction of children by strangers often results in sexual abuse and murder. Only a small number of these cases result in the return of the child or the capture and prosecution of the criminal. Many stranger abductions take place right on neighborhood streets, in shopping malls, and in parking lots.

Serial killers prefer strangers as victims. According to the FBI, cases of stranger abduction involve specific types of criminals: the pedophiles who seek sexual gratification from children, killers who prey on a child's innocence and lack of strength, those who grab children to sell, and the occasional individual who is obsessed with the desire to have a child. Few stranger abduction cases leave specific clues as to the type of criminal who has taken the child. Stranger abductions victimize more females than males, occur primarily at outdoor locations, victimize both teenagers and school-age children, and are associated with sexual assaults.

Four subtypes of serial killers are reported in the literature. Each is associated with the killing of strangers. Although each type is distinct, there is overlap (Holmes and De Burger, 1988):

- *Visionary* killers murder because they hear voices or see visions ordering them to kill. Their motive is responding to a higher order. These killers are usually psychotic and target persons of different races or religions.

- *Mission-oriented* killers murder individuals who they believe are unworthy of living. Their motive is to cleanse society of "undesirables." These killers usually target prostitutes and the homeless.

- *Hedonistic* killers murder for the thrill of it. Their motive is excitement, sex, or money. Their motivation is usually fueled by sexual fantasy and lust.

- *Power-oriented* killers murder because they enjoy having control over their victims. Their motive is power and control more than sex. These types may kidnap a victim and hold the victim in captivity, during which time they torture and humiliate the victim before killing the person.

BIAS AND HATE-MOTIVATED CRIMES

Buford Furrow, a white supremacist, told investigators after he shot six people in a rampage at a Los Angeles Jewish center on August 12, 1999, that he wanted the shooting to be a wake-up call to America to kill Jews. While escaping after the shootings, he killed a postal worker because the man was nonwhite and worked for the government. The worker just happened to be in the wrong place. Furrow is a typical hate criminal who may strike at anyone because of that person's race or religion.

At the national level, the systematic collection of information about **hate or bias crimes** began with the passage of the Federal Hate Crime Statistics Act in 1990. Hate or bias offenders target a victim because of the person's race, religion, sexual preference, ethnic heritage, or physical appearance. Numerous hate groups are scattered throughout the United States. They are referred to generally as skinheads or white supremacists. The specific names of some of these groups are Aryan Brotherhood, Ku Klux Klan, Neo-Nazis, the Order, the Sword, the Arm of the Lord, and Posse Comitatus. Most of these groups are located in the Midwest and the Southeast. Such groups are also called domestic terrorists. The Oklahoma City bombing of 1995, in which 168 people were killed, is an example of the work of **domestic terrorists** who targeted the government (see Chapter 8).

Bias crimes result from attacks against a specific race, religion, sexual orientation, ethnicity, person with disabilities, or the homeless. In terms of race, blacks are most likely victimized; for religion, Jews; and for sexual orientation, gay males. In 60 percent of hate crimes, the most serious offense was a violent crime, most commonly intimidation or simple assault. The majority of incidents motivated by race, ethnicity, sexual orientation, or disability involved a violent offense, whereas two thirds of incidents motivated by religion involved a property offense, most commonly vandalism. Younger offenders were responsible for most hate crimes. Thirty-one percent of violent offenders and 46 percent of property offenders were under age, 18 years. Table 4–4 depicts the types of incidents, offenses, victims, and known offenders of bias-motivated crimes.

TABLE 4–4 INCIDENTS, OFFENSES, VICTIMS, AND KNOWN OFFENDERS BY BIAS MOTIVATION, 2006

Bias motivation	Incidents	Offenses	Victims[1]	Known offenders[2]
Total	**7,722**	**9,080**	**9,652**	**7,330**
Single-Bias Incidents	**7,720**	**9,076**	**9,642**	**7,324**
Race:	**4,000**	**4,737**	**5,020**	**3,957**
Anti-White	890	1,008	1,054	1,074
Anti-Black	2,640	3,136	3,332	2,437
Anti-American Indian/Alaskan Native	60	72	75	72
Anti-Asian/ Pacific Islander	181	230	239	181
Anti-Multiple Races, Group	229	291	320	193
Religion:	**1,462**	**1,597**	**1,750**	**705**
Anti-Jewish	967	1,027	1,144	362
Anti-Catholic	76	81	86	44
Anti-Protestant	59	62	65	35
Anti-Islamic	156	191	208	147

(Continued)

TABLE 4–4 (Continued)

Bias motivation	Incidents	Offenses	Victims[1]	Known offenders[2]
Anti-Other Religion	124	140	147	63
Anti-Multiple Religions, Group	73	88	92	49
Anti-Atheism/ Agnosticism/etc.	7	8	8	5
Sexual Orientation:	**1,195**	**1,415**	**1,472**	**1,380**
Anti-Male Homosexual	747	881	913	914
Anti-Female Homosexual	163	192	202	154
Anti-Homosexual	238	293	307	268
Anti-Heterosexual	26	28	29	26
Anti-Bisexual	21	21	21	18
Ethnicity/ National Origin:	**984**	**1,233**	**1,305**	**1,209**
Anti-Hispanic	576	770	819	802
Anti-Other Ethnicity/ National Origin	408	463	486	407
Disability:	**79**	**94**	**95**	**73**
Anti-Physical	17	20	21	17
Anti-Mental	62	74	74	56
Multiple-Bias Incidents[3]	**2**	**4**	**10**	**6**

[1]The term *victim* may refer to a person, business, institution, or society as a whole.
[2]The term *known offender* does not imply that the identity of the suspect is known, but only that an attribute of the suspect has been identified, which distinguishes him/her from an unknown offender.
[3]In a *multiple-bias incident*, two conditions must be met: (a) more than one offense type must occur in the incident and (b) at least two offense types must be motivated by different biases.
Source: Federal Bureau of Investigation. 2007. Washington, DC: U.S. Department of Justice.

The irrational nature of hate and bias crimes is particularly disruptive and threatening, both to the victims and to the community. Compared with conventional crimes, hate and bias crimes are far more likely to be committed randomly against victims by complete strangers. Criminologists have concluded that far greater societal disruption occurs from random acts of violence than occurs from violent acts that have some rational cause (McDevitt, 1989). The disruption to society is of enormous significance when whole groups of citizens are placed in constant fear of **random victimization** from attackers with whom they have no direct connection.

The motives for hate crimes vary, but some research suggests certain typologies are present. The most common was based on a study of 169 cases in Boston (McDevitt, Levin, and Bennett, 2002). The researchers found four major categories of hate-crime motivation:

Thrill-seeking.   Offenders who are motivated by a desire for excitement (66 percent).

Defensive.   Offenders who commit hate crime to protect their turf or resources in a situation that they consider threatening (25 percent).

Retaliatory.   Offenders acting to avenge a perceived insult or assault (8 percent).

Mission.   Offenders who are so strongly committed to bigotry that hate becomes their career (less than 1 percent).

According to the U.S. Department of Justice, hate offenders are of several types. Some are *mission* offenders, who believe they are on a mission to cleanse the world of a particular evil. Others are *scapegoat* offenders, projecting their resentment toward the growing economic power of a particular racial or ethnic group through violent actions. History reminds us of many examples of mission and scapegoat types, such as the Nazi persecution of the Jews. Others are impromptu thrill seekers, who take advantage of vulnerable and disadvantaged groups such as the homeless.

In 2004, three Milwaukee teens murdered a homeless man at his campsite. The teens hit the 49-year-old man with rocks, a flashlight, and a pipe, before smearing feces on his face and covering his body with leaves and plastic. According to the criminal report, one of the boys "hit the victim one last time to see if he would make a sound like in *Grand Theft Auto*" and then cut him several times with a knife to make sure he was dead (National Coalition for the Homeless, 2005). This tragic example is evidence of the bias crime type referred to as thrill seekers, who are primarily teenagers and common perpetrators of violence against homeless people.

In a study by the National Institute Against Prejudice and Violence, researchers concluded that victims of hate and bias attacks suffered 21 percent more adverse psychological and physiological symptoms than did victims of the same crimes that were not hate- or bias-related. A National Gay and Lesbian Task Force study revealed that 83 percent of gay and lesbian respondents expected future victimization and 62 percent feared for their safety (Herek and Berrill, 1992). Part of the distinct trauma that hate and bias crime victims experience results from their unique vulnerability, in addition to the degradation they experience because of a characteristic that is central to their identity. Distressingly, many victims are youths for whom the emotional impact from such attacks can be particularly severe and long lasting (Henneberger, 1992).

Hate and Bias Crime Legislation

On July 3, 1996, President Bill Clinton signed the **Church Arson Prevention Act** into law. Responding to the increasing number of church arsons in recent years, the law makes it easier to prosecute church arsons as federal offenses. It enhances penalties for damaging religious property or obstructing any person's exercise of religious freedom if the offense in some way affects interstate commerce. The law also provides compensation to churches that fall prey to arsonists and extends federal hate crime and crime victim protections to churches attacked because of the ethnic or racial composition of their memberships.

More recent legislation—the **Hate Crimes Prevention Act** of 1999—prohibits people from interfering with an individual's federal rights (e.g., voting or employment) by violence or threat of violence prompted by his or her race, color, religion, or national origin. This act allows the federal government more authority to investigate and prosecute hate crime offenders who committed their crime because of the perceived sexual orientation, gender, or disability of the victim. It also permits the federal government to prosecute without having to prove that the victim was attacked because he or she was performing a federally protected activity.

As part of the 1999 Crime Prevention Act, the Hate Crimes Sentencing Enhancement Act provides for longer sentences if the offense is determined to be a hate crime. A longer sentence may be imposed if it is proved that a crime against person or property was motivated by race, color, religion, national origin, ethnicity, gender, disability, or sexual orientation. Many states also have enacted legislation against hate crimes, and legislative movements enhance many of these laws.

SUMMARY

Stranger violence is a constant threat, particularly in highly populated areas. It may not be possible to avoid victimization totally, but an awareness of how to avoid being a victim is useful. Altering routine activities, such as shopping and banking, reduces the potential for victimization. Avoiding places and people known for violence is also recommended.

KEY TERMS AND CONCEPTS

Carjacking   Home invasion robberies
Church Arson Prevention Act   Random victimization
Domestic terrorists   Robbery
Felony murder   Serial killers
Hate Crimes Prevention Act   Spontaneous murder
Hate or bias crimes   Targeted murder

DISCUSSION QUESTIONS AND LEARNING ACTIVITIES

1. How do you explain the murder of Michael Jordan's father in terms of offender motives?

2. Explain the difference between targeted murders and spontaneous murders.

3. Discuss the characteristics of serial killers. Who are likely to be their victims? In what ways did some of the victims discussed in this chapter invite their own deaths?

4. Visit your local police department and interview a crime analyst. Find out how many persons in your community are victimized by strangers (e.g., street robberies, carjacking).

5. Compare hate and bias crimes with other types of stranger crimes. In what ways are these crimes more vicious than other violent crimes?

6. How can people avoid becoming victims of random violence? Is it possible to do so?

7. Are there any business establishments in your community that are recognized as nuisance bars or trouble spots? What are the characteristics of these establishments?

8. Interview the local police crime prevention officer or contact victim counselors from your community regarding the type of crime prevention programs available in your community.

WEB SOURCES

Federal Bureau of Investigation. Crime in the U.S. 2002. www.fbi.gov/ucr/cius_02/html/web/offreported/offreported.html

U.S. Department of Justice. www.usdoj.gov/index.html

Court TV. Crime Library. www.crimelibrary.com/index.html

RECOMMENDED READINGS

Abbe Research Division. 2004. *America and Crime as Its #1 Business Includes Property, Theft, Robbery, Murder, Rape, Burglary, Graft, Bribery, Fraud and Malpractice.* Washington, DC: Abbe.

Espejo, Roman, ed. 2002. *What Is a Hate Crime?* At Issue Series. San Diego: Greenhaven Press.

Holmes, Ronald M., and Stephen T. Holmes. 2000. *Murder in America,* 2nd. ed. Thousand Oaks, CA: Sage Publications.

Newton, Michael. 2000. *The Encyclopedia of Serial Killers.* New York: Checkmark Books.

Perry, Barbara. 2001. *In the Name of Hate: Understanding Hate Crimes.* Chicago: Routledge.

Roleff, Tamara L. 2001. *Hate Crimes.* Current Controversies Series. Los Angeles: Greenhaven Press.

Schechter, Harold. 2003. *The Serial Killer Files: The Who, What, Where, How, and Why of the World's Most Terrifying Murderers.* New York: Ballantine Books.

REFERENCES

Bureau of Justice Statistics. 2003b. *Violent Crime Characteristics: Victim/Offender Relationship.* Washington, DC: U.S. Department of Justice.

Carjacking Law Takes Effect. 1997. *National Law Journal,* August 25, A-08.

Decoy Cops Take the Lumps to Sting Houston Gay Bashing. 1993. *Law Enforcement News,* September 30, 3.

Edds, Kimberely, 2005. String of Freeway Shootings in L.A. Area Has Left 4 Dead. *Washington Post,* May 3, A-3.

Erickson, Rosemary J., and Arnie Stenseth. 1996. Crimes of Convenience. *Security Management,* October, 89.

Federal Bureau of Investigation. 1996. *Hate Crimes—1995.* Washington, DC: U.S. Department of Justice.

Federal Bureau of Investigation. 1998. *Uniform Crime Reports: Crime in the United States, 1998.* Washington, DC: U.S. Department of Justice.

Federal Bureau of Investigation. 2004. *Uniform Crime Reports, 2003.* Washington, DC: Department of Justice.

Fiore, Faye. 1997. Road Rage Tied to More Traffic Deaths. *Los Angeles Times,* July 18, Part A.

Ginsburg, P. 1993. *The Shadow of Death: The Hunt for a Serial Killer.* New York: Macmillan.

Henneberger, M. 1992. For Bias Victims, a Double Trauma. *New York Newsday,* January 9, 36.

Herek, G., and K. Berrill, eds. 1992. Hate Crimes: Confronting Violence Against Lesbians and Gay Men. *Community United Against Violence, Statistical Analysis,* January–March.

Hickey, Eric W. 2002. *Serial Murderers and Their Victims.* Belmont, CA: Wadsworth.

Hickey, Eric. 2006. *Serial Murderers and their Victims.* Belmont, CA: Wadsworth Press.

Holmes, R. M., and J. De Burger. 1988. *Serial Murder.* Newbury Park, CA: Sage Publications.

Hurley, James T. 1995. Violent Crime Hits Home: Home Invasion Robbery. *FBI Law Enforcement Bulletin,* June, 5:44–48.

Hutson, Range H., Deirdre Anglin, and Michael Pratts. 1994. Adolescents and Children Injured or Killed in Drive-By Shootings in Los Angeles. *New England Journal of Medicine* 330:324–327.

Jenkins, Philip. 1993. Chance or Choice? The Selection of Serial Murder Victims. In *Homicide: The Victim Offender Connection*, ed. Anna V. Wilson. Cincinnati, OH: Anderson Publishing.

Kellerman M., Lori Westphal, Laurie Fischer, and Beverly Harvard. 1995. Weapon Involvement in Home Invasion Crimes. *Journal of the American Medical Association* 273:22.

Leyton, E. 1986. *Compulsive Killers: The Story of Modern Multiple Murder.* New York: New York University Press.

Linedecker, Charles. 1988. *Thrill Killers.* Toronto: PaperJacks.

Los Angeles Times. 1996a. *Help for Highway Hotheads: A Psychiatrist Explains How Aggressive Type A Drivers Can Learn to Go with the Flow.* March 29, 12.

Los Angeles Times. 1996b. *Two Men Accused of Robbing Harry Dean Stanton.* April 11, B-20.

Luckenbill, D. F. 1997. Criminal Homicide as a Situated Transaction. *Social Forces* 25:288–315.

Lundesgaarde, H. F. 1997. *Murder in Space City: A Cultural Analysis of Houston Homicide Patterns.* New York: Oxford University Press.

Maxson, C., and Malcolm Klein. 1995. Investigating Gang Structures. *Journal of Gang Research* 3:33–42.

McDevitt, Jack. 1989. *The Study of the Character of Civil Rights Crimes in Massachusetts (1983–1987).* Paper presented at the American Society of Criminology, Washington, DC, July.

McDevitt, J., J. Levin, and S. Bennett. 2002. "Hate Crime Offenders: An Expanded Typology," *Journal of Social Issues* 58:303–317. The researchers analyzed 169 cases handled by the Community Disorders Unit of the Boston Police Department in 1991–1992.

National Coalition for the Homeless. 2005. www.nationalhomeless.org/index.html (accessed June 2005).

National Crime Prevention Council. 1997. *Carjacking.* Washington, DC: National Crime Prevention Council.

Scheb, John M. 1996. *American Criminal Law.* Minneapolis: West Publishing.

Sherman, Lawrence W., Janell D. Schmidt, and Robert J. Velke. 1992. *High Crime Taverns: A RECAP Project in Problem-Oriented Policing.* Washington, DC: Crime Control Institute final report to the National Institute of Justice.

Simon, R. 1995. *Bad Men Do What Good Men Dream.* www.appi.org/appi.html; simonb.html.

Wolfgang, Marvin. 1958. *Patterns of Criminal Homicide.* Philadelphia, PA: University of Pennsylvania Press.

Wooden, Kenneth. 1994. *Child Lures.* Shelburne, VT: National Coalition for Children's Justice, Child Lures Inc.

5

Workplace Violence and Harassment

LEARNING OBJECTIVES

After studying this chapter, you will:

- Recognize the sources of and reasons for workplace violence.
- Be familiar with research on workplace violence.
- Recognize the warning signs and attributes of people prone to violence or harassment.
- Understand how a business can be legally responsible for acts of violence committed on its premises.
- Understand the recommended strategies for controlling violence in the workplace.
- Understand the role of employee assistance programs in recognizing and targeting violence.
- Become familiar with legislation initiated by some jurisdictions for addressing violence in the workplace.

INTRODUCTION

> *The workplace killer is typically a 37-year-old single man who worked at the company at least four years. The shooting is generally prompted by personal problems in life and at work, and often follows a firing or on-the-job altercation. The shootings are not random . . . most workplace killers harbor grudges and target certain co-workers and bosses.*
>
> —*USA Today*, July 14, 2004

The number of violent acts by intruders and employees at various workplaces has been increasing. The violence resulting in the death or physical injury of an employee or business invitee is called *workplace violence.* It is often the result of the offender's anger or perceived injustice committed by management or other coworkers.

The definition of workplace violence should also include psychological abuse at a workplace because such activities can lead to stress or physical abuse. This chapter addresses the dynamics of workplace violence. Theories on and reasons for workplace violence are discussed to enable the reader to recognize and respond to signs before violence occurs. The chapter concludes with suggested strategies that businesses can take to reduce the threat of victimization.

In the 13-year period from 1992 through 2004, there were an average of 808 workplace homicides in the United States each year, ranging from a high of 1,080 in 1994 to a low of 551 in 2004. The most common scenario of workplace homicide was a retail worker killed during the course of a robbery or other crime. Taxicab drivers have the very highest rates of workplace homicide. Other circumstances or perpetrators of workplace homicides include coworkers or former coworkers, customers, clients, or patients, and current or former domestic partners. From 1993 through 1999, there was an average of 1.7 million nonfatal violent victimizations in the United States each year, accounting for 18 percent of all violent crime during the seven-year period. Of the occupations for which data were available, police officers had the highest rate of workplace violent crime at 261 per 1,000 persons, followed by corrections officers (156 per 1,000) and taxicab drivers (128 per 1,000). The majority (75 percent) of the violent victimizations were simple assaults.

In 1997 in California, 636 workers died on the job, with more than 20 percent of those deaths resulting from homicide (Metcalfe, 1999). The **Centers for Disease Control and Prevention** reports that several thousand women die annually in the United States as a result of homicide. In other words, homicide accounts for 40 percent of all workplace death among women (Centers for Disease Control and Prevention, 2005).

Overview of Violence in the Workplace

One of the earliest reported cases of workplace violence occurred in 1917 when a disgruntled patrol officer killed a New Orleans police chief and a police captain. The officer was upset over being terminated from the force for excessive absences. He requested reinstatement, which the chief granted, but just prior to the hearing, the officer burst into the chief's office and shot him repeatedly. The officer had a history of mental illness (Workplace Violence Prevention Institute, 1994:2).

The first major study of workplace violence and crime was conducted in 1980. The study of business robberies was supported by the Southland Corporation, which was trying to curb robberies at its convenience stores. After that study, little additional research on the topic was completed until 1987, when healthcare administration journals released a number of articles on the subject. A serious academic interest is reflected in the 1988 Gainesville, Florida, study that addressed convenience store robberies. The study resulted in improvement in the security of these stores in an attempt to limit the exposure of workers to late-night robberies (Workplace Violence Prevention Institute, 1994:8).

A comprehensive study of fear and violence in the workplace was conducted by Northwestern National Life Insurance Company (1993). Some of the study's key findings were as follows:

- Violence and harassment affect the health and productivity of workers.
- A strong relationship exists between job stress and workplace harassment and violence.
- Harassers are usually coworkers or bosses; attackers are more likely to be customers.
- Improved interpersonal relations and effective preventive programs can result in lower levels of violence.

By 1990, several studies by the National Institute for Occupational Safety and Health (NIOSH) began to appear in the literature (Richardson, 1993). These studies examined death certificates to determine the location and cause of death of people on the job. The data revealed that the leading cause of work-related death was homicide. Most of the victims were women working in retail trades, and most died during robberies.

A survey of 479 human resource managers completed by the Society of Human Resource Management provided additional information on workplace violence (Harrington and Gai, 1996). The survey focused on violence in general. It reported that 33 percent of the human resource managers had experienced at least one violent incident in the workplace. In more than 54 percent of the cases, another employee attacked the victims. Males committed 80 percent of the violent acts. The most common reasons cited for the violence were personality conflicts between those persons involved and marital or family problems of the offender. More than 60 percent of the incidents resulted in serious harm or the need for medical intervention.

Of selected occupations examined from 1993 to 1999, not surprisingly police officers were most likely to be victims of workplace violence. Correctional officers, taxicab drivers, private security workers, and bartenders

TABLE 5-1 OCCUPATIONS WITH THE HIGHEST NUMBERS OF HOMICIDES

Occupation of Victim	Average Annual Number
Sales	327
Executive/manager	154
Law enforcement	69
Security guard	60
Taxi driver/chauffeur	74
Truck driver	25

Note: Based on 1993 and 1995–1996.

Source: Bureau of Labor Statistics. 1998. *Census of Fatal Occupational Injuries, 1993–1996.* Washington, DC: U.S. Department of Justice.

were also vulnerable. Between 1993 and 1999, police officers were victims of nonfatal violent crimes while they were working or on duty at a rate of 261 per 1,000 officers. A listing of the likely occupations of victims of nonfatal violence is presented in Table 5–1.

In 1995, the University of Southern California Center for Crisis Management (CCM), with the financial support of the International Facility Management Association, Pepsi-Cola, Taco Bell, and Pizza Hut, initiated a research project to better understand the phenomenon of workplace violence (Harrington and Gai, 1996:2). A questionnaire was mailed to 1,500 corporate human resource managers and security directors. The intent of the research was to measure the scope of workplace violence, explore the association between violence and the type of organization, and identify management practices for responding to violence.

The research provided some interesting findings. More than 43 percent of the respondents reported having experienced incidents of violence in the previous 3 years. The most common incidents were threatening phone calls, bomb threats, and fights between employees. One disturbing finding of the study was that 64 percent of the respondents reported having no training programs to help them address workplace violence. Harrington and Gai (1996) indicate, however, that businesses with employee assistance programs (EAPs) that address topics such as outplacement, grievances, and harassment experienced fewer acts of workplace violence.

In a report on violence in the workplace between 1993 and 1999, the following are some of the major findings of workplace violence (U.S. Department of Justice, 2001):

- Each year between 1993 and 1999, more than 2 million U.S. residents were victims of a violent crime while they were at work or on duty.

- More than 1,900 workplace homicides occurred annually.

- The most common type of workplace victimization was simple assault, with an estimated 1.4 million occurring each year. U.S. residents also suffered 51,000 rapes and sexual assaults and approximately 84,000 robberies while they were at work.

- Annually, more than 230,000 police officers were victims of a nonfatal violent crime while they were on duty.

- About 40 percent of victims of nonfatal violence in the workplace reported that they knew their offenders.

- Women were more likely than men to be victimized by someone they knew.

- Approximately 12 percent of the nonfatal violent workplace crimes resulted in an injury to the victim. Of those injured, about half received medical treatment.

- Intimates (current and former spouses, boyfriends, and girlfriends) were identified by the victims as the perpetrators of about 1 percent of all workplace violent crime.

No one particular business type is prone to violence; however, information gathered from the *National Crime Victimization Survey (NCVS)* indicates that government employees are most prone to violent victimization, such as shootings. The organizations most likely to be victimized by workplace violence are government organizations and agencies at the local, state, and federal levels. Post offices have the worst experience, with more than 40 postal employees murdered on the job since 1986. The U.S. Department of Labor reports that between 1993 and 1999, most victimizations were by strangers or casual acquaintances (see Table 5–2).

Although violence seems to occur in certain workplace environments more than in others, it can happen in any occupational setting. As on the streets or in public areas, no workplace is safe from a predatory attack by a determined offender. Workplace crime has been, in part, attributed to disgruntled current or former employees and domestic disputes involving intimates. The following example indicates that no place or occupation is immune from violence.

On April 25, 1996, a 32-year-old firefighter shot his wife in the head and then proceeded, armed with several weapons, to a firehouse. Using an assault rifle, he shot six coworkers, all supervisors, killing four of them and wounding the other two. He then fled the scene and led the police on a wild chase for 10 miles. At the end of the chase, he exchanged gunfire with a police officer, whom he wounded, before shooting himself in the head. The president of the union representing the shooter described him as "a time bomb waiting to go off" (Kelleher, 1996).

TABLE 5–2 ANNUAL WORKPLACE HOMICIDE BY VICTIM–OFFENDER
RELATIONSHIP, 1993–1999

Relationship	Average Annual Number	Percentage of Total
Work association	899	100
Stranger	753	84
Work associate	103	11
Coworker, former coworker	67	7
Customer, client	36	4
Intimate	28	3
Husband	17	2
Wife		
Boyfriend	10	1
Other relative	5	1
Other acquaintance	9	1

Source: Bureau of Labor Statistics. 2001. *Census of Fatal Occupational Injuries.* Washington,
DC: U.S. Department of Labor.

Violence is a particular concern in healthcare settings. According to the
Bureau of Labor Statistics, 2,637 nonfatal assaults on hospital workers
occurred in 1999—a rate of 8.3 assaults per 10,000 workers. Violence often
takes place during times of high activity and interaction with patients, such
as at mealtimes, during visiting hours, and during patient transportation.
Assaults may occur when service is denied, when a patient is involuntarily
admitted, or when a healthcare worker attempts to set limits on eating,
drinking, or tobacco or alcohol use. Violence may occur anywhere in the
hospital, but it is most frequent in psychiatric wards, emergency rooms,
waiting rooms, and geriatric units (National Institute for Occupational
Safety and Health, 2002).

A study of 9,187 nurses in British Columbia and Alberta hospitals
showed that 38 percent experienced emotional abuse in the last five shifts
they worked (Bains, 2000). Some 66 percent of those who worked in emergency rooms said they had been emotionally abused during the same
period. Approximately 22 percent of emergency room nurses said they had
also experienced physical abuse. While most physical abuse traditionally
occurs in emergency rooms, the study showed that the same number of
nurses, 22 percent, experienced physical abuse in surgical and medical
wards. Approximately 56 percent of nurses in psychiatry wards said they
had been emotionally abused during the last five shifts worked, while
21 percent said they had also experienced physical abuse, according to the
study. The culprits were mostly patients, but nurses also cited visitors
as offenders.

CATEGORIZATION OF WORKPLACE VIOLENCE

The State of California Department of Industrial Relations, Division of Occupational Safety and Health Administration (2001) classifies workplace violence into four major types. In Type I (Criminal Intent) incidents, the perpetrator has no legitimate relationship with the business or its employees and is usually committing a crime in conjunction with the violence. These crimes can include robbery, shoplifting, and trespassing. The vast majority of workplace homicides (85 percent) fall into this category. A typical example is an employee at a convenience store, bank, or service station being assaulted during the course of a robbery.

In Type II (Employer-Directed) incidents, the perpetrator is generally a customer or client who becomes violent during the course of a normal transaction. Service providers, including healthcare workers, schoolteachers, social workers, and bus and train operators, are among the most common targets of Type II violence. Attacks from "unwilling" clients, such as prison inmates on guards or crime suspects on police officers, are also included in this category.

Type II incidents have the following characteristics:

- The perpetrator is a customer or a client of the worker.
- The violent act generally occurs in conjunction with the worker's normal duties.
- The risk of violence to some workers in this category (e.g., mental health workers, police) may be constant, even routine.

Type III (Worker-on-Worker) violence occurs when an employee assaults or attacks his or her coworkers. In some cases, these incidents can take place after a series of increasingly hostile behaviors by the perpetrator. Worker-on-worker assault is often the first type of workplace violence that comes to mind for many people, possibly because some of these incidents receive intensive media coverage. For example, the phrase "going postal," referring to the scenario of a postal worker attacking coworkers, is sometimes used to describe Type III workplace violence. In truth, the U.S. Postal Service is no more likely than any other organization to be affected by this type of violence.

Type III violence accounts for about 7 percent of all workplace homicides. No specific occupations or industries appear to be more or less prone to Type III violence. Because some of these incidents appear to be motivated by disputes, managers and others who supervise workers may be at greater risk of being victimized.

Type III incidents have the following characteristics:

- The perpetrator is an employee or former employee.
- The motivating factor is often one or a series of interpersonal or work-related disputes.

Type IV violence is *domestic* related. Because of the insidious nature of domestic violence, it is given a category all its own in the typology of workplace violence. Victims are overwhelmingly, but not exclusively, female. The effects of domestic violence on the workplace are many. They can appear as high absenteeism and low productivity on the part of a worker who is enduring abuse or threats or as the sudden, prolonged absence of an employee fleeing abuse.

Occasionally, the abuser—who usually has no working relationship with the victim's employer—will appear at the workplace to engage in hostile behavior. In some cases, a domestic violence situation can arise between individuals in the same workplace. These situations can have a substantial effect on the workplace even if one of the parties leaves or is fired.

None of the four types should be regarded as mutually exclusive. Retail establishments, for example, are at risk of Type I events such as robbery and Type III events involving combative coworkers. Hospital emergency rooms are at risk of Type I and Type II events.

SOURCES OF WORKPLACE VIOLENCE

The sequence of events leading to workplace violence follows a pattern. First, a traumatic event that produces extreme anger and anxiety occurs. This experience may be triggered by a single event (such as denial of a promotion, a demotion, or termination) or by a number of events that occur over time (such as negative performance ratings). Second, the employee then becomes obsessed with the negative experience, suffering from a great deal of internal conflict and blaming others for the problem. This stage may continue for weeks or months. Finally, the employee seeks revenge for the experience, perhaps focusing on a supervisor or other employees who are seen as the cause of the problem.

A variety of traumatic events contribute to anger in the workplace. In the 1990s, **corporate downsizing** became a common event. Corporations sought to control costs by trimming their labor force, displacing workers, and eliminating many jobs. According to Jones (1996), to help avoid violence, employers should consider the following guidelines when downsizing:

- Practice responses to a range of emotions such as anger, shock, and silence; keep the meeting short.
- Never say negative things to the terminated employee such as, "You are being let go because we need new blood."
- Know the telephone numbers of security or have security personnel nearby.
- Change computer passwords and secure credit cards and company cars immediately on termination.
- Stress that upper management has approved the layoff decision.

A study of 125 workplace homicides found that half of the perpetrators had recently been laid off or terminated in a downsizing effort. Thus, the possibility of losing a job and then actually being dismissed can result in violent behavior (Johnson, 1994). One study indicates that assailants often have a history of frustrating life experiences and personal failures (Fox and Levin, 1994). These frustrations may have developed over many years for older individuals; thus, the growing number of middle-aged workplace assailants reflects the increasing age of the general population. As discussed, many employees who commit acts of workplace violence had been the subject of grievances or had disciplinary actions pending at the time of attack. In several instances, the assailant sought retribution for being passed over for promotion, for feeling that he or she was the victim of favoritism, or for other arbitrary managerial decisions.

The Northwestern National Life Insurance Company study (1993:8) found job stress to be both a cause and an effect of workplace violence and harassment. Feelings of lack of control, little managerial support, and other psychological symptoms have been reported for many occupations (Burke, 1991). In other words, uncertainty about steady employment, adversarial relations with supervisors or peers, and perceived unfair workplace policies and procedures are sources of stress that, if undetected and unaddressed, can result in violent confrontations.

A study of postal workers found that they experience high levels of stress-related physical and psychological symptoms, low levels of job satisfaction, and little supervisory support. Many workers claimed that they lacked control over their work because of the regimented atmosphere and uncaring management (Smith, 1993:32).

Many of our nation's youth have jobs in fast-food restaurants, which are described as low-end, low-wage, time-consuming positions that they find demeaning and degrading. The pressure to please customers increases workers' frustrations, which may result in violence (Howe and Strauss, 1993). Thus, employees from different backgrounds working together in organizations in which they see no future and who feel pressure to perform often become pessimistic, angry, and, perhaps, violent.

The data in a 1993–1994 study of 50 fast-food restaurants in the East, Midwest, and South were obtained through 300 employee interviews. Most of the respondents worked night shifts and were females employed in the management ranks. The study revealed that the most frequent event reported by employees was drunken/threatening behavior by employees reporting to work or visiting the workplace while off duty. This behavior was the most common reason for termination. Supervisors were often the target of retaliatory threats by these employees. The next most common event was nonsexual harassment, which involved threats and insults exchanged between employees. The third most common complaint was fighting. It was not uncommon for fights to break out between customers or between employees, usually late at night. Approximately 50 percent of the complaints resulted from these three events (O'Connor, 1997).

Violence occurs in other organizational settings where political or religious beliefs collide. An example is abortion clinics. Opponents of abortion view employees of abortion clinics, especially doctors, as murderers. Since 1977, anti-abortionist factions have been responsible for more than 1,000 reported acts of violence, including bombings, arson, kidnappings, assaults, shootings, and clinic invasions aimed at abortion providers. The seriousness of abortion violence gained national attention on March 10, 1993, when pro-life advocate Michael Griffin mortally wounded abortion clinic doctor Dr. David Gunn as he arrived for work at the Pensacola (Florida) Women's Medical Services Center. The motive for the killing was Griffin's hatred for abortion and the doctors who performed abortions. Dr. Warren Hern, medical director of an abortion clinic in Colorado, stated, "Death threats are so common they are not remarkable" (Hall, 1992:36).

WARNING SIGNS OF VIOLENCE

A number of signs may indicate potential violence. Some of the blatant indicators are threatening phone calls, stalking, and unwelcome attention, such as love letters and gifts (romantic obsession). A psychological view of the potentially violent person involves a three-part profile addressing the general characteristics of the violent worker, the characteristics of the employee who may be capable of murder, and the characteristics of the nonviolent employee. By examining past cases of violence, the perpetrators, and settings in which violence occurs, we can learn a great deal.

A technique to identify employees most likely to commit murder in the workplace was developed by **Anthony Baron** (1993). Dr. Baron, considered a leading researcher on workplace violence and the chief executive officer of the Scripps Center for Quality Management, in San Diego, California, conducted research on employees who committed murder in the workplace. He found that most were white males between 25 and 40 years of age. They had a history of violence, either on the job or in their personal lives, and had requested some form of counseling. He indicated that workplace murderers tend to be loners and appear withdrawn, exhibit bursts of anger, and have conflicts with other employees. They often have a history of marital problems, as well as drug and alcohol abuse.

Most displayed feelings of paranoia. They often owned weapons. Based on his research, Dr. Baron found that there is an 80 percent chance that those who commit violence will be male, a 75 percent chance that they will be white, and a 90 percent chance that they are between 25 and 50 years old. There is a 90 percent probability that the offender has one or more of the following characteristics:

- History of violence
- Evidence of psychosis
- Evidence of erotomania
- Evidence of chemical or alcohol dependence
- Depression
- Pattern of pathological blaming
- Impaired neurological functioning
- Elevated frustration level
- Interest in weapons
- Evidence of personality disorder
- Vocalization of violent intentions prior to a violent act
- Evidence of strange or bizarre behavior over a period of time

Human resource experts have found that employees who explode into a murderous rage fit a similar demographic and psychological profile. In other words, predictors and profiles of impending violence exist. According to one such profile (DiLorenzo and Carroll, 1995), the violent employee generally fits one or more of the following characterizations:

- A loner with a history of violence and a fascination with weapons
- An angry person who has few outlets for that anger, but who has requested some type of assistance in the past
- A socially withdrawn person with a history of interpersonal conflict, family problems, and marital strife
- Someone who often gives verbal expression to complaints about and to management, but then stops
- Someone who exhibits paranoia about others or engages in self-destructive behavior, such as drug or alcohol abuse

One of the most celebrated cases of workplace violence occurred in California in 1991. As Chapter 3 indicates, stalking is a threat that can lead to physical violence. In the case of Laura Black (Focus 5–1), a romantic obsession by a coworker led to her stalking and the subsequent murder of several employees.

Focus 5–1   Obsession with Laura

Richard Farley's complete obsession with coworker Laura Black exemplifies the violence that can result from a particularly virulent delusional disorder.

Electromagnetic Systems Labs (ESL) was a premier defense contractor and a respected member of the burgeoning electronics industry located in the heart of Silicon Valley. ESL provided its employees with a comfortable working environment and a camaraderie unique to high-tech firms. Richard Ward Farley was a software technician who had left the military with a much-demanded skill and a high security clearance during a 10-year stint with the Navy.

From the moment Farley was introduced to Laura Black, an electrical engineer who had worked at ESL for less than a year, he was obsessed with her. Later recalling their first meeting during court testimony, Farley said, "I think I fell instantly in love with her. It was just one of those things, I guess." Black at first had no inkling of Farley's obsession with her. During the three and a half years following that meeting, Farley wrote some 200 letters to her, constantly followed her to and from work, left gifts on her desk, and rifled through confidential personnel files to learn more about her personal life. At one point, learning that Black was to visit her parents in Virginia in December 1984, Farley broke into her desk at the office, obtained the address of her parents, and wrote letters to her in Virginia. His letters in 1984 and 1985 were not overtly threatening, but that changed as Black continued to thwart his advances. Farley frequently drove

(Continued)

(*Continued*)

past her home at night and telephoned her at any hour, and, at one point, joined her aerobics class to remain as close as possible to her, day and night.

Although Farley dated another woman and eventually lived with her in his San Jose bungalow, he twice attempted to move into the same apartment building where Black lived. Farley often asked for a date but would inevitably be turned down by the polite and naturally gentle Black. These rejections inevitably brought on recurring protestations and endless restatements of his limitless love for her. She did what she could to avoid him and deter his advances; he responded by redoubling his efforts with more telephone calls, more harassment, more gifts, and incessant car trips past her home.

Black was forced to move twice during these years as Farley's harassment continued unabated at work, at her apartment complex, and even on shopping trips. Eventually, Farley's tactics became aggressive and cruel. He made derogatory statements about her and rifled through her locked desk in search of more information about her personal life and activities away from work. It seemed that every effort that Black made to avoid Farley resulted in more encounters with him, each contact becoming more offensive than the previous one.

By the fall of 1985, Farley had pursued Black so unceasingly that she turned to the human resources department at ESL for help. Farley was told he must attend psychological counseling sessions and stop harassing Black if he wanted to keep his job. Although he attended the required counseling sessions regularly, the harassment did not diminish, it escalated. During the period he was attending counseling, Farley made a duplicate copy of Black's house key that she had inadvertently left on her desk. Rather than using the key to gain entry to her apartment, Farley displayed it and a handwritten note on the dashboard of his car so that Black and others would know that he could get to her at any time. His driving excursions past her home and his telephone calls to her late at night increased. The letters he wrote became more threatening, sometimes referring to his large gun collection.

Finally, in 1986, Farley could no longer control his growing anger at Black's continuing rejections. He publicly and vehemently threatened her life if she would not submit to his desire to have her for himself. Farley also began threatening other employees at the company, including a manager whom he warned about his gun collection, his expertise with guns, and the fact that he "could take people with [him]" if provoked.

ESL management, by now very concerned about Farley's bizarre behavioral patterns, dismissed him in May 1986. Managers were clearly concerned about Black's safety as well as that of others in the organization. Even as Farley was being fired from his job, an ESL manager warned Black once more about Farley's uncontrollable obsession and the company's concern for her safety. Still, even the termination from his $36,000-a-year position could not dissuade Farley. In fact, in a letter to Black just before he was fired from his job, Farley wrote, "Once I'm fired, you won't be able to control me ever again. Pretty soon, I'll crack under the pressure and run amok and destroy everything in my path." His words proved prophetic in the extreme.

(*Continued*)

(*Continued*)

For the next year and a half, Farley continued to harass Black. He was experiencing economic hardships, lost two houses, and found himself in trouble with the IRS for back taxes. But none of this seemed to matter. He thought constantly about Black and increased his efforts to gain her affection. The fact that he could no longer see her at work did nothing to check his pursuit of her. The telephone calls continued, as did his habit of following her whenever he could. By November 1987, his letters to Black were voluminous and overtly threatening. In that month he wrote, "You cost me a job, $40,000 in equity taxes I can't pay, and a foreclosure. Yet I still like you. Why do you want to find out how far I'll go?" Closing his letter, Farley threatened her again: "I absolutely will not be pushed around, and I'm beginning to get tired of being nice."

Black, in fear for her life and completely victimized by the ever-present Farley, eventually sought, and was granted, a temporary restraining order that forbade him from approaching within 300 yards of her and ordered him not to contact her in any manner. The order was served against Farley on February 8, 1988, with a hearing scheduled for the matter on February 17. For Farley, this temporary restraining order was an act of ultimate abandonment on Black's part. He knew, without question, that Black would never submit to his advances. All that was left for Farley was revenge—and he already had much of what he needed to take that course.

On February 9, 1988, Farley purchased a new 12-gauge semiautomatic shotgun and ammunition for his arsenal of personal weapons. He spent $2,000 that day, despite his financial problems, just to be sure he had everything he needed. When Farley returned to the offices of his former employer on Tuesday, February 16, 1988, he was clearly prepared for maximum violence. It was just after 3 P.M. as he drove his motor home into the ESL parking lot armed with his new shotgun, a rifle, two handguns, bandoleers of ammunition strapped across his chest, and a container of gasoline. In all, Farley carried nearly 100 pounds of firearms and ammunition on his body. Walking across the parking lot to the office building, Farley shot and killed his first victim, a 46-year-old data processing specialist whom he knew. He then approached the building entrance and blasted his way through the locked glass doors, heading directly for Black's office. Making his way to her location, Farley fired indiscriminately at anyone in his path. Before reaching Black, he shot six employees, killing four instantly with powerful blasts from his semiautomatic shotgun. Hearing the chaos outside of her office, Black slammed and locked her door, hoping to find some refuge. It was to no avail. Farley leveled his shotgun at the office door and blew it off the hinges. Jumping past the shattered door and moving swiftly toward her desk, he raised the shotgun again and fired twice. The first shot missed, but the second critically wounded her, severing arteries, tearing muscles, and destroying bone in her shoulder. Although losing a great deal of blood and in unimaginable pain, she was able to hide in an adjoining office and then make a run for the parking lot where, by that time, waiting ambulances and a SWAT team had arrived. During his rampage, Farley killed seven employees and wounded another four, including Laura.

(*Continued*)

(Continued)

At the end of his five-hour rampage, Farley surrendered to a police SWAT team. Throughout the standoff, law enforcement personnel later recounted, Farley expressed no remorse for what he had done and, in fact, appeared to delight in the mayhem and chaos surrounding his actions.

The day after Farley's rampage, Family Court Commissioner Lois Kittle declared the restraining order obtained by Black a few weeks earlier as permanent. It was clearly a symbolic, but important, act. A tearful Commissioner Kittle said, "Pieces of paper do not stop bullets." On that day it was uncertain if Laura Black would survive to testify against Richard Wade Farley.

Farley went on trial in 1991, charged with seven counts of capital murder and four additional felonies. In his testimony, he admitted that he knew he should not have harassed Laura Black but claimed he could not help himself. He argued that he had "instantly" fallen in love with his former coworker, saying, "The more she tries to push me away, the more I try to not have her push me away." According to his testimony, Black's final response to his incessant attempts to date her was that she would not go out with him even if "I was the last man on Earth."

During the course of the trial, Black, obviously still in pain from her injuries and permanently disabled, testified that she had not encouraged Farley in any way but had, in fact, made extraordinary efforts to avoid him and deter his advances. Having been grievously wounded during the February 16 siege, Black made a compelling witness against the remorseless Farley. It was clear that she had truly been through hell with Richard Farley.

Source: Based on material originally published in M.D. Kelleher, *New Arenas for Violence: Homicide in the American Workplace* (Praeger Publishers, an imprint of Greenwood Publishing Group, Inc., Westport, CT, 1996). Used with permission.

It is a textbook case of violence escalation and how a company was slow to recognize the problem. A different kind of romantic obsession is described in Focus 5–2, regarding an office romance gone completely out of control.

FOCUS 5–2   An Office Romance Gone Crazy: Who Is to Blame and Who Are the Victims?

In September 1992, Elizabeth Saret-Cook was hired by a law firm as a paralegal. She worked with Clifford Woosley, a partner in the law firm, who also agreed to assist her in preparing for her bar exam. Although both were married, both were at the time experiencing difficulties in their respective marriages. Woosley feared that his marriage might soon end, and Saret-Cook was unhappy in her marriage. At this time, Woosley was 41 years old with two sons. His wife was apparently about the same age. Saret-Cook

(Continued)

(Continued)

was 30 years old with one son and an adopted daughter. Her husband was in his early 60s. Saret-Cook and Woosley soon began a sexual affair. Saret-Cook later stated that she had fallen in love with Woosley when she first met him, admitted that she deliberately planned to seduce him, and admitted that she, in fact, had seduced him.

The affair between Saret-Cook and Woosley resulted in Saret-Cook's pregnancy. Woosley reported the affair and pregnancy to the managing partner. Although he told the managing partner that he and Saret-Cook had earlier talked about marriage, he also explained that he had decided to break off the affair and to recommit to his existing marriage. The office manager then spoke with Saret-Cook. He suggested that in view of the circumstances and possible future complications, it would be better if a new supervising attorney were found to mentor Saret-Cook.

In response, Saret-Cook "went absolutely bonkers." She insisted that Woosley continue to act as her supervising attorney in the study program, giving as an explanation for this insistence her claim that she would lose credit in the study program should she change supervising attorneys and be delayed in taking the bar exam.

Woosley was a partner with the firm's insurance bad faith appellate section. Saret-Cook was employed as a paralegal in that section and sometimes performed work assignments directly for him. Several weeks after the affair and resulting pregnancy were reported to the managing partner, a delegation of three female attorneys complained to the managing partner that Saret-Cook was disrupting the office by continually arguing with personnel on her floor, insisting on discussing the intimate sexual details of her affair, and publicly theorizing how she might rekindle the affair. The attorneys complained that Saret-Cook's conduct was interfering with productivity. Perceiving a developing morale problem, the managing partner transferred Saret-Cook (over her objection) to a different department on a different floor. Pursuant to her demand, however, the individual respondent continued to act as her mentor in the study program.

After her transfer, Saret-Cook continued disruptive behavior in the new office locale and continued her efforts to rekindle the affair. She falsely told Woosley that she had divorced her husband and did induce Woosley briefly to resume their affair. In October, however, Woosley irrevocably ended it. He later told colleagues that he could not believe that at one time he thought he might have been in love with Saret-Cook.

Other strange and dishonest behavior developed as well. Although Saret-Cook learned 8 weeks into her pregnancy that she was bearing a single child, she consistently told the individual respondent and others that she was pregnant with twins, even naming them "Claire" and "Clark." Shortly before her delivery, Saret-Cook asked the individual respondent for a check to pay for Clark's circumcision, which the individual respondent provided. After giving birth to a single female child, Claire, by emergency cesarean, Saret-Cook phoned Woosley from the hospital and told him that Clark had been stillborn. This news was particularly wrenching to Woosley, because he himself was a surviving twin. Saret-Cook knew this when she

(Continued)

(*Continued*)

lied about Clark because the individual respondent had told her about his dead twin before the affair began. Saret-Cook also told others that Clark had died. However, there was never a baby Clark.

The baby Claire had multiple complications and medical problems and needed significant ongoing medical attention. Saret-Cook told the individual respondent that she wanted to concentrate on the living, and, therefore, wanted no public mourning for the loss of Clark. Saret-Cook stated that she would make arrangements with the hospital for the disposition of Clark's remains. There was no funeral. In late February, Saret-Cook began telling the individual respondent that Clark's death was the individual respondent's fault, saying, "How does it feel to have killed your own son?" and "Clark is dead because you refused to give me the emotional support that I deserved when I was pregnant." In June 1994, while the individual respondent was engaged in obtaining care for Claire, Saret-Cook changed her story about Clark. She now told the individual respondent that Clark had not actually been stillborn, but instead had miscarried in October. She stated that Clark's remains had been buried at Forest Lawn. The individual respondent promptly went to Forest Lawn in an unsuccessful search for the burial site. Not until later did the individual respondent learn that Saret-Cook's statements about Clark's existence and death were part of an elaborate lie.

Two weeks after Claire's birth, Saret-Cook returned to work. She told the managing partner that she intended to resign from the firm, that it was her own personal decision, and that she had not been pressured to resign. She stated, however, that she first needed to complete her study program. In March 1994, Saret-Cook had told her psychologist that she was threatening a scandal at the firm, that she loved Woosley and hoped he would leave his wife and marry her. Saret-Cook also told the managing partner that she intended to sue the firm. Settlement negotiations consequently commenced. Even after execution of the settlement documents, Saret-Cook's disruptive behavior continued, including continued public discussions of her relationship with the individual respondent and arguments. She also began to use her phone excessively for personal calls. From mid-February to July 1994, Saret-Cook made 3,600 calls from her office phone alone, over half of which were confirmed to be personal calls. She also began bringing Claire into the office, often leaving the baby unattended and crying.

She also commenced other bizarre deceptions. On one occasion, Saret-Cook reported that she was being threatened by opposing counsel in a case she was working on, that she was being followed, that one of her tires had been slashed, and that her son had been accosted. The partner in charge removed her from the case and spent considerable time investigating, but found her allegations inconsistent and contradictory. When he asked her to provide substantiation of her claims, she instead asked a paralegal to confirm a false story about being followed. The quality of her work also deteriorated with missed deadlines and unfinished administrative tasks.

Her disruptive behavior also escalated as her obsession with Woosley apparently intensified. She told a paralegal that she wanted to get pregnant by the individual

(*Continued*)

(Continued)

respondent a second time because she felt he would then be forced to marry her. She told another employee that she had hired a private detective to investigate the individual respondent's wife. In July 1994, she used the firm printer to print a letter stating that the individual respondent's wife had had an affair and that the individual respondent was not the father of his son. The pages were left in the printer and were found by a secretary. On another occasion, she followed the female attorney who had declined to intervene on her behalf into the women's room, screaming that she was a "loud-mouth bitch," while the office manager escorted visitors through the office nearby.

Her harassment of the individual respondent also intensified. She phoned Woosley in his office, at his home, and on his car phone, and phoned his wife as well. When the individual respondent stopped answering the repeated calls shown by the firm's internal caller ID system to be from Saret-Cook's office, she would dial "9" for an outside line and call again. The incessant phone calls prevented the individual respondent from working productively. A paralegal testified that Saret-Cook admitted "wreaking havoc" on Woosley. She repeatedly entered the individual respondent's office and refused to leave, forcing him to work with his door locked to keep her out. She would bang on his locked door, shouting that she needed to talk with him. She refused to leave after study program sessions, insisting instead on staying to talk about personal matters. Woosley began holding the study program sessions in empty offices so that he could leave and return to his own office when the study session had ended. On one occasion, she blocked the exit from the empty office, daring him to physically move her to escape. Saret-Cook also hounded the individual respondent by continually following him, on two occasions even following him into the men's room. She told her psychologist that she hoped to marry him.

The situation was so severe that in June 1994 he began commuting 3 days per week to GKCJ's Riverside office in order to avoid Saret-Cook's hounding. He had to continue to come into the Los Angeles office on Tuesdays and Thursdays, however, to mentor Saret-Cook in her study program. On September 1, Saret-Cook attended her last study session with the individual respondent and refused to leave afterward. When the individual respondent attempted to leave, Saret-Cook first feigned fainting, then yelled, "I'm going to destroy you, and I'm going to destroy your family and everything that's near and dear to you!"

Despite the fact that September was her agreed-on separation date, Saret-Cook nevertheless came into the office on September 2. A number of heated exchanges between Saret-Cook and GKCJ attorneys occurred, with conflicting evidence as to their cause and content. The managing partner received an emergency call on his car phone from the office administrator while the managing partner was en route to the firm's Orange County office, reporting on Saret-Cook's continuing disruption. He spoke to Saret-Cook by telephone from the Orange County office, asking her to just "leave with dignity." She hung up.

After her resignation date, Saret-Cook obtained employment at another law firm on the strength of her false representation that she had taken the bar exam. During her

(Continued)

(Continued)

time at that firm, she continued her incessant calls to Woosley. On October 31, she phoned him and stated that she must see him outside the office because she was about to do something that would destroy them both. He refused to see her, but later that day he was hospitalized and remained hospitalized for four days. Saret-Cook continued to phone him at the hospital. She also repeatedly phoned his wife at home and at work, calling her a "slut" and asking scurrilous questions. At times, Saret-Cook would claim she was a reporter with the *National Enquirer* or say she was calling about the *Sally Jesse Raphael* program. On the birthday of the individual respondent's youngest son, Saret-Cook phoned Woosley's wife pretending to be a reporter for the *L.A. Times* and asking about her husband's affair and illegitimate child. In November 1994, Woosley changed the home phone number his family had used for 8 years. Yet after only 3 weeks, phone calls from Saret-Cook began again. The individual respondent testified that he felt oppressed and that his family was frightened.

Woosley reported the incessant phone calls to the police, and a tracer was installed on the family phone. The calls continued. On January 26, 1995, for example, the family received six calls from Saret-Cook, each made one minute apart. In her many calls, she would ask the individual respondent's wife, "How many illegitimate children do you have?" or would ask the 14-year-old son, "Who is your daddy?" or tell him to ask his mommy about her lover. The family changed its phone number four times in an attempt to stop the calls. By March 1995, the calls that could be positively identified as from Saret-Cook had stopped, but untraceable crank hang-up calls persisted. Some of these calls were made from public pay phones near Saret-Cook's home and workplace.

Friction and tension between Saret-Cook and Woosley continued due to their necessary interactions relating to Claire's need for medical care. The individual respondent became increasingly distraught and increasingly unable to focus on his work. By May 1995, he was experiencing weight loss and muscle spasms. A psychiatrist diagnosed him as suffering from depression and treated him until July 1995 when he (rather than the psychiatrist) discontinued the treatments.

By the winter of 1995, however, neither his condition nor his productivity had improved. As a consequence, Woosley was asked to step down from his partnership. He testified that he felt that he had lost something he had worked for his entire life. His income was reduced by over half. Because he was no longer able to afford the family home, he had to sell it. He also began taking medication to control muscle twitching. In February 1996, he resumed psychiatric care. He had lost over 30 pounds, could not sleep, was extremely anxious, and suffered from muscle spasms, restlessness, and suicidal thoughts. He was diagnosed as having major depression, placed on disability, and prescribed antidepressant and antianxiety medications. On a depression scale of 1 to 10, his psychiatrist placed him at an 8 or 9. As of the time of the trial in July 1996, he remained on disability.

Source: Facts taken from California Supreme Court case *Saret-Cook v. Gilbert, Kelley, Crowley and Jennett* et al., California Super. Ct. No. BC 116590, 1999.

In Focus 5–2, a story fit for a Hollywood horror film, the office romance had severe implications and numerous warning signs of possible violence. That incident, however, occurred in a prestigious law firm. Many lessons are to be gained from such a scenario. Although no murder or physical violence took place, as in the case of Laura Black in Focus 5–1, many lives were ruined. In both cases, abnormal obsession, harassment, intimidation, and threats compromised the workplace, causing organizational dysfunction and victimization. After years of civil litigation, the male victim received a judgment against the harasser. But, should he or his supervisors share in the blame?

It is imperative that management, particularly immediate supervisors, be aware of the characteristics of problem employees. One characteristic is repeated tardiness or excessive absences, or both. These indicators are particularly important if the employee usually is prompt and reliable and are suggestive of a personal problem or low morale. A second characteristic is the need for increased supervision. Employees requiring close supervision may be signaling a need for help; constant or repetitive mistakes may be a clue to behavioral problems, particularly if the employee has not required close supervision in the past. A third characteristic is reduced productivity. A previously productive employee whose performance level suddenly drops requires intervention. Another classic warning sign is a strained workplace relationship or conflict with other employees. A worker displaying disruptive, argumentative behavior with other employees needs help. This type of behavior can deteriorate, as in the case of Richard Farley (see Focus 5–1).

Other characteristics of problem employees are changes in health and hygiene and exhibiting unusual behavior, such as radical changes in dress or personality. These changes suggest possible substance abuse or depression, which may result from dissatisfaction with the job or domestic problems. These characteristics may also indicate that an employee is in need of help and may be prone to violence or other disruptive antisocial behavior. Other typical characteristics include the following:

- Evidence of feelings of being victimized by the company, supervisors, or coworkers
- Displays of unwarranted anger or sudden outbursts
- Romantic obsession with another employee
- Inability to take criticism
- Taking up much of the supervisor's time with personal problems
- Lack of concern for the safety of others
- Lack of concern for company property and equipment

- Complaints by coworkers or others regarding inappropriate behavior (sexual harassment, etc.)
- Becoming withdrawn or socially isolated from other workers

Approaching a person who demonstrates any one or a combination of these characteristics requires caution and patience. The actions suggested in Table 5–3 can deescalate potentially violent situations or people (Timm and Chandler, 1995). The goal in dealing with a possible problem employee is to defuse that person by using nonthreatening language and gestures. Be patient and empathetic, and allow the person to speak or vent his or her frustrations. Use accommodating language such as, "I know you're upset; it sounds as if the world is falling down around you. . . . Let's talk about it; maybe we can work something out." Avoid challenges and threats that may further inflame the issue.

TABLE 5–3   WAYS TO MINIMIZE VIOLENCE WITH A PERSON EXHIBITING THE CHARACTERISTICS OF A PROBLEM EMPLOYEE

The following can be used to deescalate potentially violent situations. If at any time a person's behavior begins to escalate beyond your comfort zone, disengage.

Do	Do Not
Project calmness; move and speak slowly, quietly, and confidently.	Generate hostility by using styles of communication such as apathy, brush-off, coldness, condescension, robotism, going strictly by the rules, or giving the runaround.
Be an empathetic listener; encourage the person to talk and then listen patiently.	
Focus your attention on the other person to let him or her know you are interested in what he or she has to say.	Reject all of the person's demands from the start.
Maintain a relaxed yet attentive posture and position yourself at a right angle to rather than directly in front of the other person.	Pose in challenging stances such as standing directly opposite the person with hands on hips or arms crossed. Avoid any physical contact, finger pointing, or long periods of fixed eye contact.
Acknowledge the person's feelings; indicate that you can see that he or she is upset.	Make sudden movements that can be perceived as threatening.
Ask for small, specific favors such as asking the person to move to a quieter area.	Challenge, threaten, or dare the individual. Never belittle the person or make him or her feel foolish.
	Criticize the person or act impatient.

(continued)

TABLE 5–3 (continued)

Do	Do Not
Establish ground rules if unreasonable behavior persists; calmly describe the consequences of any violent behavior.	Attempt to bargain with a threatening individual.
Use delaying tactics to give the person time to calm down. For example, offer a drink of water (in a disposable cup).	Try to make the situation less serious than it is.
Be reassuring and point out choices; break big problems into smaller, more manageable ones.	Make false statements or promises you cannot keep.
Accept criticism in a positive way. When a complaint might be true, use statements such as "You're probably right" or "It was my fault." If the criticism seems unwarranted, ask clarifying questions.	Try to impart technical or complicated information when emotions are high.
Ask for the person's recommendations; repeat what you believe the person is requesting of you.	Take sides or agree with distortions. Invade the individual's personal space. Make sure there is enough space between you and the person.
Arrange yourself so that a visitor cannot block your access to an exit.	

Source: Howard Timm and Callie J. Chandler. 1995. *Combating Workplace Violence.* Washington, DC: U.S. Department of Justice, Bureau of Labor Statistics.

The type of business, its geographical location, and its configuration or layout may be contributing factors to victimization. Based on previous research on violence in the workplace, the following conditions are considered **business risk predictors** (Meadows, 1990). The list is not inclusive but is offered as a guide to identify a business that may be at risk.

BUSINESS RISK PREDICTORS: QUESTIONS TO CONSIDER

1. Has the business experienced previous criminal intrusions?
2. Does the business operate during evening hours?
3. Is there public access (a number of public access points)?
4. Is alcohol served on the premises?
5. Are there several points of uncontrolled entry into the business?
6. Is there uncontrolled access to parking areas or structures?

7. Does the business deal in cash transactions?

8. Have any employees complained of harassment or assaults by other employees, customers, or other people?

9. Does the business offer public entertainment?

10. Have incidents of crime (robbery, assaults, gang activity) occurred in the area immediately surrounding the business?

11. Is the business located near an entrance to a freeway or an interstate highway?

12. Is the business located in a metropolitan area?

13. Have firearms or other deadly weapons been reported on the premises?

14. Have there been reports by employees or others regarding loitering on or near the premises?

15. Have there been reports of illegal drug usage by employees or others on the premises?

16. Have there been physical confrontations or fights between employees or others?

17. Have any discharged or disgruntled employees made threats?

Obviously, a business manager or owner who answers yes to a number of these questions should give serious thought to ways to address the problems. Predictors, especially when they occur frequently or when the business has a history of criminality on the property, raise the specter of crime and potential legal problems' foreseeability.

BULLYING IN THE WORKPLACE

Associated with workplace violence is the problem of bullying of employees by coworkers or supervisors. Bullying is a form of harassment but without the same legal protections as sexual harassment. In other words, bullying is a type of aggression against a coworker that may not involve physical contact or sexual suggestions. Thus, bullying is a form of same-sex harassment, which is usually not actionable except when unwanted sexual overtures are involved (Namie, 2003).

Bullying is a serious concern in the workplace because it can lead to victimization and violence; however, the victimization may not always be violent. Bullies use a number of tactics. Figure 5–1 rank orders the top 25 tactics commonly used by the workplace bully. As described, some of these tactics could lead to violence or retaliation against the bully, or at the very least result in lower productivity and negative working environments.

FIGURE 5–1   TOP 25 TACTICS OF WORKPLACE BULLIES

Rank

1. Falsely accused someone of "errors" not actually made (71 percent)
2. Stared, glared, was nonverbally intimidating, and was clearly showing hostility (68 percent)
3. Discounted the person's thoughts or feelings ("oh, that's silly") in meetings (64 percent)
4. Used the "silent treatment" to "ice out" and separate from others (64 percent)
5. Exhibited presumably uncontrollable mood swings in front of the group (61 percent)
6. Made up own rules on the fly that even he/she did not follow (61 percent)
7. Disregarded satisfactory or exemplary quality of completed work despite evidence (58 percent)
8. Harshly and constantly criticized having a different "standard" for the target (57 percent)
9. Started, or failed to stop, destructive rumors or gossip about the person (56 percent)
10. Encouraged people to turn against the person being tormented (55 percent)
11. Singled out and isolated one person from coworkers, either socially or physically (54 percent)
12. Publicly displayed "gross," undignified, but not illegal, behavior (53 percent)
13. Yelled, screamed, and threw tantrums in front of others to humiliate a person (53 percent)
14. Stole credit for work done by others (47 percent)
15. Abused the evaluation process by lying about the person's performance (46 percent)
16. "Insubordinate" for failing to follow arbitrary commands (46 percent)
17. Used confidential information about a person to humiliate privately or publicly (45 percent)
18. Retaliated against the person after a complaint was filed (45 percent)
19. Made verbal put-downs/insults based on gender, race, accent or language, disability (44 percent)
20. Assigned undesirable work as punishment (44 percent)
21. Made undoable demands—workload, deadlines, duties—on person singled out (44 percent)
22. Launched a baseless campaign to oust the person and was not stopped by the employer (43 percent)
23. Encouraged the person to quit or transfer rather than to face more mistreatment (43 percent)
24. Sabotaged the person's contribution to a team goal and reward (41 percent)
25. Ensured failure of person's project by not performing required tasks: signoffs, taking calls, working with collaborators (40 percent)

Source: WBTI 2003 Report on Abusive Workplaces, 2003. Bellingham, WA: Workplace Bullying and Trauma Institute.

Bullying in the workplace also assumes some different dynamics. Women bullies, for example, tend to target their own sex, with women bullies choosing women targets 87 percent of the time. However, men bullies choose women targets 71 percent of the time. Women bullies are more likely than are men bullies to adopt the tactics of silent treatment and encouraging colleagues to turn against the target. Men bullies, on the other hand, choose tactics that range from blatantly illegal through different forms of aggression to threats of physical force (Namie, 2003).

Legal movements address workplace bullying. Laws have been introduced in Washington state and Hawaii to criminalize bullying. In a civil case in Indiana, a heart surgeon was ordered to pay a former hospital employee $325,000 for perpetrating extreme verbal abuse, profanity, and insults against the person (Martin, 2005). As in this precedent-setting case, workplace bullying may be viewed as actionable if the pattern of conduct is extensive.

EMPLOYER LIABILITY FOR WORKPLACE VICTIMIZATION

With growing concern over workplace violence, employers and business owners are also becoming increasingly interested in their legal obligations should a violent event occur. Loss control and safety experts warn that businesses that do not implement security measures increase their exposure to lawsuits (Roberts, 1994:4). Workers' compensation may cover most employee injury claims, but the employer may still be responsible in other ways. The **foreseeability** of violent events, such as prior complaints and dangerous working conditions, is important in establishing employer liability.

The cost of workplace violence to an employer can be high. The National Safe Workplace Institute in Chicago, for example, reported in 1 year that jury verdicts against employers average $2.2 million for wrongful deaths, $1.8 million for rapes, and $1.2 million for assaults (McCune, 1994:55). Violence in the workplace can result not only in lawsuits but also can invite a great deal of adverse publicity for a business. The reputation, credibility, and employee morale of a business can be damaged by publicity resulting from litigation. Workplace violence often results in loss of time from work, increased workers' compensation claims, and increased insurance premiums.

In the event that litigation does occur, attorneys for crime victims can use a number of legal precedents or doctrines, depending on the facts of the case. One theory, **premises liability**, considers the defendant employer/business to be liable if it can be proved that the employer failed to exercise reasonable care in securing the premises; for example, security measures were inadequate, security guards failed to patrol the property, security personnel had not been trained properly, or the employer failed to provide security as required by law. If laws requiring parking lots to be lighted or a business to develop a security plan are not followed, the business may be liable (*Lopez v. Rouse Co.*, 1994).

A number of cases have claimed premises liability resulting from the failure of a business to provide reasonable security in its parking area. For example, the Connecticut Supreme Court found a department store negligent and awarded $1.5 million to the estate of a woman killed in the store parking lot (*Stewart v. Federated Department Stores*, 1995). This lawsuit alleged negligent security. Evidence presented during the case indicated that no security officers were on duty in the garage at the time of the incident, although four were on duty inside the store. Records indicated that in the previous year, more than 1,000 serious crimes had been committed within two blocks of the garage (issue of foreseeability). Other evidence indicated that customers and employees had previously been robbed in the garage. In addition, more than 300 fluorescent lights were burned out or were inoperative on the day of the incident. Premises liability was also claimed in *Doe v. First Gibraltar Bank* (1993). In this case, an employee was assaulted in a parking lot that had been the site of previous crimes and assaults.

Another theory used in such cases is that a **legal duty** may exist if the premises have a history of crime problems, particularly violent crimes. Generally, an entity (business or person) has no legal duty to prevent harm to another citizen unless some **special relationship** exists. If you see someone under attack, you are under no legal duty to assist that person unless a special relationship between you and the victim exists, such as between a lifeguard and a drowning swimmer. In these situations, the relationship establishes the duty. Under the doctrine of legal duty, employers can be held liable for damages resulting from criminal attacks against their employees and other invitees. Thus, if the employer or agent (e.g., supervisor) knows that a former employee has threatened to return to a business to harm another employee, a special relationship exists and the employer/agent must take action to prevent the attack and must warn the intended victim of a threatened attack. In *Duffy v. City of Oceanside* (1986), an employer was aware of both the threatening employee's previous convictions for kidnap and sexual assault and the victim employee's complaints that the other employee had been sexually harassing her. The court held that the employer had a duty to the victim and was thus liable for the sexual assault of the victim employee because the employer did not take steps to protect her.

An employer's liability for workplace violence can result from owning or leasing the property. In many states, landowners and persons in possession of property are legally obligated to protect people who enter the premises from situations that are known to be dangerous, such as providing adequate security for the employer's premises. In one case, a jury awarded an employee $1.75 million because she was robbed in a parking lot controlled by her employer. Although the employer's security officers regularly patrolled that parking lot, the employer did not replace an officer who called in sick on the day that the employee was attacked (Johnson and Toner, 2006).

If a business advertises to employees that its property is safe, when in fact it is not, and an employee or other invitee relies on those representations but becomes the victim of violence, that person may sue the employer for fraud. The **fraud doctrine** states that it is fraudulent for a business to falsely represent itself in terms of security. If a criminal attack occurs, the business is guilty of fraud.

An employer's potential for liability increases when current employees commit the violence. A number of legal doctrines pertain to an employer's liability regarding the injury of an employee or a third party caused by another employee. Under the **respondeat superior doctrine**, an employer may be held liable for injuries to others caused by an employee. Two conditions apply. First, the crime or act of violence must occur within the course and scope of employment. Thus, an employer can be held liable if an employee uses the employer's equipment or the crime is motivated by the job duties. For example, a police officer who arrests a drunk driver and then commits a sexual assault against the arrestee has committed an act for which the employer is liable (*Mary M. v. City of Los Angeles*, 1991). The second condition requires that the employer has knowledge that the employee is violent and also the employer does nothing to correct the problem; thus, the foreseeability of a criminal act by an employee is one key to holding an employer liable under respondeat superior. An employee who is being sexually harassed by a coworker and who alerts the employer who does nothing about the problem may be able to sue the employer if an assault actually occurs.

Under the doctrine of **negligent hiring**, an employer can be liable for the criminal actions of an employee if it can be proved that the employer failed to do an adequate background check on the employee during the hiring process. Thus, if an employee has displayed violence toward others or has been fired from a previous job for violence, an employer who did not do the adequate background check may be liable (*Underwriters Ins. Co. v. Purdie*, 1983).

Related to negligent hiring is **negligent supervision or retention**. Under this doctrine, an employer who knows that an employee is unfit for duty because of violent tendencies may be liable if the employee commits a violent act while on the job. In other words, an employer may not have any evidence of employee violence before the hiring but may later become aware of violent tendencies on the job. To illustrate, a car rental company was found liable for approximately $800,000 after an employee violently assaulted a customer. The court reasoned that the company knew that the employee had a history of fighting outside work and arguing with customers but failed to discharge the employee after learning of these previous behaviors (*Greenfield v. Spectrum Investment Corp.*, 1985). A key to employer negligence under this theory is that actual knowledge of violence is not required, only a reasonable knowledge that violence could occur.

In the California case *Bryant v. Livigni* (1993), a supermarket employee attacked a customer's 4-year-old child. Liability determination was based on the employee's prior violence toward other coworkers and the fact that the assailant's coworkers knew of his violent temper and propensity for violence. In another case, an employer was held liable for an employee's murder of a coworker. The murderer had worked for the company for 2 years but then was convicted of manslaughter. After his release from prison, he was rehired and began sexually harassing a female employee. After an investigation of the complaint, he resigned. Eight days later, however, he shot and killed the employee who brought the complaint. A Minnesota court found that the employer had a duty to take steps to protect employees. By hiring a person whom the company knew to be violent, the company violated that duty (*Yunker v. Honeywell, Inc.*, 1993).

Another doctrine related to employer liability is **negligent training**. An employer who supervises others who carry instruments as weapons and who then commit violent acts may be liable for negligent training. In *Gonzales v. Southwest Security and Protection Agency, Inc.* (1983), a security firm was held liable for the act of one of its officers who caused serious injury to the plaintiff by using a nightstick. The court held that the security firm had failed to train the officer on the proper usage of a nightstick and failed to train employees on how to properly detain persons. Another facet of this doctrine involves negligence in selling a weapon. A Kmart employee sold a gun to a drunk customer. The customer later shot and paralyzed his girlfriend. The court found that Kmart had failed to train its sales force on firearm sales and issued an $11 million judgment against Kmart. Thus, liability for negligent training may extend beyond those who use dangerous weapons to those who sell weapons (Workplace Violence Prevention Institute, 1994:8).

In addition to civil liability, an employer may bear criminal liability for violence in the workplace (Workplace Violence Prevention Institute, 1994:8). In 1991, Congress passed legislation that requires federal sentencing guidelines to be applied to corporations found liable under the vicarious liability theory; that is, an employer is guilty if an employee commits an act of violence with the employer's actual or apparent authority. In addition, many states have enacted legislation making employers who conceal or fail to prevent hazardous workplace conditions subject to liability for such conditions. Several states have enacted laws that penalize an individual, including a business manager or owner, whose negligence causes death or serious injury in the workplace. Thus, an employer who negligently ignores a threat of workplace violence could face civil or criminal liability under these state laws.

The California Corporate Criminal Liability Act imposes criminal liability for a corporation's failure to disclose "serious concealed dangers," such as hazardous conditions. Therefore, if an employer knows of dangerous conditions but fails to warn employees of the danger, the employer can be fined or sent to prison if an injury occurs. Section 6400 of the California Labor Code requires that every employer furnish a place of employment that is safe and healthful for employees. Employers should always be aware that they may face criminal or civil negligence charges for acts of violence in the workplace.

SEXUAL HARASSMENT AND LEGAL LIABILITY

Claims of sexual harassment in the workplace have become common, and sexual harassment itself is a potential source of violence. Sexual harassment involves people in positions of power (usually men although women have been accused of harassment as well) doing or saying offensive things, usually to women under their supervision. Women who conduct their daily work activities in male-dominated job settings are more likely to be victimized than those who do not. These women are in closer proximity to potentially motivated offenders, because men are their most likely assailants. Women who work at locations with many workers are more likely to be victimized than those who work in smaller work locations. Women who work with the public are at increased risk of sexual harassment victimization (De Coster, Estes, and Mueller, 1999).

Investigations into claims of sexual harassment must be handled in such a way that disclosure of improper conduct will result in the prompt resolution of valid complaints. Reports of sexual harassment claims indicate a sharp increase in this problem. It has been estimated that 90 percent of all sexual harassment claims are bona fide (Collier and Associates, 1995).

Sexual harassment was not defined until the 1980s when the **Equal Employment Opportunity Commission (EEOC)**, under Title VII of the Civil Rights Act of 1964, formulated guidelines to define it. Sexual harassment is conduct that has the purpose or effect of creating an intimidating, hostile, or offensive working environment; has the purpose or effect of unreasonably interfering with an individual's work performance; or otherwise adversely affects an individual's employment opportunities. According to EEOC guidelines and federal and state case law reflecting those EEOC guidelines, behavior is considered to be sexual harassment if one of three elements is present: (1) unwelcome sexual advances, (2) requests for sexual favors, or (3) verbal or physical conduct of a sexual nature. Employers have a duty to maintain a work environment free of sexual harassment; this duty requires taking positive action when necessary to eliminate it or remedy its effects. Employers who knew or should have known of such conduct but failed to take immediate and appropriate corrective measures are liable for the sexual harassment. Evidence that the sexual harassment is pervasive in the organization may establish knowledge.

The EEOC and the courts recognize two distinct forms of sexual harassment: quid pro quo and hostile work environment. The most common form is quid pro quo, or the exchange of sexual favors in return for keeping a job or getting a promotion. The essence of a quid pro quo claim is that an employee with the authority to control or alter employment opportunities asks or demands that a subordinate employee grant sexual favors to obtain or retain an employment opportunity or benefit. The conduct must be of a sexual nature, and the alleged victim must belong to a protected group. Although an express demand for sexual favors is not required, the conduct of the harasser must be reasonably interpreted as a demand for sexual favors in exchange for tangible job benefits such as promised promotion. The conduct of the harasser must also be unwelcomed; thus, the position taken by the EEOC is that if the alleged victim actively participates in the conduct, the conduct is presumed to be welcome. To overcome this presumption, the victim must give the harasser notice that the conduct is no longer welcomed (Collier and Associates, 1995).

For the purposes of sexual harassment claims, a work environment is considered hostile when conduct at the workplace has the purpose or effect of unreasonably interfering with an individual's work performance, creating an intimidating or offensive work environment. The hostile environment must be sufficiently pervasive to alter the conditions of the victim's employment and create an abusive work environment. The victim need not be subjected to sexual harassment for any extended period of time; one act of severe conduct may be sufficient to prove a hostile work environment. The more severe the conduct, the less pervasive the conduct needs to be to create a hostile work environment. One rape is enough; one dinner invitation is not. Trivial unwelcomed sexual conduct, such as asking for a date, is not considered harassment unless it is pervasive or continuous. Unwelcomed intentional touching of intimate body areas is sufficiently offensive to alter the conditions of the working environment. Sexual flirtation or innuendos, however, probably

---

Focus 5–3 Staring: A Case of Sexual Harassment

A female employee (plaintiff) worked on an assembly line at an automotive manufacturing plant. A male coworker asked the plaintiff for a date three or four times, and each time, she declined the invitation. The coworker approached her and told her he wanted to "eat her." The plaintiff told him to leave her alone. He remained in her work area for a while before departing. A couple days later, he approached her at the worksite and told her he was having fantasies about bathing her, drying her off, carrying her into his room, and putting her down on his bed covered with rose petals. She again told him to leave her alone. He did not respond and continued to stay in her area before leaving. Fearful after these incidents, the plaintiff began to carry mace to work. She also complained about her coworker to management. Following her complaint to management, the coworker never spoke to her again. Instead, he began a campaign of staring at her. For the next 6 months, he would go to her workstation five or more times a day. He would stare directly at her "for at least several seconds" each time. This sort of conduct would occur "at least five to ten times a day." In response, the plaintiff gave him dirty looks and waved at him to go away, but he would not. He would continue to stare at her and on at least one occasion placed his hand on his crotch. The court ruled in the case that staring was actionable and is a form of sexual harassment. The court reasoned that the prior actions of the male coworker combined with his staring were sufficient. Also, "to plead a cause of action for sexual harassment, it is only necessary to show that gender is a substantial factor in the discrimination and that if the plaintiff had been a man, she would not have been treated in the same manner."

Source: Birschtein v. New United Motor Mfg., Inc., 92 Cal. App. 4th 994 (2001).

---

would not be considered to cause a hostile environment (Collier and Associates, 1995). Focus 5–3 discusses a case in which staring was judged to be sexual harassment.

Research on sexual harassment in the workplace reveals that the threat diminishes as guardianship increases. In other words, supportive supervisors and coworkers possess guardianship potential, which reduces the harassment victimization. Supportive supervisors and coworkers in solidaristic work groups and/or in work groups characterized as supportive, help protect women from harassment victimization (De Coster et al., 1999).

Many states are becoming proactive in addressing sexual harassment in the workplace. A law passed in California in 2005 (SB 1825) requires California employers of 50 or more persons to provide supervisors with at least 2 hours of sexual harassment training every 2 years. Employers must include their full-time, part-time, and temporary service employees as well as independent contractors. The training incorporates information and practical guidance regarding federal and state sexual harassment laws, including harassment prevention and correction, and the remedies available to victims. The training must be interactive, requiring participation by the trainee (California Chamber of Commerce, 2005).

REDUCING THE VIOLENCE THREAT: THE TARGETED HUMAN RESOURCE APPROACH

Although no method can guarantee the prevention of workplace violence or threats of harassment, certain strategies have been used successfully to reduce the potential for workplace violence. All aspects of the workplace environment must be considered and proactive approaches taken to identify hazards and risks.

The **Targeted Human Resource Approach (THRA)** is a proactive approach by which an employer assembles a human resource team and assesses the threats for which the business may be at risk. This requires considering several types of hazards, such as environmental and situational risks. As part of the process, the employer develops policies and procedures to address violence and natural disasters. These policies become corporate goals and procedures that define the corporate methods to achieve them. If a corporation determines that crime prevention is a goal, it writes a policy outlining steps to take to protect employees from harm and to protect corporate assets. These policies should address a wide area, from handling money and dealing with the public to reacting to a criminal action. Policies on preemployment screening, incident training, and threat responses should be developed.

One necessary policy concerns the company's guidelines on background checks of potential employees. Employers must investigate the background of prospective employees without violating the applicant's right to privacy. Kraft Foods (Anfuso, 1994) developed a three-pronged prescreening system using interviews, attitude tests, and reference checks. The latter involve contacting the applicant's previous employer to determine employment responsibilities and reasons for termination. Kraft retains an outside firm to conduct the background checks.

The background check involves two issues, a potential employer's right to information concerning an applicant's qualifications and the applicant's right to privacy. It is generally permissible to ask an applicant on an application or during an interview whether he or she has a criminal record. However, the fact that an applicant has a criminal record does not always mean that he or she is unqualified, nor does lack of a criminal record mean that the applicant will not become violent on the job. The record must be examined for job-related issues (Quirk, 1993).

A proper preemployment investigation must be fair to the applicant and must seek information that would protect the employer from a negligent hiring action. Some companies use diagnostic tests for preemployment assessment that attempt to evaluate specific characteristics; however, no test accurately measures an applicant's propensity for violence. The U.S. Postal Service has explored a number of behavioral tests but has not found one that is a true predictor of violence (Anfuso, 1994). In failing to identify characteristics that measure the propensity for violence, diagnostic tests can be challenged on the grounds of bias and for violating the **Americans with Disabilities Act (ADA)**. Passed in 1990, the ADA protects people with mental and physical disabilities, including past substance abuse (Anfuso, 1994). Under ADA, employers risk being sued for discharging a mentally unfit or unstable employee who may pose a risk to customers or other employees (Morris and Jakubowski, 1995). Thus, the employer must be careful when denying employment or dismissing someone because of a mental disability. A federal court in Pennsylvania recently found that an employee who was discharged because her employer "perceived" her to be an alcoholic or substance abuser may have a claim against her employer under ADA (*Ackridge v. Philadelphia Department of Human Resources*, 1994).

In addition to taking appropriate steps to screen prospective employees, companies should develop policies and procedures to train supervisors to properly discipline and discharge employees. Employee assistance programs (EAPs) are crucial in providing outplacement services and in assessing the violence potential of employees terminated for cause. EAPs and human resource approaches are based on investigating the possibility for violent incidents, ways to prevent them, and ways to control them should they occur.

The human resource team can assist in developing procedures for handling violent situations. The following short list explains how to approach a violent person during an investigation:

- Remain calm, and move and speak slowly and confidently. Invite the person to go to a quiet location or place away from others. Do not arouse or excite the person.
- Be an empathetic listener. Allow the person to speak, and listen patiently.
- Let the person know you are listening. Make comments such as, "I know you're upset," "Let's see what we can do to resolve the problem."

- If an employee is terminated, be sympathetic and offer solutions or referrals for other jobs. However, listen for clues of reprisal.

- Do not get too close to the person. Allow personal space for your safety as well as the person's dignity. In other words, "getting in someone's face" is demeaning as well as dangerous and can cause an escalation in violence.

- Have protection personnel nearby (but not too close), in the event of violence.

A quality EAP approach provides opportunities for employees to air grievances and for open communications between management and employees. The human resource team model requires a threat management response by employees, security personnel, human resources, labor relations, corporate counsel, and other management personnel. Incorporated in this model is a threat assessment program (Fein, Vassekul, and Holden, 1995).

The threat assessment program requires three major functions. The first is *identification of a potential perpetrator.* This process involves defining conditions that could cause a person to become a threat. It includes determining who in the organization is responsible for investigating complaints concerning improper conduct and establishing the procedures for initiating a complaint.

The second major function of a threat assessment program is *evaluation of the risks.* An employee who is violent or threatening should be investigated immediately. The investigation includes interviewing the person (if a known employee), coworkers, or others who know him or her. Interviewing the person can also provide information on the situation. The purpose is to determine whether the subject has exhibited violence in the past and whether the person has been involved in criminal or civil cases since the time of employment. Obtaining information about the person's lifestyle may also be beneficial. Information on whether he or she has a fascination with weapons, is suicidal, or has displayed anger toward others in the past is important. The person's right to privacy may become an issue; seeking legal advice is suggested if questions are raised about background information.

Once the person has been identified and the risks assessed, the next step, and third function of the program, is *intervention.* This involves confronting the person. If the person has threatened a coworker, the coworker must be informed and told how to respond. If the person threatening violence is unknown, the target's coworkers and associates need to be notified to protect them and to assist in identifying the person.

Protective strategies may involve transferring the target to a more secure location within the business, offering him or her a leave of absence, assisting him or her in securing legal advice and counseling support, and providing escorts to parking areas. Employees experiencing threats from estranged spouses can be offered flex time, short-term paid leave, or extended leave without pay to seek protection and legal recourse against violence.

After a violent event occurs, employees need help in dealing with their experiences. This is the humane response, and it helps to prevent absenteeism, loss of productivity, and workers' compensation claims. After a violent incident, the following should occur (Fein et al., 1995):

- A debriefing to discuss the cause of the violence, address a plan of action, and identify those needing further counseling should be held with all affected employees 24–72 hours after a serious violent incident.
- After a serious incident of violence, a group debriefing should be held for immediate coworkers to tell them how to interact with a victim/coworker who is returning to work after an absence and to provide ongoing follow-up treatment, as needed.
- Employers should support prosecution of offenders to prevent additional incidents from occurring and to show their support for the victims.
- Employees involved in a violent incident should be allowed to make court appearances and work with the prosecution.
- Employers should cooperate with law enforcement authorities to help prevent crime and to identify and prosecute offenders.

According to Behavior Analysts and Consultants, which conducts corporate training on managing workplace violence, one of the key responsibilities of a human resource management team is assessing vulnerability to crime (Johnson, 1994). The assessment should incorporate a study of past incidents as well as the particular business and the surrounding community. With assistance from law enforcement personnel, this assessment should attempt to identify crime patterns and incidents occurring on the premises and in the immediate neighborhood. The nature of a business and its location, services, hours of operation, and so forth, should be assessed. Previously discussed studies have identified restaurants, especially fast-food restaurants, and service stations as being particularly vulnerable to crime and disruptions.

SUMMARY

We live in a world where many people feel unimportant or disconnected. A person's work often defines his or her relationship with and importance to society. If workers feel threatened on the job or have dysfunctional lives, violence in the workplace will continue to pose a threat. It is important to recognize that no institution is immune from violence. Therefore, planning and understanding are crucial if such threats are to be diverted. People victimized in the workplace or on private property may have legal recourse if they can establish that there was negligence on the part of the property owner or manager.

KEY TERMS AND CONCEPTS

Americans with Disabilities
  Act (ADA)
Baron, Anthony
Business risk predictors
Centers for Disease Control and
  Prevention
Corporate downsizing
Equal Employment Opportunity
  Commission (EEOC)
Foreseeability
Fraud doctrine

Legal duty
Negligent hiring
Negligent supervision
  or retention
Negligent training
Premises liability
Respondeat superior doctrine
Sexual harassment
Special relationship
Targeted Human Resource
  Approach (THRA)

DISCUSSION QUESTIONS AND LEARNING ACTIVITIES

1. List the types of workplace violence discussed by the State of California Department of Industrial Relations/OSHA.
2. List different sources of workplace violence.
3. In the cases discussed in Focus 5–1 and Focus 5–2, what could the organizations have done to prevent the harassment and/or violence?
4. What are some personal indicators (profile) of a potentially violent employee?
5. Visit a corporation or institution (hospital, post office, etc.) and interview a security manager on what programs have been implemented to address the threat of workplace violence. What evidence is there of use of the THRA model?
6. Conduct a search of news articles in major newspapers and analyze their reports of violence in the workplace. Try to determine the reasons for the violence and the type of offender.

7. Visit a law library and search the jury verdicts for your state on trials pertaining to premises liability and crime. List the types of businesses or locations where the victimizations occurred to determine whether they are located in high-crime areas.

8. Conduct a class study of events of workplace violence. Collect cases and news articles and determine whether any of the profiles or characteristics of violent employees discussed in this chapter were present.

9. Discuss the two types of claims arising from sexual harassment cases. Search news articles for cases of sexual harassment. Discuss these cases in class.

10. Why is domestic violence a threat to the workplace? Are some work environments more susceptible to violence than others?

11. Discuss the relationship between workplace violence and foreseeability.

12. Explain the association of bullying and harassment to workplace violence.

WEB SOURCES

Centers for Disease Control and Prevention. www.cdc.gov/page.do
U.S. Department of Labor. www.osha.gov/sltc/workplaceviolence/
   index.html
Violence in the Workplace. www.cdc.gov/niosh/violcont.html

RECOMMENDED READINGS

Baron, Anthony. 2001. *Violence in the Workplace: A Prevention and Management Guide for Businesses*, 2nd ed. New York: Pathfinder Publishing.

Christensen, Loren. 2005. *Surviving Workplace Violence: What to Do Before a Violent Incident; What to Do When the Violence Explodes.* Chicago, IL: Paladin Press.

Drobac, Jennifer Ann. 2004. Sexual Harassment Law: History, Cases, and Theory (Carolina Academic Press Law Casebook). Durham, NC: Carolina Academic Press.

Gilbert, Steven, and Maureen Harrison, ed. *Sexual Harassment Decisions of the United States Supreme Court.* Carlsbad, CA: Excellent Books.

Goldschmidt, Jona, and Irvin H. Perline. 2003. *The Psychology and Law of Workplace Violence: A Handbook for Mental Health Professionals and Employers.* New York: C. C. Thomas.

Johnny, Lee. 2004. *Addressing Domestic Violence in the Workplace.* Amherst, MA: Human Resource Development Press.

McElhaney, Marc. 2004. *Aggression in the Workplace: Preventing and Managing High-Risk Behavior.* Bloomington, IN: Authorhouse.

Moses, Daniel. 2004. *A Descriptive Study of Issues Associated with Sexual Harassment in the Workplace.* Chicago, IL: Cork Hill Press.

REFERENCES

Ackridge v. Philadelphia Department of Human Resources, W.L. 184421 (E.D. Pa., 1994).

Anfuso, Dawn. 1994. Deflecting Workplace Violence. *Personnel Journal* 73:10.

Bains, Camille. 2000. Violence, Abuse against Nurses a Serious Problem: Nurses, Survey. *National News* (Alberta, Canada).

Baron, A. 1993. *Violence in the Workplace: A Prevention and Management Guide for Business.* San Jose, CA: Pathfinders Publishing.

Bryant v. Livigni, 250 Ill. App. 3rd. 303 9 (1993).

Burke, T. 1991. *The Relationship between Dispatcher Stress and Social Support, Job Satisfaction and Locus of Control.* PhD diss., City University of New York.

California Chamber of Commerce. 2005. http://www.calchamber.com/Pages/Default.aspx (accessed July 10, 2005).

California Department of Industrial Relations, Division of Occupational Safety and Health Administration. 2001. *Guidelines for Workplace Security.* San Francisco, CA: California Department of Industrial Relations.

Centers for Disease Control and Prevention. 2005. *Violence in the Workplace.* Atlanta, GA. cdcinfo@cdc.gov

Collier and Associates. 1995. *Defining and Avoiding Sexual Harassment,* Dallas, Texas, 1995. http://collierlaw.com/

De Coster, Stacy, Sarah Beth Estes, and Charles W. Mueller. 1999. Routine Activities and Sexual Harassment in the Workplace. *Work and Occupations* 26:21–49.

DiLorenzo, Louis P., and Darren J. Carroll. 1995. Screening Applicants for a Safer Workplace (Part 2). *Human Resources Magazine* 40:55.

Doe v. First Gibraltar Bank, 36 Atla, L. Rep (1993).

Duffy v. City of Oceanside, 179 Cal. App. 3rd 666 (1986).

Fein, Robert A., Bryan Vassekul, and Gwen A. Holden. 1995. *Threat Assessment: An Approach to Prevent Targeted Violence.* Washington, DC: U.S. Department of Justice, National Institute of Justice.

Fox, James, and Jack Levin. 1994. Mass Murder—America's Menace. Cited in Worker's Despair May Fuel Killings. *Sarasota Herald-Tribune,* September 24, 34.

Gonzales v. Southwest Security and Protection Agency, Inc., 100 N.M. 54 New Mex. Ct. App. (1983).

Greenfield v. Spectrum Investment Corp., 174 Cal. App. 3rd 111 (1985).

Hall, Mimi. 1992. Abortion Foes Target Doctors. *USA Today,* August 21, 36.

Harrington, Katherine L., and Eric J. Gai. 1996. Research on Workplace Violence, Summary Report. In *Workplace Violence: An Increasing Problem in Our Society,* by Michael B. Wishes, ed. Master's thesis, California Lutheran University.

Howe, N., and B. Strauss. 1993. *Abort, Retry, Ignore, Fail?* New York: Vintage Books.

Johnson, Dennis. 1994. Breaking Point: The Workplace Violence Epidemic and What to Do About It. *Corporate Security* 20:26.

Johnson, Jewelle and Janine Elizabeth Toner. 2006. Dealing with Anger in the Workplace: Avoiding Liability for Workplace Violence. *Construction Business Owner.*

Jones, Del. 1996. Managers Study Up for Downsizing. *USA Today,* February 19.

Kelleher, M. D. 1996. *Profiling the Lethal Employee.* Westport, CT: Greenwood Publishing.

Lopez v. Rouse Co., 37 Atla, L. Rep. (1994).

Martin, Eric. 2005. Doctor Must Pay in Bullying Case; Heart Surgeon Owes a Former Co-worker $325,000 to Cover Lost Wages, Jury Says. *Indianapolis Star*, March 5.

Mary M. v. City of Los Angeles, 54 Cal. 3rd 202 (1991).

McCune, Jenny C. 1994. Companies Grapple with Workplace Violence. *Management Review*, March.

Meadows, Robert J. 1990. Violence in the Workplace: Establishing the Nexus between Security Practices and Premises Liability. *Security Management* 13:30–32.

Metcalfe, Coll. 1999. More Firms Act to Boost Security for Employees. *Los Angeles Times*, B-1.

Morris, Frank, and Teresa L. Jakubowski. 1995. ADA Places Employers of Mentally Ill in a Bind: Companies Risk Violating the Disabilities Act If They Dismiss a Worker Who May Be Dangerous. *National Law Journal* 17:33.

Namie, Gary. 2003. Report on Abusive Workplaces. The Workplace Bullying and Trauma Institute. www.bullyinginstitute.org/home/2003results.pdf (accessed July 2005).

National Institute for Occupational Safety and Health (NIOSH). 2002. *VIOLENCE Occupational Hazards in Hospitals.* Washington, DC: U.S. Department of Health and Human Services.

Northwestern National Life Insurance. 1993. *Fear and Violence in the Workplace. A Survey Documenting the Experiences of American Workers.* New York: Northwestern National Life Insurance.

O'Connor, Thomas R. 1997. Social Correlates of Workplace Violence within the Fast Food Domain: A Qualitative Analysis. *Security Administration* 20:1.

Quirk, James H. 1993. Human Relations Face Legal Aspects of Workplace Violence. *Human Resources Magazine* 38:11.

Richardson, Scott. 1993. Workplace Homicides in Texas, 1990–1991. *Compensation and Working Conditions* 45:1–6.

Roberts, Sally. 1994. Curbing Workplace Violence: $12 Million Settlement Stresses Need to Act. *Business Insurance* 28.

Smith, S. L. 1993. Violence in the Workplace: A Cry for Help. *Occupational Hazards* 55.

Stewart v. Federated Department Stores, Conn. S.Ct. 15124 (1995).

Timm, Howard, and Callie J. Chandler. 1995. *Combating Workplace Violence.* Washington, DC: U.S. Department of Justice, Bureau of Justice Statistics.

Underwriters Ins. Co. v. Purdie, 145 Cal. App. 3rd. 57 (1983).

U.S. Department of Justice. December 2001. *Violence in the Workplace 1993–1999.* Washington, DC: Bureau of Justice Statistics.

Workplace Violence Prevention Institute. 1994. *Complete Workplace Violence Prevention Manual.* Newport Beach, CA: Workplace Violence Prevention Institute.

Yunker v. Honeywell, Inc., 496 N.W. 2nd. 419 Minn. (1993).

6

School Violence
and Victimization

LEARNING OBJECTIVES

After studying this chapter, you will:

- Understand the major research findings on school violence.
- Learn why some youth become violent.
- Understand how schools influence violence and student disruption.
- Identify the warning signs of violent youth.
- Become familiar with the strategies for controlling school violence.

INTRODUCTION

On April 16, 2007, on the Virginia Tech campus in Blacksburg, Virginia, student Seung-Hui Cho killed 32 people and wounded many more, before committing suicide. The school shooting was the deadliest school shooting in U.S. history. Cho viewed himself as a victim. He was a South Korean who moved to the United States at age eight. Cho had a history of mental disorders and relationship problems, who prior to the shooting, had been accused of stalking female students.

At the high school level, an armed 15-year-old youth entered his school with three guns and fired 51 bullets at students and staff. When it was over, two students were dead and 22 injured. Back home, the police found the boy's parents also shot dead. It soon turned out that the accused assailant, Kip Kinkel, had been arrested the day before for trying to buy a stolen weapon.

Public schools and universities confront a number of challenges, such as how to educate students and provide a safe learning environment for students and staff. Despite overcrowding and other distractions in some districts, our schools are generally doing a good job, educating and providing a safe environment for our children. However, recent violence in some of our schools has dispelled the notion that schools are safe. The 1999 school shootings at Columbine High School in Littleton, Colorado, in which 12 students and one teacher were fatally gunned down by two students, and a shooting at a suburban high school in Conyers, Georgia, where a student gunman opened fire on a group of students, reject this view of school safety.

A number of shooting incidents and acts of violence have been directed at teachers and students throughout the nation following these shootings, and undoubtedly there will be more. In some communities, gang intimidation and drug dealing on campus are added to the school violence scenario. But we must remember that schools are a collection of young people, most with serious aspirations to achieve in academic or extracurricular activities. School is a place of growth, a rite of passage before jumping into the uncertainties of adulthood. And for a few, it is a stressful environment, full of negativity and empty experiences, leading to violence or dropping out.

Schools, like workplaces, are miniature societies bringing together people from varied backgrounds, personalities, and cultural experiences. In other words, stress, mental illness, disruptive behavior, and poor attitudes enter the school doors with students. Whatever the source of that violence, whether from the home, the community, or elsewhere, the effects of violence on learning are so destructive that educators are placing school security on the education agenda. Teachers cannot teach and students cannot learn in an environment of intimidation and fear.

RESEARCH ON SCHOOL CRIME AND VIOLENCE

Studies of school violence have variously used such terms as *teen aggression, conflict, delinquency, conduct disorders, criminal behavior*, and *antisocial behavior* to describe the sources of the problem. In simple terms, drugs, hormonal imbalances, conflicts with peers or parents, rejection of authority, and so forth fuel the anger many youth harbor. If the anger is not displaced at home, on the streets, or in some legitimate activities, then the schools are targeted.

Because of the opportunities presented by some school environments, school violence has increased dramatically in the past decade.

A study of 10 inner-city public high schools in California, Louisiana, New Jersey, and Illinois funded by the National Institute of Justice (Sheley, McGee, and Wright, 1995) found that one in five inner-city students (one of three males) surveyed had been a victim of a shooting or stabbing while at school or in transit to or from school. Most students knew someone who carried a weapon to school; one in four reported carrying weapons while in school. The National Center for Education Statistics reported that 10 percent of U.S. public schools experienced at least one serious violent crime in the 1996–1997 school year. These incidents included murder, rape or other types of sexual battery, suicide, a physical attack or fight with a weapon, or robbery. There were nearly 190,000 physical attacks or fights without a weapon, as well as high numbers of thefts or larceny and vandalism.

The use or sale of drugs, as well as gang membership, was part of the students' experiences. Although only 4 percent of inner-city school students in one study reported using hard drugs, 13 percent reported either dealing drugs or working for a drug dealer (Sheley, McGee, and Wright, 1995). The National Parents' Resource Institute for Drug Education reported in 1994 that almost 1 in 13 (7.4 percent) of all high school students carried a gun to school in 1993–1994, that 13.8 percent joined a gang, and that 35 percent threatened to harm another student or a teacher.

In 1978, the **National Institute of Education** undertook the first comprehensive study of school crime and safety. Its purpose was to investigate the extent of student and teacher victimization. This study collected data from more than 4,000 principals, 31,000 students, and nearly 24,000 teachers representing rural and urban schools (Berman and McLaughlin, 1978:35–36). Some results of the study are reported here. Although students spend only about 25 percent of their active time in school, about 36 percent of all robberies of teenagers occur in schools. Campus robberies may seem less severe than those occurring on our streets, but to some students, it is a traumatic experience. Thus, taking a student's lunch money or clothing article under the threat of violence qualifies as robbery. The problem of school violence is more serious in cities with populations of more than 500,000. The findings from the **Safe School Study** reported in *School Crisis Prevention and Response* include the following (National School Safety Center, 1990):

- Approximately 7 percent of high school students stay at home at least one day each month because they fear being victimized.

- Approximately 24 percent of students avoid three or more places at school because they fear being victimized.

- More than 29 percent of teachers are threatened with physical harm each month.
- More than 28 percent of teachers hesitated in the month preceding the study to confront misbehaving students because they feared for their own safety.

The authors of the report concluded that crime, violence, and the fear of both are present in our schools, especially in schools located in large cities. In 1987, the American School Health Association (1989) surveyed approximately 11,000 eighth- and tenth-grade students in 20 states about a wide range of issues concerning school experiences. Of the students surveyed, about 2 percent admitted carrying a handgun to school at least once a year and 33 percent of those had carried a pistol daily; about 8 percent said they had carried knives. The potential for violence is great, especially when more than one-third of tenth graders reported that "bullies" and others had threatened to hurt them while at school. Clearly, juvenile victimization on school property and in the surrounding community is a major concern.

A study by Sheley, McGee, and Wright (1995) asked students for their perceptions regarding the following: the difficulty of obtaining drugs or alcohol at school; the prevalence of street gangs in school; and the degree to which students fear being attacked at school. The findings are based on a nationally representative sample of more than 10,000 youths who were interviewed from January through June 1989 and who attended school during the 6 months before the interview. Some findings of the study follow:

- Students older than age 17 were generally less likely to be victims of crimes at school than were younger students.
- Students living in families that had moved three or more times in the preceding 5 years were nearly twice as likely to have experienced a criminal victimization as were students who had moved no more than once.
- Victimization by violent crime at school had no consistent relationship to the income level of the victims' families. For property crime, however, students in families with annual incomes of $50,000 or more were more likely to be victimized than students whose families earned less than $10,000 a year.
- Public high school students (9 percent) were more likely to be crime victims than were private school students (7 percent).
- High school seniors were the least likely students to be crime victims. Ninth-grade students were more likely to be crime victims than were students in all higher grades.

- In the first half of 1989, about 30 percent of the students interviewed believed that marijuana was easy to obtain at school, 9 percent said crack was easy to obtain, and 11 percent claimed cocaine was readily available.

- A larger proportion of males than females knew whether drugs were available in school.

- Similar percentages of black (67 percent) and white (69 percent) students claimed that drugs were available at school; these students were significantly more likely than students belonging to other racial groups to say that drugs could be obtained.

- Victims of violent crimes were about three times as likely as nonvictims to report that they were afraid of being attacked at school (53 percent versus 19 percent). The overwhelming majority of students who had not been victimized reported no fear of attack, either at school (81 percent) or on the way to and from school (87 percent).

- Students who had been robbed or assaulted during the previous 6 months were more likely to avoid certain places at school, such as stairwells and restrooms, out of fear of attack or harm (25 percent) than were those who had experienced a theft or attempted theft (10 percent).

- Six percent of students indicated that they avoided some place in or around their school because they thought that someone might attack or harm them there. School restrooms were most often mentioned as a place students avoided (3 percent), followed by school hallways (2 percent).

- About the same percentage of male and female students feared an attack at school and avoided certain places because of that fear. However, female students expressed more fear of attack while going to and from school than did male students.

- Seventy-nine percent of students said no gangs existed at their schools; 15 percent reported gangs, and another 5 percent were not sure whether gangs existed at their schools.

- Of those students who said there were or could be gangs at their school, 37 percent reported that the gang members never fought at school, 19 percent claimed that gang members fought once or twice a year, and 12 percent said that members fought once or twice a week or even every day.

- The 15 percent of students who reported the presence of gangs at their schools were more likely than students from schools without gangs to be victims of some type of crime (12 percent versus 8 percent, respectively).

A study by the **U.S. Department of Education** of a nationally representative sample of 1,234 regular schools in the 50 states and the District of Columbia revealed some interesting data on school violence (Dwyer, Osher, and Warger, 1998). One in 10 public schools experienced at least one of those crimes, which occurred at a rate of 53 incidents per 100,000 students, during 1996–1997. Serious violent crimes were more likely to occur in large schools. Thirty-three percent of schools with 1,000 or more students experienced a serious violent crime compared with 4 to 9 percent in small- and medium-sized schools. Large schools also had a ratio of 90 incidents per 100,000 public school students, compared with medium-sized schools that had 38 serious violent crimes per 100,000.

Interviews with students have revealed perceptions on the causes of violence among youth. The following list and its order is based on interviews with youth in the nation's most violent neighborhoods, conducted by the National Campaign to Stop Violence (Anderson, 2000).

Top 10 causes of violence in the order that children cited them:

The media
Substance abuse
Gangs
Unemployment
Weapons
Poverty
Peer pressure
Broken homes
Poor family environment/bad neighborhoods
Intolerance/ignorance

Higher percentages of middle and high schools experienced serious violent crime than did elementary schools. Schools in central cities, although more likely to experience serious violent crime than those in towns and rural locales, did not differ significantly from urban fringe schools in terms of the percentage of schools reporting at least one incident. City and urban fringe schools reported a higher ratio of violence than did those in towns or rural areas. School size along with such characteristics as minority enrollment and percentage of students eligible for free or reduced school meals are variables associated with levels of reported violence (see Table 6–1). In addition, schools were more likely to take serious disciplinary action against physical attacks or fights among students. Forty-eight percent of public schools (approximately 39,600 schools) took at least one serious disciplinary action

TABLE 6–1 PERCENTAGE OF PUBLIC SCHOOLS EXPERIENCING INCIDENTS OF CRIME PER 1,000 STUDENTS SCHOOL FY 2005–2006.

School characteristic	Violent incidents[1]				Serious violent incidents[2]			Theft[3]			Other incidents[4]		
	Number of schools	Percent of schools	Number of incidents	Rate per 1,000 students	Percent of schools	Number of incidents	Rate per 1,000 students	Percent of schools	Number of incidents	Rate per 1,000 students	Percent of schools	Number of incidents	Rate per 1,000 students
Total	83,200	77.7	1,489,400	31.2	17.1	59,100	1.2	46.0	242,700	5.1	68.2	458,900	9.6
School level[5]													
Primary	48,600	67.3	561,700	25.2	11.0	19,300!	0.9!	27.8	36,000	1.6	54.8	105,800	4.7
Middle	15,500	94.4	522,200	51.6	25.2	18,900	1.9	68.7	79,300	7.8	87.8	120,800	11.9
High school	11,700	95.2	313,500	25.7	31.8	17,500	1.4	85.6	105,500	8.7	93.6	192,000	15.7
Combined	7,400	83.5	92,000	29.2	17.4	3,500	1.1	54.9	21,900	7.0	75.0	40,400	12.8
Enrollment size													
Less than 300	20,800	63.7	148,400	34.5	11.4	12,000	2.8	29.6	‡	‡	53.2	52,800	12.3
300–499	23,800	77.3	325,000	34.0	11.7	6,800	0.7	37.2	31,600	3.3	63.4	63,600	6.7
500–999	29,300	82.1	609,700	30.9	19.2	21,100	1.1	52.1	89,800	4.5	74.2	151,800	7.7
1,000 or more	9,300	96.5	406,400	28.6	37.2	19,100	1.3	85.8	102,800	7.2	95.1	190,700	13.4
Urbanicity													
City	21,000	82.3	547,400	38.1	23.9	29,800	2.1	46.8	77,500	5.4	72.7	158,900	11.1
Urban fringe	27,600	78.2	524,700	27.1	15.9	16,800	0.9	46.9	89,800	4.6	69.9	162,000	8.4
Town	8,200	82.2	129,400	31.9	15.2	3,700	0.9	48.4	23,000	5.7	70.6	38,500	9.5
Rural	26,400	72.3	287,900	28.7	13.6	8,800	0.9	43.7	52,300	5.2	62.1	99,500	9.9
Percent minority enrollment[6]													
Less than 5 percent	16,600	71.6	174,000	26.9	13.1	5,700	0.9	42.8	31,100	4.8	62.4	55,300	8.6
5–20 percent	20,600	73.5	269,900	22.9	15.7	11,100	0.9	43.4	60,900	5.2	63.4	109,200	9.3
20–50 percent	18,600	79.7	326,200	28.4	16.6	15,700	1.4	47.9	63,300!	5.5!	71.5	109,700	9.6
50 percent or more	25,600	82.9	677,500	39.9	21.6	25,700	1.5	48.4	81,900	4.8	71.9	171,600	10.1

Percent of students eligible for free or reduced-price lunch												
0–20 percent	19,200	68.0	209,600	16.4	12.5	7,100	0.6	45.9	63,100	4.9	61.7	101,600	8.0
21–50 percent	27,600	79.7	501,700	30.1	19.2	16,400	1.0	52.5	97,100	5.8	72.3	165,900	10.1
More than 50 percent	36,400	81.4	778,100	42.3	18.0	35,600	1.9	41.0	82,400	4.5	68.5	185,500	10.3
Student/teacher ratio[7]												
Less than 12	42,200	73.0	598,300	33.2	14.3	22,100	1.2	40.1	89,220	5.0	62.3	161,900	9.0
12–16	27,000	82.4	550,700	30.8	17.1	23,800	1.3	50.6	94,630	5.3	71.9	169,800	9.5
More than 16	14,000	83.0	340,400	28.6	25.8	13,200	1.1	54.9	58,930	4.9	78.8	127,300	10.7

!Interpret data with caution.

‡Reporting standards not met.

[1]Violent incidents include rape or attempted rape, sexual battery other than rape, physical attack or fight with or without a weapon, threat of physical attack with or without a weapon, and robbery with or without a weapon. Serious violent incidents are also included in violent incidents.

[2]Serious violent incidents include rape or attempted rape, sexual battery other than rape, physical attack or fight with a weapon, threat of physical attack with a weapon, and robbery with or without a weapon.

[3]Theft/larceny (taking things worth over $10 without personal confrontation) was defined for respondents as "the unlawful taking of another person's property without personal confrontation, threat, violence, or bodily harm. Included are pocket picking, stealing a purse or backpack (if left unattended or no force was used to take it from owner), theft from a building, theft from a motor-vehicle or of motor vehicle parts or accessories, theft of bicycles, theft from vending machines, and all other types of thefts."

[4]Other incidents include possession of a firearm or explosive device, possession of a knife or sharp object, distribution, possession, or use of illegal drugs or alcohol, and vandalism.

[5]Primary schools are defined as schools in which the lowest grade is not higher than grade 3 and the highest grade is not higher than grade 8. Middle schools are defined as schools in which the lowest grade is not lower than grade 4 and the highest grade is not higher than grade 9. High schools are defined as schools in which the lowest grade is not lower than grade 9. Combined schools include all other combinations of grades, including K–12 schools.

[6]These estimates exclude data from the 73 schools that did not report estimates of student race/ethnicity.

[7]Student/teacher ratio was calculated by dividing the total number of students enrolled in the school by the total number of full-time-equivalent (FTE) teachers and aides. The total number of FTE teachers and aides is a combination of the full-time and part-time teachers and aides, including special education teachers and aides, with an adjustment for part-time status.

Note: Responses were provided by the principal or the person most knowledgeable about crime and safety issues at the school. "At school" was defined for respondents to include activities that happen in school buildings, on school grounds, on school buses, and at places that hold school-sponsored events or activities. Respondents were instructed to respond only for those times that were during normal school hours or when school activities or events were in session, unless the survey specified otherwise. Population size is 83,200 public schools. Detail may not sum to totals because of rounding. Estimates of number of incidents and schools are rounded to the nearest 100.

Source: U.S. Department of Education, National Center for Education Statistics, 2005–2006 School Survey on Crime and Safety (SSOCS), 2006.

against a student—including suspensions lasting 5 days or more, removals with no services (i.e., expulsions), and transfers to specialized schools—for specific offenses during the 2005–2006 school year.

The offenses included physical attacks or fights; insubordination; distribution, possession, or use of alcohol; distribution, possession, or use of illegal drugs; use or possession of a weapon other than a firearm or explosive device; and use or possession of a firearm or explosive device. Of the 830,700 serious disciplinary actions taken during the 2005–2006 school year, 74 percent were suspensions for 5 days or more, 5 percent were removals with no services, and 20 percent were transfers to specialized schools (NCES, 2007). In Figure 6–1[1] we see an increase in firearms and explosive devices over the years, while other types have been basically the same.

FIGURE 6–1 PERCENTAGE OF PUBLIC SCHOOLS THAT TOOK A SERIOUS DISCIPLINARY ACTION, BY TYPE OF OFFENSE: VARIOUS SCHOOL YEARS, 1999–2000, 2003–2004, AND 2005–2006

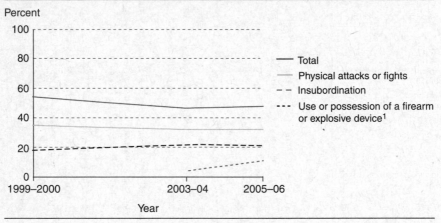

Note: Responses were provided by the principal or the person most knowledgeable about crime and safety issues at the school. Serious disciplinary actions include removals with no continuing services for at least the remainder of the school year, transfers to specialized schools for disciplinary reasons, and out-of-school suspensions lasting 5 or more days, but less than the remainder of the school year. Respondents were instructed to respond only for those times that were during normal school hours or when school activities or events were in session, unless the survey specified otherwise. Population sizes of public schools are 82,000 in 1999–2000, 80,500 in 2003–2004, and 83,200 in 2005–2006.

Source: U.S. Department of Education, National Center for Education Statistics, 1999–2000, 2003–2004, and 2005–2006 School Survey on Crime and Safety (SSOCS), 2000, 2004, and 2006.

---

[1]Data not available prior to 2003–2004.

Despite a recent wave of high-profile incidents of violence committed in schools across the United States, statistics show that violent crime—particularly homicide—is relatively rare in our schools. From July 1, 2005, through June 30, 2006, there were 35 school-associated violent deaths in elementary and secondary schools in the United States. In each school year, youth were over 50 times more likely to be murdered and were over 150 times more likely to commit suicide when they were away from school than at school (NCES, 2007).

TEACHERS AT RISK

Students are not the only victims of violence and crime at school. Over the 5-year period from 1998 to 2003, teachers were the victims of approximately 234,000 total nonfatal crimes at school, including 144,000 thefts and 90,000 violent crimes (rape, sexual assault, robbery, aggravated assault, and simple assault). The average annual rate of violent victimization for teachers varied according to their sex, instructional level, and location. Over the 5-year period from 1998 to 2002, male teachers were more likely than female teachers to be victims of violent crimes, and senior high school and middle/junior high school teachers were more likely than elementary school teachers to be victims of violent crimes (National Center of Educational Statistics, 2003). In addition to the personal toll that violence may take on teachers, those who worry about their safety may have difficulty teaching and may leave the profession altogether (Elliott, Hamburg, and Williams, 1998). Information on the number of crimes against teachers at school can help show the extent of the problem.

Although the majority of teachers believe that they are unlikely to be victims of violence in and around school, the opposite is true. Most teachers feel safe in their schools during the day, but after school hours, many teachers, especially those in urban areas, do not. Women and younger, less experienced teachers are targets, but they are not the primary victims of violence among school staff. Teachers who are considered to be strict, insisting that students adhere to rigorous academic and behavioral standards, are most at risk of being victimized. Thirty-eight percent of teachers and 57 percent of students rank strict teachers as more at risk of victimization than any other members of the teaching staff (*American Teacher*, 1993).

Another dilemma confronting teachers is their response to violence. In other words, teachers are not only concerned about being victimized; they are also concerned about being sued if they intervene in student fights or acts of violence. They may not intervene aggressively because of fear of being accused of child abuse. In this age of litigation, some parents are eager to sue teachers for the slightest mishandling of their child, even if teachers may be justified in their actions.

EXPLAINING SCHOOL VIOLENCE

The troubled youngster becomes increasingly isolated, leaving him—the typical offender is male—with no counterbalance for his violent thoughts. He wants to make people pay attention to him. If he has seen enough examples of violence and bizarre behavior on television and in movies, video games, and comic books, similar feats may seem a good way to impress others. Being kicked out of class may trigger an impulsive act of aggression.

—Richard Harding, Vice president and clinical professor
of pediatrics and psychiatry at the University of South Carolina
School of Medicine, Columbia.

A number of theories explain violence and deviance in youth (see, generally, Seigel and Senna, 1999). A full discussion of these theories is beyond the scope of this book. Suffice it to say that many offenders are also victims of biological, social, and psychological conditions that drive their propensity toward violence. This is not to say that we should excuse violent behavior because of background or social conditions, but we must recognize that these trappings do influence antisocial as well as proper behavior. Likewise, we cannot predict who will turn violent or when.

We can only look at the research and past cases to make any kind of projection as to who may be on the road to violence. Over the years, however, attempts have been made to identify factors that may lead to violence and victimization in some youth. For purposes of this discussion, the risk factors are presented in eight categories. Children suffering from these risks are also victims because many of these conditions are beyond their control.

The first factor is referred to as **character risks**. In this group, researchers hypothesize that birth complications result in brain dysfunction and associated neurological and neuropsychological deficits that directly and indirectly predispose an individual to violent behavior (Moffitt and Silva, 1988). Birth complications, for example, could lead to cognitive deficits that translate to school failure, occupational failure, and, ultimately, engagement in violent behavior. Similarly, birth complications may contribute to a lack of self-control, resulting in explosive, impulsive aggression. Some of these children meet the diagnostic criteria for disorders such as **Attention**

Deficit/Hyperactivity Disorder (ADHD) or **Oppositional Defiant Disorder (ODD),** conditions where the child resists authority, often aggressively. Although these are different disorders, they have related symptoms. The former is associated with poor attention and inappropriate behaviors, while the latter is more of open defiance to authority. There exists a significant relationship between ADHD and ODD and risk for delinquency and violence (Moffitt and Silva, 1988).

In other words, many of these teens simply are unable to control themselves, and for years have constantly been criticized for their nonconformist impulsive behavior. Some of these youth resort to bullying to gain recognition or power over others. They feel that by bullying others, usually younger, weaker children, they gain a sense of satisfaction or getting even with authority (Olweus, 1994).

Some argue that violent youth are victims of environmental toxicants. A toxicologist researcher from the University of California at Santa Barbara argues that heavy metals and pesticides might hamper mental development and drive hyperactivity and impulsive behavior of youth. In other words, lead poisoning, which has already been established as a cause for poor mental development in youth, might be the culprit in teen violence. The researcher believes that hair samples should be taken from violent juvenile offenders to determine if such a relationship exists (Kisken, 1999).

A second risk factor is **underdeveloped mental abilities**. This factor is related to low verbal IQ, which ultimately leads to poor school achievement. This risk factor differs from the previous risk factor in that many children with ADHD have above average intelligence. Yet, children who do poorly in school, who cannot keep pace with their peers, are more likely to be truant or to stop attending altogether (Cairns, Cairns, and Neckerman, 1989). When they are not attending school, these youth are usually hanging out with others who are truant or who have dropped out of school. These deviant groups provide a setting where the opportunity for engaging in delinquent and violent behavior is significantly greater than it would be if a youngster enjoyed school and was doing well.

A third risk factor is the **presence of early aggressive behaviors**. There exists a relationship between aggressive and violent behavior and childhood impulsivity and child temperament. In other words, children who are aggressive and violent in adolescence most often exhibited the same behavior in kindergarten and first grade. Research has indicated that early conduct problems in kindergarten and first grade lead to poor school achievement in later grades, which, in turn, leads to delinquency in adolescence (Tremblay et al., 1992). A "difficult" temperament may be the cause of this continuum. Thus, a temperament characterized by high activity levels, inflexibility, easy frustration, impulsive behavior, and distraction usually will render a child more noncompliant and out of control. This may also relate to mental conditions such as ADHD, previously discussed.

A fourth risk factor is **family relationships and influences**. Children are socialized from a very young age about how to handle frustration, how to react to limits and consequences, and how to solve problems effectively and resolve disputes. Most of this socialization first occurs at home and in the family. The evidence is clear: parents of aggressive children punish more frequently, but inconsistently and ineffectively. They also tend to negatively reinforce coercive and manipulative child behavior and fail to adequately reinforce positive, prosocial behavior. Psychologists argue that raising boys to be strong and silent is promoting the outbreak of school shootings and violence, subsequently causing the smoldering climate of despair among male teenagers. In other words, American boys are reared largely in keeping with the traditional code of male toughness, which encourages boys to take action while inhibiting expressions of feeling and gestures of physical affection.

Related to this concept is the **coercive style of parent–child interaction**. This occurs when parents reinforce coercive child behavior and are inadvertently reinforced themselves—by giving in to their coercive child. In other words, children learn that aggressive behavior often leads to parents' giving them what they want. By reacting to a parental request with an aggressive response that is modeled on parental problem solving, "the child escapes punishment, controls the social exchange, and continues desired behaviors" (Patterson, 1992). One risk is that this learned style of interaction may be generalized by the child from home to school, where it becomes part of a child's social repertoire with peers and teachers (Fraser, 1996). If a child learns from parents to respond to authority with aggression and manipulation (as in the case of bullies), he or she will have difficulty interacting successfully in a school environment where other adults and authority figures make daily requests of the child. Obviously, parental harshness can increase the risk of delinquency, possibly by increasing child resentment and defiance, which are then expressed through truancy, poor school performance, and antisocial behavior. It is well researched that parental abuse and neglect cause delinquency and antisocial behavior. The case of Rod Ferrell, detailed in Focus 6–1, referred to as the vampire killer, illustrates a violent youth who was exposed to a poor family environment. He was sentenced to death in 1998 for the brutal killing of the parents of one of his followers.

Fifth is the **exposure to violence and victimization.** Evidence is quickly mounting that exposure to violence, and particularly victimization by violence, is associated with increased risk of perpetrating violence (Thornberry, 1994). One study showed that adolescents victimized by

---

FOCUS 6–1 Case of Rod Ferrell

Rod Ferrell was born in 1980. His mother was Sondra Ferrell, a 17-year-old married to Rick Ferrell, also a teen. Rick filed for a divorce and joined the military, while Sondra kept the child. Her parents also looked after Rod, who claimed Sondra's father—his grandfather—raped him when he was 5 years old. Rod also claimed that as a young child, he was exposed to occult rituals and human sacrifices and was introduced to the "Dungeons & Dragons" role-playing game. Sondra eventually remarried and moved frequently with Rod before leaving him in Murray, Kentucky, and moving with her new husband to Michigan. His mother's new husband allegedly told Rod that they were never coming back, and Sondra apparently became so upset that she divorced the man and moved back to Murray to be with Rod. (Her second husband also allegedly engaged in satanic rituals.) Around this time, Rod began to undergo some sort of transformation. He walked in cemeteries at night, cut himself so others could drink his blood, and told people he was a 500-year-old vampire named "Vesago." His schoolwork slipped, and he began flagrantly disobeying his school's policies, skipping class, smoking on campus, and generally defying teachers and school officials. He also indulged in playing "Vampire: The Masquerade," a realistic role-playing game in which players act out vampiric scenarios in real time. His mother allowed him to stay out all night, use drugs, and skip school, and he frequently spent time with a young man named Stephen Murphy, who brought the teenage Ferrell into the vampire world and "crossed him over," turning him into a presumptive vampire and giving him his name. By the spring of 1996, Rod was also talking long-distance to Heather Wendorf, who apparently told Rod that her parents were hurting her and that she wanted him to come get her, but that he would have to kill them to do so. In September 1996, Murphy attacked Ferrell, who refused treatment when taken to a local hospital. Murphy was convicted for the attack. Shortly after, Rod's mother Sondra was charged with soliciting a minor—Murphy's 14-year-old brother—to whom she wrote love letters, imploring him to "cross her over" and have her as his vampire bride.

---

assault were more likely to have a history of criminal activity or to develop criminal behavior subsequent to their assault (Rivara et al., 1995). Singer et al. (1997) showed that even after controlling for the effects of demographic variables, parental monitoring, and watching aggressive television shows, recent violence exposure was the most significant predictor of self-reported violent behavior among third- to eighth-grade students, accounting for 24 percent of the overall variance. Farrell and Bruce (1997) also showed that exposure to **community violence** for urban sixth graders was related to their self-reported violent behavior, although they did not find increases over time in the frequency of violent behavior related to violence exposure. Many of our children grow up in environments where

they see violence daily. This is particularly true in gang-infested urban settings, where walking to school or the store becomes an exercise in victimization avoidance.

The sixth risk factor is the **role of the media and its impact on violence**.
It is estimated that by the time a child reaches the age of 18 he or she will
have witnessed more than 200,000 acts of television violence, including
33,000 murders (American Psychological Association, 1993). Violent acts,
defined as acts intended to injure or harm others, appear approximately
8 to 12 times an hour on prime-time television and about 20 times an hour
on children's programming (Sege and Dietz, 1994). There appear to be
three main effects of violence in the media. One effect is that children who
are exposed to high levels of media violence are more accepting of aggressive attitudes and, after watching violence, behave more aggressively with
peers (Centerwall, 1992). A second effect is that more chronic and long-
term exposure to violence can lead to desensitization to violence and its
consequences, as in youth exposed to the consequences of a shooting or
frequent violence. Third, children who watch a lot of violence on television
seem to develop a "mean world syndrome." In other words, viewing violence may increase a child's fear of becoming a victim of violence because
he or she comes to view the world as a mean and dangerous place.
Furthermore, younger children may have particular difficulty distinguish-
ing fantasy from reality and may not be able to differentiate science fiction
from their everyday experiences. In general, violence on television occurs
frequently and is typically inconsequential, effective, and rewarded. It is
practiced as often by the heroes as by the villains. Violence ends confrontations quickly and effectively, without the need for patience, negotiation, or
compromise (Sege and Dietz, 1994).

A seventh factor is the **general influence of our culture**. Our culture is
made up of many influences and seductions (other than the media) leading to temptations of the worst sort, especially for the emotionally insecure
teen. Wooden (1995) addresses the influences of culture and how some
youth respond by joining counterculture groups, such as the pale-faced
gothics, to gain recognition. In other words, we live in a society thriving on
a **toxic culture** (Criner, 1998). We see scantily dressed women advertising
beer and profiteers selling toys glorifying gang lifestyles (Larrubia, 1999).
Our youth are constantly bombarded with messages and images of defiance and independence in the form of tattoos, body jewelry, and clothing
resembling gang attire. Although a youth with pierced nipples and
tongue, green hair, or tattoos of Satan is not necessarily a threat to society,
these popular symbols do suggest something negative about the person.
For the delinquent computer genius in our culture, pornography and
instructions on bomb design can be downloaded from the Internet, where

novel ways to act on hatred or to harass others can also be found (Brogan, 1999). It is ironic that many youth are poisoned by the very culture that supposedly promotes values and order. In other words, there are mixed messages and contradictions present in our culture that many youth are unable to digest or understand.

A *final risk factor is the* **schools**. Research has concluded that the following school conditions are contributing sources of violence: (1) overcrowding; (2) high student-to-teacher ratios; (3) insufficient curricular and course relevance; combined with (4) low student academic achievement and apathy, which give rise to disruptiveness; (5) poor facilities design and portable buildings that both increase isolation and hamper internal communication (Rossman and Morley, 1996). In addition, the perception of violence and crime makes it difficult to attract and retain good teachers, particularly in inner-city schools. School discipline may suffer as teachers hesitate to confront misbehaving students because the teachers fear for their own safety. In addition, students are sophisticated enough to recognize a teacher's limitations with respect to using discipline or force to gain compliance and retain order in his or her classroom (Rossman and Morley, 1996).

EARLY WARNING SIGNS OF VIOLENT BEHAVIOR

Based on the previous discussion explaining youth violence, we can come to some conclusions on predicting or explaining violent behavior and victimization. Obviously, a teen who has been severely abused at home or reared in a dysfunctional family environment with criminal parents has an excellent chance of turning violent and becoming a client of the criminal justice system. Teachers are often in a pivotal position to recognize certain early warning signs indicating some internal conflict of the teen. It has been reported that troubled teens often give potential signals, such as writing a note or a journal entry or making a threat to a teacher or student. In other words, in more than half the incidents, some type of signal was given (Anderson et al., 2001).

Bullying

"Bullying is nothing but child abuse by peers," according to Peter Fonagy, an internationally recognized authority on infant and child development.

Related to the risk factors of youth violence and victimization is bullying. **School bullying** is a type of antisocial behavior associated with violence. Bullying involves students intimidating or threatening others (as in the workplace) or making students do things they do not want to do. It has been reported that the link of bullying to violent crime is clear, with 60 percent of playground bullies having a criminal conviction by age 24, and 90 percent of young juvenile offenders victimized by bullying. In more than two-thirds of school shootings, there was clear and obvious influence of bullying by social groups and individuals (Holmes, 2003).

Bullying is more common in public schools than in private schools but decreases as grade level increases. If not addressed, bullying can contribute to an environment of fear and intimidation in schools (Arnette and Walsleben, 1998; Ericson, 2001). The movement toward private school education may be attributed to the perception by some parents that private schools are safer and less intimidating for their children. In response to bullying, many states have passed laws to address harassment, intimidation, and bullying in school. The primary intent of almost all these legislative efforts is to define bullying, to establish school or district-level policy that firmly prohibits such behavior, and to communicate that policy to students and their parents.

Under federal law, specifically the No Child Left Behind law of 2001, each state must define a so-called dangerous school and allow parents to transfer their children out of them. Each state establishes its own definition of "dangerous." The courts are getting involved in bullying, as evidenced by a recent 2007 decision. The New Jersey Supreme Court ruled that anti-discrimination protections extend to schoolchildren subjected to bias-based bullying and harassment. The decision requires schools to take necessary steps to ensure that students are protected from bias-based harassment and makes clear that schools must address the entire school environment instead of merely viewing specific incidents of bullying as isolated events (*L.W. v. Toms River Regional Schools Board of Education*, 2007).

Understanding School Violence

In response to school violence and associated victimization, the U.S. Department of Education has published a guide to understanding school violence and possible warning signs of violent youth (Dwyer, Osher, and Warger, 1998). The following signs are offered as a guide:

- *Social withdrawal.* In some situations, gradual and eventually complete withdrawal from social contacts can be an important indicator of a troubled child. The withdrawal often stems from feelings of depression, rejection, or lack of confidence. Students who suddenly drop out of school activities may be experiencing problems.

- *Feelings of being alone.* Feelings of isolation and not having friends are associated with children who behave aggressively and violently. These feelings may result from divorce or other home problems.

- *Excessive feelings of rejection.* In the process of growing up, and in the course of adolescent development, many young people experience emotionally painful rejection. Children who are troubled often are isolated from their mentally healthy peers. Thus, those teens with ADHD, for example, may be cut off from others as a result of their mental state. Their responses to rejection may be violent.

- *Being a victim of violence.* Children who are victims of violence— including physical or sexual abuse—in the community, at school, or at home are sometimes at risk themselves of becoming violent toward themselves or others.

- *Feelings of being picked on and persecuted.* The youth who feels constantly picked on, teased, bullied, singled out for ridicule, and humiliated at home or school may initially withdraw socially.

- *Low school interest and poor academic performance.* Poor school achievement can be the result of many factors. It is important to consider the reasons for these behaviors.

- *Expression of violence in writings and drawings.* Children and youth often express their thoughts, feelings, desires, and intentions in their drawings and in stories, poetry, and other written expressive forms. Many children produce work about violent themes that for the most part is harmless when taken in context. However, an overrepresentation of violence in writings and drawings that is directed at specific individuals (family members, peers, or other adults) consistently over time may signal emotional problems and the potential for violence.

- *Uncontrolled anger.* Everyone gets angry; anger is a natural emotion. However, anger that is expressed frequently and intensely in response to minor irritants may signal potential violent behavior toward self or others.

- *Patterns of chronic hitting and bullying behaviors.* Children often engage in acts of shoving and mild aggression. But, when the behavior becomes constant, it may escalate into more serious behaviors.

- *History of discipline problems.* Chronic behavior and disciplinary problems both in school and at home may suggest that underlying emotional needs are not being met. These problems may cause the child to violate norms and rules, defy authority, and engage in aggressive behaviors with other children and adults.

- *Past history of violent and aggressive behavior.* Youth who show an early pattern of antisocial behavior are particularly at risk for future aggressive and antisocial behavior. Similarly, youth who engage in overt behaviors (such as bullying, generalized aggression, and defiance) and covert behaviors (such as stealing, vandalism, lying, cheating, and firesetting) are also at risk for more serious aggressive behavior. Research suggests that age of onset may be a key factor in interpreting early warning signs. Thus, children who engage in aggression and drug abuse at an early age are more likely to show violence later on than are children who begin such behavior at an older age.

- *Intolerance for differences and prejudicial attitudes.* Teens who pick on minorities, join hate groups, or victimize individuals with disabilities or health problems should be treated as exhibiting early warning signs.

- *Drug use and alcohol use.* Drug and alcohol use reduces self-control and exposes children and youth to violence, either as perpetrators, victims, or both.

- *Affiliation with gangs.* Youth gangs that support antisocial values and behaviors—including extortion, intimidation, and acts of violence toward other students—are a source of fear and stress among other students. Youth who are influenced by these groups—those who emulate and copy their behavior, as well as those who become affiliated with them—may adopt these values and act in violent or aggressive ways in certain situations.

- *Inappropriate access to, possession of, and use of firearms.* Children who have a history of aggression, impulsiveness, or other emotional problems should not have access to firearms and other weapons.

- *Serious threats of violence.* Recent incidents across the country clearly indicate that threats to commit violence against oneself or others should be taken very seriously. Steps must be taken to understand the nature of these threats and to prevent them from being carried out.

An added dimension to identifying problem students is the concept of "student profiling." The Federal Bureau of Investigation (FBI) has been providing local law enforcement and school officials access to programs to forecast future criminal behavior. This program has been developed by the FBI to provide a list of behavior traits to help those closest to the students—their teachers and school leaders—identify children who might be at risk.

To the FBI, telltale signs of trouble include having parental troubles, disliking popular students, experiencing a failed romance, and listening to songs with violent lyrics (Billups, 1999). In a similar profiling program, the

Capital Times in Springfield, Illinois, reports that one school district's administrators are measuring students against a behavior checklist that includes use of abusive language, cruelty to animals, and writings reflecting an interest in "the dark side of life." Students who fit the profile can undergo counseling, be transferred to an alternative education program, or even be expelled (Greenberg, 1999).

What does all this suggest? In simplistic terms, teens who constantly fight, steal, set fires, show disrespect for the rights of others, threaten violence, destroy property, and so forth need swift and immediate attention. Parents or teachers who ignore these signs are either in denial, fearful of confronting the issue or problem student, or lacking in native intelligence. It is recognized that many teens hate school because it places stresses on them that they are unable to handle. It may be the curriculum, the preppy atmosphere, rejection by so-called popular "in" groups, or the general social setting. But, however trivial these circumstances may seem to the outsider, they are very real and serious to adolescents. Renegade students can victimize anyone at any time, and schools (teachers, students, and even a parent) are potential targets—not for what they have done, but for what they represent. Yet, schools must guard against overreactive policies that are counterproductive and harmful.

RESPONDING TO SCHOOL VIOLENCE

Now that you have some idea of the risks and contributing factors to teen violence and victimization in schools, the focus shifts to what to do about it. Clearly, schools, society, or parents cannot prevent all teen violence. The best we can hope for is to develop plans and try to intervene if there is evidence of impending violence. Many schools are increasing their security policies and systems to address the problems of crime and violence. A number of school districts employ security officers. For example, the Los Angeles school district employs more than 300 security officers who have full police powers. They patrol campuses and investigate crimes occurring on or near school property. In some communities, schools have formed special police units to address violence in the schools. In 1991, Cleveland public schools, in collaboration with the local police, created a Youth Gang Unit. A relatively small contingent of half a dozen officers service 127 schools and more than 73,000 students. From 1991 to 1993, the schools noted a nearly 40 percent reduction in school gang incidents, dropping from 381 in 1991 to 231 in 1993 (Huff and Trump, 1996). The police presence in 1997 continued to deter gang activity at schools in the Cleveland district. Other districts have installed metal detectors to reduce the risk of gang-involved youth bringing firearms or other weapons into schools.

Some safety measures at schools are implemented specifically to reduce gang activity and children's exposure to gangs at school. More than half of school administrators report they have banned gang clothing and insignias (Thayer, 1996). Sometimes schools partner with communities to restrict vehicle access to school parking lots (to decrease loitering and quick drug sales) or with local law enforcement agencies to create violence-free school zones.

The **National School Safety Center** (1990) recommends that a security plan be prepared to decrease the chances of school violence. It recommends that the following general security measures be taken:

- School districts should establish a local school security committee or task force of school districts.

- This task force should plan and implement needed safety measures, including regular review of safety and security measures.

- Crime prevention expertise should be developed and greater responsibility should be taken by school administrators in working with the school boards and districts.

- Students, parents, law enforcement agencies, state government officials, and community-based groups should become involved in developing and implementing crime prevention efforts.

- A comprehensive crisis management plan that incorporates resources available through other community agencies should be developed by schools. Regular updates on safety plans and in-service training should be conducted for certified staff, classified staff, part-time employees, and substitute teachers to keep them informed.

- Volunteers from the community, as well as parents, should help patrol surrounding neighborhoods and supervise the campus before, during, and after school.

- Students should be taught to take responsibility for their own safety by learning personal safety and conflict resolution techniques.

- A curriculum committee should be established to focus on teaching students nonviolence, conflict resolution, and good decision-making techniques; developing prosocial skills; and incorporating a law-related education series.

- Alternative schools should be established to handle problem students. When these offenders are expelled from school, other programs must be in place to keep them off the streets where they may perpetrate violent incidents.

Mirroring the recommendations of the National School Safety Center of 1990, the U.S. Department of Education offers additional strategies for providing a safe physical environment for students (Dwyer, Osher, and Warger, 1998). In other words, prevention starts by making sure the school campus is a safe and caring place. Responsible student behavior begins with a well-organized, attractive school environment.

The U.S. Department of Education recommends:

- Supervising access to the building and grounds.
- Reducing class size and school size.
- Adjusting scheduling to minimize time in the hallways or in potentially dangerous locations. Traffic flow patterns can be modified to limit potential for conflicts or altercations.
- Conducting a building safety audit in consultation with school security personnel and/or law enforcement experts. Effective schools adhere to federal, state, and local nondiscrimination and public safety laws and use guidelines set by the state department of education.
- Closing school campuses during lunch periods.
- Adopting a school policy requiring uniforms.
- Arranging supervision at critical times (e.g., in hallways between classes) and having a plan to deploy supervisory staff to areas where incidents are likely to occur.
- Prohibiting students from congregating in areas where they are likely to engage in rule-breaking or intimidating and aggressive behaviors.
- Having adults visibly present throughout the school building. This includes encouraging parents to visit the school.
- Staggering dismissal times and lunch periods.
- Monitoring the surrounding school grounds, including landscaping, parking lots, and bus stops.
- Coordinating with local police to ensure that there are safe routes to and from school.

The physical condition of the school building also has an impact on student attitude, behavior, and motivation to achieve. Typically, more incidents of fighting and violence tend to occur in school buildings that are dirty, too cold or too hot, filled with graffiti, in need of repair, or unsanitary.

Arguments have been raised supporting the idea that school violence and victimizations can be reduced by eliminating the mandatory age for attending (Toby, 1995). By allowing other options to those who do not want to be in school, the learning climate will improve and schools will be safer. Some of these teens may simply be productive elsewhere. However, if these troubled adolescents are not provided with constructive options, their violent behaviors will only be shifted from the school to the streets.

The proponents of mandatory schooling argue that schools offer supervision, albeit often imperfect. Requiring students to be in school several hours a day reduces the threat of community violence and victimizations, at least for the time students are in school. In addition, crime targets are not as numerous in school as they are outside of school. The general school atmosphere interferes with student deviance, such as drinking and drug use, and schooling helps to contain crime and identify the perpetrators to appropriate authorities.

> *Zero tolerance is code language for no patience, no mercy and no empathy. The school system has failed children, law enforcement has failed, parents have failed and now they want to lock up our children.*
>
> —Captain Dennis Muhammad, Educating Neighborhoods to Obey
> Those in Authority (ENOTA Program)

Consider the following:

- A third grader in Alabama was suspended from school for five days for violation of the school's substance abuse policy when he took a purple multivitamin with his lunch.
- A 12-year-old boy in Texas was suspended for violation of the school's sexual harassment policy. His offense? Sticking out his tongue at a girl who declined to be his girlfriend. And a little kindergarten boy in North Carolina was suspended for sexual harassment after he kissed a little kindergarten girl.
- Four kindergarteners in New Jersey were suspended after they violated the anti-violence policy by playing "cops and robbers" during recess and using their fingers as "guns."

The above situations are true accounts on the use of zero-tolerance policies. Such policies were originally developed by many states and the federal government to address problems of weapons and drugs in schools. The **Gun-Free Schools Act of 1994**, for example, provides that no federal financial assistance under the Elementary and Secondary Education Act of 1965 is available to school districts that do not have at least one year of mandatory expulsion for students who bring firearms to school. Ninety-one percent of schools have adopted zero-tolerance policies for bringing a weapon to school (Cauchon, 1999).

Most schools also have zero-tolerance policies for alcohol and drugs, and violations often require mandatory expulsion, no matter how small the infraction. It stands to reason that states, confronted with the possibility of losing federal funds, have encouraged school districts to pursue zero-tolerance policies zealously. There are now accounts of students across the country being unjustly punished because any student found with a weapon or drug, regardless of reason or the student's background, faces the possibility of sanctions such as expulsion or arrest. For example, a 10-year-old girl was handcuffed and taken to a police station and held for 8 hours because she brought a pair of scissors to school. The scissors were necessary to work on a school project.

The intent of **zero tolerance** is both preventive and punitive. In other words, when students have knowledge of such policies, they may be less likely to bring weapons or drugs to school (and parents are more likely to monitor their children's behavior), and if there are infractions, swift and severe punishment will result.

Although zero-tolerance polices have a place in school security, there is the threat of overenforcement, which may undermine school–community relations and label students unfairly. Focus 6–2 indicates how zero-tolerance policies can be applied too harshly and result in injustice.

Focus 6–2   A Father's Mistake Penalizes Honor Student

An honor student maintained a straight-A average the entire sophomore year while participating in first-string varsity athletics. The student was a very focused youth with plans to attend the U.S. Naval Academy. One day a random drug search was carried out on students' autos in the school parking lot. The search revealed no drugs. But during the search of one car, a scraper blade and small pocketknife were found in the auto, which was registered to the student's father. The student's father had used the instruments the night before to replace the metal anchor for the rearview mirror on the front windshield of the car. The father had carelessly left the instruments in the vehicle. However, the student, who had no history of trouble, was informed that he would receive a penalty of 3 days' suspension and 45 days of alternative school. Although the father took responsibility, it made no difference to school officials.

Expulsion of students and their referral to the juvenile justice system under the zero-tolerance philosophy are forms of victimization, as in the case at a middle school in Dallas, Texas, of an honor student who also was a violinist, cheerleader, and student council member. The student, who had never been in trouble at school, was expelled and faced confinement in a juvenile boot camp for bringing a 20-ounce bottle of Cherry 7-Up mixed with a few drops of grain alcohol to school (Cauchon, 1999). Thus, although zero-tolerance policies have become standard operating procedure in the nation's public schools, there have been a number of criticisms. Although supporters have credited zero-tolerance policies with helping to reduce drugs and firearms and with making students feel safer in school, such policies have been condemned for inflexibility, for failure to apply discretion on a case-by-case basis. A number of state cases reject zero-tolerance policies (see *Stone v. Prosser*, 971 P.2d 125 [Wash. App. 1999]; *Wood v. Henry County Public Schools*, 495 S.E. 2d 255 [Va. 1998]).

An appellate court in Pennsylvania held that a school's policy of zero tolerance exceeded the authority of the school board in that it denied the superintendent, the school board, and the students the exercise of discretion specifically provided by the school code. In that case, a seventh-grade A student was expelled for possessing a miniature Swiss army knife. The student found the knife in the school hallway and was asked to turn it over when a teacher observed him with it. The student was expelled with no consideration of his record or background. The Pennsylvania court made clear that this zero-tolerance policy, even though not in writing, was nonetheless a school board policy that frustrated the legislative intent that the state's expulsion statute not be "blindly applied" (*Lyons v. Penn Hills School District*, 1999).

SUMMARY

Schools are subcultures, mirroring the problems and trappings of society. Students struggling in their personal lives or suffering from assorted risk factors are candidates for failure and victimization. They bring to school fears, insecurities, and anger, often making poor decisions in their daily lives. A student who is rejected by his or her peers or who is performing poorly will not bond well. At an age when impressions are important, a number of students will fall through the cracks, victimized by the very institution that is designed to educate and prepare them for the adult world. Schools must become proactive in identifying problem students. Yet, this does not mean that schools should embark on witch hunts or demand that students conform to strict dress codes and unreasonable zero-tolerance polices. It may be that schools are falling behind in their mission, or perhaps some students would be better served if they left school a year or so early, instead of being forced into curricula that serve neither their interests nor those of society.

KEY TERMS AND CONCEPTS

Attention Deficit/Hyperactivity
  Disorder (ADHD)
Coercive style of parent–child
  interaction
Community violence
Gun-Free Schools Act of 1994
National Institute of Education

National School Safety Center
Oppositional Defiant Disorder (ODD)
Safe School Study
School bullying
Toxic culture
U.S. Department of Education
Zero tolerance

DISCUSSION QUESTIONS AND LEARNING ACTIVITIES

1. Discuss several risk factors that contribute to youth violence.
2. Explain how schools are a source of victimization.
3. Interview a school counselor or administrator and determine what is being done to reduce the threat of school violence.
4. Should some public schools require dress codes? What are the advantages and disadvantages of this requirement?
5. Should student rights regarding search and seizure and other forms of privacy be eliminated to combat violence and drugs? Which is more important, the rights of the student or of society at large?
6. Observe students after the school day and determine where they congregate. Are there particular hangouts that are potential trouble spots? What can be done about them?
7. Interview a police officer and determine what types of problems occur around schools.
8. What can teachers do to minimize their risk for victimization at school?

WEB SOURCES

National Center for Education Statistics.
  http://nces.ed.gov/
Indicators of School Crime and Safety: 2004.
  http://nces.ed.gov/pubs2005/crime_safe04/index.asp
U.S. Department of Education.
  www.ed.gov/index.jhtml

RECOMMENDED READINGS

Barbour, Scott, ed. 2005. *How Can School Violence Be Prevented?* At Issue Series. San Diego, CA: Greenhaven Press.

Benbenishty, Rami et al. 2005. *School Violence in Context: Culture, Neighborhood, Family, School, and Gender.* New York: Oxford University Press.

Davis, Stan. 2005. *Schools Where Everyone Belongs: Practical Strategies for Reducing Bullying,* 2nd ed. Washington, DC: Stop Bullying Now.

Egendorg, Laura K. 2002. *School Shootings.* At Issue Series. San Diego, CA: Greenhaven Press.

Grapes, Bryan J., ed. 2000. *School Violence.* Contemporary Issues Companion. San Diego, CA: Greenhaven Press.

Martin, Gregory M., and Kimberly A. McCabe. 2004. *School Violence, the Media, and Criminal Justice Responses.* Studies in Crime & Punishment. Chicago: Peter Lang Publishing.

Newman, Katherine S. 2005. *Rampage: The Social Roots of School Shootings.* New York: Basic Books.

REFERENCES

American Psychological Association. 1993. *Summary Report of the American Psychological Association Commission on Violence and Youth* (Vol. 1). Washington, DC: American Psychological Association. (ERIC Abstract).

American School Health Association. 1989. *The National Adolescent Student Health Survey.* Oakland, CA: Third Party Publishing.

American Teacher. 1993. *Violence in America's Public Schools. The Metropolitan Life Survey.* New York: Louis Harris and Associates. (ERIC Documents).

Anderson, Jack. 2000. Lucifer on the Loose. *Meridian Magazine.*

Anderson, Mark, et al., and the School-Associated Violent Deaths Study Group. 2001. School-Associated Violent Deaths in the United States, 1994–1999. *Journal of the American Medical Association* 286:2695–2702.

Arnette, J. L., and M. C. Walsleben. 1998. *Combating Fear and Restoring Safety in Schools* (NCJ 167888). Bulletin. Washington, DC: U.S. Department of Justice, Office of Justice Programs, Office of Juvenile Justice and Delinquency Prevention. Government Printing Office.

Berman, P., and M. McLaughlin. 1978. *Federal Programs Supporting Educational Change VIII: Implementing and Sustaining Innovations.* Washington, DC: U.S. Department of Health, Education and Welfare.

Billups, Andrea. 1999. FBI Teaches Ways to Prevent Violence: Schools Search for Solutions. *Washington Times.* September 19.

Brogan, Pamela. 1999. New Technology Delivers Increasingly Graphic Images of Violence to Youth. *Gannett News Service,* May 10.

Cairns, R., B. Cairns, and H. Neckerman. 1989. Early School Dropout: Configurations and Determinants. *Child Development* 60 (6):1437–1452. (ERIC Abstract).

Cauchon, Dennis. 1999. Zero-Tolerance Policies Lack Flexibility. *USA Today.* April 13.

Centerwall, B. S. 1992. Television and Violence. *Journal of the American Medical Association* 267:3059–3063.

Criner, Lawrence. 1998. A Society Drenched in Toxic Culture. *Washington Times*, January 4.

Dwyer, D., D. Osher, and C. Warger. 1998. *Early Warning, Timely Response: A Guide to Safe Schools*. Washington, DC: U.S. Department of Education.

Elliott, D. S., B. Hamburg, and K. R. Williams. 1998. Violence in American Schools: An Overview, In *Violence In American Schools*, eds. D. S. Elliott, B. Hamburg, and K. R. Williams, pp. 3–28. New York: Cambridge University Press

Ericson, N. 2001. *Addressing the Problem of Juvenile Bullying*. OJJDP Fact Sheet #27. Washington, DC: U.S. Department of Justice, Office of Justice Programs, Office of Juvenile Justice and Delinquency Prevention. U.S. Government Printing Office.

Farrell, A. D., and S. E. Bruce. 1997. Impact of Exposure to Community Violence on Violent Behavior and Emotional Distress Among Urban Adolescents. *Journal of Clinical Child Psychology* 26:214.

Fraser, M. W. 1996. Aggressive Behavior in Childhood and Early Adolescence: An Ecological Developmental Perspective on Youth Violence. *Social Work* 41:347–361.

Greenberg, Brigette. 1999. "Student Profiling" Launched to Combat Violence. *Springfield (IL) Capital Times*, September 7.

Holmes, Leonard. 2003. Peaceful Schools Project Tackles Bullies. In *Your Guide to Mental Health Resources.* Tucson, AZ: Arrow Press.

Huff, C. R., and K. Trump. 1996. Youth Violence and Gangs: School Safety Initiatives in Urban and Suburban School Districts. *Education and Urban Society* 28 (4):492–503.

Kisken, Tom. 1999. Professor: Toxicants Contribute to Violence. *Moorpark Star* (Ventura, CA), A6.

Larrubia, Evelyn. 1999. Homies Toys Anger Anti-Gang Forces. *Los Angeles Times*, A–1. August 2.

L.W. v. Toms River Regional Schools Board of Education, A-111–05 (2007).

Lyons v. Penn Hills School District, 723 A.2d 1073 (Pa. 1999).

Moffitt, Terrie, and Phil Silva. 1988. Self-Reported Delinquency, Neuropsychological Deficit, and History of Attention Disorder. *Journal of Abnormal Psychology* 16:326–330.

National Center of Educational Statistics. 2003. Incidents of Crime and Violence in Public Schools. Washington, DC: U.S. Department of Education.

National Center for Education Statistics. NCES (2007). *Digest of Education Statistics, 2006.* Washington, DC: Center for Education Statistics, Institute of Education Sciences, U.S. Department of Education.

National School Safety Center. 1990. *School Crisis Prevention and Response.* Malibu, CA: Pepperdine University.

Olweus, D. 1994. Bullying at School: Long-Term Outcomes for the Victims and an Effective School Based Intervention Program. In *Aggressive Behavior, Current Perspectives*, ed. L. R. Huesmann. New York: Plenum Press.

Patterson, G. R. 1992. Developmental Changes in Antisocial Behavior. In *Aggression and Violence Throughout the Lifespan*, eds. R. D. Peters, R. J. McMahon, and V. L. Quinsey. Newbury Park, CA: Sage.

Rivara, F. P., J. P. Shepherd, D. P. Farrington, P. W. Richmond, and P. Cannon. 1995. Victim as Offender in Youth Violence. *Annals of Emergency Medicine* 26:609–614.

Rossman, S. B., and E. Morley. 1996. Introduction. *Education and Urban Society* 28 (4): 395–411.

Sege, R., and W. Dietz. 1994. Television Viewing and Violence in Children: The Pediatrician as Agent for Change. *Pediatrics* 94:600–607.

Scigel, Larry, and Joseph Senna. 1999. *Juvenile Delinquency*. St. Paul, MN: West Publishing.

Sheley, Joseph, Sinca McGee, and James Wright. 1995. *Weapon-Related Victimization in Selected Inner-City High School Samples*. Washington, DC: National Institute of Justice, U.S. Department of Justice.

Singer, M., D. Miller, K. Slovak, and R. Frierson. 1997. *Mental Health Consequences of Children's Exposure to Violence*. Cleveland, OH: Case Western Reserve University, Mandel School of Applied Social Sciences.

Thayer, Y. 1996. The Virginia Model: School to Community Intervention Techniques to Prevent Violence. In *Schools, Violence and Society*, ed. A. Hoffman. Westport, CT: Praeger.

Thornberry, T. P. 1994. *Violent Families and Youth Violence*. Washington, DC: U.S. Department of Justice, National Institute of Justice, Office of Justice Programs.

Toby, Jackson. 1995. The Schools. In *Crime*, ed. James Q. Wilson and J. Petersilia. San Francisco: ICS Press.

Tremblay, R., B. Masse, D. Perron, M. LeBlanc, A. Schwartzman, and J. Ledingham. 1992. Early Disruptive Behavior, Poor School Achievement, Delinquent Behavior, and Delinquent Personality: Longitudinal Analyses. *Journal of Consulting and Clinical Psychology* 60:64–72.

Wooden, Wayne S. 1995. *Renegade Kids, Suburban Outlaws*. Belmont, CA: Wadsworth Publishing.

7

Criminal Justice Injustice

LEARNING OBJECTIVES

After studying this chapter, you will:

- Understand the sources and types of police injustice.
- Be able to identify injustices in the judicial process.
- Understand how well-intended legislation and legal practices victimize some.
- Learn how the correctional process creates victimization.
- Learn through case studies how and why injustices occur.

INTRODUCTION

> *Injustice anywhere is a threat to justice everywhere.*
>
> —Martin Luther King Jr.

The justice system, in its attempt to serve and protect, is also a source of victimization through poor discretion, lack of resources, and inefficiency or incompetence by those sworn to protect and serve. Although these abuses are relatively rare, they do occur and invite scrutiny about the capability or capacity of the justice process. Various types of injustice exist, such as police use of excessive force, prosecutorial misconduct, jury tampering, or criminal activity on the part of the system's practitioners. Questionable jury decisions can also invite criticism about the justice system. In addition, when a poorly supervised parolee victimizes a citizen or a defendant in a criminal case and is released on a technicality only to commit other crimes, a lack of faith in the system may develop. In either circumstance, when criminal justice professionals make mistakes, intentional or not, society is victimized.

SOURCES OF INJUSTICE

The criminal justice system is designed to respond to and be accountable to the public. In theory, it is based on fairness, order, justice, and due process. The operation of the criminal justice system and decisions by its agents, however, sometimes create victims inadvertently or deliberately through its vast discretionary process. **Inadvertent injustice** is unintentional—the result of carelessness or neglect, such as releasing prisoners into society who then commit another crime. The lack of funds to hire more police to patrol high-crime areas or more probation and parole officers to supervise offenders contributes to inadvertent victimization. Also, the jury conviction of a crime although the defendant may be factually innocent is another crime (unless the jury was corrupt, etc.). In such cases juries only consider the evidence before them. **Deliberate victimization,** on the other hand, is more intentional, as in cases in which a police officer or prison guard wrongfully use force or when prosecutors intentionally conceal evidence beneficial to the accused. There is also the insidious side of injustice—discrimination in the administration of justice. Whether in policing, criminal prosecutions, trials, sentencing, or imprisonment, discrimination or racism can cause extraordinary harm to individuals and society alike and has lasting consequences for future generations. It has often been reported that members of racial, ethnic, and other minorities or vulnerable groups often face harassment, arbitrary detention, and abusive treatment by the law enforcement apparatus and disparate treatment by prosecutors and the courts.

This chapter presents a number of injustices resulting in primary victimization of individuals, as well as secondary victimization, the rippling effect victimization has on the victim's family and community. In other words, if a citizen is wrongfully convicted of a crime, it can have disastrous effects on the immediate family, both financially and emotionally. Likewise, an acquittal of a seemingly guilty person can also undermine our faith in the justice system. The injustices addressed are divided into the main components of the criminal justice process: the police, the courts and sentencing process, and corrections. Also addressed is how crime legislation can be a source of injustice.

THE POLICE

Most police officers are dedicated professionals performing their sworn duties well. Yet, one important source of deliberate injustice is the wrongful behavior of the police. A variety of police injustices result in civil rights violations. Policing decisions are highly discretionary, often operating without close supervision in extremely emotional environments. In the course of policing, excessive use of force, wrongful shootings, search and seizure violations, corruption, falsifying reports, false testimony, and other misconduct can and does occur.

Fueling the perception of police injustice is the media's quick reporting of police use of excessive force, particularly those cases involving minorities or disfranchised persons living in low-income communities. The renowned Rodney King incident focused attention on what many in the minority communities have complained about for years: brutal treatment by the police. Although it can be argued that King was not totally blameless for his victimization at the hands of four Los Angeles police officers, the police response was excessive and criminal. In the aftermath of the famed incident, an oversight commission, the Christopher Commission, was created to review the conduct of the Los Angeles police. The commission found that the Los Angeles police wound and kill more citizens than police in any other big-city department (per 1,000 officers). The Los Angeles police are about eight times more likely than police in New York City to shoot and wound citizens (Pate and Hamilton, 1990:138).

In 1999, the Los Angeles Police Department was again under fire for the actions of several officers. A key officer targeted in this probe was Rafael Perez, a former narcotics policeman. Perez told police that he and his partner handcuffed and shot a Honduran immigrant and then planted a gun on him, framing him for assaulting a police officer. The defendant was freed from prison after serving 2 years of a 23-year jail term. Others may be freed for the following reason:

> When a state officer acts under a state law in a manner violative of the Federal Constitution, he comes into conflict with the superior authority of that Constitution, and he is in that case stripped of his official or representative character and is subjected in his person to the consequences of his individual conduct. The State has no power to impart to him any immunity from responsibility to the supreme authority of the United States.
>
> —(*Scheuer v. Rhodes*, 416 U.S. 232, 94 S.Ct.1683, 1687 [1974])

Thus, the Perez corruption probe has forced the local district attorney to reexamine hundreds of police cases. During the investigation, additional examples of wrongful arrests and misconduct were uncovered.

In 1995, several New York City police officers were indicted for robbing drug dealers and brutally beating innocent people (Senna and Siegel, 1996). Another brutal example of direct victimization by the New York police is the case of Abner Louima, a Haitian immigrant arrested outside a New York nightclub during the summer of 1997. The sadistic events that took place afterward are difficult to believe. After being arrested, four New York City police officers beat Louima in the squad car. At the precinct station, one officer also was accused of holding him down while another sodomized him with a stick. Louima was taken to the hospital with serious injuries, including torn tissue between his bowel and bladder. The main defendant in the case, Officer Justin Volpe, entered a plea of guilty in 1999. The officer admitted in court he had struck Louima in the car and assaulted him in the lavatory. Shortly after the assault, Volpe reportedly bragged about sticking the stick six inches up Louima's rectum (Usborne, 1999:20).

There are also cases where the police have employed questionable tactics against affluent members of society. The case of Donald Scott (Focus 7–1) serves as a reminder of how overzealous police tactics can also wrong wealthy, more established people.

There is no question that policing is a stressful, dangerous job, requiring integrity and accountability. Although most police do a credible job, a number of officers exceed boundaries of reason and due process and so violate the civil rights of others. The unnecessary use of force is a relatively rare occurrence in American policing, but previous studies suggest that when it does occur, it often escalates to the level of injuring force. For example, a 1996 reexamination of 5,688 cases in the 1977 *Police Services Study* data found that reasonable force was used in 37 cases (0.65 percent) and that improper force was used in 23 cases (0.40 percent). The study

---

Focus 7–1   Donald Scott

On October 2, 1992, a pounding at the door awakened Donald Scott and his wife, Frances Plante. As Plante attempted to open the door, a narcotics task force from the Los Angeles County Sheriff's Department burst into the home, weapons in hand. Plante was pushed forcefully from the door at gun point. She cried out, "Don't shoot me, don't kill me!" With a gun aimed at her head, she looked to her right and saw Donald charging into the room, waving a revolver above his head. She heard a deputy shout, "Put the gun down! Put the gun down! Put the gun down!" As Scott was doing so, she heard three gun shots ring out, apparently from two sources. Her husband was killed instantly. Scott was a millionaire, heir to the Scott paper fortune. He owned 250 acres of breathtakingly beautiful land adjacent to federal parklands in Malibu, California. Attempts had been made by the government to buy the property, but Scott was not interested in selling. Claims that there might be pot growing on the land, made by agents who did aerial surveillance, were used to get a search warrant of Scott's home. An official inquiry later suggested that agents were hoping this raid would lead to asset forfeiture of the property Scott would not sell. No marijuana was found in the home. Scott did not smoke it.

suggests that improper force was used in 38 percent of encounters that involved force (Worden, 1996). When this occurs, not only is the individual citizen victimized but the agency and other responsible officers are labeled as corrupt, brutal racists or incompetent buffoons. In other words, such cases cause negative community relations, which can undermine public trust and confidence as well as police morale.

The reasons for police injustice have been debated for years. Blame has been pointed at job stress, poor supervision, inadequate recruitment or training, lack of agency policies designed to ferret out corruption, zealous enforcement of controversial laws, or simply the basic culture of policing. Officers may be hired with the best intentions of fair and impartial enforcement, but the police culture, the environment in which they serve, provides temptations and opportunities to commit injustices, such as skimming money from drug dealers or applying unreasonable force against resisting disenfranchised offenders.

Remedies for Police Injustice

It is imperative to identify remedies for police injustice. A variety of federal laws, both criminal and civil, address police misconduct. These laws cover the actions of state, county, and local officers, including those who work in prisons and jails. In addition, several laws also apply to federal law enforcement officers. The laws protect all people in the United States—both citizens and noncitizens.

Under federal law, it is a crime for one or more persons acting under color of law willfully to deprive or conspire to deprive another person of any right protected by the Constitution or laws of the United States (18 U.S.C. §§ 241–242 2002). *Color of law* simply means that the person doing the act is using power given to him or her by a governmental agency (local, state, or federal). A law enforcement officer acts "under color of law" even if he or she is exceeding his or her rightful power. The types of law enforcement misconduct covered by these laws include excessive force, sexual assault, intentional false arrests, or the intentional fabrication of evidence resulting in a loss of liberty to another.

Enforcement of these provisions does not require that any racial, religious, or other discriminatory motive existed. Violations of these laws are punishable by fine and/or imprisonment, which was the result when several Los Angeles police officers were convicted under federal law in the Rodney King incident.

Another federal law is referred to as the police misconduct provision. This law makes it unlawful for state or local law enforcement officers to engage in a pattern or practice of conduct that deprives persons of rights protected by the Constitution or laws of the United States (42 U.S.C. § 14141). The types of conduct covered by this law include, among other things, excessive force, discriminatory harassment, false arrests, coercive sexual conduct, and unlawful stops, searches, or arrests.

To be covered by this law, the misconduct must constitute a "pattern or practice"—it may not simply be an isolated incident. The Department of Justice (DOJ) must be able to show in court that the agency has an unlawful policy or that the incidents constituted a pattern of unlawful conduct. However, unlike the other civil laws discussed later, the DOJ does not have to show that discrimination has occurred to prove a pattern or practice of misconduct. The remedies available under this law are different from the previous laws discussed. There is no monetary relief, only injunctive relief, such as orders to end the misconduct and changes in the agency's policies and procedures that resulted in or allowed the misconduct.

Police injustice may also be inadvertent, as when the police make an arrest and it later turns out they arrested the wrong person. If the police reasonably believe, based upon complaints or other evidence, that a certain person is responsible for a crime, an arrest may be made. However, faulty witness reports or other misinformation can cause errors. Although the police may be exonerated in some of these cases, potential liability may still result.

PROSECUTION AND THE JUDICIAL PROCESS

> At current levels of incarceration, newborn Black males in this country have a greater than 1 in 4 chance of being sentenced to prison during their lifetimes, while Latin-American males have a 1 in 6 chance, and White males have a 1 in 23 chance of serving time.
>
> —Department of Justice, March 1997

Both inadvertent and deliberate injustice arise during the judicial process, including the prosecution stage. The judicial process incorporates pretrial, prosecution, trial proceedings, including jury decision making, sentencing, and plea bargaining. The injustices that may result are convicting the factually innocent or acquitting the factually guilty. Additional examples of injustice during the judicial process involve misconduct by a judge or jury resulting in an unfair dispensing of justice.

Let's begin with an example of an injustice leading to the acquittal of a seemingly guilty person, the appalling jury acquittal of O. J. Simpson of double murder charges. In this case, two people were brutally slain, a suspect with a motive was arrested, evidence was presented, but the jury had reasonable doubt as to Simpson's guilt. Whether the jury made a deliberate or inadvertent decision in acquitting Simpson is a subject for continuous debate. In other words, the jury felt compelled to acquit Simpson because of perceived racism and misconduct on the part of the police. The prosecution strategy and media circus around the trial have been widely criticized as contributing to the injustice. While Simpson went free, the true victims of this injustice are the family and friends of the slain pair, who must live with the knowledge that two people have been murdered, no one has been convicted of the crimes, and no one is under investigation. However, the family was exposed to another round of litigation, which resulted in the bittersweet victory of winning a $38 million judgment against Simpson in a 1997 civil suit.

As another example, on June 13, 2005, pop star Michael Jackson was acquitted of all charges stemming from accusations of child molestation, contributing to the delinquency of minors, and other related charges. The jury found no compelling evidence to convict Jackson. Some believed that the *Jackson* verdict is just another example of injustice, whereby a famous celebrity beat the system. However, it can also be argued that a conviction, if delivered by the jury, would be an injustice because of the credibility of the witnesses and quality of evidence presented by the prosecution. Or, retaining high-profile legal representation, as did O. J. Simpson, is the key to celebrity acquittals.

In another high-profile case, Edgar Ray Killen, once an outspoken Mississippi white supremacist and Ku Klux Klan member, was convicted on June 20, 2005, of manslaughter for masterminding the killing of three civil rights workers in 1964. The conviction was based on transcripts of earlier cases (there was a hung jury in an earlier case). Although no other factual evidence was presented, the jury believed in his guilt. Questions can be raised as to why it took so long to try the case or whether there was enough evidence to convict. In other words, one can argue an injustice from various points of view in any of these cases.

The most damaging victimization occurs when the justice system victimizes citizens through its accusatory or decision-making process, as when a person is wrongfully charged, convicted, imprisoned, or punished. Although the person is not the victim of overt violence or physical injury, he or she has been harmed, either financially or emotionally, in the name of justice.

Consider the Duke University lacrosse scandal of 2006 that drew national attention and polarized races. Several all-white members of the Duke University lacrosse team held a party at an off-campus house and hired two black strippers to perform. One of the dancers later claimed she was raped in a bathroom by some of the team members. The rape and sodomy accusations resulted in the coach resigning and the team's season to be cancelled. Two of the players were suspended from school by the university. Subsequent case investigation revealed that the evidence against the players was insufficient to support a case. The initial police investigation did not establish a rape due in part to inconsistent statements by the accused. Furthermore, DNA test results failed to connect any of the 46 members of the team to the alleged victim. And, the other stripper at the scene later admitted that no rape occurred. The district attorney in the case, Mike Nifong, for political or personal motives, pressed on with the case despite evidence to the contrary. He made misleading and inflammatory statements to the press about the accused players and failed to verify important evidence brought forth by the accused. In the end, Nifong was found to be responsible for withholding evidence from the defense, lying to the court, and lying to the bar investigators. He later resigned and was disbarred. This is an example of deliberate injustice which ultimately resulted in lawsuits and embarrassment for the University and the District Attorney's office. It also addresses the power of prosecution.

Another deliberate example involving prosecutorial misconduct was the *McMartin* case in which false accusations of child abuse, facilitated by an overzealous prosecution, victimized a family. Whether or not one believes the accusations, the defendants were found not guilty of any crime. The case remains as one of the most expensive criminal trials in U.S. history, riddled with mistakes and flawed pretrial investigations, so much for the sensible use of justice resources and tax funds (see Focus 7–2).

Focus 7–2 McMartin Ritual Abuse Cases: Guilt by Accusation

The *McMartin* case was one of the first multivictim, multioffender (MVMO) child abuse cases. Lasting 6 years, it was the longest U.S. criminal trial in history; at a cost to the state of $15 million, it was also the most expensive. No one was convicted. The case has become the most famous of its type. The McMartin preschool, located in Manhattan Beach, California, was owned by Peggy Buckey and her mother, Virginia McMartin. Ms. Buckey's son, Ray, was a part-time school aide there. On August 12, 1983, Judy Johnson complained to the police that her son, a student at the school, had been molested by Ray. Although no physical evidence or confirmation from other children at the school was available, Ray was arrested on September 7. Because of the lack of evidence, the district attorney decided to not prosecute him.

The chief of the Manhattan Beach Police then created a local panic by circulating a confidential letter to about 200 parents of present and past McMartin school

(Continued)

(*Continued*)

students. The letter specified that Ray might have forced the children to engage in oral sex; fondling of genitals, buttocks, or chest area; and sodomy. The parents were urged to question their children to seek confirmation. A local TV station was first with the news, reporting that the preschool might be linked to child pornography rings and various sex industries in nearby Los Angeles. Hundreds of children were later interviewed by the Children's Institute International (CII). It was later determined that CII interviewers had used leading, suggestive questions when interviewing the children and that rewards were given for disclosing the "right" answers. By spring 1984, 360 kids had been diagnosed as having been abused. One hundred fifty children received medical exams, but no physical evidence could be found; in spite of this, physicians concluded that about 120 had been sexually abused. The whole town, particularly the parents of the children, became enraged. Parents pressured their children to tell their stories. Ultimately, the children said that they

- had been sexually abused
- had been forced to act in pornographic movies and submit to the taking of millions of "kiddy-porn" photographs
- had seen the mutilation and killing of animals
- had been forced to engage in Satanic rituals, including ritual murder of infants, and to drink a baby's blood
- had seen dead and burned babies, flying witches
- had been forced into a coffin and buried
- had been molested at a market and in a car wash
- had been forced to watch while Ray Buckey killed a sea turtle by stabbing it with a knife as a demonstration of what would happen to the children if they told
- had been taken to the airport, flown to Palm Springs, abused, and returned
- had been taken through trapdoors in the floor of the center and through underground tunnels

In spite of this strong bias by the residents, the judge refused the defense request for a change of venue. Judy Johnson continued to make allegations of abuse; among other charges, she said that her ex-husband had sodomized their son and the family dog; that her son had been injured by an elephant and lion during a school field trip; and that her son had been tortured by teachers who put staples in his ears, nipples, and tongue, and scissors in his eye. There was, of course, no physical evidence of these traumas. She was later diagnosed as suffering from acute paranoid schizophrenia, was hospitalized, and died at home of alcohol-related liver disease before the trial began, but information of her mental illness was kept from the defense. Armed with search warrants, the police searched 11 locations but found no

(*Continued*)

(Continued)

evidence to support the charges. Groups of parents searched the school yard for signs of tunnels, underground rooms, and sacrificed infants or animals. They did find the remains of a sea turtle; a forensics exam showed that the sand inside the shell was foreign to the area, indicating that the remains had been dug up on a beach and planted in the yard. In March 1984, 208 counts of abuse of 40 children (some sources say 42) were brought against several adults: the owners of the school, Ray Buckey, and four schoolteachers. After 20 months of preliminary hearings, the state's case appeared weak. Prosecutors offered the defendants immunity from prosecution or leniency if they would testify against the other defendants. None accepted the offer. The prosecution produced a pair of rabbit ears, black candles, and a black cape as evidence of Satanic ritual abuse. The defense lawyers were able to prove that these items were totally unrelated to the McMartin case.

In January 1986, Ira Reiner was elected district attorney. He dropped all charges against five of the adults, leaving 52 charges against Ray Buckey and 20 counts against Peggy Buckey, plus a single count of conspiracy. The results of an area telephone survey in 1986 were as follows:

96 percent of the adults had heard of the case.

97 percent of those with an opinion believed that Ray Buckey was guilty.

93 percent believed that Peggy Buckey was guilty.

On January 18, 1990, after almost 3 years of trial testimony and 9 weeks of deliberation, the jury cleared Peggy Buckey of all 13 remaining counts. Ray was acquitted on 39 of 52 counts; the jury's vote was split on the remaining counts, with large majorities in favor of acquittal. Ray was retried on some of the 13 counts; the second jury delivered a hung verdict later that year. The prosecution gave up at this point.

Peggy Buckey immediately filed a civil suit against the city, county, the CII, and an ABC television station for a shopping list of improper behaviors. A few months later, Virginia McMartin and two of the defendants who were charged but never tried also filed suits. These actions failed because state law and previous court decisions granted absolute immunity from prosecution to child protective services workers and persons involved in the prosecution. This protection was extended to the CII in this case because it was working for the prosecution.

Many lives were disrupted by the events at *McMartin*. Hundreds of children, now teenagers, believe that they were abused during bizarre rituals. Seven adults have been financially impoverished. The school was closed and leveled to the ground. Many copy-cat prosecutions occurred across North America. Mysterious tunnels were reported in various other MVMO cases around the world.

There are a number of reasons why a wrongful conviction may occur. However, most reasons for wrongful conviction are factors such as **overzealous prosecutors** or police officers, **eyewitness misidentification** or fabrication of evidence, and so forth (Gross et al., 2004; Radelet and Bedau, 1992). In a study of wrongful convictions in the United States from 1989 through 2003, a total of 328 exonerations were found. One hundred forty-five were cleared by DNA and 183 by other evidence. Defendants served an average of 10 years in prison. Some died in prison before their release. Most were convicted of murder or rape through faulty eyewitnesses or sloppy police work. It was also revealed that nearly 90 percent of the juvenile defendants exonerated were black or Hispanic, suggesting a racial injustice as well (Gross et al., 2004).

In a study of wrongful convictions, Scheck, Neufeld, and Dwyer (2001) found that the leading cause of these gross errors was faulty eyewitnesses. Other leading mistakes resulting in wrongful convictions were serology errors and police and prosecutorial misconduct (Figure 7–1).

The case of Steve Titus illustrates how uncorroborated testimony can send a man to prison (Focus 7–3). Although Titus finally prevailed, his life savings were depleted, he lost his job, and he died of a massive heart attack in 1985. As in the *McMartin* case, the effects of the victimization are lifelong and can be life threatening.

FIGURE 7–1   FACTORS LEADING TO WRONGFUL CONVICTIONS

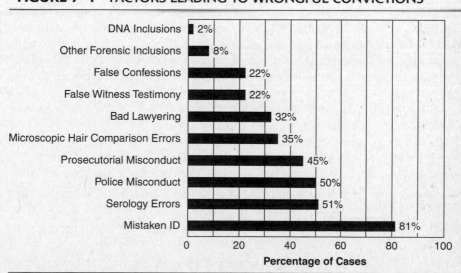

Source: B. Scheck, P. Neufeld, and J. Dwyer. 2001. *Actual Innocence: When Justice Goes Wrong and How to Make It Right.* New York: Penguin Books.

Focus 7–3 What Did They Really See? The Problems of Eyewitness Identification: The Case of Steve Titus

On the night of October 12, 1980, a teenage girl became a rape victim after hitchhiking on the Pacific Coast Highway near the Seattle-Tacoma airport. She gave the police a description of her assailant: He was a bearded white man about 6 feet tall, wearing a three-piece, cream-colored suit. He had threatened her with a knife. She had been able to recall something about the car that she had entered: it was a royal blue compact with a temporary license plate displayed in the rear window. She was not certain of all the numbers on the license plate, but she seemed to recall that the first digits were either 667 or 776.

Armed with this information, Port of Seattle police searched the area and came across a bearded man by the name of Steve Gray Titus, who was to become the only suspect in the case. He was driving a light blue Chevette and was spotted by the police outside a restaurant, not far from the rape scene, from which he had just emerged with his fiancée after they had had a drink together. Titus, taken by surprise when approached by the police, was asked a few questions, and then police asked him if he had any objection to his picture being taken. Neither suspicious nor frightened, and certain that he was innocent, he consented without hesitation. He then asked the officers to take an additional picture of him with his girlfriend.

Steve Titus was tried and convicted based on the uncorroborated testimony of the victim, the similarity of his car to the one she had described, and deliberate distortions by a Port Authority police corporal. Titus remained free on bail while protesting his innocence and waiting for sentence to be imposed, while deeply worried and trying to work on leads for an appeal. He never did go to prison, because his complete exculpation was established before the gates had an opportunity to open and devour him. His innocence was established not through the efforts of the police or the prosecutor, but because of the continuing and relentless efforts of Paul Henderson, a *Seattle Times* reporter, who was convinced that a miscarriage of justice was unfolding before his eyes. The reporter called attention to Titus's airtight alibi, his spotless record, the failure of the authorities to conduct proper forensic tests, and the many inconsistencies and errors in the prosecutor's case (some of which had appeared to be remedied by last-minute distortions by the Port Authority corporal). Henderson called for the case to be reopened and insisted on a new investigation.

Ultimately, Titus was exonerated. Eventually, a 28-year-old man was linked to the crime and made a complete confession. When the victim recognized her mistake, she broke down and cried, agonized over having made such a serious error.

Source: Ronald Huff, Arye Rattner, and Edward Sagarin. 1996. *Convicted but Innocent.* Thousand Oaks, CA: Sage Publications.

The case of Kevin Lee Green serves as another shocking example of injustice. In 1979, the Marine was convicted of killing his pregnant wife, which led to the death of their unborn baby. Despite professing his innocence, he was convicted; he had no believable alibi and could not afford to pay for DNA tests during his trial. He served 17 years in prison for the crimes. In 1996, Green was cleared of the crimes after DNA tests revealed that another Marine, Gerald Parker, had committed the crimes. Parker confessed to the crimes and other murders as well (Hua, 1996).

A recent example is the Charles Chatman case. Chatman served 27 years in the Texas prison system for a crime he did not commit. Convicted of sexual assault in 1981, he was released in February 2008. The primary evidence was the fact that he lived near the victim and that she identified him in lineup. Through the aggressive efforts of the innocence project in Texas and volunteer law students, DNA evidence proved innocence. It was also revealed that Texas has the most exonerations than any other State (Johnson, 2008).

A report released by the Washington, DC-based **Death Penalty Information Center (DPIC),** a death penalty opposition group, says that between 1993 and 1997, the courts exonerated 21 death row prisoners. Previous reports showed that, on average, 2.5 innocent defendants were released annually from death row between 1973 and 1993. The DPIC says an average of 4.8 innocent defendants were released each year since 1993. The 21 cases cited bring the total of such wrongful convictions to 69 since 1973. Add to the list of justice mistakes the cases of Rolando Cruz and Alejandro Hernandez, convicted in Illinois of the murder of a 10-year-old girl. Eventually, after a convicted murderer admitted to the killing, both were released. Prosecutors and police were charged with obstruction of justice (Rovella, 1997).

Other death row inmates have not been so lucky. In May 1990, Jesse Tafero was executed in Florida. His case gained notoriety because the electric chair malfunctioned and his head caught on fire before he died. Surprisingly, 2 years later, Jesse's co-defendant, Sonia Jacobs, who had been convicted and sentenced to death on exactly the same evidence, was released after a U.S. Court of Appeals concluded that her conviction was based on prosecutorial suppression of exculpatory evidence and perjury by a prosecution witness, who was later found to be the real killer (*Jacobs v. Singletary*, 952 F.2d 1282 11th Cir. 1992]. Had he been alive, the evidence that led to Jacobs's release would have led to Tafero's release, too.

We like to believe, or indeed hope, that criminal jury trials are completely unbiased and fair for both the defendant and victim. Unfortunately, juror misconduct, ranging from deliberate acts by jurors who callously disregard their oaths to inadvertent or unintentional actions by jurors, bailiffs, and judges who do not understand jury protocol, has been cited as a cause of injustice. Jury misconduct has been found to result from juror disobedience; inappropriate communications with bailiffs, third parties, and/or alternate jurors; contact with extraneous reading materials and/or inadmissible evidence; race and ethnic prejudice; improper jury deliberations; and official misconduct by bailiffs, judges, and other court personnel. There are many bizarre and egregious examples of juror misconduct. Fortunately, most have resulted in cases being overturned or new trials ordered. Regardless of whether a defendant is factually guilty or innocent, the duty of a juror is to devote his or her full attention to the case. An example of juror misconduct is the case of *Spunaugle v. State* (946 P.2d 246 Okla. 1997). In that case, an appellate court ruled that the trial court committed reversible error by failing to grant the defendant's timely motion to replace a sleeping juror. The record clearly reflected that during trial a juror had, in fact, been asleep.

A further response to the problem of wrongful convictions was a law created in 1994. The Justice for all Act was signed into law by President Bush. The Justice for All Act includes legislation that grants any federal inmate the right to petition a federal court for DNA testing to support a claim of innocence. It also encourages states—through the power of the purse—to adopt adequate measures to preserve evidence and make postconviction DNA testing available in inmates seeking to prove their innocence. Other key provisions include helping states that have the death penalty to create effective systems for the appointment and performance of qualified counsel, together with better training and monitoring for both the defense and prosecution. It provides substantial funding to states for increased reliance on DNA testing in new criminal investigations, increases the amount of compensation available to wrongfully convicted federal prisoners, and expresses the sense of Congress that all wrongfully convicted persons should be reasonably compensated.

CRIME LEGISLATION AND INJUSTICE

> *I don't like mandatory sentences, I think they can lead to injustice.*
>
> —Supreme Court Justice Anthony M. Kennedy

A young single mother with no prior convictions or any evidence of involvement in drug sales drove her aunt from Miami to a drug dealer's home in Palm Beach County. For that, she was sentenced to 12.5 years in prison, which the sentencing judge, Federal District Judge Jose Gonzalez Jr., termed an outrage. A 44-year-old carpenter in Portland, Oregon, with no criminal record, whose savings were wiped out paying for his wife's cancer treatment, was asked to help unload a cargo boat of hashish onto a truck. He did so and ended up sentenced to 12 years in prison without parole (Koppel, 1995).

In recent years, **crime control legislation,** along with assorted state or federal laws, has been passed to prevent and respond to criminal violence;

however well meaning the laws, inadvertent or unintentional victimization has resulted. Since 1984, Congress has added vast numbers of new **mandatory minimum sentences,** particularly for federal crimes involving drug or firearms offenses. And, since then, more than 60,000 individuals have been sentenced under these guidelines. The expectation that mandatory minimum sentences for drug dealers would affect the availability of drugs by reducing the number of suppliers has not been realized. Offenders receiving these new mandatory minimum sentences have generally been only small-time dealers.

Ninety-four percent of federal mandatory minimum cases involve four laws covering drugs or weapons. Beginning with New York's **Rockefeller Law** in 1973, almost every state has enacted its own mandatory minimum sentences.

The war on drugs resulted in mandatory minimum sentences, designed to be extremely tough on narcotics offenders and make drugs almost the sole factor in sentencing. For instance, the mandatory minimum for people possessing more than 5 grams of crack cocaine is 5 years in federal prison (an individual packet of sugar in a restaurant weighs about one gram). The only factors other than drug weight that may be considered in the sentencing are the defendant's prior convictions, in which case the mandatory minimum is raised, and whether the U.S. attorney asks for a sentence less than the mandatory minimum because the defendant provided substantial assistance in obtaining the conviction of another accused drug offender.

Because of harsh new sentencing guidelines, such as "three-strikes, and you're out," a disproportionate number of young black and Hispanic men are likely to be imprisoned for life under scenarios in which they are guilty of little more than a history of untreated addiction and several prior drug-related offenses. States will absorb the staggering cost not only of constructing additional prisons to accommodate increasing numbers of prisoners who will never be released but also of warehousing them into old age (Haney and Zimbardo, 1998).

The federal mandatory minimums are not limited to people who possess specific amounts of drugs for sale. In 1988, Congress added conspiracy to commit a drug offense to the list of crimes with mandatory minimums. Thus, if a person gives an undercover federal agent a tip as to who will sell LSD and if this other person does possess 5 grams of LSD, the person giving the tip is considered a conspirator and subject to the same mandatory minimum as the person who actually possessed the LSD.

As a result of these mandatory minimums, one-quarter of all federal inmates are serving sentences of 15 years or more; half are serving sentences of more than 7 years. At both the federal and state levels, mandatory minimum sentences result in disproportionate sentencing.

The drug war is also credited with legalized racism because more minorities are arrested, prosecuted, convicted, and jailed, reinforcing the perception that drug trafficking is primarily a minority activity. This perception creates the profile that results in more stops of minority drivers, called "driving while black" or **racial profiling.** It is reported that white drivers receive far less police attention. Many white drug dealers and drug possessors go unapprehended, fueling the perception that whites commit fewer drug offenses than minorities. In short, the pervasiveness of racial profiling by the police in the enforcement of our nation's drug laws is the consequence of escalating the so-called war on drugs.

Mandatory legislation for unlawful weapons possessions has also created controversy. In Massachusetts, the **Bartley Fox law** requires one year in prison for carrying a gun without a permit. An early test case under Bartley–Fox involved the prosecution of a teenager who had inadvertently allowed his gun license to expire. To raise money to buy his high school class ring, he was driving to a pawnshop to sell his gun. Stopping the youth for a traffic violation, a policeman noticed the weapon. The teenager spent the mandatory year in prison with no parole.

The **American Civil Liberties Union** of Massachusetts lobbied against Bartley–Fox because of the likelihood that people would be sent to prison inappropriately (Koppel, 1995).

In many states, there is what is known as the **felony murder rule.** The rule states that any killing, whether intentional or not, occurring during the course of committing certain serious crimes, such as robbery or rape, can result in life imprisonment or a death sentence. The intent of the law is to hold offenders accountable to the fullest extent of the law when a death results from the offender's misconduct. The problem with the law is interpretation or overenforcement, as in the case of Brandon Hein (Focus 7–4).

Focus 7–4 Brandon Hein

On August 21, 1996, Brandon Hein was sentenced to life in prison without the possibility of parole for being at the wrong place at the wrong time.

On May 22, Brandon and four other teenagers went to the backyard clubhouse of another teenager, Mike, to purchase marijuana. Mike was known to sell marijuana out of his clubhouse, the "Fort," where he and his friends hung out. Mike's best friend and frequent companion at the Fort was Jimmy, the son of an LAPD police officer. Most of the teenagers were stoned or drunk.

A 15-year-old called Micah was first into the small, dark Fort. By the time the others entered, words had been exchanged between Micah and Mike and a fight was

(Continued)

(*Continued*)

in progress. The bigger Mike had Micah in a headlock. Micah's older, teenaged brother, Jason, jumped in and a melee was under way. During the 60-second fight, Jason pulled a two-inch Swiss Army-type knife from a holder on his belt and stabbed at Mike. Mike's friend Jimmy jumped in, and Jason stabbed him, too. In 60 seconds it was over. Brandon was in the fistfight, though he didn't know who was swinging or why. Nothing was taken from the clubhouse.

After the fight, Brandon, Jason, Micah, and another teen left the Fort, joined another teen who was sitting in a truck nearby, and drove off. Jason would later tell the incredulous boys, "I think I stabbed them." Mike and Jimmy ran to Mike's house where Jimmy collapsed on the floor. Mike's family dialed 911 and also called Jimmy's mother who lived down the street.

Jimmy died of the knife wounds. The emergency room doctor who treated him would write to the judge that "Jimmy Farris did not die of grossly brutal wounds. A single small puncture wound penetrated his chest and into his heart. Had that stab wound been one inch further to the left, he perhaps would still be alive today." Because of the severity of the stab wound to the heart, most of the bleeding was internal.

The DA immediately began to portray all of the boys as gang members—something for which there was absolutely no evidence—and the LAPD and Los Angeles County Sheriff's Department closed ranks around their own. Although Brandon was ready for trial, he was denied his constitutional right to a speedy trial and forced to wait in Los Angeles County Jail almost a year until his case was heard. His case was combined with that of the others by the court. All were tried as one. Although Jason took the stand and claimed full responsibility for his actions, the district attorney, reeling from a series of public humiliations, including loss of the O. J. Simpson trial, charged all the boys under California's felony murder rule. Under that rule, everyone is caught up in the same net, regardless of any culpability in the crime, foreknowledge, or even knowledge that a crime had been committed. All the DA needed to do was convince the jury that although nothing had been taken, the boys intended to steal and not buy pot. Although he changed his story many times, by the time of the trial, Mike's testimony had become that the boys came to steal, not buy, his marijuana. Mike was the sole witness claiming the boys came to steal, and for his testimony, he was granted immunity. From the beginning, the DA effectively used the media to plant the idea in the minds of potential jurors that this was a gang killing, even though any gang testimony was so flimsy as to not be allowed in court. The jurors believed Mike's testimony and found the boys guilty of attempted robbery, which meant they automatically became guilty of murder under the felony murder rule.

Source: Information taken directly from the Brandon Hein Web site, www.BrandonHein.com/

Another type of well-meaning legislation stirring controversy in recent years is the so-called **three strikes law.** In March 1994, California passed this law in response to violent crimes committed by repeat offenders. Between 1993 and 1995, 24 states passed "three strikes and you're out" laws, which prolong prison terms for comparatively few criminals with a particular pattern of prior felony convictions. Under the law, a defendant convicted of a third felony that is violent or serious could be sent to prison for life. There is little argument that repeat violent offenders should be locked up for life. However, the law has included populations not considered to be the most violent in society.

The three strikes measures have resulted in prison overcrowding, with many male offenders in their 30s getting life sentences. And, unfortunately, the three strikes law is inconsistently applied, costly, and targets more nonviolent, low-level felons than it does violent career criminals. It results in life sentences for offenses that would otherwise be billed as short-term county jail time. The average third striker enters prison at age 36 and will serve about 21 years. The average cost of incarcerating an inmate in California is about $25,600 per year, a figure that triples when an inmate becomes elderly and requires more health care. The figures add up—it costs about $1.5 million to incarcerate a third-strike prisoner for 25 years (Fannon, 2001).

Another potential impact of the law, as argued by Reynolds (2001), is that the law may encourage some career criminals to commit more grievous crimes. The criminal can reduce his chances of apprehension and conviction by killing a witness, without fear of more severe punishment. If apprehended and convicted of a third serious violent crime, for instance, the penalty would equal that for homicide anyway in terms of years served in prison. So, too often the criminal will kill to reduce the chances of being caught. In recent years, there have been modifications and court challenges to the three strikes laws.

The California Supreme Court ruled in 1996 that the law was too strict because many were being sent to prison for nonviolent crimes. This decision allows judges to use discretion in sentencing after the third conviction. As a final note, the law makes sense if the most violent are incarcerated for life after the third conviction for a serious and violent crime (i.e., rape). It can be seriously argued that locking up these repeat, sociopathic, violent predators may prevent future victimizations. However, incarcerating nonviolent offenders for life terms may be counterproductive to the goals of justice. Research suggests that three strikes laws have had little significant impact on crime and arrest rates. According to the *Uniform Crime Reports,* states without a three strikes law have lower rates of index crimes, whereas index crime rates were highest in states with get-tough laws (Turner, et al., 2000).

Another aspect of legislation or the failure of legislation to control crime is illegal immigration and gangs. In 2007, crimes committed by alien criminals, such as rape, murder, or drug distribution, cost U.S. taxpayers

$1.6 billion in prison costs alone. The figure doesn't include the cost of lost property, medical bills of the victims, time lost from work to recover, higher insurance costs, and so on. In 2007, it is reported that illegal aliens make up 29 percent of the U.S. prison population—or 500,000 illegals. As a tragic example, in Los Angeles in 2008, a high school football star named Jamiel Shaw was shot and killed by an illegal alien who belonged to a notorious street gang. The man charged with shooting was found to have been living illegally in this country for more than a decade. The shooter was released from jail a day before the shooting. Had the shooter been checked more thoroughly, he would have been deported and not released. However, the city has what is referred to as special order 40, which prevents officers from checking on the immigration status of suspects in most cases. This event has prompted a call for reform in Los Angeles and other cities to initiate a law known as Jamiel's law.

CORRECTIONS

In 1993, 12-year-old Polly Klaas was abducted from her home at knifepoint and murdered. Her body was found in a shallow grave 65 days later. Richard Allen Davis, a convicted sex offender on parole, was convicted of the brutal and senseless crime and is currently awaiting execution. This case is an unfortunate reminder of the failure of the court and correctional institutions to rehabilitate habitual offenders or to see that fear of incarceration prevents new crimes. It is also a warning that predatory victimization can occur anywhere, instilling fears about personal security (LaGanga, 1994). The *Klaas* case served as a stimulus to pass more stringent laws, such as the three strikes law previously discussed and postrelease supervision for repeat violent offenders. Criminal injustice in the corrections system must be viewed as serious. Whenever an offender is placed on probation or released on parole, there is a risk of recidivism.

The risks become paramount if the offender has a drug problem, is unemployed, or is thrust back into a dysfunctional environment. Add to the mix the fact that many probation and parole officers are overburdened with high caseloads, which makes the job of quality supervision more difficult.

A study of burglary victims by Reingert (1989) found that people previously convicted of crime or poorly supervised parolees often victimize the poor and people living in communities undergoing transition. These recidivist offenders are often released because of prison overcrowding and seek communities where they can achieve anonymity and prey on innocent victims.

According to statistics released by the Justice Department, a record 7 million adults nationwide were either in prison or jail, were on probation, or parole at the end of 2005. This number amounts to about one in every 32 people in the United States. Furthermore, statistics show there was an increase of nearly 3 percent of people behind bars from the previous year. Most offenders sentenced to prison will eventually be released. Unfortunately, many of these offenders are mentally ill, requiring medical assistance. The United States currently has more mentally ill men and women in jails and prisons than in all state hospitals combined. The statistics show that over half of all state and prison inmates report mental illnesses including psychotic disorders, mania, and major depression. The rate of reported mental illnesses in prisons is increasing and is greater than mental health problems experienced by the general adult population.

These care issues have plagued prisons and jails for years. And they will carry over to the community when the mentally ill are released. Problems include inadequate services, undertrained staff, lack of interagency collaboration, managing different populations (i.e., juveniles, racial minorities, and elderly offenders), and funding. According to Fitzgibbons and Gunter-Justice (2000), many jails, because of their size or locale, have little or no mental health assistance available, either internally or within the community. Not surprisingly, inmates with mental illness are more prone to commit crimes, are at a greater likelihood for arrest, are more likely to commit violent crimes, and have the highest rates of recidivism of any offenders (Sigurdson, 2000).

The injustice of overcrowded and understaffed prisons, filled with idle prisoners facing long terms of incarceration, are precursors for extortion, violence, and other abuses. Because of public reluctance to spend any more than necessary to warehouse the criminal population, inmates generally have limited work training, education opportunities, treatment, or counseling services. There is also the problem of a small minority of correctional staff who physically abuse inmates.

Guard violence, if not endemic, is more than sporadic in many facilities. In 1999, for example, news stories detailed a series of horrific cases of guard abuse—stories of inmates being beaten with fists and batons, fired at unnecessarily with shotguns, stunned with electronic devices, slammed face first onto concrete floors, and even raped by correctional officers (Human Rights Watch, 2001). In some instances, entire state prison systems were full of abuse.

A March 1999 federal court decision concluded, for example, that the frequency of "wholly unnecessary physical aggression" perpetrated by guards in Texas prisons reflected a "culture of sadistic and malicious violence" found there (*Ruiz v. Johnson*, 1999). Violence between inmates includes extortion, harassment, rape, and other types of physical abuse. It has been reported that such violence is common, with estimates that as many as 70 percent of inmates are assaulted by other inmates each year (McShane and Williams, 1996). The case of Larry serves as a brutal example of the violence occurring in some prisons (Focus 7–5). As reported in 1998, 79 inmates were killed in prison, and many thousands more were injured so severely that they required medical attention (Camp and Camp, 1998).

Many readers probably are not concerned about inmate victimization. But the reality is that most prisoners will be released back into society someday, and a number of them will be mentally ill, angry, or disfranchised, with little hope or family support. The question is not why are they being released, but how to deal with these offenders during incarceration and upon release.

Focus 7–5   The Rape of Larry

At age 22, Larry received a 6-year sentence for possession of cocaine. In April 1995, he was sent to a notoriously dangerous prison in Texas. Larry was one of a handful of white prisoners on the wing to which he was assigned, and he was immediately subject to racial harassment, threats, and violent assaults. Fearful for his life, he later told Human Rights Watch that he purposely broke prison disciplinary rules in order to be placed on special cell restrictions, which left him locked in his cell 23 hours a day and, therefore, more protected. Another inmate, S.R., was assigned to share his cell. The inmate was African American, told Larry that he was a member of the Crips, and displayed identifying tattoos. He immediately began to threaten Larry, demanding that Larry give up his personal belongings and that he submit to sex. Larry alerted a guard to his situation, stating that he was afraid for his safety and did not want to be housed with S.R. The guard dismissed his fears. For several days, Larry was threatened, and he repeatedly informed guards of his fears for his safety. On the third night, the inmate again demanded that Larry submit to sex. When Larry refused, the inmate yanked him from the top bunk where he had been resting. Larry fell to the floor, and the inmate began punching and kicking him. After a struggle, Larry was knocked unconscious. When he gained conscious, the inmate was holding a shank (homemade knife) to his throat. He then anally raped Larry. Early the next morning, when guards were delivering the breakfast trays, Larry, who was visibly injured, demanded that he be taken from the cell and brought to the prison infirmary. For an entire day, the guards ignored his plea. Prison medical staff did not examine Larry until 9:00 A.M. the following morning. Larry was transferred to another prison, but still felt extremely insecure and unsafe. Two months later, he attempted suicide by cutting his wrists. He was transferred to the prison psychiatric unit for treatment, where he stayed for the remainder of his sentence.

Source: Human Rights Watch, www.hrw.org/reports/2001/prison/case_histories.

SUMMARY

Injustice by the criminal justice system is harmful to society as well as to the individual victim. It can occur at any stage of the justice process, from arrest to postsentencing confinement. An injustice to an individual, such as a wrongful conviction, also victimizes the family of the falsely accused and destroys public confidence in the system. Likewise, releasing the violent or acquitting the guilty is also a travesty of justice. Although most injustice is inadvertent or unintentional, society must be vigilant to the threat of mistakes. For acts of deliberate injustice, vigorous prosecution is needed to remove those responsible for such egregious behavior.

KEY TERMS AND CONCEPTS

American Civil Liberties Union   218
Bartley–Fox law   218
Crime control legislation   216
Death Penalty Information
    Center (DPIC)   215
Deliberate victimization   204
Eyewitness misidentification   213

Felony murder rule   218
Inadvertent victimization   204
Mandatory minimum sentences   217
Overzealous prosecutors   213
Racial profiling   218
Rockefeller Law   217
Three strikes law   219

DISCUSSION QUESTIONS AND LEARNING ACTIVITIES

1. Select an injustice committed by the police, and discuss why it occurred. How could the injustice have been prevented?

2. Scan news articles for examples of system injustice. What appear to be the reasons for the injustices committed? Were they deliberate? Inadvertent?

3. Do you feel that the acquittal of O. J. Simpson was an injustice? Why or why not?

4. Do you feel that the felony murder rule is unjust? How should it be changed?

5. How can crime legislation be a source of injustice?

6. Are the poor and disenfranchised victimized more by the justice system? What example can you provide?

7. Interview a judge, prosecutor, police officer, and a probation officer about what they feel are examples of criminal justice injustice.

8. Visit the American Civil Liberties Union (ACLU) homepage and search for examples of injustices. Do you agree with the ACLU positions?

9. Discuss the case and varieties of victimizations experienced by the McMartin family. Who was most responsible for causing the victimization? (There is also a film on the case titled *Indictment*.)

10. Regarding violent victimizations occurring in prisons, develop an argument as to why citizens should be concerned about the problem.

11. Identify the reasons for system injustice during the adjudication process.

12. What legal remedies are available to a citizen victimized by police misconduct?

WEB SOURCES

Center on Wrongful Convictions: Northwestern Law. www.law.northwestern.edu/wrongfulconvictions/

American Bar Association   A Statistical Look at Criminal Justice and Injustice. www.abanet.org/irr/hr/winter04/statistical.html

Justice for All—A Criminal Justice Reform Organization. www.jfa.net/

RECOMMENDED READINGS

Huff, C. Ronald. 2002. What Can We Learn from Other Nations About the Problem of Wrongful Convictions? *Judicature* 86:2, 91–97.

Huff, C. Ronald. 2002. Wrongful Conviction and Public Policy: The American Society of Criminology 2001 Presidential Address. *Criminology* 40:1–18.

Liebman, James S., Jeffrey Fagan, Valerie West, and Jonathan Lloyd. 2000. Capital Attrition: Error Rates in Capital Cases. *Texas Law Review* 78:1839–1865.

Scheck, Barry, Peter Neufeld, and Jim Dwyer. 2000. *Actual Innocence.* New York: Doubleday.

Westervelt, Saundra D., and John A. Humphrey, eds. 2001. *Wrongly Convicted: Perspectives on Failed Justice.* New Brunswick, NJ: Rutgers University Press.

REFERENCES

Camp, Camille, and George M. Camp. 1998. *The Corrections Yearbook 1998.* Middletown, CT: Criminal Justice Institute.

Fannon, Charles. 2001. The Insanity of the Three Strikes and You're Out Law. www.frictionmagazine.com.

Fitzgibbons, M., and T. Gunter-Justice. 2000. Telemedicine and Mental Health in Jails: New Tool for an Old Problem. *Corrections Today* 62 (6):104–107.

Gross, Samuel, et al. 2004. *Exonerations in the United States: 1989–2003.* New York: Gideon Project of the Open Society Institute.

Haney, Craig, and Philip Zimbardo. 1998. The Past and Future of U.S. Prison Policy: Twenty-Five Years after the Stanford Prison Experiment. *American Psychologist* 53 (7):718.

Hua, Thao. 1996. New Suspect Charged as Man Held 17 Years Is Freed. *Los Angeles Times,* June 21, A-1.

Human Rights Watch. 2001. *World Report 2000.* New York. Jailing the Mentally Ill. 2000. www.americanradioworks.org/features/mentally_ill/poll/stats.html.

Johnson, Kevin. DNA tests fuel urgency to free the innocent. *USA Today* February 19, 2008 1A.

Koppel, David. 1995. Sentencing Policies Endanger Public Safety. *USA Today*, 24:32, 64.

LaGanga, Maria. 1994. Haunted City Girds for Klaas Case Trial. *Los Angeles Times*, July 11, 14.

McShane, Marilyn D., and Frank P. Williams III, eds. 1996. *Encyclopedia of American Prisons.* New York: Garland Publishing.

Pate, Anthony, and Edwin Hamilton. 1990. *The Big Six: Policing America's Largest Cities.* Washington, DC: Police Foundation.

Radelet, M. L., and H. G. Bedau. 1992. *In Spite of Innocence: Erroneous Convictions in Capital Cases.* Boston: Northeastern University Press.

Reingert, George F. 1989. Spatial Justice and Criminal Victimization. *Justice Quarterly,* 6:4.

Reynolds, Morgan. 2001. *Murderous Impact of Three Strikes.* Washington, DC: U.S. Department of Labor.

Rovella, David E. 1997. Danger of Executing the Innocent on the Rise. *National Law Journal* 4 August, A-101.

Ruiz v. Johnson. 1999. U.S. Dist. LEXIS 2060, at 236–37 (March 1, 1999).

Scheck, B., P. Neufeld, and J. Dwyer. 2001. *Actual Innocence: When Justice Goes Wrong and How to Make It Right.* New York: Penguin Books.

Senna, Joseph, and Larry Siegel. 1996. *Introduction to Criminal Justice.* Minneapolis, MN: West Publishing.

Sigurdson, C. 2000. The Mad, the Bad and the Abandoned: The Mentally Ill in Prisons and Jails. *Corrections Today,* 62:70–78.

Turner, Susan, RAND Corporation Criminal Justice Program, and Justice Research and Statistics Association. 2000. Impact of Truth-in-Sentencing and Three Strikes Crime Legislation. *Crime and Justice Atlas 2000.* Washington, DC: U.S. Department of Justice.

Usborne, David. 1999. NYPD Officer Admits Torture. *Independent,* May 26, 20.

Worden, Robert E. 1996. The "Causes" of Police Brutality: Theory and Evidence on Police Use of Force. In *Police Violence: Understanding and Controlling Police Abuse of Force*, eds. William A. Geller and Hans Toch. New Haven, CT: Yale University Press.

8

The Violence of Terrorism

LEARNING OBJECTIVES

After studying this chapter, you will:

- Be familiar with the meaning of terrorism.
- Understand the types of terrorism.
- Understand the motives of terrorists.
- Learn how terrorists use violence.
- Understand the responses to terrorism.

INTRODUCTION

Is one man's terrorist another man's freedom fighter?

—Boaz Ganor

Since September 11, 2001, fighting terrorism is a major priority for the U.S. government and a serious reminder of our own vulnerability to dedicated attacks. However, the violence terrorism presents has deep historical roots, with many motives and often very sophisticated tactics. Terrorist tactics have been used to fight oppression, as well as for criminal purposes.

As suggested in the opening quote, terror tactics may be considered essential to overcome oppression, which is why this form of violence is difficult to explain or rationalize. The *Zealots* in Israel (A.D. 100) fought Roman occupation with hit-and-run tactics in public places. The *Assassins* in Iraq (A.D. 1100) fought the Christian Crusaders by using suicide tactics much like the present-day suicide attacks occurring in Iraq and other nations.

During the Revolutionary War, terrorist attacks against the British forces were commonplace.

Although terrorism has been practiced for centuries, the actual term can be traced to the French Revolution (1789–1795) to describe the actions of the French government. During the period of the French Revolution, also known as the Reign of Terror, thousands of so-called enemies of the state were put on trial and executed (O'Connor, 2005a). Terrorist acts are the clash of political, religious, or social beliefs that results in violence. Much has been written about terrorism in recent years, particularly addressing motives, organization, and tactics of various terrorist groups (see, generally, Hoffman, 1999; Jenkins, 1985; Kushner, 2003; Laqueur, 1999; Martin, 2003). A full treatment of terrorism is beyond the scope of this chapter. However, an overview of the violence and victimization of terrorism is given along with a discussion of the distinctions between terrorist groups and the various methods and motives used.

DOMESTIC AND INTERNATIONAL TERRORISM

It is not unusual for criminal groups to employ terrorist tactics to accomplish particular objectives. Some groups are well organized, with strong financial backing, whereas others have little cohesion and structure. Some terrorist groups operate within a particular country, while others transport terror to other nations. There are generally two broad types of terrorism: domestic and international. Both types employ intimidation, threats, property destruction, and murder albeit with different motives and strategies.

Domestic Terrorism

Timothy McVeigh, a former U.S. Army soldier and a right-wing extremist, was executed by the federal government by lethal injection in 2001 for bombing the Alfred P. Murrah Federal Building in Oklahoma City in 1995. McVeigh's conviction resulted from 11 counts of murder and conspiracy for the bombing, which killed 168 people. The execution was the first application of the death penalty by the federal government in more than 30 years. **Domestic terrorism** occurs when the violence and terror associated with it are confined to national territories and do not involve targets abroad. The terrorists may be organized crime groups, inner-city street gangs, white supremacist groups, or others with a particular agenda or ideology. Some are single-issue oriented, whereas others are against government policies or business practices in general.

The Federal Bureau of Investigation (FBI) defines domestic terrorism as acts of violence by persons who reside in the United States, who are not acting on behalf of a foreign power, and who may be conducting criminal activities in support of terrorist objectives. In other words, domestic terrorism refers to activities that involve acts dangerous to human life that are a violation of the criminal laws of the United States or of any state; appear to be intended to intimidate or coerce a civilian population; intend to influence the policy of a government by mass destruction, assassination, or kidnapping; and occur primarily within the territorial jurisdiction of the United States (Jenkins, 1985).

The U.S. Department of Justice further adds to the definition the following:

> The unlawful use of *force or violence*, committed by a group(s) of two or more individuals, against *persons or property* to *intimidate or coerce* a government, the civilian population, or any segment thereof, in furtherance of *political or social objectives.*

> —(U.S. Department of Justice, 1994, Washington DC)

Unlike many international terrorist groups, domestic terrorists function more on emotional issues rather than broader political ideologies. (See Focus 8–1.) Members of domestic radical groups, for example, are

---

Focus 8–1   Profile of a Domestic Terrorism Group: Christian Identity

Christian Identity is a religious ideology popular in extreme right-wing circles. There are more than 50,000 members throughout the United States. It is a racist and anti-Semitic religious sect whose adherents believe that white people of European descent are the descendants of the Lost Tribes of ancient Israel. Many consider Jews to be the Satanic offspring of Eve and the Serpent and nonwhites are "mud peoples" created before Adam and Eve. Its racist and anti-Semitic beliefs are usually accompanied by extreme anti-government sentiments. Christian Identity influences virtually all white supremacist and extreme anti-government move- ments. In the summer of 1995, Christian Identity members committed a series of bombings in the wake of the Oklahoma City bombing by Timothy McVeigh. In 1998, Eric Rudolph became a fugitive after allegedly bombing gay bars, the Atlanta Summer Olympics, and an abortion clinic. In 1999, Buford Furrow, a former Aryan Nations security guard, went on a shooting spree at a Jewish Community Center in Los Angeles, wounding four children and an adult, and later killing a Filipino-American postal worker.

Source: Anti-Defamation League, 2005 (http://www.adl.org/).

usually loners or associate with rebellious groups whose beliefs have little support from the larger mainstream American society. In these cases, fear, anger, hatred, or ignorance motivate group membership and methods of operation. Many demonstrate hate violence against other racial/ethnic groups, such as blacks, Jews, or Asians. Others target the government or particular businesses for supporting practices they deem wrong (i.e., abortion, animal slaughter). The emotional responses of domestic groups are significantly "less entrenched and thus more transient than the ideological beliefs of their overseas counterparts" (Gilmartin, 1999).

Who are domestic terrorists and what are their goals? Domestic terrorists range from white supremacists, anti-government types, and militia members to eco-terrorists and lawless inner-city street gangs. They include violent anti-abortionists and black and brown nationalists who envision a separate state for blacks and Latinos (Copeland, 2004). See Focus 8–2 discusses **Eric Rudolph,** a domestic terrorist.

FOCUS 8–2   Profile of a Domestic Terrorist: Eric Rudolph

Eric Rudolph was born in 1966. After his father's death, he moved with his mother and siblings to North Carolina. He dropped out after the ninth grade and worked as a carpenter with his older brother Daniel. His mother believed in survivalism and instilled this ideology in Rudolph. After Rudolph received his general equivalency diploma (GED), he attended Western Carolina University and later enlisted in the U.S. Army. He was discharged in 1989 while serving with the 101st Airborne Division, reportedly for smoking marijuana. Rudolph committed several bombings for political reasons. Of the bombings committed by Rudolph, the most notoriety came from the Centennial Olympic Park bombing in Atlanta on July 27, 1996, during the 1996 Summer Olympics. The blast killed one person and wounded 111 others. Rudolph's motive for the bombings was political, with the purpose of angering the government in "the eyes of the world for its abominable sanctioning of abortion on demand" and force the cancelation of the Games; Rudolph also confessed to the bombings of an abortion clinic in Atlanta in 1997, a gay and lesbian nightclub in Atlanta in 1997, and an abortion clinic in Birmingham, Alabama, in 1998, killing one person. Rudolph's bombs were made of dynamite surrounded by nails, which act as shrapnel, increasing the destructive power of the bomb. He targeted health clinics and office buildings sponsoring abortions and venues for gays and lesbians. Rudolph is an adherent of the extremist group known as the Christian Identity, a sect that holds that white Christians are God's chosen people and that others will be condemned to hell. Rudolph was finally arrested in 2003 and sentenced to four consecutive life terms.

Source: Wikipedia, 2005.

As reported by the congressional subcommittee on street gangs, the domestic terrorist family is growing, including street gangs. Is it reported in 2005 that there are approximately 30,000 street gangs, with 800,000 members, impacting 2,500 communities across the United States. The gangs represent the very real threat of homegrown terror because they are tied to numerous acts of murder, extortion, robbery, kidnapping, and violent assaults, as well as drug, auto, and weapons smuggling, which resemble terrorist tactics (Hyde, 2005).

Another type of domestic terrorist group is the so-called inner-city street gang. Many names are given to these gangs, and their presence is becoming more recognized throughout the country. Street gangs may not fit the profile of a traditional terrorist group, but their tactics of intimidation and random violence do. Regarding the violence of street gangs, there is no shortage of examples. One of the most violent street gangs is termed the **MS-13,** composed mainly of Central American immigrants from El Salvador, Honduras, and Guatemala. Their violence has been reported in Northern Virginia, New York, California, Texas, as well as Oregon and Nebraska. The group is estimated to have 8,000 to 10,000 hardcore members—and they are growing increasingly sophisticated, widespread, and violent (Hyde, 2005). In fact, news reports have indicated that MS-13 gang members and Middle Eastern aliens are using the U.S. border to illegally enter the country, suggesting a connection with international terrorists (McPhee, 2005).

Los Angeles is the major population center for MS-13 members, with Washington, DC, the next largest center. The violent methods of MS-13 surpass those of other gangs because of

- their willingness to use overt violence to punctuate their activities
- their paramilitary type structure and order that comes from years of civil wars and insurgencies in Central America
- the concern that MS-13 could form an alliance with terrorists or other violent gangs

Law enforcement in 28 states have reported MS-13 members are engaged in international retail drug trafficking, primarily trafficking in powdered cocaine, crack cocaine, marijuana, and, to a lesser extent, in methamphetamine and heroin. The drug proceeds are then laundered through seemingly legitimate businesses in those communities. MS-13 members are also involved in a variety of other types of criminal activity, including rape, murder, extortion, auto theft, alien smuggling, and robbery (Swecker, 2005). And, it is not uncommon for a deported gang member, having benefited from newly established links to the drugs, weapons, and other criminal networks in Central America, to return to the United States within a matter of months (Reisman, 2006).

A visit to some inner cities such as Los Angeles and Chicago reveals territorial conflicts between many rival ethnic gangs with such identities as the Crips, Bloods, and so forth. Many of these gangs not only terrorize other gangs but target citizens living in neighborhoods where the gangs congregate. These violent gangs are known to retaliate against anyone who reports their activities or becomes a police informant. Living in these gang communities invites victimization.

In some of the toughest gang areas in Los Angeles, residents are afraid to go out at certain times of day or even to report gang violence to the police. To many, the streets are a war zone and violence is an everyday occurrence. It is reported that gang members in some communities patrol their neighborhoods exacting "taxes" from nongang members to sell drugs or work as prostitutes (Barrett, 2004). In response to the gang problem in California, Governor Schwarzenegger introduced the California Gang Reduction, Intervention and Prevention (CalGRIP) initiative in May of 2007 to confront the dramatic increase in gangs across the state. Reportedly, there are more than 420,000 gang members statewide, responsible for crimes including money laundering, extortion, narcotic production and sales, prostitution, human trafficking, assassinations for hire, theft, and counterfeiting. In spite of an overall decrease in crime in most California cities since the 1990s, rates of gang-related violent crime remain steady (Imperial Valley News, 2008).

A more clandestine type of domestic terrorist is the so-called eco-terrorist. Two examples are the Animal Liberation Front (ALF) and the Earth Liberation Front (ELF). Both of these groups are often referred to as eco-terrorists because their primary purpose is to protect animals or the environment through violence or intimidation. Both groups advocate tactics including arson and vandalism, resulting in losses of millions of dollars from damage to homes, equipment, and research facilities. The **Animal Liberation Front (ALF)** is against the abuse of animals such as fox hunting and raising animals for clothing (minks, rabbits). This group is active in protesting against businesses such as medical labs that use animals for research (FBI, 2003).

The **Earth Liberation Front (ELF)** is an environmental group that uses economic sabotage to stop the exploitation and destruction of the natural environment. In 2003, arsonists associated with the group attacked several car dealerships in Los Angeles, burning down a warehouse and vandalizing several cars. Most vehicles such as sport utility vehicles (SUVs) and Hummers were targeted because of their lower-than-average fuel efficiency, which the group feels is an energy threat to the environment (FBI, 2003a).

The FBI reports that animal and environmental rights extremists have claimed credit for more than 1,200 criminal incidents since 1990. In 2004, the FBI had 150 pending investigations associated with animal rights or eco-terrorist activities, and Bureau of Alcohol, Tobacco, and Firearms (ATF) officials say they have opened 58 investigations in the past 6 years related to violence attributed to ELF and ALF (Frieden, 2005).

Attacks committed by eco-terrorists are also growing in frequency and size:

> Harassing phone calls and vandalism now co exist with improvised explosive devices and personal threats to employees. ELF's target list has expanded to include sports utility vehicle dealerships and new home developers. It is anticipated that these trends will persist, particularly within the environmental movement, as extremists continue to combat what they perceive as "urban sprawl."

> —(Lewis, 2005)

Terrorists may even attempt to contaminate the food supply of a nation. **Agroterrorism** is a term associated with attacks on the food supply that can affect the health of a nation and commerce. One tactic is to spread a virus among meat-producing animals, causing such diseases as hoof-and-mouth disease. Any such disease requires the slaughter of contaminated animals and forces quarantine procedures that seriously disrupt the food supply and the economy (Knowles, 2005).

International Terrorism

International terrorism activities are violent terrorist acts committed by U.S. citizens or foreign nationals in the United States who are targeting national security interests on behalf of a foreign power (FBI, 2004). Since 1968, the U.S. State Department tallied many deaths caused by terrorism, and undoubtedly there will be many more in years to come.

In 1985, the U.S. State Department reported 816 deaths caused by terrorism, the highest annual toll until then. The deaths decreased in the subsequent years and then rose to 3,295 in 2001, mostly as a result of the September 11, 2001, attacks. In 2003, more than 1,000 people died as a result of terrorist acts. Many of these deaths resulted from suicide (homicide) bombings in countries such as Iraq, India, and Israel (U.S. Department of State, 2005a).

There are many examples of international terrorists operating in many countries and frequently directing hostility toward American interests such as the U.S. military, American businesses, and U.S. citizens. Sadly, terrorists target other countries that are aligned with the United States. On July 7, 2005, several bombs exploded in a London subway and a double-decker bus during the morning rush hour. The blasts resulted in more than 50 deaths with hundreds more wounded. The bombings were blamed on Islamic militants associated with **Al-Qaeda** and other terrorists in Europe, who reportedly are targeting governments providing troops in Iraq and Afghanistan.

According to the U.S. Department of State (2005a), well over 50 foreign terrorists organizations throughout the world are considered threats to Americans. The organization of the groups varies from highly organized to loosely affiliated extremists. The loosely affiliated type includes Sunni Islamic extremists, such as Osama bin Laden (see Focus 8–3) and those affiliated with his Al-Qaeda organization. The common element among these diverse individuals is that they are committed to the radical international jihad movement, whose ideology includes promoting violence

---

Focus 8–3   Profile of an International Terrorist: Osama bin Laden

Osama bin Laden, who instigated the terror attacks on the United States on September 11, 2001, is the most recognized terrorist in the world. He is on the FBI Top (Ten) Most Wanted list. Bin Laden was born in 1957 to a wealthy Saudi Arabian construction magnate. He reportedly has 24 children from several marriages. In 1979, he joined the Afghan Moslem rebels fighting the USSR. Bin Laden used his money to recruit an army from around the Middle East. Throughout the 1980s, and with help from the CIA, bin Laden fought the Soviet-backed regime. He viewed the United States as much of an evil as the Soviet Union. After the war, he returned to Saudi Arabia, but the Saudi government feared his brand of militant Islam and stripped him of his Saudi citizenship. He went to Sudan, but pressure from the West forced him to return to Afghanistan in 1995. He developed a following and is allegedly responsible for bombing the World Trade Center in New York in 1993 and the Egyptian Embassy in Pakistan 2 years later. His backers have fought wars and insurgencies in Bosnia, Chechnya, Kashmir, and Tajikistan. He is responsible for backing the September 11, 2001, terrorist attacks. As of 2005, the U.S. Department of State is offering a reward of up to $25 million for information leading directly to the apprehension or conviction of Osama bin Laden. An additional $2 million is being offered through a program developed and funded by the Airline Pilots Association and the Air Transport Association. As of June 2005, bin Laden's location is unknown.

Source: Wikipedia, 2005.

against the "enemies of Islam." to overthrow all governments not ruled by conservative Islamic law. The primary terrorist threat to the United States in 2005 continued to be Al-Qaeda, which remained intent on attacking the U.S. homeland as well as U.S. interests abroad (U.S. Department of State, 2005a).

In response to the growing threats, the Antiterrorism and Effective Death Penalty Act of 1996 authorizes the Secretary of State to designate organizations as Foreign Terrorist Organizations. This list of designations is officially updated every 2 years, but the secretary may add organizations to the list at any time and frequently does in annual reports titled *Patterns of Global Terrorism*, which are mandated under the U.S. Criminal Code (O'Connor, 2005a).

There are three criteria for designation as an international terrorist group:

1. The organization must be foreign.
2. The organization must engage in terrorist activity as defined by law.
3. The organization's activities must threaten the security of U.S. nationals or the national security (national defense, foreign relations, or the economic interests) of the United States.

As for state-sponsored terrorism, the U.S. Department of State identifies Iran as the most active sponsor of terrorism. State sponsors of terrorism pose a grave WMD terrorism threat. A WMD program in a state sponsor of terrorism could enable a terrorist organization to acquire sophisticated WMD. State sponsors of terrorism and nations that fail to live up to their international obligations deserve special attention as potential facilitators of WMD terrorism. Its Islamic Revolutionary Guard Corps (IRGC) and Ministry of Intelligence and Security (MOIS) were directly involved in the planning and support of terrorist acts and continued to exhort a variety of groups, especially Palestinian groups with leadership cadres in Syria and Lebanese Hezbollah, to use terrorism in pursuit of their goals. In addition, the IRGC was increasingly involved in supplying lethal assistance to Iraqi militant groups, which destabilizes Iraq.

Iran maintained a high-profile role in encouraging anti-Israeli terrorist activity—rhetorically, operationally, and financially. Supreme Leader Khamenei and President Ahmadinejad praised Palestinian terrorist operations, and Iran provided Lebanese Hezbollah and Palestinian terrorist groups—notably Hamas, Palestinian Islamic Jihad, the al-Aqsa Martyrs Brigades, and the Popular Front for the Liberation of Palestine-General

Command—with extensive funding, training, and weapons (U.S. Department of State, 2008).

Whatever the brand or source of terrorism, the key variable is the infliction of random violence, usually on a civilian population as reported in Iraq and many other nations. Employing the most horrific violence is viewed as necessary because that is what terrorists do and it garners attention for their cause in the hope of inciting citizens to revolt against the government. It is the only method extremists can use because direct battlefield confrontation with their enemies would only result in their defeat. (See Focus 8–4.)

Focus 8–4   Profile of a International Terrorist Group: Jemaah Islamiya

Jemaah Islamiya (JI) is a Southeast Asian–based terrorist network with links to Al-Qaeda. The network recruited and trained extremists in the late 1990s, following the stated goal of creating an Islamic state comprising Brunei, Indonesia, Malaysia, Singapore, the southern Philippines, and southern Thailand. The Jemaah Islamiya organization is responsible for numerous high-profile bombings, including the bombing of the J. W. Marriott Hotel in Jakarta on August 5, 2003, and the Bali bombings on October 12, 2002. Members of the group have also been implicated in the September 9, 2004, attack outside the Australian Embassy in Jakarta. The Bali attack, which left more than 200 dead, was reportedly the final outcome of meetings in early 2002 in Thailand, where attacks in Singapore and against soft targets such as tourist spots were also considered. In June 2003, authorities disrupted a JI plan to attack several Western embassies and tourist sites in Thailand. In December 2001, Singaporean authorities uncovered a JI plot to attack the U.S. and Israeli Embassies and British and Australian diplomatic buildings in Singapore. JI is also responsible for the coordinated bombings of numerous Christian churches in Indonesia on Christmas Eve 2000 and was involved in the bombings of several targets in Manila on December 31, 2000. Recent investigations also linked JI to the December 2000 bombings when dozens of bombs were detonated in Indonesia and the Philippines. Exact numbers are currently unknown, and Southeast Asian authorities continue to uncover and arrest additional JI elements. Singaporean officials have estimated total JI members to be approximately 5,000. The number of actual operationally oriented JI members probably is several hundred.

JI is believed to have cells spanning Indonesia, Malaysia, Singapore, the Philippines, and southern Thailand and may have some presence in neighboring countries. The JI receives money and logistic assistance from Middle Eastern and South Asian contacts, nongovernmental organizations (NGOs), and other groups, including al-Qaeda.

Source: U.S. Department of state. 2005. *Country Reports on Terrorism, 2004.* Washington, DC: U.S. Department of State.

THE VIOLENCE AND VICTIMS OF TERRORISM

The objectives of terrorists, whether domestic or international, are to instill fear through violence, extortion, threats, or other acts of property or commerce destruction. As suggested earlier, the targets of terrorists may be select persons or a particular group or property not necessarily related to the aim of the incident, with the hope of coercing a government or civil population to act or not to act according to certain principles (Botha, 2005).

The violence perpetrated by terrorists can be homegrown (domestic) or operated under the guidance of governments as well as anti-government groups. It is well known that terrorism violence was adopted as a state policy by totalitarian regimes such as Nazi Germany under Adolf Hitler and the Soviet Union under Joseph Stalin. During these times, torture and execution were applied without legal guidance or restraints to create a climate of fear and to encourage adherence to the national ideology or the economic, social, and political goals of the state.

In recent years, terrorist tactics resulting in slaughter and torture have been used by various groups backed by the government. In Sudan, many atrocities including rape and murder were committed against certain citizens with the aim of displacing the black Sudanese tribes. The systematic slaughter was committed by the so-called Arab militia known as the Janjaweed, which reportedly was backed by the Khartoum government of Sudan (MSNBC News, 2004). Another brutal example is the corrupt regime of North Korea orchestrated by its dictator Kim Jong-il. Citizens have been murdered and tortured during government purges, with millions dying of starvation or as prisoners in one of the many death camps (Becker, 2005).

Whatever the purpose or ideology, a terrorist group or government commits acts of violence to accomplish selected goals, and violence is a means to intimidate citizens to achieve the aims of a corrupt, brutal regime or group. The following are some reasons for terrorist violence (Terrorism Research Center, 2005):

- Produce widespread fear
- Obtain worldwide, national, or local recognition for a cause by attracting the attention of the media
- Harass, weaken, or embarrass government security forces so that the government overreacts and appears repressive
- Steal or extort money and equipment, especially weapons and ammunition vital to the operation of the group
- Destroy facilities or disrupt lines of communication to create doubt that the government can provide for and protect its citizens

- Discourage foreign investments, tourism, or assistance programs that can affect the target country's economy and supports of the government in power
- Influence government decisions, legislation, or other critical decisions
- Satisfy vengeance

Terrorism is a process that has three elements:

1. The act of violence
2. The reaction or fear produced by the act
3. The social impact that follows the fear

As depicted in Figure 8–1, the **terrorism process** begins with an act, followed by a reaction to the act, followed by a social or legal impact. The violent acts are varied but usually include sabotage, assassination, hostage taking, murder, kidnapping, and bombing.

The reactions to terrorism include fear of travel, lifestyle changes, or suspicion and loathing of persons from other nations or cultures. The social impact can include legislation such as passage of the Patriot Act in 2001 (discussed later in this chapter) or changes in security as evidenced in airports, transportation venues, and business practices.

After the September 11th attacks, for example, the suicidal act of crashing airplanes into the Twin Towers in New York and into the Pentagon instilled fear in many American citizens. Lifestyles changed, and paranoia and suspicions rose. In a phone survey by the Rand Corporation, it was revealed that nearly half of American adults (44 percent) reported having one or more substantial symptoms of stress in the hours and days immediately following the September 11th terrorist attacks, and 9 out of 10 had stress reactions to some degree. Among children 5 years old or older, more than a third displayed one or more stress symptoms and almost half expressed worry about their own safety or the safety of loved ones. Stress reaction rates were highest in the New York City region and among women, nonwhites, and people with preexisting psychological disorders. But significant rates and symptoms were found in all subgroups and across the entire country, in large cities and small towns (Shuster et al., 2001).

FIGURE 8–1   MODEL OF THE TERRORISM PROCESS

Act $\Longrightarrow$ Reaction $\Longrightarrow$ Impact

The impact of terrorist attacks follows the reaction phase and includes a change in legislation and business practices. The insurance industry began offering affordable terrorism coverage to homeowners and businesses because of a federal law known as the Terrorism Risk Insurance Act of 2002. The federal law requires insurers to offer coverage for terrorism losses. The government acts as a reinsurer by pledging billions of federal dollars to help pay claims if terrorists attack the United States again (Associated Press, 2004).

A study of 600 U.S. clients of one insurance company found that nearly 25 percent had terrorism coverage in 2003. Less than a year later, 44 percent had coverage. Not surprisingly, the biggest rise came from large property owners, with coverage most common in the transportation industry, often a target in terrorist attacks (Associated Press, 2004).

In the United States, most terrorist incidents have involved small extremist groups who use terrorism to achieve a designated objective. Such groups are involved in hate crimes (church arsons, etc.) or crimes of violence against organizations or businesses performing acts contrary to the ideology of a particular group (abortion clinics, automobile manufacturing, etc.).

The violence of terrorism abroad, on the other hand, is usually in response to political or religious conflicts between competing factions attempting to control or change a system. In other words, politics and religion are often intertwined in the terrorist ideology, and there are many examples of these overlapping conflicts. Political and religious conflicts between the Catholics and Protestants in Northern Ireland and the violence occurring in Israel and Palestine are frequent reminders of terrorist intensity, which often results in innocent parties being killed or injured in the process.

Motives of Violence

Most violence has a motive, although the motive may not be rational or acceptable to others. For terrorists or other dedicated criminals, motives are genuine and necessary. There are a number of reasons motivating terrorism, whether domestic or international. The following are some brief explanations (O'Connor, 2005a):

1. *Political.* Heavily armed groups tending to be focused around supremacy, government intrusion, or religious revisionism (Aryan Nation)
2. *Cause-based.* Groups devoted to a social or religious cause using violence to address their grievances (Islamic Holy War, abortion clinic bombings, street gangs)

3. *Environmental.* Groups dedicated to slowing down development they believe is harming animals (ALF)

4. *State-sponsored.* When a repressive regime forces its citizens into total obedience (Peru, Iraq, Sudan, Haiti)

5. *Genocide.* When a government seeks to wipe out a minority group in its territory (Rwanda, Bosnia)

6. Although there are various overlapping philosophies motivating terrorism, terrorism can be divided into secular and nonsecular types. Note, however, that both types may be present and in some cases are difficult to distinguish.

Secular Motivations.   Groups with secular ideologies or nonreligious goals often attempt highly selective and discriminate acts of violence to achieve a specific political aim. This often requires them to keep casualties at the minimum to attain the objective. This is both to avoid a backlash that might severely damage the organization and also to maintain the appearance of a rational group that has legitimate grievances. By limiting their attacks, **secular terrorists** reduce the risk of undermining external political and economic support. Groups that comprise a "wing" of an insurgency or that are affiliated with political organizations often operate under these constraints. Some of these groups are also referred to as left-wing terrorists out to destroy capitalism and replace it with socialism or anarchism.

Groups on the far left tend to justify violent actions as struggles requiring civil disobedience or riots. In other words, revolution is needed for change as in the case of communism. For groups professing secular political or social motivations, their targets are usually symbolic, representing authority: government offices, banks, airlines, multinational corporations, and so forth. Likewise, these groups conduct attacks on representative individuals whom they associate with economic exploitation, social injustice, or political repression (Terrorism Research Center, 2005).

There are numerous examples of secular groups, and many are termed domestic terrorists. Examples are the ALF and anti-government groups that specifically target certain government operations or businesses, avoiding injury to the general citizenry. However, often innocent people are killed or injured as collateral damage.

Nonsecular Motivations.   As opposed to secular groups, religiously oriented groups typically attempt to inflict as many casualties as possible in their acts of terrorism. The loss of innocent life is irrelevant, and the more casualties, the better (as with the London bombings). Losses among their coreligionists are of little account because such casualties will reap benefits in the afterlife, as with the Islamic fundamentalists' homicide bombers. In other words, nonbelievers, whether they are the intended target or injured or killed as collateral damage, deserve death, and killing them may be considered a moral duty.

The Kenyan bombing against the U.S. Embassy in 1998 inflicted casualties on the local inhabitants in proportion to U.S. personnel of more than 20 to 1 killed, and an even greater disparity in the proportion of wounded (more than 5,000 Kenyans were wounded by the blast; 95 percent of total casualties were non-American). Fear of backlash rarely concerns these secular groups because it is often one of their goals to provoke overreaction by their enemies and hopefully widen the conflict (Terrorism Research Center, 2005).

Violence Dissemination

How violence is planned and delivered are other matters. Groups may differ on how they inflict violence or select their victims. The FBI categorizes violence of terrorists into two areas: **weapons of mass destruction** (the use of chemical, biological, and radiological agents) and **cyber terrorism.** Additionally, the 1999 *Emergency Response to a Terrorism Self-Study Manual*, published by the Federal Emergency Management Agency, lists four categories of terrorist incidents: nuclear, incendiary, chemical, and explosive. Chemical agents fall into five classes: nerve agents, blister agents, blood agents, choking agents, and irritating agents (Federal Emergency Management Agency, 1999).

As suggested, a terrorist attack can take several forms depending on the means available and motives of the terrorist. Bombings and arson have been the most frequently used terrorist methods in the United States. Other possibilities include an attack on transportation facilities, an attack on utilities or other public services, or an incident involving chemical or biological agents.

As for international terrorist attacks against American interests, the U.S. State Department reports that in 2003 most attacks occurred in the Middle East and involved bombings of businesses or other locations where Americans congregate (see Figure 8–2).

Before discussing the categories of weapons of mass destruction and cyber terrorism, a review of one of the most common types of tactics used by international extremist organizations follows: the practice of suicide (homicide) bombings, which occur in many countries.

FIGURE 8–2 TERRORIST ATTACKS AGAINST THE UNITED STATES
BY REGION, TYPE OF EVENT, AND TARGETS IN 2003

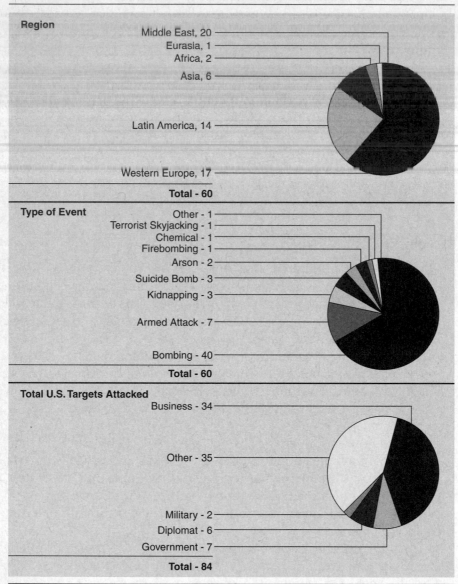

Region

Middle East, 20
Eurasia, 1
Africa, 2
Asia, 6
Latin America, 14
Western Europe, 17

Total - 60

Type of Event

Other - 1
Terrorist Skyjacking - 1
Chemical - 1
Firebombing - 1
Arson - 2
Suicide Bomb - 3
Kidnapping - 3
Armed Attack - 7
Bombing - 40

Total - 60

Total U.S. Targets Attacked

Business - 34
Other - 35
Military - 2
Diplomat - 6
Government - 7

Total - 84

Source: U.S. Department of State, 2004.

Suicide Terrorism

September 11, 2001, was for Americans a wake-up call to suicide terrorism, as
were the London bombings in June 2005 for citizens of the United Kingdom.
The rash of suicide bombings in Iraq and other nations is a further reminder

of the dedication of these killers. Suicide bombers are basically homicide bombers who are mission oriented and believe in state-sponsored terror.

The beginning of modern-day suicide bombing operations was in 1983 when Muslim guerrillas trained by Iran blew up 241 American servicemen and 58 French paratroopers in Beirut, Lebanon. The strategy was later adopted by the Palestinians, leading to a series of bombings on Israeli buses and in marketplaces that have continued to the present day. Although the religion of Islam condemns suicide killings, many radical Muslims view such acts as leading to martyrdom, which justifies its use (*Daily Telegraph*, 2001).

Suicide terrorism is viewed as a desperate last-resort measure, but with certain advantages over conventional terrorism. For a terrorist group supporting such tactics, it is less costly and a simple process requiring no major preparation or escape plans. In addition, suicide terrorism increases mass and public hysteria because it is unpredictable and usually produces mass carnage. The life of a bomber is considered a necessary sacrifice for the greater good of the cause, much like the Japanese suicide (kamikaze) pilots of World War II.

WEAPONS OF MASS DESTRUCTION

> *We know that the terrorists seek an even deadlier technology. And if they acquire chemical, biological or nuclear weapons, we have no doubt they will use them to cause even greater harm.*
>
> —President George W. Bush

Weapons of mass destruction are a serious threat to governments and citizens. Although there has been no widespread use of these weapons, there is a fear that these weapons may be used by terrorists in the future, which explains why nuclear nations are opposed to unstable nations or extremist leaders developing nuclear technology. The following sections discuss the various types of weapons of mass destruction.

Biological and Chemical Weapons

Biological agents are infectious microbes or toxins used to produce illness or death in people, animals, or plants as used in **biological terrorism.** Biological agents can be dispersed as aerosols or airborne particles. Terrorists may use biological agents to contaminate food or water because such agents are extremely difficult to detect.

An example of a deadly biological agent is anthrax. Anthrax is caused by bacteria that normally reside in soil in the form of microscopic spores. The spores are odorless and tasteless bacteria, which produce a toxin fatal to humans and animals. Although it may take thousands of spores to cause an infection, the amount needed to cause illness is smaller than a speck of dust (Mayo Foundation, 2004). In 2001, the threat was realized after two Washington, DC, postal workers died from the disease after handling mail.

Like biological agents, chemical agents can kill or incapacitate large populations when used in acts of **chemical terrorism.** Some chemical agents are odorless and tasteless and are difficult to detect. They can have an immediate effect (a few seconds to a few minutes) or a delayed effect (several hours to several days).

In contrast to biological weapons, chemical weapons can kill rapidly, often within hours or minutes, and sometimes with just a small drop. An example of a chemical agent is ricin, which is a poison taken from castor bean plants. The agent can be inhaled or ingested from poisoned food or a contaminated water supply. The symptoms of ricin poisoning are weakness, fever, chest tightness, cough, and severe respiratory problems including fluid buildup in the lungs. The poison can also cause intestinal bleeding and organ damage. Medical sources report that no vaccine or antidote is available for ricin (Mayo Foundation, 2004).

Biological and chemical weapons have been used primarily to terrorize an unprotected civilian population and not as weapons of war because of fear of retaliation and the likelihood that the agent would contaminate the battlefield for a long period of time. The Persian Gulf War in 1991 and other confrontations in the Middle East were causes for concern in the United States regarding the possibility of chemical or biological warfare. Although no incidents occurred, there remains a concern that such weapons could be involved in an accident or be used by terrorists (Federal Emergency Management Agency, 2005).

In response to the threat, President George W. Bush signed a law in 2004 known as the **Project Bioshield Act,** which authorizes $5.6 billion over 10 years for the government to purchase and stockpile vaccines and drugs to fight anthrax, smallpox, and other potential agents of bioterror. The Department of Health and Human Services has taken steps to purchase 75 million doses of an improved anthrax vaccine for the Strategic National Stockpile.

Nuclear or Radiological Terrorism

Another fear is nuclear or radiological attacks. The world's nuclear weapons stockpiles are concentrated in the following nations: Britain, China, France, India, Israel, Pakistan, Russia, the United States, and possibly North Korea.

In addition, enough plutonium for many nuclear weapons exists in more than 40 countries, sometimes in quantities large enough to make a bomb (International Atomic Energy Agency, 2000).

The danger of nuclear weapons or nuclear materials falling into the hands of terrorists or hostile nations is a global one, especially with the collapse of the Soviet Union and the threat of so-called Third World nations seeking nuclear weapons or materials. To date, there has been no evidence of a terrorist group obtaining a nuclear weapon, although reportedly there have been attempts by Osama bin Laden (Allison, 2004).

Related to **nuclear terrorism** threats are so-called **dirty bombs.** A dirty bomb uses conventional explosives such as dynamite to spread radioactive material. A dirty bomb is easier to make, requiring no more than a stick of dynamite and some radioactive material in a shoebox. The only known dirty bomb-related incident occurred when Chechen rebels planted a radioactive package with dynamite in a Moscow park. The authorities quickly located the material before it was dispersed (Allison, 2004).

Cyber Terrorism

Other than WMD, terrorists are using cyber tactics to disrupt the economy and security. As defined by the FBI, "cyber terrorism is the premeditated, politically motivated attack against information, computer systems, computer programs, and data which result in violence against noncombatant targets by sub national groups or clandestine agents" (Dick, 2002).

These days, practically every aspect of American life is dependent on computer technology. The U.S. economy is increasingly dependent on electronic transactions, which are vulnerable to a cyber terrorist attack. A dedicated hacker or cyber terrorist can do much to harm the environment, businesses, or government operations.

There are a number of examples of cyber terrorism, which can be committed by domestic or international groups, as well as disgruntled individuals. In 2000, a computer hacker was able to log on to a waste management control system and release millions of gallons of raw sewage on an Australian town (Scott, 2002). In 2001, two postgraduate students cracked a bank system used by banks and credit card companies to secure the personal identification numbers of their customers' accounts (Pritchard, 2001). Consider also the possibility of a terrorist hacking into the computer system of an air traffic control center and altering information about aircraft positions and so forth.

It is clear that a cyber terrorist, as with other types of offenders that use technology for illegal purposes, can cause extreme damage to a government, private corporation, individual, or civilian population. Terrorism violence whether by bombings (suicide or traditional), biological or chemical agents, or cyber threats suggests that terrorists are dedicated to a cause and will sacrifice their own lives to achieve their objectives.

COMBATING TERRORISM

What are our responses to terrorism? On the domestic front, a number of laws were initiated in recent years to address hate crimes and street violence. Various states have enacted laws that enhance the penalties for gang-related offenses, and many local jurisdictions have adopted ordinances that are designed to curb or outlaw gang related activities. Some of these laws are referred to as state terrorism acts, which target gang-initiated crime (Institute for Intergovernmental Research, 2005). As a result of the September 11th attacks, major legislative changes also occurred. A number of weapons and drug laws are also in effect.

Los Angeles has taken steps to address MS-13 and other gang members who are also illegal immigrants. In 2007, the Los Angeles City Attorney and Los Angeles County District Attorney agreed to partner more closely with federal immigration officials and attorneys to prosecute and depart gang members for immigration violations. The announcement was significant for Los Angeles because it is a place that has historically "kept federal immigration authorities at arm's length and largely prohibits its police officers from asking the immigration status of either crime victims or suspects" (McGreevy and Winton, 2007).

The partnership allows local law enforcement officials to check the immigration status of all suspected gang members who commit violent and nonviolent or petty crimes, including violating gang injunctions, graffiti, and loitering. This agreement represents a realization on the part of local, state, and federal officials that gangs may have local origins but eradicating or reducing gang crimes and violence cannot be addressed without harnessing the resources of all levels of government. However, there is also a growing awareness that gang activities extend beyond national borders and are proliferating throughout the Western Hemisphere, especially in Central American countries.

Homeland Security

In an effort to increase homeland security following the September 11th terrorist attacks on the United States, President George W. Bush issued the National Strategy for Homeland Security in July 2002 and signed legislation creating the **Department of Homeland Security (DHS)** in November 2002 (U.S. Department of Homeland Security, 2005). The strategy set forth the overall objectives, mission areas, and initiatives to prevent terrorist attacks within the United States, reduce U.S. vulnerability to terrorism, and minimize the damage and assist in the recovery from attacks that may occur. The strategy also called for the creation of the DHS, which began operations in March 2003 and represents a fusion of 22 federal agencies responsible for coordinating and centralizing the leadership of many homeland security activities under a single department. In response to terrorism, the department uses a color-coded system to indicate the level of security and awareness needed. For example, after the London bombings in July 2005, the U.S. government raised the threat level from Code Yellow—or Elevated—to Code Orange—or High—for the mass transit portion of the transportation sector.

THE USA PATRIOT ACT

On October 26, 2001, President George W. Bush signed into law the Terrorism Act of 2001 (USA PATRIOT Act). A number of changes were made under the law in national security, criminal law, modifications of immigration law, money-laundering statutes, victim assistance statutes, as well as in other areas. The **USA PATRIOT Act** also created a new definition of "domestic terrorism" to correspond to the existing definition of international terrorism. The term *domestic terrorism* refers to activities occurring primarily within the territorial jurisdiction of the United States involving acts dangerous to human life that are a violation of the criminal laws of the United States or any state and appear to be intended to intimidate or coerce a civilian population, influence the policy of a government by intimidation or coercion, or affect the conduct of a government by mass destruction, assassination, or kidnapping. On the criminal side, the definition of a federal crime of terrorism was modified to include several offenses likely to be committed by terrorists, including a number of aircraft violence crimes and certain computer crimes.

New federal offenses include perpetrating attacks on mass transportation systems, vehicles, facilities, or passengers; harboring or concealing persons who have committed or are about to commit a variety of terrorist offenses; providing material support or resources to terrorists, now including expert advice and assistance; and possessing a biological agent or toxin of a type or in a quantity that is not reasonably justified for specifically defined purposes.

SUMMARY

Terrorism violence is unpredictable and is becoming an increasing threat to the domestic as well as the global community. When more persons continue to see themselves as victimized by social or government policies or perceive religious persecution, terrorism—domestic or international— will continue to spread its violence. Add to the problem our porous national borders, which provide terrorists easy access to our nation's infrastructure. To address these threats, additional compromises and lifestyle changes by the public are necessary to increase security and safety. The country must reexamine its immigration policies because many terrorists and other criminals can enter the country harboring violent intent. There is some concern that a number of foreign nationals who enter the United States legally (e.g., with student visas) may actually have terrorist connections and may one day carry out attacks against civilian targets such as what occurred in London. It is predicted that there will be struggles between civil libertarians and the government as we weigh individual rights against the overall safety needs of society.

KEY TERMS AND CONCEPTS

Agroterrorism
Al-Qaeda
Animal Liberation Front (ALF)
Biological terrorism
Chemical terrorism
Christian Identity
Cyber terrorism
Department of Homeland
  Security (DHS)
Dirty bombs
Domestic terrorism

Earth Liberation Front (ELF)
International terrorism
Jemaah Islamiya (JI)
MS-13
Nuclear terrorism
Project Bioshield Act
Rudolph, Eric
Secular terrorists
Terrorism process
USA PATRIOT Act
Weapons of mass destruction

DISCUSSION QUESTIONS AND LEARNING ACTIVITIES

1. Differentiate between domestic and international terrorism. How are they similar?
2. Differentiate between secular and nonsecular terrorism.
3. Explain why terrorism flourishes in some countries and some regions of the world more than it does in others.

4. Research a terrorist group and discuss the group's motivations or reasons for why it supports terror.

5. Is the government doing enough to defend against terrorism or should more laws or programs be established?

6. Discuss why street gangs are considered terrorists. Is the terrorism label incorrect?

7. Research some recent federal legislation on terrorism. What do the laws provide or protect against?

8. Should the government negotiate with terrorist groups? Are there circumstances in which negotiation is necessary? Explain.

9. Visit one of the Web sources and compare so-called right-wing and left-wing terrorist groups. How do they differ? How are they similar?

10. Apply the model of the terrorism process (Figure 8–1) to a terrorist act in any country.

WEB SOURCES

Terrorism Research Center.
   www.terrorism.com/
Terrorism and Homeland Security.
   www.rand.org/research_areas/terrorism/
Intelligence and Terrorism Information Center.
   http://terrorismexperts.org/
Department of Homeland Security.
   www.dhs.gov/dhspublic/

RECOMMENDED READINGS

Alexander, Yonah, and Milton Hoenig. 2001. *Super Terrorism: Biological, Chemical and Nuclear.* Ardsley, NY: Transnational Publishers.

Chomsky, Noam, and Takei Masakuzu. 2003. *Power and Terror: Post 9–11 Talks and Interviews.* Chicago: Seven Stories Press.

Cronin, Isaac. 2002. *Confronting Fear: A History of Terrorism.* Washington, DC: Thunder's Mouth Press.

Essig, Christopher G. 2001. *Terrorism: Criminal Act or Act of War: Implications for National Security in the 21st Century.* Strategy Research Project. Carlisle Barracks, New York: U.S. Army War College.

Henderson, Harry. 2003. *Terrorist Challenge to America.* New York: Facts On File.

Kushner, Harvey W. 2002. *Encyclopedia of Terrorism.* Sage Publications.

Laqueur, Walter. 2001. *A History of Terrorism.* New Brunswick, NJ: Transaction.

Levy, Barry S., and Victor W. Sidel, eds. 2004. *Terrorism and Public Health: A Balanced Approach to Strengthening Systems and Protecting People.* New York: Oxford University Press.

Maniscalco, Paul M., and Hank T. Christen. 2002. *Understanding Terrorism and Managing the Consequences.* Upper Saddle River, NJ: Prentice Hall.

Smith, James M., and William C. Thomas. 2001. *The Terrorism Threat and U.S. Government Response: Operational and Organizational Factors.* Colorado Springs, CO: USAF Institute for National Security Studies.

REFERENCES

Allison, Grahman. 2004. *Nuclear Terrorism: The Ultimate Preventable Catastrophe.* New York: Belfer Center for Science and International Affairs, John F. Kennedy School of Government.

Anti-Defamation League. www.adl.org/ (accessed June 15, 2005).

Associated Press. 2004. Fear of Terrorism in Boston, New York: The Threat of Attacks at Political Conventions Prompts Property Owners in Host Cities to Add Insurance Coverage. *St. Petersburg (Florida) Times,* July 20.

Barrett, Beth. 2004. Homegrown Terror: Special Report on Gang Violence. *Los Angeles Daily News,* September 26.

Becker, Jasper. 2005. *Rogue Regime.* New York: Oxford University Press.

Botha, A. 2005. *The Multi-Headed Monster: Different Forms of Terrorism.* www.iss.co.za/Pubs/Monographs/No63/Chap1.html (accessed June 1, 2005).

Copeland, Larry. 2004. Domestic Terrorism: New Trouble at Home. *USA Today,* November 14, 6.

Daily Telegraph (England). 2001. New Assassins Queue Eagerly for Martyrdom. September 13. www.apologeticsindex.org/ (accessed June 18, 2005).

Dick, Ronald L. 2002. Cyber Terrorism and Critical Infrastructure Protection. July 24. www.fbi.gov/congress/congress02/nipc072402.htm 2. Id.

Federal Bureau of Investigation. 2003a. *Terrorism in the United States, 1994.* Washington, DC: U.S. Department of Justice, National Security Division, Terrorist Research and Analytical Center.

Federal Bureau of Investigation. 2003b. *Terrorism 2000–2001.* Washington, DC: U.S. Department of Justice.

Federal Bureau of Investigation. 2004. Violence in the Name of the Environment: The Case of the Calculating Eco-terrorist. May 3. www.fbi.gov/ (accessed June 13, 2005).

Federal Emergency Management Agency (FEMA). 1999. *Emergency Response to Terrorism Self-Study Manual.* Washington, DC: U.S. Department of Justice, Office of Justice Programs.

Federal Emergency Management Agency (FEMA). 2005. Backgrounder: Terrorism. Washington, DC. www.fema.gov/hazards/terrorism/terror.shtm (accessed June 11, 2005).

Frieden, Terry. 2005. FBI, ATF Address Domestic Terrorism Officials: Extremists Pose Serious Threat. May 19. www.cnn.com/ (accessed May 26, 2005).

Gilmartin, Kevin M. 1999. Lethal Triad: Understanding the Nature of Isolated Extremist Groups. http://www.fbi.gov/publications/leb/1996/sept961.txt.

Hoffman, Bruce. 1999. *Inside Terrorism.* New York: Columbia University Press.

Hyde, Henry J. 2005. Gangs and Crime in Latin America. *Subcommittee on the Western Hemisphere.* Washington, DC: Committee on International Relations, U.S. House of Representatives. March 16.

Institute for Intergovernmental Research. 2005. *Analysis of Gang-Related Legislation* Tallahassee, FL: Institute for Intergovernmental Research.

International Atomic Energy Agency. 2000. *Nuclear Research Reactors of the World.* Vienna, Austria: IAEA.

Jenkins, Brian. 1985. *Terrorism and Beyond.* Santa Monica, CA: RAND Corporation.

Knowles, Terry. 2005. Agro-Terrorism. Presentation given to Crime Research Conference. Washington, DC, July 18.

Kushner, Harvey. 2003. *Encyclopedia of Terrorism.* Thousand Oaks, CA: Sage.

Laqueur, W. 1999. *The New Terrorism.* New York: Oxford University Press.

Lewis, John. 2005. Deputy Assistant Director, Counterterrorism Division Federal Bureau of Investigation, statement given before the Senate Committee on Environment and Public Works. www.fbi.gov/ (accessed July 2005). May 18.

Martin, Gus. 2003. *Understanding Terrorism.* Thousand Oaks, CA: Sage.

Mayo Foundation. 2004. Biological and Chemical Weapons: Arm Yourself with Information. www.mayoclinic.com/invoke.cfm?id = MH00027 (accessed June 16, 2005).

McPhee, Michele. 2005. Hub "Should Be Worried": U.S. Rep: MS-13 Gang Is True Terror Threat. *Boston Herald,* January 7.

MSNBC News. 2004. www.msnbc.msn.com/id/4739647/ (accessed June 7, 2005).

O'Connor, Tom. 2005a. Terrorism Syllabus. http://faculty.ncwc.edu/toconnor/429/429lect01.htm (accessed June 11, 2005).

O'Connor, T. R. 2005b. In MegaLinks in Criminal Justice. http://faculty.ncwc.edu/toconnor/ (accessed June 2005, May 27, 2005).

Pritchard, Carolyn. 2001. Cracks in the System. http://journalism.berkeley.edu/projects/newworld/cyberterrorism.html (accessed May 10, 2005).

Scott, Berinato. 2002. The Truth About Cyberterrorism. March 15. www.cio.com/archive/031502/truth_content.html.

Shuster, Mark A., et al. 2001. A National Survey of Stress Reactions after the September 11, 2001, Terrorist Attacks. *New England Journal of Medicine* 345:1507–1512.

Terrorism Research Center. 2005. www.terrorism-research.com/goals/ (accessed July 10, 2005).

U.S. Department of Homeland Security. 2005. www.dhs.gov/dhspublic/ (accessed August 6, 2005).

U.S. Department of State. 2005a. *Patterns of Global Terrorism.* Released by the Office of the Coordinator for Counterterrorism. April 29.

U.S. Department of State. 2005b. *Terrorism 2005.* www.state.gov/ (accessed July 20, 2005).

U.S. Department of State 2008. Washington, DC. http://www.state.gov/

Wikipedia, the Free Encyclopedia. 2005. Eric Robert Rudolph. http://en.wikipedia.org/ (accessed June 12, 2005).

Swecker, Chris. 2005. *Congressional testimony provided to the Subcommittee on the Western Hemisphere, U.S. House of Representatives.* Washington, DC, April 20.

Reisman, Lainie. 2006. Breaking the Vicious Cycle: Responding to Central American Youth Gang Violence. *SAIS Review* 26.2:147–152.

McGreevy, Patrick and Winton, Richard. 2007. Feds Bolster War on Gangs, *Los Angeles Times.* Retrieved on April 5, 2007 from http://www.latimes.com. April 5.

"Governor Schwarzenegger Announces Millions in Grants to Combat Gang Violence." *Imperial Valley News.* Retrieved on March 3, 2008 from http://www.streetgangs.com/ topics/2008/030308govenor.html.

9

Responding to Criminal Victimization

Learning Objectives

After studying this chapter, you will:

- Identify the various measures of personal protection.
- Know the history of major crime prevention programs.
- Be familiar with the effectiveness of various crime prevention programs.
- Understand how victim compensation programs operate.
- Be familiar with proposed and recently passed crime victim legislation at both the state and federal levels.
- Learn about various court decisions affecting victims' rights.
- Understand how a crime victim can seek civil remedies for injuries resulting from criminal attack.
- Recognize how victim advocacy programs operate.
- Know the various programs available for crime victims.
- Learn the recommended approaches for developing a crime prevention program.

Introduction

It is recognized that the roots of violence are greed, jealousy, mental illness, lack of social bonding, economic strife, perceived persecution or oppression, and other assorted life maintenance problems. The instruments of violence—weapons, drugs, and automobiles—fuel these passions and facilitate crime and violence. Although it is important to understand the sources of violence, it is equally important to find ways to prevent or control such acts. Violence and the threat of criminal victimization have prompted serious debate regarding what society as a whole and as individuals can do to protect themselves from violent predators. As Cohen and Felson (1979) discuss, the supply of offenders is constant, whether it is petty offenders, robbers, or thrill-seeking predators. A motivated offender, a suitable target, and a good chance of completing the crime without detection are necessary for the commission of a crime. Law enforcement is unable to protect citizens from all victimizations, forcing citizens and institutions to undertake measures to protect against intrusions and violence.

Two major responses to counter the threat of violence and criminal victimization are the proactive and the reactive. A **proactive response to crime** involves a preventive approach through instituting defense measures and learning opportunity reduction strategies. A **reactive response to crime** is a postcrime response, which generally entails legal responses to victimization. A reactive response is crime control legislation or legislation designed to compensate victims for expenses related to the crime. Another reactive approach is holding property owners or predators legally responsible in civil proceedings or **civil justice for the victim.**

PROACTIVE RESPONSES

In chapter one, problems with familial relationships and social disorganization accounted for some of the causes of violence. To reduce the potential of victimization, measures must be taken to address the threat. Proactive measures are designed to prevent violence; they include community–family action programs, personal protection measures, lifestyle changes, and other crime prevention and security measures designed to divert opportunistic offenders at one's home, business, or other institutional settings.

Community Violence Prevention Strategies

A number of proactive strategies address violence in the community. Generally, these strategies focus on community interaction, family bonding, personal skill development, quality health care, youth activities, and so forth. The following strategies resulted from research work with at-risk youth in the Chicago public schools. The research may be applied to strategies designed to reduce violence in any community.

Rebuilding the Village.   The adage that "it takes an entire village to raise a child" has merit. Unfortunately, if the village is disorganized or founded on morally weak principles, the statement may not be accurate. Social disorganization theories of deviance suggest that poverty, lack of job opportunities, single-head households, isolation from neighbors, and weakened community networks and institutions lead to reduced informal and formal social control, which, in turn, promotes violence and victimization (Sampson, Raudenbush, and Earls, 1997).

This strategy focuses on the need to strengthen community organizations. One prevention strategy would be to pair schools with community-based secular or religious organizations to develop activities to reduce violent and disruptive behavior by and against youth in the schools and surrounding communities. There is evidence that school-based interventions that shift how high-risk children are managed—by increasing parental involvement in school and collaboration with school personnel—can reduce risk, particularly for in-school violence (Elliott and Tolan, 1999).

Providing Access to Health Care. It is well accepted that neuropsychiatric disorders, particularly neuropsychological brain impairments acquired since birth, among adolescents and children may predispose them to violence. Environmental factors may also create physiologic responses that influence antisocial behavior. Research, for example, indicates that children with high levels of exposure to lead may be predisposed to violence (Moffitt, 1997). With proper health care, along with the early identification of those at risk for violence, violence may be reduced in at-risk youth. In other words, early medical interventions, such as counseling or medication, may be effective in preventing violence in at-risk people. But the health care must be available and reasonably priced.

Improving Bonding, Attachment, and Connectedness Dynamics. The lack of parental warmth, acceptance, and affection; poor family cohesion; and incidents of family conflict and hostility have been associated with delinquent and violent behavior. Providing early intervention programs for infants, toddlers, and preschoolers and their parents can teach both parents and children the skills to enhance their sense of personal mastery and to encourage strong intrafamily attachments. A major strategy here is helping parents bond with their infants. Infants who grow up with basic trust and security are provided the groundwork for future stable relationships, which may be necessary to prevent violence. Such attachments have been shown to reduce the risk of serious antisocial behavior and violence (Henggeler, Melton, and Smith, 1992).

Improving Self-Esteem. People need opportunities to gain recognition to improve their self-esteem. Poor self-esteem is frequently at the base of violence. Suicide and other self-destructive behaviors are often the result of poor self-esteem or lack of recognition. Schools and other social institutions can assist by providing service-learning opportunities and constructive activities that help youths develop social skills and self-esteem.

The objectives of these initiatives are to reduce racial, ethnic, and religious intolerance through education and to provide youths with models on how to communicate, solve problems, plan, develop leadership skills, manage resources, and remove barriers to success. Being involved in constructive activities helps youths develop social skills and self-esteem and helps to reduce their engagement in risky behaviors (Bell, 1997). These approaches will help reduce their engagement in risky behaviors and assist in developing an attachment to respected people, places, and activities.

Increasing Social Skills. Educating parents about the importance of supervising and monitoring their children, becoming more involved in their children's lives, and increasing their knowledge of their children's activities and whereabouts can also reduce the possibility of violence. Providing youths with opportunities to serve their community, resolve disputes peacefully, and develop leadership skills that will enable them to promote healthy alternatives to violence will decrease tendencies to resort to violence in a variety of circumstances. The Chicago public school system uses a peer mediation program to teach students how to manage conflict and disagreements effectively without resorting to violence and other forms of aggressive and antisocial behavior. There is evidence of success here in reducing violent encounters among at-risk youth (Bell et al., 2001).

Reestablishing the Adult Protective Shield. Research demonstrates the need for and the value of positive adult role models and adult involvement in the lives of youths. Many studies link adolescent participation in delinquent and violent behavior to the lack of parental monitoring—represented at its extreme by neglect and conflict-ridden or poor discipline (Gorman-Smith et al., 1996). By increasing the predictability of parenting and the level of parental monitoring of children and by decreasing negative parenting methods, violent tendencies among children can be averted. In other words, this approach utilizes adult, not just parental, supervision to address student violence. Increased adult involvement and supervision, along with security and surveillance systems, are valuable in maintaining safer communities (Bell et al., 2001).

Minimizing the Residual Effects of Trauma. Research shows that it is important to provide prevention, intervention, and follow-up counseling to reduce the possibility and impact of violent acts. Schools, therefore, frequently have counseling, nursing, psychological, and social services (U.S. Department of

Justice, 2000). A new program, found to be successful in violence reduction, was initiated by the City of Chicago. The program facilitates the collaboration among the Chicago police, the Metropolitan Family Services' Domestic Violence Program, the Community Mental Health Council Psychiatric Emergency Room/Crisis Intervention Program, and the Community Mental Health Council Children's and Adolescents' Outpatient Services in an effort to provide the full range of needed services to children exposed to violence (U.S. Department of Justice, 2000).

Law and Prevention. In 1996, a federal law required the U.S. Attorney General to provide Congress with an independent review of the effectiveness of state and local community crime prevention assistance programs funded by the U.S. Department of Justice. These programs combine both proactive and reactive philosophies of crime prevention. Many of the programs emphasize youth or community violence. They employ rigorous and scientifically recognized standards and methodologies (Sherman et al., 1996).

Programs that show promise for infants and younger children at risk include frequent home visits by nurses, teachers, and other professionals. For delinquent or at-risk preadolescents, family therapy and parent training are promising approaches. For schools, programs such as organizational development for innovation, teaching of social competency skills, and coaching of high-risk youth in thinking skills have helped. For older male ex-offenders, vocational training has produced good results; thus, meaningful job training helps some offenders to return to society.

For rental housing areas with drug dealing problems, nuisance abatement actions against landlords have improved living conditions, including a reduction in crime. For high-crime hot spots, additional high-profile police patrols are effective. To prevent high-risk offenders from repeating their crimes, monitoring by specialized police units and, of course, incarceration are the best methods. In other words, there is an important place in society for maximum-security prisons, and more such facilities will be needed in the future. Domestic abusers who are employed seem to be deterred by on-scene arrests. These are a few of the community-based social programs that seem to show promise in preventing certain types of offenses (Sherman et al., 1996).

Personal Defense Measures and the Gun Debate

> *A skillful warrior strikes a decisive blow and stops. He does not continue his attack to assert his mastery. He will strike the blow, but be on his guard against being vain or arrogant over his success. He strikes it as a matter of necessity, but not from a wish of mastery.*

> —Lao-tzu, Chinese philosopher

Another proactive strategy to reduce the potential for victimization is personal protection measures. It is a citizen's right to defend against physical attack by using reasonable force. Generally, **reasonable force** is the amount of force needed to defend oneself against imminent and serious attack to which no other alternatives, such as escape, are possible (Reid, 1997: 474–476). An example of reasonable and necessary force is a situation in which a victim is at home and an intruder unlawfully enters and threatens to use deadly force. Although state laws should be consulted, any force used to defend against the attack, including deadly force, is appropriate. The force used, however, must not exceed what is reasonable or necessary. For example, if two persons were arguing over a card game and one strikes at the other with his fists, the one struck would not generally be justified in getting a gun and shooting the other person. Such response is neither reasonable nor necessary because no imminent danger of serious harm or death is involved.

A number of self-defense programs are available to the public. Many of them stress martial arts training or the use of chemical agents. Some people are taking self-protection to a higher level by purchasing handguns. Whether guns present a deterrent to crime or invite injury has been and continues to be debated. It is no secret that guns are the weapon of choice for criminals, resulting in a significant number of victimizations each year.

Data from the Federal Bureau of Investigation (FBI) *Uniform Crime Reports (UCR)* and National Institute of Justice indicate that nearly one-third of the murders, robberies, and aggravated assaults reported to police involved firearms. Many prisoners serving sentences in a state or federal prison carried a firearm when they committed the crime for which they were serving time. In 1997, 32,436 deaths resulted from firearm-related injuries, making such injuries the second leading cause of injury mortality in the United States after motor-vehicle-related incidents. That same year, an estimated 64,207 people sustained nonfatal firearm-related injuries and were treated in U.S. hospital emergency rooms (Hoyert, Kochanek, and Murphy, 1999).

Despite the fact that victimization is associated with guns, there is also evidence that gun ownership saves lives. Probably less than 5 percent of U.S. homicides are committed in the victim's home by killers using guns kept in that home (Kleck and Hogan, 1996). Further, the slight risk of such an event occurring is almost completely confined to unusually high-risk subsets of the population because, contrary to widespread belief, gun violence is largely confined to people with a prior history of criminal behavior. Even within these high-risk groups, it is not known if the net causal effect of gun ownership is to increase the risks of homicide victimization because the gun–homicide association found in the previous research of high-risk populations was at least partly spurious. High-risk groups have a higher-than-average probability of both violence-increasing offensive uses of guns and of violence-reducing defensive uses; however, it cannot yet be firmly stated whether the net effect is to increase homicides (Kleck, 1998a).

A conservative estimate by a major study on gun ownership by Kleck and Gertz (1995) revealed 2.5 million protective uses of guns by adults annually. For every life lost to a gun, as many as 65 lives are protected by them. Likewise, for every case of gun abuse dramatized by the media, many more cases of abuse are prevented, but these go unreported. The author of a *University of Tennessee Law Review* article argues that the benefits of guns, as tools to avoid violence, have been ignored for years (Kates, 1995).

Studies have shown that in any year, approximately 1 million to 2.5 million Americans use guns to protect themselves and their families, and 400,000 of them believe that they would have been killed or seriously injured if they had had no gun (Kleck, 1998b). Some evidence indicates that the criminal population fears citizens with guns. A 1986 survey of 1,900 incarcerated felons by sociologists James Wright and Peter Rossi found that 40 percent had at some time decided not to commit a crime because they believed the intended victim was armed. Three-fifths of the felons said criminals are more worried about meeting an armed victim than meeting the police (Witkin, 1994).

Errors in measurement exist in many studies, but even if the figures of saved lives are only 10 percent accurate, guns save more lives each year than they cause deaths. As Leape (1994) reported in the *Journal of the American Medical Association*, more lives are lost through physician negligence than through gun deaths each year: Approximately 180,000 persons die each year from inadvertent physician-induced injury. This number is about five times the rate for gun deaths. One might conclude from this study that doctors pose a greater threat to society than do firearms. In addition, the abuse of alcohol and the misuse of automobiles (e.g., drunk driving and gang drive-by shootings) cause many victimizations each year. However, the idea of prohibiting alcohol or driving is not considered.

The government provides further evidence of the benefits of guns. U.S. Bureau of Justice Statistics (1994) data indicate that defense with a gun results in fewer injuries to the defender (17.4 percent) than does resisting with a less powerful weapon, such as a knife (40 percent), physical force (50.8 percent), evasion (34.9 percent), or not resisting at all (24.7 percent). Guns are the safest means for self-defense (Kleck, 1998b). Some researchers found, however, that jurisdictions that have strengthened their laws on gun ownership have not experienced increases in gun violence (McDowell, Loftin, and Wiersema, 1991).

Many states have reformed gun ownership laws, requiring waiting periods and background checks on prospective owners. The federal Brady Law requires a 5-day waiting period before a person can purchase a handgun. Some states require a longer waiting period. California requires a 15-day waiting period before a permit is issued. From the inception of the Brady Act on March 1, 1994, to December 31, 2000, nearly 30 million applications for firearm transfers were subject to background checks. Approximately 691,000 applications were rejected. In 2000 alone, 155,000 (2.0 percent) of approximately 7,699,000 applications for firearm transfers or permits were rejected by the FBI or state and local agencies (Bureau of Justice Statistics, 2001). Some states have also revised laws to allow citizens to protect themselves outside their homes by allowing more discretion in defending themselves. Florida passed a law in 2005 which gives a gun owner the right to shoot an attacker in a public area (Roig-Franzia, 2005).

Data on shootings of innocent people by the police, as compared with shootings by other citizens, are interesting. Citizens use guns to repel crime about 7 to 10 times more frequently than do the police; 11 percent of the police shootings as compared with about 2 percent of the citizen shootings result in injury to an innocent person (Kleck, 1991). The debate regarding citizen ownership of guns will undoubtedly continue for some time. However, one fact is clear. The more than 20,000 American gun laws, including national gun laws, have done nothing to reduce violent crime or the availability of guns to criminals (Suter, 1995). A 1995 study (Decker, Pennell, and Caldwell, 1997) of 7,000 arrestees in 11 major urban areas found that firearms used by these offenders were obtained through black market contacts.

The offenders interviewed stated that firearms were easy to obtain, suggesting that traditional methods of firearm control may not be effective. Citizens desiring to own a firearm should consult with their local law enforcement agency, a reputable gun dealer, or the National Rifle Association regarding firearms training and other legal requirements in their state.

Security Measures

Security measures incorporate strategies to prevent crime and protect assets. This approach incorporates the following three protection measures: physical protection, protection officers, and security procedures. The measures are widely used in a number of institutions to address a variety of criminal threats.

The first measure, *physical protection*, encompasses measures necessary to protect one's home or business from unauthorized access by intruders. The use of barriers (fences, walls, etc.) provides protection. Fences cannot keep all intruders out, but they do define the property boundaries and reduce the potential for casual intrusions.

Adequate lighting is essential; standards regarding the quality of lighting needed for parking areas and so forth are available. Many city ordinances specify lighting standards. Lighting is universally considered to be the most important security feature in a parking facility. Good lighting deters crime and produces a more secure atmosphere in private areas and public streets (Girard, 1996). For example, the Fairmount Fair Mall in Camillus, New York, was experiencing a high number of car break-ins. The installation of a lighting system eliminated these break-ins, boosted mall patronage, and allowed the scope and frequency of security patrols to be reduced. Similarly, the installation of an effective lighting system at the parking lot in Spring Valley Park in San Diego, California, eliminated robberies, vandalism, and burglaries. Vehicular accidents were also reduced, and children and the elderly began to use the park at night once again (Smith, 1996).

In addition to lighting and fencing, a number of electronic surveillance devices are on the market. These include **closed-circuit television cameras**, often referred to as CCTV systems, and electronic card key access systems. Various types of intrusion detection systems or alarms are available. Some are proprietary, which means that when activated, the property's security staff will respond. Other alarms are silent and alert a security company or a police department; when the alarm is activated, the police or a security agency automatically respond. Some employees have what are referred to as panic buttons at their workstations; when activated, these devices alert the security staff or the local police. Some security measures are illusionary; that is, they are present to deter the opportunistic offender. The use of "dummy cameras" is an example. The use of these methods, however, may be ineffective against more experienced criminals. As discussed in Focus 9–1, preventing crime through the use of monitored cameras has been successful.

Improved technology is being used to seek terrorists and keep other criminals from entering the country. One such approach is the use of an Automated Fingerprint Identification System that assists Border Patrol agents in searching various identification systems such as the FBI's criminal fingerprint database. The technology enables agents to rapidly identify people with outstanding warrants and criminal histories. During a 3-month period in 2004, the agents identified and detained 84 homicide suspects, 37 kidnapping suspects, 151 sexual assault suspects, 212 robbery suspects, 1,238 suspects for assaults of other types, and 2,630 suspects implicated in dangerous narcotics-related charges (Seper, 2004).

Focus 9–1   Closed-Circuit Television and Crime Control

The most prevalent use of CCTV by law enforcement agencies in the United States is in the taping of traffic stops by cameras mounted in police vehicles. Until recently, cameras were rarely used to monitor public spaces in the United States. Most of the research on the effectiveness of such use has been done in the United Kingdom. A study by the Home Office Police Research Group examined the effectiveness of CCTV systems in three English town centers. Among the findings was that analysis of crime data showed that the presence of CCTV can have a deterrent effect on a variety of offenses, especially property offenses; however, such reductions in crime can disappear as publicity about and awareness of the cameras fade. New computer technology allows CCTV systems to match recorded faces against a computer database of photos. The use of facial recognition technology in public areas is not yet readily accepted in the United States. By allowing small police forces to cover larger areas, however, facial recognition systems can lead to a greater number of arrests, at least in theory. Privacy advocates are uneasy about the use of CCTV to monitor public meetings and demonstrations. Training programs, clear policies and procedures, personnel background checks, and strict supervision of camera operators can help to mitigate some abuses. Courts have generally ruled that people do not have a reasonable expectation of privacy when in public, because their actions are readily observable by others. It is likely the use of CCTV will continue to expand, as will its use in enforcing traffic laws.

Source: National Criminal Justice Reference Service. U.S. Department of Justice 2006. http://www.ncjrs.gov/App/Publications/abstract.aspx?ID = 200909.

Another security measure is the presence of trained *protection personnel.* The key to a successful security plan is the availability of protection officers. Protection personnel outnumber public law enforcement by a ratio of three to one. The police cannot be expected to respond quickly to every property crisis, but properly selected and trained protection officers can be employed to control and detect property intrusions. Their duties are basically to prevent crime, to control access, to escort employees, and to respond to unusual incidents. The number of protection personnel required varies with the size of the business. In other words, the larger the business (as measured by the number of employees and premises square footage), the greater the need for protection personnel. Some businesses, such as hospitals and financial institutions, must comply with industry requirements for protection personnel and security plans. The effectiveness of security personnel in preventing crime and violence should be studied seriously.

Some evidence indicates that the presence of a trained security force has reduced criminal activity. In a study of a parking facility where predatory crime is a serious threat, the visible presence of uniformed officers is one of the best crime prevention methods and should be considered in high-risk facilities. Unscheduled patrols who vary their routes throughout the shift appear to be most effective (Smith, 1996). All security personnel should be trained to properly monitor and operate all security equipment within the facility and respond to alarms. In some cities, private security companies are under contract to assist overburdened police departments. The security officers are able to reduce prostitution, drug activities, and other disorderly offenses (Corwin, 1993; Doherty, 1993). According to a study by Zappile (1991: 22–23), the use of trained security officers to patrol the downtown area of Philadelphia reduced the number of crimes and disturbances.

An interesting fact regarding deterrence and security personnel was revealed in a study of inmates incarcerated for armed robbery. The study, which was conducted in 12 state prisons throughout the United States (Erickson and Stenseth, 1996), indicated that one of the most important deterrents of robbery is the presence of armed security officers. The robbers reported that they were less likely to rob a store that had armed security officers on the premises. They also avoided stores from which there is a poor escape route or where the clerks may be armed (generally privately owned stores). A convicted armed bank robber serving a 65-year sentence stated in an interview that he avoided banks with armed security officers and tellers behind bullet-resistant booths (Hubler, 1996). In other words, most robbers seek to avoid detection, conflict, and security obstacles.

The final protection measure is *security procedure,* which addresses the heart of the protection plan. Protection policies must be established and followed by all employees. Employees need to know what to do in the event of an intrusion, unusual occurrence, or disaster. They need to learn code words to alert other employees and supervisors when help is needed. Procedural protection encompasses such measures as requiring employees to wear photo identification and periodically changing access codes. In large corporations, the prompt deactivation of gate passes of terminated employees is a crucial procedure. Procedural protection includes informing employees on how to respond to bomb threats, report suspicious persons, and control access to the property. Requiring employees to enter or exit through designated doors and controlling public access through selected points are part of an overall plan. Office furniture and partitions should be arranged so that employees in daily contact with the public are surrounded by "natural" barriers—desks, countertops, partitions—to separate them from customers and visitors.

To attempt to deter crimes at automatic teller machines (ATMs), a number of banks in Los Angeles have installed their machines in police stations, supermarkets, and convenience stores. The police report that ATM crime has been reduced dramatically as a result of these changes (Hubler, 1996). This effective procedural approach simply reduces the opportunity for crime by placing ATM machines where detection and apprehension are likely to be high. To deter other threats, banks are increasingly relying on a variety of security measures to prevent robberies, including special metal-detecting doors and, in some cases, armed security guards. Commonly applied security measures include the following:

- Silent alarm and bulletproof teller windows inside banks
- Plainclothes security guard
- Single-entry security doors that lock if a large metal object is detected
- Uniformed security guard allowing only one person at a time to enter
- Video cameras

The three measures of protection discussed here are not mutually exclusive but are best utilized together. They are not, however, a guarantee against property intrusion. Determined offenders will seek a way to commit a crime regardless of the obstacles. The measures discussed will assist, however, in detecting, deterring, delaying, or denying certain offenders trying to complete acts of violence. The best proactive defense against criminal violence and victimization is an integrated approach utilizing all available human and physical resources.

Opportunity Reduction Strategies

Opportunity reduction attempts to decrease victimization by focusing on geography or the physical environment that may be conducive to crime. This approach is often referred to as **environmental criminology**, which is a combination of defensible space theory (Newman, 1972), crime prevention through environmental design (Jeffrey, 1971), and situational crime prevention approaches (Clarke, 1980).

Defensible Space Theory.   Newman's (1972) work represents a novel idea in the use of architectural designs to save public housing from crime. His work extends early views that a relationship exists between crime, street use, and the layout of the land. In one study, Jacobs (1961) pointed out that the more diverse the land use (residential, commercial, leisure, and institutional), the more likely people are to pay attention to their environment and report crime. Thus, offenders are attracted to areas where they can commit crime and avoid detection. Newman suggested the **defensible space theory**. Residents living in large, anonymous public housing units, with multiple access points, had little control over visitors. The design of the building made it difficult to separate residents from outsiders. The crux of defensible space theory is the empowerment of residents to develop a sense of community and territoriality by designing buildings that allow increased resident privacy. When residents live in housing units with private areas, they are more likely to identify outsiders and to have a sense of belonging and control.

In the past, public housing units have been abandoned because of the crime and violence committed there. In the early 1970s, a 2,740-unit housing project in St. Louis was torn down because of high vacancy rates as a result of crime there. The housing project, built in 1957, looked like a deteriorated high-rise hotel built in the 1920s. Residents constantly lived in fear, stayed behind fortified locked doors, and avoided most other residents. They had no sense of control or privacy in the hallways or perimeter areas. Because there was no access control to the property, transients and various criminal types were often attracted to the property (Newman, 1972: 17). In addition, run-down neighborhoods or structures attract predators and deviant persons because they present the perception that no one really cares. Once one window is broken others will be, unless there is an organized effort to improve the community (Wilson and Kelling, 1982).

Physically deteriorating property not only influences behavior and attracts potential offenders, but also shapes how people feel about each other. In the preceding photo, a stolen and stripped vehicle is parked in an alley (note the graffiti on the walls). Making physical improvements and caring for property can reduce incivilities and negative attitudes that

A stolen, stripped vehicle abandoned in an alley. Photo by Robert J. Meadows.

people have about their environment. The fear of victimization can affect how we feel and live. One of the most impressive examples of defensible space is the Five Oaks neighborhood of Dayton, Ohio (Newman, 1992), a half-square-mile area with 2,000 households located about a mile from Dayton's central business district.

In the 1990s, property values decreased, and many homeowners, unable to find buyers, converted their property to low-cost rentals. Crime increased, and prostitution and drug dealing became common in the area. Residents feared victimization. The city retained Oscar Newman to study the area. Newman is concerned about the interaction of social and physical factors. He believes that the physical characteristics of a building or environment can strongly influence the social behavior of its residents. The following statement summarizes his position (Newman, 1972: 26):

> The more complex and anonymous the environment, the more difficult it is for a code of behavior following societal norms to become established and to be maintained. It is difficult for moderate-income families with two adult heads of household to cope with crime and vandalism problems in poorly designed environments. But when poor and broken families are grouped together in such a setting, the results prove disastrous. The public housing projects now being abandoned consist of the worst mixture of social and physical aggregates.

Newman recommended, among other things, closing side streets to through traffic and adding portals made of attractive brick pillars to the ones that remained open. Other streets were blocked by attractive iron gates, which could be opened in emergencies, making many streets cul-de-sacs. Criminals driving through the portals found leaving the area more difficult. Blocking the streets also increased neighborhood identity and social interaction of the neighbors and led to an awareness of suspicious persons in the area. Traffic and crime decreased. Residents became involved with each other and their environment.

The idea of blocking streets and developing gated communities has become popular. After the 1992 riots in Los Angeles, more than 40 neighborhoods applied to the city for street barriers (see photo on page xxx). Neighborhood groups are incorporating communities and developing their own gated communities, offering increased security and social interaction, which are the bases of defensible space theory and crime prevention through environmental design (Stewart, 1996).

Crime Prevention Through Environmental Design. The concept of **crime prevention through environmental design (CPTED)** goes beyond defensible space theory. It focuses on the location rather than the offender. The work of Jeffrey (1971) encompassed a set of principles broader than defensible space and extending beyond the residential context to the community and business setting. Jeffrey's concept of making an area safe and secure is known as crime prevention through environmental design. According to the rational offender perspective (Clarke, 1992), criminal behavior and victimization result from the physical environment or the layout of an area. Offenders decide whether to commit a crime in a location after they determine a number of factors:

1. How easy will it be to enter the area?
2. How visible, attractive, or vulnerable do targets appear?
3. What are the chances of being seen?
4. Will the people in the area do something if they see a problem?
5. Is there a quick, direct route for leaving the location after committing a crime?

Accordingly, some properties provide the opportunity for crime. An ATM machine located in an isolated area with poor lighting, abundant foliage, and several routes of undetected escape is an environment conducive to crime. A cash-oriented business situated in a high-crime area with lax security standards and controls is an invitation to victimization of employees and customers. As a result, victims of crime are seeking

A residential street is gated to prevent access from a major highway.
Photo by Robert J. Meadows.

compensation from property owners and managers for their victimization. These cases are commonly known as **premises liability** cases. They are based on allegations made by the victim that the property owner failed to provide adequate security and thereby contributed to the crime. Claims of inadequate security include systemic, organizational, human, and environmental design flaws.

Crime prevention through environmental design (CPTED) is emerging as a basis for liability suits brought by victims against property owners and managers under premises liability discussed in Chapter 4. (See also Gordon and Brill, 1996.) Plaintiffs have used poor property design or the lack of CPTED in demonstrating the causation element. The lack of security measures (poor lighting, places on property to hide) increases the risk of crime and the likelihood of liability.

The work of Hunter and Jeffrey (1992) focused on preventing convenience store robbery through environmental design. Convenience stores historically have been attractive crime targets. Their location, cash-handling procedures, store layout, and lack of security procedures made them ideal targets. In 1989, 36,434 convenience store robberies were reported nationwide, representing a 28 percent increase since 1985 (Sessions, 1990).

A study of 7-Eleven stores in Florida found that several prevention strategies reduced robbery. According to Hunter and Jeffrey (1992: 202), such strategies led to Florida legislation known as the Convenience Store Act, which includes the following:

- Silent alarms
- Security cameras
- Drop safe or cash management devices
- Well-lighted parking lots
- Posted signs indicating less than $50 cash on hand
- Clear and unobstructed windows
- Height markers at entrances
- No concealed access/escape routes
- Cash-handling policies to limit available cash
- Employees trained in robbery deterrence and safety
- Two clerks during night hours

The results of these prevention efforts are encouraging. Other strategies used in preventing store robberies are locating cashiers near the middle of the store, locating the store on a busy street, installing gasoline pumps to increase customer visibility, and locating the store near other evening commercial activities. Altering the physical environment according to specific design considerations was found to be a factor in controlling robberies.

The theories of defensible space and CPTED have been tested in a number of studies. One such study was conducted in Atlanta, Georgia, in the early 1980s (Greenberg, Williams, and Rohe, 1982). The study focused on three pairs of neighborhoods. The basic research focused on why some neighborhoods that would be expected to be unsafe because of their proximity to dangerous areas and their social and economic characteristics are relatively safe. The study considered criminal opportunity and the relationship to territoriality (spatial identity, social cohesion) and physical characteristics (land use, housing and street types, etc.) of the neighborhoods. Among the study's results are the following:

1. High-crime neighborhoods had fewer residential properties and more vacant land than demographically similar and physically adjacent low-crime neighborhoods. High-crime neighborhoods had fewer single-family residences.

2. High-crime neighborhoods had significantly more blocks with major thoroughfares and fewer blocks with small neighborhood streets.

3. High-crime neighborhoods had mixed land use, that is, a combination of commercial and residential areas.

4. Areas surrounding high-crime neighborhoods were low in socioeconomic status.

5. Low-crime neighborhoods had private parking facilities—fewer parking lots but more driveways than did high-crime neighborhoods.

6. Residents of low-crime neighborhoods were more likely to own their own homes, as opposed to high-crime neighborhoods, whose residents were more transient.

7. Residents of low-crime areas identified more with their neighborhoods in terms of affective attachment than did residents of high-crime areas and were, therefore, more likely to report intruders.

Areas with increased residential land use dominated by single-family homes had fewer crime problems than areas with mixed commercial and residential areas. In addition, low-crime neighborhoods had fences, curbs, clearly marked addresses, smaller streets, and few major thoroughfares. The basic conclusion of the study is that a mixture of commercial and residential land use, combined with transient residents (apartments), increases the potential for criminal activity. Offenders such as robbers are drawn to these areas and are more likely to move about unnoticed. This is not to suggest that apartment dwellers are criminal types but that the opportunity for criminal attacks increases with the degree of anonymity. Furthermore, neighborhoods populated with convenience stores, bars, fast-food restaurants, and other late-night businesses are invitations to the public, some of whom may have criminal intent. These facts should be considered in planning communities.

The CPTED approach is basically a combination of property design, land use, circulation patterns, territorial features, and property maintenance (Taylor and Harrell, 1996). This approach incorporates such features as improved lighting, signage, citizen involvement, and street design. In Seattle, Washington, some neighborhood parks experiencing crime instituted a program called "adopt-a-park," which entailed removing overgrown trees and shrubs and improving the lighting to discourage drug dealing and vandalism. It was reported to be a success in reducing victimization (Weisel, 1994).

Another successful twist to the concept of CPTED is community policing, which incorporates many of the principles of CPTED by developing close cooperation between police and residents to reduce both crime and fear of it. According to research conducted by the National Institute of Justice (Fleissner and Heinzelmann, 1996), cooperation between the police and citizens can go a long way to reduce community crime. Community policing is a partnership among community groups, the police, and businesses to reduce crime by making the environment more attractive. Both CPTED and community policing rely on partnerships with the community, government, and educational and social agencies to implement crime prevention strategies. The following are some approaches to community policing:

- Police involvement within neighborhoods can include assigning officers to foot patrol and working with community groups to increase citizens' sense of security and involvement in solving neighborhood problems that contribute to crime and fear of crime.
- Residents can work together to improve neighborhood appearance and deter criminals.
- Government can use building codes and inspection power to increase environmental security and discourage drug use and other criminal activities.

If gang violence is a problem, the community and police can develop solutions that could include more aggressive patrol strategies and street blockage in areas where drive-by shootings have occurred. That is, pro-active arrests of repeat offenders and directed patrols at crime hot spots are examples of effective law enforcement strategies (Sherman et al., 1996).

Situational Crime Prevention. **Situational crime prevention** is an extension of the defensible space theory and CPTED. Another aspect of environmental criminology, it is concerned with strategies to reduce crime opportunity through management or manipulation of the environment. Situational crime prevention is directed at specific forms of crime. It is an attempt to make crime more difficult to commit, increase the risks of offending, and reduce the rewards of offending. Clarke and Eck (2003) developed 25 techniques of situational crime prevention presented in Table 9–1. Each technique has examples to better explain the meaning of each.

A number of businesses and institutions use situational crime prevention techniques. In some communities, citizens are fortifying their environments to reduce crime threats. As mentioned, situational prevention incorporates defensible space theory and CPTED. A criticism of situational prevention is that it may serve only to displace crime; that is, when one area uses this prevention method, the criminal may turn to an area less protected or try another approach. Criminals seek the path of least resistance. As discussed in Chapter 4, the increase in home robbery invasions may be attributed to increased security used by businesses. The fortress mentality described in Focus 9–2 is an unpleasant reminder of living conditions in many communities.

REACTIVE RESPONSES TO VICTIMIZATION

Victimization cannot be totally prevented, and even the best crime prevention efforts are not guarantees against crime. Reactive responses to victimization include community programs and laws implemented in response to a crime problem. The reactive responses discussed here are restorative approaches such as victim compensation and support programs, legislation, and civil justice responses. The restorative programs deal directly with victim assistance, although civil justice is designed to punish those responsible or associated with the victimization, a full treatment of restorative approaches is not offered in this book but may be found in many contemporary readings in criminology and corrections.

Restorative approaches emphasize repairing the harm caused by criminal behavior. This restoration is accomplished through cooperative

TABLE 9–1 TWENTY FIVE TECHNIQUES OF SITUATIONAL PREVENTION

Increase the Effort	Increase the Risks	Reduce the Rewards	Reduce Provocations	Remove Excuses
1. Target harden • Steering column locks and immobilisers • Anti-robbery screens • Tamper-proof packaging	**6. Extend guardianship** • Take routine precautions: go out in group at night, leave signs of occupancy, carry phone • "Cocoon" neighborhood watch	**11. Conceal targets** • Off-street parking • Gender-neutral phone directories • Unmarked bullion trucks	**16. Reduce frustrations and stress** • Efficient queues and polite service • Expanded seating • Soothing music/muted lights	**21. Set rules** • Rental agreements • Harassment codes • Hotel registration
2. Control access to facilities • Entry phones • Electronic card access • Baggage screening	**7. Assist natural surveillance** • Improved street lighting • Defensible space design • Support whistleblowers	**12. Remove targets** • Removable car radio • Women's refuges • Pre-paid cards for pay phones	**17. Avoid disputes** • Separate enclosures for rival soccer fans • Reduce crowding in pubs • Fixed cab fares	**22. Post instructions** • "No Parking" • "Private Property" • "Extinguish camp fires"
3. Screen exits • Ticket needed for exit • Export documents • Electronic merchandise tags	**8. Reduce anonymity** • Taxi driver IDs • "How's my driving?" decals • School uniforms	**13. Identify property** • Property marking • Vehicle licensing and parts marking • Cattle branding	**18. Reduce emotional arousal** • Controls on violent pornography • Enforce good behavior on soccer field • Prohibit racial slurs	**23. Alert conscience** • Roadside speed display boards • Signatures for customs declarations • "Shoplifting is stealing"

4. Deflect offenders
- Street closures
- Separate bathrooms for women
- Disperse pubs

5. Control tools/weapons
- "Smart" guns
- Disabling stolen cell phones
- Restrict spray paint sales to juveniles

9. Utilize place managers
- CCTV for double-deck buses
- Two clerks for convenience stores
- Reward vigilance

10. Strengthen formal surveillance
- Red light cameras
- Burglar alarms
- Security guards

14. Disrupt markets
- Monitor pawn shops
- Controls on classified ads
- License street vendors

15. Deny benefits
- Ink merchandise tags
- Graffiti cleaning
- Speed humps

19. Neutralize peer pressure
- "Idiots drink and drive"
- "It's OK to say No"
- Disperse trouble-makers at school

20. Discourage imitation
- Rapid repair of vandalism
- V-chips in TVs
- Censor details of modus operandi

24. Assist compliance
- Easy library checkout
- Public lavatories
- Litter bins

25. Control drugs and alcohol
- Breathalyzers in pubs
- Server intervention
- Alcohol-free events

Source: Clarke, R.V and Eck, J. (2003) *Become a Problem-Solving Crime Analyst: In 55 Small Steps.* London: Jill Dando Institute of Crime Science, University College London. www.jdi.ucl.ac.uk/publications/manual/crime_manual_content.php.

Focus 9–2   Fortification

Fortification epitomizes the ghetto in America today, just as back alleys, crowded tenements, and lack of play areas defined the slums of the late nineteenth century. Buildings grow claws and spikes; their entrances acquire metal plates; their roofs get fenced in; and any additional openings are sealed, cutting down on light and ventilation. Glass windowpanes in first-floor windows are rare. Instead, window openings are bricked in or fitted with glass bricks. In schools and in buses, Plexiglas, frosty with scratches, blurs the view outside. Even in areas where statistics show a decrease in major crime, fortification continues to escalate and, as it does, ghettos lose their coherence. Neighborhoods are replaced by a random assortment of isolated bunkers, structures that increasingly resemble jails or power stations, their interiors effectively separated from the outside.

Throughout the nation's cities, we are witnessing the physical hardening of a new order, streetscapes so menacing, so alien, that they would not be tolerated if they were found anywhere besides poor, minority communities. In brick and cinder block and sharpened metal, inequality takes material form. The U.S. Post Office is the main symbol of the federal government in the ghetto. But where one might expect reassuring classical buildings decorated with eagles and images of the old Pony Express, there are instead squatty concrete blocks with iron gratings. The only unifying national symbols are the American flag on the outside and, on the inside, the FBI most-wanted poster. . . .

In South Central Los Angeles, a basic fortress is a bungalow with a small green lawn. The dwelling's first line of defense is an iron door, usually painted black. Metal bars on the windows add further protection, changing the once-friendly character of the wood and stucco houses. Less visible are the iron spikes to ward off trespassers.

In urban sections where apartment buildings are the typical abode, outsiders are discouraged from loitering in lobbies, harassing residents, selling drugs, and stealing mail by locked extensions using iron fencing that jut out, removing sections of sidewalk from public use. Courtyard entrances are closed off with heavy gates topped with razor-ribbon wire. Inside buildings, a guard dog chained to the stairway railing calls attention to suspicious movements. In dangerous projects, metal doors to apartments have as many as four locks, including one at the center that releases two cross-shaped bars. Between the dogs and the door locks, however, are often-dark hallways, and little can be done to defend those.

Source: Camilo José Vargara. 1994. Dwellings, Safety, and Security Measures. *New Statesman and Society* 7: 18. Copyright © 1994 *New Statesman and Society*. Reprinted with permission.

processes that include victims and the community. Restorative approaches may include encouraging the victim and the offender to play active roles in resolving conflict through discussion and negotiation. A number of restorative approaches are used in addressing victims of crimes. While some are considered proactive, most are reactive approaches to victimization. Some typical programs defined as restorative approaches are:

- Victim offender mediation
- Victim assistance
- Restitution

Involvement in restorative justice processes gives victims the opportunity to express their feelings about the offense and the harm done to them and to contribute their views about what is required to put things right. In theory, restorative approaches to justice create better responsiveness to victims and communities, while also helping offenders to understand the impact of their behavior and to repair the harm done (National Institute of Corrections, 2005).

Victim Rights and Compensation Programs

In recent years, crime victims have received the attention of public policy-makers. Every state includes protections for victims of crime within its statutory code. Victims' rights statutes have significantly influenced the manner in which victims are treated within the federal, state, and local criminal justice systems. Victim rights are also established by constitutional amendment. The first state to adopt a constitutional amendment providing rights to crime victims was California, in 1982. While modest in scope, the Victims' Bill of Rights amendment provided California victims a right to restitution from the offender and specifically recognized the importance of enacting "comprehensive provisions and laws ensuring a bill of rights for victims of crime." To date, 32 states have incorporated crime victims' rights in their constitutions (National Center for victims of Crime, 2008).

The core rights for victims of crime include:

- The right to attend criminal justice proceedings;
- The right to apply for compensation;
- The right to be heard and participate in criminal justice proceedings;
- The right to be informed of proceedings and events in the criminal justice process, of legal rights and remedies, and of available services;
- The right to protection from intimidation and harassment;
- The right to restitution from the offender;

- The right to prompt return of personal property seized as evidence;
- The right to a speedy trial; and
- The right to enforcement of these rights.

One of the most crucial rights are **victim compensation programs**. Victim compensation is defined as money paid from a public fund to innocent victims to enable them to recoup some of their financial losses. It is not a new concept, however. Victim compensation has been traced back to ancient Greece and Rome, where families of crime victims received funds for food and clothing. Victim rights compensation was recognized in the courts of the United States as early as 1960, when a New York case defined an eligible victim as "an aggrieved party whose rights, person or property were invaded by the defendant as a result of which criminal proceedings were successfully concluded" (*People v. Grago*, 1960). The federal definition is broader. It includes "any victim of the offense."

In the United States, California initiated the first victim compensation program in 1966. Since 1966, all states have passed some form of victim compensation program, which enables victims of violence to obtain some form of compensation for out-of-pocket expenses. Efforts to pass federal legislation began in 1964; in 1984, the Victim of Crime Act (VOCA) was passed. It authorized federal funding to induce states to implement compensation programs and victim outreach programs. In essence, the act was a major step in reacting to violent crime. Revenues for VOCA funds come from offender fines, penalty assessments, and forfeited appearance bonds. Most of the funds are used to provide grants to states to compensate crime victims.

In addition to federal assistance, most states receive compensation funds from convicted offenders in the form of fines, assessments, and penalties. Compensation funds also come from money earned by offenders engaged in prison work or work release assignments. Furthermore, many jurisdictions have laws that prohibit convicted offenders from making a profit from their crime. These are often called "notoriety-for-profit" laws. Under these laws, the offender is typically required to notify a state agency when he or she enters into a contract related to the crime. The state agency then freezes or holds the profit and notifies the victim. The victim has a certain amount of time to bring a civil suit against the offender (National Center for Victims of Crime, 2008).

Related to the notoriety-for-profit laws is the Son of Sam provision of VOCA, which requires that royalties from the sale of books written by offenders be deposited in the crime victim fund. The funds must be held in escrow for 5 years, however, to satisfy any civil judgments the victim may obtain against the offender (Parent, Auerbach, and Carlson, 1992). The concept behind the Son of Sam provision is to prohibit criminals from profiting by telling their stories while their victims continue to suffer financially. Since 1977, 42 states have enacted laws with Son of Sam provisions. In 1991, the New York law was challenged on the grounds that it was too broad and that it violated the First Amendment right to freedom of expression (*Simon & Schuster, Inc. v. New York Crime Victims Board*, 1991). In response to the Supreme Court's decision in *Simon & Schuster*, the state of New York and several other states have enacted new legislation. The key provisions of the new law in New York include the following:

- The law applies to any economic benefit to the offender derived by the crime, not just proceeds from the sale of the offender's story.
- Once notified, victims have 3 years in which to obtain a civil judgment for damages and to collect against any of the profits derived from the crime.
- The Crime Victim Compensation Board can freeze and seize all profits before victims have the opportunity to sue.

In upholding the Son of Sam law in California, a California state court of appeal ruled in 1999 that a man who kidnapped Frank Sinatra's son in 1963 cannot make any money from a movie about the crime. The court rejected a challenge to a 1986 California law that requires convicted felons to pay their victims when they sell their stories. The convicted person was the leader of three kidnappers who abducted a 19-year-old Frank Sinatra Jr. from Harrah's Casino at Lake Tahoe in 1963. He was released unharmed after a ransom payment. All three kidnappers were caught and convicted. After a magazine interview, the offender sold the movie rights of the case to Columbia Pictures. But Sinatra sued the kidnappers, the writer, and Columbia and got a court order preventing the studio from paying the convicted offender (O'Neil, 1999: B-2).

As a general rule, only victims who are directly harmed as a result of violent crime are eligible for compensation. In some cases, however, dependent family members of victims as well as good Samaritans can receive compensation. Most statutes require that the victim be physically harmed; however, some exceptions allow compensation for psychological counseling and treatment for children who witnessed violent crimes. A victim must not have provoked or contributed to the crime and must report the crime to the police, cooperate with the investigation, and apply for the compensation within a reasonable time (normally within 1 year) to be eligible for compensation. If the victim initiated a fight but was beaten in the process, eligibility is denied. Likewise, a victim who was a participant in a crime but was injured by the other offender is not eligible. The amount of compensation awards varies by state.

In most states, family members are allowed to recover losses incurred by homicide victims, including medical and funeral expenses. The types of losses for which victims may obtain restitution vary from jurisdiction to jurisdiction. Almost all states allow recovery of the victim's actual costs, such as medical expenses, which may include mental health counseling, psychiatric care, physical therapy, tests for human immunodeficiency virus (HIV), and property damage or loss. Restitution may be ordered during pretrial hearings or during sentencing. Of course, the offender's ability to pay is considered in ordering restitution. However, a number of methods ensure that offenders repay their victims.

Laws have granted the courts a variety of ways to enforce restitution orders beyond revocation of probation or parole. Several jurisdictions have allowed courts to garnish offenders' wages. For example, California and Florida mandate an income deduction order when restitution is required. In Texas, sentencing judges can require offenders to send letters to employers authorizing payment of a portion of the offenders' salaries directly to the victims. Some states have laws authorizing the attachment of offenders' assets (i.e., bank accounts, holdings, financial instruments). Some states have required offenders to disclose the nature and location of such assets or to post a cash bond to ensure payment of restitution. A California law makes it a misdemeanor or, in some instances, a felony for a convicted offender to sell or conceal property to reduce his or her financial ability to pay restitution (National Victim Center, 1995).

All states cover medical costs and funeral expenses, but only a few cover attorney costs. Victim compensation is a last resort remedy. Benefits do not include expenses covered by other sources, such as medical and auto insurance, employee benefits, and other public assistance programs (National Association of Crime Victim Compensation Boards, 1995). For crimes committed while the victim was on the job, workers' compensation is the primary benefit for the victim.

The average award generally ranges between $10,000 and $25,000, although a few states have higher or lower amounts. For example, the maximum award in Alabama is $10,000; in Minnesota it is $50,000. The crime victim compensation program in Texas (National Victim Center, 1995) covers sexual assault, kidnapping, aggravated assault and robbery, homicide, and other crimes in which the victim is injured and suffers physical or emotional harm or death. The following are the basic requirements:

- *Residency.* The crime must occur in Texas to a resident of Texas or the United States or must involve a Texas resident who becomes a victim in another state that does not have a crime victim compensation program.

- *Reporting the crime.* The crime must be reported to a law enforcement agency within 72 hours unless the victim is under 18 years of age or the reason that the crime was not reported within this time period is acceptable (e.g., in a kidnapping).
- *Filing for compensation.* An application must be filed within a year of the crime unless the person is under 18 years of age or there is a good reason that it was not submitted.
- *Cooperation.* The victim must cooperate fully with law enforcement officials.
- *Qualification.* The following qualify: an innocent victim of a crime who suffers physical and/or emotional harm or death, immediate family members needing counseling as a result of the crime against the victim, and household members related to the victim by marriage or blood and requiring counseling as a result of the crime.
- *Ineligibility.* The following may not receive benefits: a victim whose behavior contributed to the crime, a victim or claimant who knowingly and willingly participated in the crime, an offender or an accomplice of the offender, anyone incarcerated in a penal institution when the crime occurred or on probation or parole for a felony involving criminally injurious conduct, and victims of motor vehicle accidents except those victims of accidents involving driving under the influence or other crimes involving vehicles.

In most states, information on crime victim compensation is available from law enforcement agencies and prosecutors' offices. Victims always have had a common law right to restitution for criminal harm inflicted, and virtually all states have adopted laws that codify those rights in some form. A vast majority of states allow courts to make payment of restitution a condition of probation, parole, or both. Most important for victims, at least 23 states have passed laws requiring that restitution be ordered in all cases or that the court state on the record its reason for failing to do so (Beatty, 1991). Although laws vary as to the exact definition of who is eligible to make a claim, virtually all jurisdictions allow restitution to direct victims of crime. Table 9–2 lists the funds allocated to crime victims by state in 2003 and 2004.

An example of a typical victim services program is presented here. The program is operated by the Ventura County, California District Attorney Victim Services Division (1999). As described in a 1999 brochure titled *Information for Crime Victims and Witnesses,* the program purposes are as follows:

- To reduce trauma and ensure the sensitive treatment of crime victims
- To provide victims with faster, more complete recovery from the effects of crime through crisis intervention and related support services

TABLE 9–2 VOCA VICTIM COMPENSATION ALLOCATIONS IN FYS 2003 AND 2004

State or Territory	FY 2003	FY 2004	Total
Alabama	$1,740,000	$2,792,000	$4,532,000
Alaska	504,000	543,000	1,047,000
Arizona	1,374,000	1,258,000	2,632,000
Arkansas	1,148,000	1,187,000	2,335,000
California	44,234,000	64,796,000	109,030,000
Colorado	3,558,000	3,707,000	7,265,000
Connecticut	808,000	780,000	1,588,000
Delaware	399,000	859,000	1,258,000
District of Columbia	1,643,000	2,313,000	3,956,000
Florida	13,256,000	8,822,000	22,078,000
Georgia	2,304,000	1,706,000	4,010,000
Guam*	0	0	0
Hawaii	512,000	522,000	1,034,000
Idaho	462,000	821,000	1,283,000
Illinois	8,974,000	10,431,000	19,405,000
Indiana	1,588,000	638,000	2,226,000
Iowa	1,560,000	1,238,000	2,798,000
Kansas	1,058,000	1,222,000	2,280,000
Kentucky	491,000	339,000	830,000
Louisiana	988,000	771,000	1,759,000
Maine	186,000	175,000	361,000
Maryland	1,291,000	2,058,000	3,349,000
Massachusetts	1,142,000	1,520,000	2,662,000
Michigan	866,000	757,000	1,623,000
Minnesota	948,000	1,241,000	2,189,000
Mississippi	539,000	713,000	1,252,000
Missouri	2,563,000	2,279,000	4,842,000
Montana	309,000	356,000	665,000
Nebraska	170,000	127,000	297,000
Nevada	1,995,000	1,561,000	3,556,000
New Hampshire	200,000	211,000	411,000
New Jersey	2,283,000	4,842,000	7,125,000
New Mexico	490,000	734,000	1,224,000
New York	12,129,000	9,938,000	22,067,000
North Carolina	2,643,000	3,830,000	6,473,000
North Dakota	135,000	98,000	233,000
Ohio	8,783,000	6,777,000	15,560,000
Oklahoma	1,525,000	1,659,000	3,184,000
Oregon	753,000	1,046,000	1,799,000
Pennsylvania	3,863,000	2,071,000	5,934,000
Puerto Rico	131,000	139,000	270,000
Rhode Island	1,941,000	1,248,000	3,189,000
South Carolina	3,075,000	4,116,000	7,191,000

State or Territory	FY 2003	FY 2004	Total
South Dakota	158,000	184,000	342,000
Tennessee	5,095,000	4,971,000	10,066,000
Texas	16,020,000	18,489,000	34,509,000
U.S. Virgin Islands	100,000	103,000	203,000
Utah	1,794,000	2,332,000	4,126,000
Vermont	267,000	212,000	479,000
Virginia	1,095,000	1,244,000	2,339,000
Washington	4,018,000	4,444,000	8,462,000
West Virginia	749,000	646,000	1,395,000
Wisconsin	846,000	841,000	1,687,000
Wyoming	230,000	442,000	672,000
Totals	$164,933,000	$186,149,000	$351,082,000

*Due to several natural disasters, Guam's government elected not to participate during the biennium.

- To sensitize law enforcement officials, criminal justice personnel, and the community to the needs of crime victims and to reinforce a concerned approach to crime
- To ensure that crime victims are an integral part of the case in which they are involved
- To maintain a comprehensive program of services for victims of all types of crimes

Once a case comes to the district attorney's office, a trained victim advocate will be assigned to the case. The victim advocate works as part of a team with the deputy district attorney and the investigator who have been assigned to the case. It is not necessary for a case to be prosecuted for a victim to utilize the services of the Victim Services Division. A number of services are provided by the victim advocates. They are trained to assist victims for such crimes as domestic assault, families of homicide victims, child abuse, and other felonies and misdemeanors.

Services include the following:

- Assistance with domestic violence temporary restraining orders
- Orientation to the criminal justice system
- Crisis intervention
- Information about the case in question
- Property return assistance
- Interview accompaniment

- Support during court proceedings
- Referrals to community agencies
- Help with Victims of Crime Compensation
- Assistance with therapist referrals

In addition, victims often incur expenses as a direct result of the crime. Sometimes victims or families do not have medical insurance or the financial ability to pay for these expenses. The State of California has a compensation fund for crime victims to help with these expenses. The monies for this fund come entirely from fines assessed to criminals at the time they are sentenced (restitution fines). The apprehension or prosecution of the suspect is not necessary to file a Victims of Crime Compensation application. The Victim Services Division has a trained victim advocate who helps victims and family members complete the paperwork and determine whether they may be eligible for help through this program.

Eligible persons are the following:

- A victim who was injured as a result of a crime
- A person who was not directly injured or killed as a result of the crime but who was the parent, sibling, spouse, or child of the victim *and who was a resident of California at the time of the crime*
- A person living with the victim at the time of the crime or who had lived with the victim for at least 2 years in a relationship similar to a parent, sibling, spouse, or child of the victim
- A person who is another family member of the victim, including the victim's fiancé(e), *and witnessed the crime*
- Anyone who pays for the medical, funeral, or burial expenses of a deceased victim

Some requirements are the following:

- The crime must have occurred in California.
- The crime must have been reported to appropriate law enforcement agencies.
- The victim or witness must cooperate with law enforcement agencies.

Losses that may be covered include the following:

- Medical/dental
- Mental health counseling

- Wages/income
- Financial support
- Funeral/burial
- Job retraining

Losses that are *not* covered include the following:

- Personal property losses, including cash
- Compensation for pain and suffering

Legislation to Protect Victims

The federal government and a number of states pressed for increased rights for crime victims in the 1990s. A victim rights amendment to the U.S. Constitution has been proposed. The amendment, endorsed by a number of interest groups, such as Mothers Against Drunk Driving (MADD) and Parents of Murdered Children, would guarantee certain rights to crime victims and their families. Their efforts have already resulted in additional federal protection for crime victims.

Under federal law, as indicated in Focus 9–3, the Victim and Witness Protection Act of 1982 (VWPA) includes rights of all crime victims, including victims of domestic abuse and victims who are children.

Focus 9–3   Victim and Witness Assistance

The VWPA of 1982 was enacted for the following reasons:

To enhance and protect the necessary role of crime victims and witnesses in the criminal justice process; to ensure that the federal government does all that is possible within limits of available resources to assist victims and witnesses of crime without infringing on the constitutional rights of defendants; and to provide a model for legislation for state and local governments.

[Bill of] Rights of Crime Victims—42 U.S.C. 10606 (B)

1. The right to be treated with fairness and respect for the victim's dignity and privacy.
2. The right to be reasonably protected from the accused offender.
3. The right to be notified of court proceedings.

(Continued)

(Continued)

4. The right to be present at all public court proceedings related to the offense, unless the court determines that testimony by the victim would be materially affected if the victim heard other testimony at trial.

5. The right to confer with the attorney for the government in the case.

6. The right to restitution.

7. The right to information about the conviction, sentencing, imprisonment, and release of the defendant.

Additional Rights of Victims of Violent Crime/Domestic Abuse

Victims of violent crime have the right to speak at the sentencing of a defendant or submit a victim impact statement. In the case of a victim under the age of 18 or who is incompetent, a parent or legal guardian may exercise the victim's right to speak. If the victim is deceased or incapacitated, the victim's right to speak may be exercised by one or more family members or relatives designated by the court and present at the sentencing hearing.

Victims of domestic violence have the right to be heard at any detention·hearing of the defendant.

Rights of Child Victims/Witnesses

The rights of children are outlined in 18 U.S.C. Section 3509. In brief, they are as follows:

1. Alternatives to live, in-court testimony
2. Competence examination
3. Privacy protection
4. Closed courtroom
5. Victim impact statements
6. Multidisciplinary child abuse teams when feasible
7. *Guardian ad litem*
8. Adult attendant
9. Speedy trial
10. Testimonial aids

The concern for victims' rights has caught the attention of Congress. The 103rd Congress (1995–1996) passed a number of victims' rights laws. The Open Campus Police Logs Act of 1995 amends the Higher Education Act of 1965 (HEA) to require any higher education institution that participates in any student aid program under HEA Title IV and maintains a police or security department to keep a daily log of specified information about crimes that is open to public inspection (42 U.S.C. 14020, 1996). The Interstate Stalking Punishment and Prevention Act of 1996 amends the federal criminal code to prohibit and prescribe penalties for interstate stalking (i.e., traveling across a state line or within the special maritime and territorial jurisdiction of the United States) with the intent to injure or harass another person and, in the course or as a result of such travel, placing that person in reasonable fear of death or serious bodily injury to that person or a member of that person's immediate family.

Federal law is further recognizing the privacy of victims. It is unlawful to breach the confidentiality between sexual assault or domestic violence victims and their counselors (42 U.S.C. 13942, 1996). It is unlawful to threaten or retaliate against witnesses and crime victims (18 U.S.C. 1513, 1996). The Victim's Family's Access to Justice Act of 1996 amends the federal criminal code to require the attorney general to permit the adult members of a murder victim's family and others to attend the murderer's execution. Too often, offenders, particularly sex offenders convicted of serious crimes, have been released and then have committed new crimes. As a result, legislatures in many states have begun reacting to this threat by enacting community notification statutes. By 1995, most states required the registration of sex offenders.

The Violent Crime Control Act passed in 1994 represents the bipartisan product of several years of work. It is the largest crime bill in the history of the country. It allows victims of federal violent and sex crimes to speak at the sentencing of their assailants, referred to as **victim impact statements.** A number of states already had such a provision. In California, the passage of Proposition 8 in 1984 gave victims the right to attend and speak at sentencing and parole hearings, which is an attempt to provide input to the judge or jury about the victim's experiences. In 1991, the U.S. Supreme Court upheld the use of victim impact statements (*Payne v. Tennessee,* 1991). Although it is uncertain whether these statements affect sentencing, they do allow victims to speak out. The statements provide another method of informing the sentencing authority about the specific harm caused by the offender.

Related to victim impact statements is the right of crime victims to confer with prosecutors regarding plea agreements with offenders. Plea bargaining is a fundamental process in the criminal justice system. Yet, concerns are raised as to the fairness of bargaining from the perspective of the crime victim. In at least 22 states, the victim's right to confer with the prosecutor requires a prosecutor to obtain the victim's views concerning the proposed plea (Office for Victims of Crime, 2007). Whereas the laws in some of these states do not address how victims will make their concerns known, others specifically provide for written input. When victims have been permitted to provide input into plea agreements, the right has typically been granted at two stages of the criminal justice process: (1) when conferring with the prosecutor during plea bargaining and (2) when addressing the court, either orally or in writing, before the entry of the plea. Depending on the law of a particular state, a victim may be given the opportunity to comment on the proposed plea at either or both of these stages.

SEXUAL OFFENDER NOTIFICATION LAWS

In 1994, the New Jersey state legislature passed **Megan's Law**. The law was named after Megan Kanka, who was brutally raped and killed by a paroled sex offender living across the street from her home. The offender, Jesse Timmendequas, confessed to the killing and was finally convicted and sentenced to death in 1997.

A majority of states limit access to information to law enforcement and, in some cases, criminal justice officials. However, some states permit public access, with specific guidelines. California and New York, for example, have adopted a "900" telephone number that can be called by members of the public to find out about a certain offender. These states also provide a directory of registered sex offenders distributed to law enforcement officials and open to public inspection (National Victim Center, 1996). A computer-based retrieval system, similar to that used by banks in allowing customers to access their accounts, is being used in some jurisdictions. The system is referred to as the **Victim Information and Notification Everyday (VINE) system** (VINE Bears Some Appealing Fruit, 1995). The system gives callers information about times and locations of court dates and the status of inmates incarcerated in the county correctional system and also allows victims to register so they can be automatically notified when an inmate is to be released from jail.

Sexually Violent Predator Act

The Sexually Violent Predator Act was passed in Washington State in 1993 and has been imitated by a number of other states (e.g., California, Kansas) in recent years. The act calls for the civil confinement of sexual predators after they have served their criminal terms. The act is based on a predictive philosophy that convicted sexual offenders, such as pedophiles, are potential recidivists and a danger to society. In other words, these offenders are in need of further treatment even though they have served time for a criminal offense. These acts follow a preventive detention approach to reduce victimization by sexual predators by civilly confining them indefinitely for what they might do if released. Kansas defines a sexual predator as "a person who has been convicted of or charged with a sexually violent offense and who suffers from a mental abnormality or personality disorder which makes the person likely to engage in the predatory acts of sexual violence" (Kansas Civil Code Section 59–29a02[a]).

The act continues by defining a sexual predator and the required civil commitment procedures: (1) "a presently confined person who has been convicted of a sexually violent offense" and is scheduled for release; (2) a person who has been "charged with a sexually violent offense" but has been found incompetent to stand trial; (3) a person who has been found "not guilty by reason of insanity of a sexually violent offense"; and (4) a person found "not guilty" of a sexually violent offense because of a mental disease or defect (Kansas Civil Code Section 59–29a03[a], Section 22–3221, 1995).

The Kansas Sexual Predator Act was challenged constitutionally on the grounds of double jeopardy, due process, and so forth. However, the U.S. Supreme Court ruled in June 1997 that the act was constitutional (*Kansas v. Hendricks*, 1997). The ruling may set a precedent for other states to follow for sex offenders as well as for other violent offenders.

Anti-Gang Legislation

For years, many cities have struggled with gang violence and the victimization it creates. Arrest for the commission of substantive criminal offenses, defined by federal or state statute, is the main mechanism used by law enforcement to prosecute youth and adult gangs (Bureau of Justice Assistance, 1997). The use of penalty enhancements has been developed for use against gang members. These laws provide more severe sentences for crimes that are often gang related, although they are not limited in application to gang members. They enhance penalties against principals charged with offenses such as drug trafficking, homicide, assault with a weapon, robbery, home invasion, arson, extortion, and auto theft. Under federal conspiracy laws, accomplices may also be charged with such offenses by aiding and abetting overt criminal acts (Bureau of Justice Assistance, 1997).

Although a number of federal measures are available, aggressive legal approaches are under way in many local jurisdictions. The California **Street Terrorism, Enforcement, and Prevention (STEP) Act** of 1988 has served as a model for Florida, Georgia, Illinois, Louisiana, and other jurisdictions. A unique notification process is used to inform people that they can be prosecuted under STEP (Klein, 1995). Police and/or prosecutors gather evidence that a targeted gang fits the STEP Act's definition. This information is presented to the court, resulting in a judicial order. Gang members are then notified in writing that they are known members of such a group. Following such notice, the act can then be applied to these members, enhancing penalties for subsequent offenses because of the commission of crimes while involved in a gang.

Cities have enacted a number of measures that restrict or prohibit youth and adult gang activities, such as banning gang member use of public parks that have been gang confrontation sites and prohibiting cruising and many forms of belligerent public behavior. Court injunctions, aimed at the heart of one of the nation's largest and most vicious gangs in Los Angeles, are an ambitious approach to curb gang activities. The gang known as the 18th Street Gang has its roots in central Los Angeles. It deals in drugs and is responsible for numerous killings. The gang is an organization of terrorists bringing fear to many residents and business owners. The injunctions would ban all gang gatherings and bar members from possessing pagers and cellular phones. The court order would impose an 8:00 P.M. curfew for any gang member under the age of 18 unless accompanied by a parent or on a lawful errand (Krikorian and Connell, 1997).

Since 1993, about a dozen California cities have requested or received similar court injunctions. In 1997, the California Supreme Court upheld this gang suppression tactic. Clearly, the injunctions provide the police with greater powers of detention and arrest. Although the injunctions may simply displace gang members to other areas or represent harassment strategies to some, communities and lawmakers are tiring of the victimization caused by violent street criminals.

Crime Control Legislation in 2000 and Beyond

At the beginning of the new millennium, Congress was active in the area of crime control legislation. Even before the September 11th events, Congress passed the Victims of Trafficking and Violence Protection Act, which provides aid for victims of terrorism and expands authority to respond to incidents of terrorism outside the United States. In essence, the program seeks to address the unique needs and circumstances of international terrorism victims. On the domestic front, the following are a list of several pieces of legislation signed into law passed by Congress after 2000.

- The Justice for All Act of 2004 was signed into law by President Bush in October 30, 2004. The act contains several major sections related to crime victims and the criminal justice process. Some of the purposes of the act are to protect crime victims' rights, eliminate the substantial backlog of DNA samples collected from crime scenes and convicted offenders, and improve and expand the DNA testing capacity of federal, state, and local crime laboratories. More specifically, the act provides crime victims:

(1) The right to be reasonably protected from the accused.

(2) The right to reasonable, accurate, and timely notice of any public court proceeding or any parole proceeding involving the crime, or of any release or escape of the accused.

(3) The right not to be excluded from any such public court proceeding, unless the court, after receiving clear and convincing evidence, determines that testimony by the victim would be materially altered if the victim heard other testimony at that proceeding.

(4) The right to be reasonably heard at any public proceeding in the district court involving release, plea, sentencing, or any parole proceeding.

(5) The reasonable right to confer with the attorney for the Government in the case.

(6) The right to full and timely restitution as provided in law.

(7) The right to proceedings free from unreasonable delay.

- *Aimee's Law.* **Aimee's Law** penalizes states that release a person previously convicted of murder, rape, and dangerous sexual offenses in cases in which that person goes on to commit one of those crimes in another state. The releasing state must pay prosecution and incarceration costs, from federal law enforcement funds, to the second state. The law is a warning to states to exercise caution before releasing a violent offender on parole.

- *Campus Sex Crimes Prevention Act.* In addition to registering with local law enforcement authorities, the **Campus Sex Crimes Prevention Act** requires notice to be given to each institution of higher education that a sex offender will be attending or employed by them. Such information must be made available to area law enforcement and to the campus community.

- *Child Abuse Prevention and Enforcement Act.* This law increases funding for child abuse prevention and victim assistance programs. It doubles the amount of money to be set aside under the Victims of Crime Act (VOCA) formula for these programs, with a cap of $20 million. The act also includes the so-called Jennifer's Law, which is a measure creating $2 million in grants each year for 3 years to improve states' reporting of unidentified and missing persons.

- *Kristen's Act.* **Kristen's Act** authorizes grants to organizations to find missing adults who may be endangered because of diminished mental capacity, age, the circumstances of the disappearance, or the possibility of foul play. The law authorized funds to establish a national clearinghouse to provide resources and referrals for families of missing adults, assist law enforcement in locating missing adults, maintain statistics on missing adults, and create a national database to aid in the tracking of such persons.

- *Violence Against Women Act (VAWA) Reauthorization.* The **Violence Against Women Act (VAWA) Reauthorization** reauthorizes existing VAWA grant programs and establishes new grant programs. Some of the key provisions of the law include the following:
  (1) Pilot programs for transitional housing and for supervised visitation
  (2) Grants for civil legal assistance
  (3) Programs to address violence against elderly women and women with disabilities
  (4) Expansion of the federal stalking statute to include cyberstalking

In 2005, following a trend of sexual violence against children across the country, and specifically the brutal rape and killing of 9-year-old Jessica Lunsford in Florida, the state of Florida enacted the country's broadest and harshest legislation against sexual offenders. Known as the **Jessica Lunsford Act**, the law requires a minimum sentence of at least 25 years for offenders who molest children under the age of 12. Offenders could get a life sentence and would be placed on lifetime satellite monitoring if they are ever released from prison. The law further requires satellite monitoring of offenders who have molested children between the ages of 12 and 15 once the offenders are released from prison and put on probation. The law makes it a felony to harbor a sex offender, as in the case of the Lunsford crime where the offender was hiding with friends after the crime (Stockfisch, 2005).

As to the effectiveness of GPS monitoring, a Florida State University study of over 5,000 parolees showed that electronically monitored sex offenders were 44.8 percent less likely to commit a new offense than sex offenders not on electronic monitoring (Padget, Bales, and Bloomberg, 2006). In 2008, 22 states and over 400 cities nationwide have enacted residency restrictions on sex offenders in an attempt to keep predators away from areas where children congregate.

As an example, California, which has one of the highest number of sex offenders in the nation, enacted Proposition 83 in 2007. The law prohibits ex-offenders from living within 2,000 feet of places where children gather. Some argue the law may be too strict since it may create homelessness or force sex offenders to relocate away from family supports. In 2006,

Congress passed the Adam Walsh Child Protection and Safety Act. The act protects children from sexual exploitation and violent crime, prevents child abuse and child pornography, promotes Internet safety, and honors the memory of Adam Walsh who was kidnapped from a shopping mall and later found murdered. The legislation organizes sex offenders into three tiers and mandates that Tier 3 offenders update their whereabouts every 3 months. Failure to register and update information is made a felony under the law. It also creates a national sex offender registry and instructs each state and territory to apply identical criteria for posting offender data on the Internet (i.e., offender's name, address, date of birth, place of employment, photograph, etc.).

Victim Advocacy Groups

Many communities operate a number of **victim advocacy groups** whose services are available to victims of violent crimes and, in some cases, the victim's family. Victim advocacy or support services may be provided by independent for-profit or nonprofit groups or by government agencies, such as the district attorney's office or police department. The purposes of these groups are the following:

- Provide shelter and counseling to victims of violence.
- Offer advice, education, and direct aid to crime victims.
- Give support during criminal trials and other justice processes.
- Provide information about compensation programs.

According to Karmen (1995), six types of victim advocacy organizations operate in most communities. The first is referred to as a general independent nonprofit group. This group is concerned with public awareness and the education and training of other victim support groups. It does not assist specific victims but operates more as a clearinghouse or information source. The National Victim Center and National Organization for Victim Assistance are examples.

A second group is referred to as the focused independent nonprofit group. It is probably the most common type of victim support group. It offers assistance for victims of domestic violence, marital and date rape, drunk drivers (such as MADD), hate violence, and more. Many of these groups also lobby politicians for stricter laws (such as Megan's Law, discussed earlier).

A third type is the self-help group. These groups are often made up of former victims who offer counseling and advice to persons who have suffered losses though violence, such as rape victims, parents of murdered children, and victims of incest.

A fourth type is private for-profit civil advocacy. This type of group is discussed in the next section on civil justice for the victim. Generally, victims hire legal counsel to represent them in a civil action against an alleged offender or other responsible party.

The fifth type is general governmental advocates. These are tax-supported government agencies that offer information, data, and direct aid to crime victims. At the national level, the Office for Victims of Crime of the U.S. Department of Justice is an example. On the county and local levels, district attorneys' offices operate victim assistance programs staffed by people who are victim witness coordinators. The coordinator offers services to the victim, such as transportation to court and referrals.

The final type is called the focused governmental agency. Like its counterpart on the nonprofit level, this group provides support for specialized needs, such as the child welfare and protection units commonly found in local jurisdictions. These groups are responsible for children who have been abused or neglected, providing counseling and foster placement.

There are many community support programs for victims of violence. Two examples are presented here. The Dignity of Victims Everywhere (DOVE) program initiated in Everett, Washington, has drawn national attention in recent years. It is a nonprofit corporation staffed by volunteers that offers services at no charge. It is the nation's oldest victim service program. Its services include the following:

- *Peer counseling.* Enables victims to help victims.
- *System intervention.* Teaches victims how to deal with the criminal justice system.
- *Searching for families.* Provides assistance in locating missing children and other family members.
- *Referrals and networking.* Assists victims in finding other support.
- *Court support.* Makes legal assistance referrals.
- *Research.* Studies the justice system.
- *Victim advocacy program.* Accompanies victims to court hearings.
- *Education.* Offers training on victimization.

Another successful innovative program is the Interface Children and Family Services Program of Ventura County, California. A nonprofit agency founded in 1973, it responds to the increasing abuse to children and families caused by drug use. The program offers a number of services and facilities, including the following:

- *Youth crisis homeless/runaway shelter.* A program for abused children of 8 to 18 years of age.
- *Youth crisis intervention.* A program offering trained volunteers 24 hours a day, 7 days a week.
- *Domestic violence services for battered women and their children.* A program that offers shelter, counseling, and life planning for up to 30 days.
- *Victim–offender reconciliation programs.* A program that allows offenders who have committed minor offenses to meet with their victims and reconcile the event through structured mediation.
- *Batterers' diversion program.* A 52-week program for court ordered education and treatment for people who are physically violent in relationships.

Another support program for victims and witnesses of crime is a protection program. Witnesses frequently are reluctant to provide information because they fear retaliation; this is especially true for crimes involving gang violence. In 1982, the VWPA expanded federal laws regarding witness security and victim services. It established penalties for witness tampering, intimidation, and harassment. Local prosecutors and law enforcement officials are dealing with this problem by establishing innovative protection programs for violent crime and gang-related cases. Funding for these services is provided through Victim of Crime Act grants and local budgets.

Research on victim and witness intimidation conducted by the National Institute of Justice was based on structured interviews with 32 criminal justice professionals from 20 urban jurisdictions, including prosecutors, law enforcement officials, victim service advocates, judges, and scholars. The study found five principal enforcement methods for victim and witness protection (Healey, 1995). The first method is to offer emergency relocation and support by registering witnesses and victims in hotels or motels under false names. The second method involves long-term relocation strategies of literally moving the victim or witness to another part of the state, out of the state, or even out of the country. The relocated person is given a living allowance, relocation expenses, and so forth. A third method involves pretrial and courtroom security measures. Prosecutors and law enforcement officials employ methods such as providing separate waiting rooms for victims and witnesses, escorted transportation to and from the courthouse, and the use of metal detectors and video cameras to screen people coming to the courthouse. A fourth method involves placing a witness in protective custody. Protective custody seeks to prevent witness intimidation. The final method is community outreach, which uses established relationships among community agencies. The intent is to make the community aware that victim–witness programs exist and that protection is available. Community outreach is an extension of community policing, which incorporates community-based strategies to combat crime.

In addition to local advocacy organizations, national resources are available for crime victims. The National Victim Center (NVC), established in 1985, has the dual mission to provide training and technical assistance to victim service providers and criminal justice professionals and to promote **victim rights** through education, information dissemination, and public policy. A not-for-profit organization with offices in Arlington, Virginia, and New York City, NVC serves as a national resource for more than 8,000 organizations and many thousands of individuals each year. It accomplishes its mission in a variety of ways, including the following:

- Providing training and technical assistance to criminal justice professionals, including law enforcement officers, prosecutors, judges, and corrections personnel
- Developing and presenting national workshops that comprehensively address the issues of HIV and acquired immune deficiency syndrome (AIDS) and victim services
- Conducting educational seminars on the issues and rights of crime victims and professionals who provide victim services
- Drafting model legislation and providing information for public policymakers
- Offering a toll-free information and referral program

NVC has one of the largest collections of crime victim and criminal justice–related information in the United States. Its comprehensive collection includes more than 10,000 books, journals, articles, research studies, dissertations, bibliographies, and other documents relevant to criminal justice and victims issues. NVC helped develop curricula for the first-ever library project designed to increase cooperation and referrals among libraries and agencies that service youth and families in crisis.

Civil Justice for Victims

The civil justice system, unlike the criminal justice process, does not attempt to determine the innocence or guilt of an offender or to punish him or her by incarceration. Rather, the civil courts attempt to ascertain whether a defendant is liable for the civil damages related to injuries caused by a crime, referred to as a tort. Most often, a civil court's finding of liability means that the defendant must pay the victim and/or the victim's family monetary damages; this is referred to as civil justice for the victim. In this respect, the civil justice system can augment the criminal justice process and sometimes can even provide victims and their families with a sense of justice that the criminal courts cannot. According to the civil justice system's concept of "a crime against the state," a defendant who is found liable is directly accountable to the victim. The civil justice system requires less proof of liability than the criminal system's proof beyond a reasonable doubt. In the civil system, the victim–plaintiff must prove his or her case by only a preponderance of the evidence to find the defendant liable. Therefore, a defendant may be found liable in a civil case even though he or she was found not guilty in a criminal case. In some civil cases, a third-party defendant may be held liable. Justice obtained through the courts for damages is known as civil justice. The O. J. Simpson civil trial is an example. Although he was acquitted of the murders of his former wife and her friend in criminal proceedings, the victims' families sued him. In 1997, they won a judgment of more than $38 million against Simpson.

In a number of civil cases, crime victims seek damages from a property owner if it can be shown that the owner was negligent in protecting employees or visitors from criminal attack. These people are known as third-party defendants. They are not the people who actually committed a crime but are found by the court to have been negligent in contributing to the factors that allowed a crime to occur. Such cases must establish that the defendant owed the plaintiff a legal duty (to protect) but breached that duty (failed to protect) and that the breach was a proximate or legal cause of the injury (the failure to protect was linked to the injury). Examples of third-party defendants are hotels and apartments that do not have proper security procedures and proper lighting, shopping malls that do not employ security patrols, and employers that do not properly check backgrounds of their employees. In one study of 1,086 cases, defendants prevailed 52 percent of the time. Plaintiffs won 21 percent of the time, and 19 percent of the cases were remanded— meaning that a case was sent back to the trial court for some further action (those cases had not resulted in a verdict for either party at the time the study was concluded). Eight percent of the cases were settled, with the results made public. About 71 percent of the plaintiffs in premises security liability suits were people invited onto the property such as customers and tenants (Anderson, 2002).

Many civil suits settle out of court, sending a message to public and private institutions about their liability for potential damages. Actions against third parties have been credited with changing security and safety practices in some businesses and institutions. By awarding huge damages, the courts are calling attention to civil liability (Meadows, 1995). The following cases are examples of third-party suits:

- In 2008, most families of victims of the mass shootings at Virginia Tech in 2007 have agreed to an $11 million state settlement that will compensate families who lost loved ones, pay survivors' medical costs, and avoid a court battle. Seung-Hui Cho, a mentally disturbed student, killed 32 victims and wounded two dozen others at Virginia Tech on April 16, 2007, before committing suicide. The university officials were criticized for waiting about 2 hours before informing students and employees about the first shootings, which police initially thought were an act of domestic violence.

- A woman was kidnapped in her own car in a parking lot. The lot attendant, who was on a 14-hour shift, was asleep and did not hear her screams as she struggled against her attacker. She was driven away and then robbed and raped. She sued the owner of the parking facility and was awarded $2.1 million in damages (*Doe v. System Parking, Inc.*, 1995).

- A nurse was arriving for work at a hospital when she was abducted and sexually assaulted. The nurse sued the hospital for inadequate security, claiming that the facility had no perimeter security, no lot attendant, and no security guards, and that there was inadequate monitoring of CCTV cameras. The jury awarded the plaintiff $400,000.

- A jury in New York awarded a woman $2 million in damages for a rape occurring on hotel property. The hotel had been on notice for prior crimes (*Splawn v. Lextaj*, 1995).

- A female convenience store clerk in Texas was awarded $13 million in damages. She was raped while working alone. About 2 weeks after the rape, she returned to the store and was raped again by the same person. The rapist testified that the store was "easy to rob." After the first rape, she had asked for a leave of absence, but it was denied. The jury returned a verdict against the store of $13 million (*Laird v. E-Z Mart*, 1995).

- A federal jury ordered the district government to pay $550,000 to the family of a boy who was terrorized and sexually abused at a city-run summer camp when he was left alone with an older camper. After hearing testimony from the victim and other young campers, a U.S. District Court jury found that the D.C. Department of Parks and

Recreation was negligent and failed to protect him during his 5-day stay in 2001.

- In 2005, the Archdiocese of San Francisco was ordered to pay $437,000 to a California man who was repeatedly fondled by a priest during the 1970s.

In a number of cases, victims have recovered huge amounts for the negligence of owners. One of the first cases to receive national attention was the victimization of singer Connie Frances. In 1974, she was raped in a Howard Johnson's motel room, and she sued the hotel chain for premises liability, proving that the motel's locking devices were inadequate. She received a $1.4 million judgment. It is clear that one way to react to victimization is to seek damages from sources other than disenfranchised or absent offenders. The process of civil litigation is an exhaustive one. If the victim prevails at trial (assuming that the parties do not settle out of court), the defendant may appeal the decision, thus blocking the victim from seeking immediate recovery. The victim may reach a settlement of less than the amount that the court awarded just to get over with it. The emotional costs to the victim can be staggering.

SUMMARY

Combating victimization requires a concerted effort between the public and private sectors. The United States is responding to violent crime in various proactive and reactive ways. The increase in the purchase of weapons reminds us of the fears many have. Community crime planning and increased security measures are a vital part of any crime prevention effort. The 1994 Federal Crime Bill was a significant step in addressing victimization and crime. The best way to curtail victimization is to address the sources of crime. In 1996, Congress required the attorney general to provide a "comprehensive evaluation of the effectiveness" of Department of Justice grants of more than $3 billion annually to assist state and local law enforcement and communities in preventing crime. The evaluation resulted in an exhaustive report analyzing various approaches to crime prevention (Sherman et al., 1996). The independent review of the relevant scientific literature included more than 500 program impact evaluations. The report found that some prevention programs work, some do not, some are promising, and some have not been tested adequately. Given the evidence of promising and effective programs, the report found that the effectiveness of Department of Justice funding depended heavily on whether it was directed to the urban neighborhoods where youth violence is highly concentrated. The report found that substantial reductions in national rates of serious crime can be achieved only by prevention in areas of concentrated poverty, where the majority of all homicides in the nation occur and where homicide rates are 20 times the national average. Reducing victimization also includes awareness of personal risks or avoidance of life styles conducive to crime and victimization. Clearly, much can be done to address violence and victimization.

KEY TERMS AND CONCEPTS

Aimee's Law
Campus Sex Crimes Prevention Act
Civil justice for the victim
Closed-circuit television cameras
Crime prevention through
environmental design (CPTED)
Defensible space theory
Environmental criminology
Jessica Lunsford Act
Kristen's Act
Megan's Law
Premises liability
Proactive response to crime

Reactive response to crime
Reasonable force
Situational crime prevention
Street Terrorism, Enforcement, and
Prevention (STEP) Act
Victim advocacy groups
Victim compensation programs
Victim impact statements
Victim Information and Notification
Everyday (VINE) system
Victim rights
Violence Against Women Act (VAWA)
Reauthorization

DISCUSSION QUESTIONS AND LEARNING ACTIVITIES

1. Do you believe that citizens should carry firearms on their person while traveling? What is the law in your state regarding citizen firearm training and possession and concealment of weapons?

2. Interview a security director of a corporation and determine what security measures the corporation finds most effective in deterring crime.

3. Regarding environmental criminology, visit a community and determine whether the physical conditions are a factor in crime. You may want to interview a police officer assigned to the area.

4. Some citizens believe that certain businesses or residential properties are a nuisance and attract crime. Do you believe that they have a valid point? What evidence do you have to support it?

5. What victim services programs are available in your community? Indicate the type of funding they receive.

6. Explain how a crime victim may receive compensation for injuries. Under what circumstances would a crime victim not be eligible for compensation?

7. Do you believe that legislation regarding victim impact statements is effective or is just an example of appeasing victims? Explain.

8. In two groups, discuss the benefits and disadvantages of laws regarding community notification of released sex offenders.

9. What evidence do you see in your community of crime prevention through environmental design?

10. In what ways can the community, police, and local businesses work together to reduce crime?

11. Search the Internet or contact your congressional representative and determine what legislative efforts are under way to increase the rights of victims.

12. Explain the difference between victim restitution and victim compensation.

WEB SOURCES

Office for Victims of Crime.
  www.ojp.usdoj.gov/ovc/
The National Crime Victim Bar Association.
  www.ncvc.org/vb/main.aspx?dbID = dash_Home
National Organization for Victim Assistance (NOVA).
  www.trynova.org/

RECOMMENDED READINGS

Baker, Thomas E. 2005. *Introductory Criminal Analysis: Crime Prevention and Intervention Strategies.* Upper Saddle River: Prentice Hall.

Brennan, Dean, and Al Zelinka. 2001. *SafeScape: Creating Safer, More Livable Communities through Planning and Design.* Madison, WI: APA Planners Press.

Crowe, Timothy. 2000. *Crime Prevention Through Environmental Design.* 2nd ed. New York: Butterworth-Heinemann.

DeConde, Alexander. 2001. *Gun Violence in America.* Boston: Northeastern University Press.

Garland, Davis, Andrew Von Hirsh, and Alison Wakefield. 2005. *Ethical and Social Perspectives on Situational Crime Prevention.* Oxford, UK: Hart Publishing.

Geffner, Robert. 2004. *Identifying and Treating Sex Offenders: Current Approaches, Research, and Techniques.* New York: Haworth Press.

REFERENCES

Anderson, Teresa. 2002. Laying Down the Law: A Review of Trends in Liability Lawsuits. *Security Management:* 88–90.

Beatty, David. 1991. Legal Issues. *Participant Manual: Offender Supervision and Restitution Project.* Lexington, KY: American Parole and Probation Association and the Council of State Government.

Bell, C. 1997. Promotion of Mental Health through Coaching of Competitive Sports. *Journal of the National Medical Association* 89(10): 657–662.

Bell, C., S. Gamm, P. Vallas, and P. Jackson. 2001. Strategies for the Prevention of Youth Violence in Chicago Public Schools. In *School Violence: Contributing Factors, Management, and Prevention,* eds. M. Shafii and S. Shafii. Washington, DC: American Psychiatric Press, 251–272.

Bureau of Justice Assistance. 1997. *Urban Street Gang Enforcement.* Washington, DC: U.S. Department of Justice, Office of Justice Programs, Bureau of Justice Assistance.

Bureau of Justice Statistics. 1994. *Guns and Crime: Handgun Victimization, Firearm Self-Defense, and Firearm Theft.* Washington, DC: U.S. Department of Justice.

Bureau of Justice Statistics. 2001. Background Checks for Firearm Transfers, 2000. *Bureau of Justice Statistics Bulletin.* Washington, DC: National Institute of Justice.

California District Attorney Victim Services Division. 1999. *Information for Crime Victims and Witnesses.* Ventura: Ventura County, California District Attorney Victim Services Division.

Clarke, R. V. 1980. Situational Crime Prevention: Theory and Practice. *British Journal of Criminology* 2.

Clarke, R.V. 1992. *Situational Crime Prevention,* Albany, NY Harrow and Heston.

Clarke, R. V., and Eck, J. 2003. *Become a Problem-Solving Crime Analyst: In 55 Small Steps.* London: Jill Dando Institute of Crime Science, University College London. www.jdi.ucl.ac.uk/publications/manual/crime_manual_content.php.

Cohen, L. E., and M. Felson. 1979. Social Change and Crime Rate Trends: A Routine Activity Approach. *American Sociological Review* 44.

Corwin, Miles. 1993. A Growing Crop of Private Cops Is the First Line of Defense for Homes and Shops. *Los Angeles Times,* November 28, B-1.

Decker, Scott H., Susan Pennell, and Ami Caldwell. 1997. *Illegal Firearms: Access and Use by Arrestees.* Washington, DC: U.S. Department of Justice, National Institute of Justice.

Doe v. System Parking, Inc., Cuyahoga County C.C.P. No. 178051 (1995).

Doherty, Jake. 1993. Private Patrol Supplements Police. *Los Angeles Times,* August 1, C-1.

Elliott, D., and P. Tolan. 1999. Youth Violence Prevention, Intervention, and Social Policy. In *Youth Violence: Prevention, Intervention and Social Policy,* eds. D. J. Flannery and C. R. Huff. Washington, DC: American Psychiatric Press.

Erickson, Rosemary J., and Arnie Stenseth. 1996. Crimes of Convenience. *Security Management,* October.

Federal Bureau of Investigation. 1994. *Uniform Crime Reports: Crime in the United States, 1993.* Washington, DC: U.S. Department of Justice.

Fleissner, Dan, and Fred Heinzelmann. 1996. *Crime Prevention through Environmental Design and Community Policing.* Washington, DC: National Institute of Justice.

Girard, Charles M. 1996. Security Lighting. In *Handbook of Loss Prevention and Crime Prevention,* ed. Lawrence J. Fennelly. Boston: Butterworth-Heinemann.

Gordon, Corey J., and William Brill. 1996. *The Expanding Role of Crime Prevention through Environmental Design in Premises Liability.* Washington, DC: National Institute of Justice, Bureau of Justice Programs.

Gorman-Smith, D., et al. 1996. The Relationships of Family Functioning to Violence Among Inner-City Minority Youth. *Journal of Family Psychology* 10:115–129.

Greenberg, Stephanie W., J. R. Williams, and W. R. Rohe. 1982. *Safe and Secure Neighborhoods: Physical Characteristics and Informal Control in High and Low Crime Neighborhoods.* Washington, DC: U.S. Department of Justice, National Institute of Justice.

Healey, Kerry Murphy. 1995. *Victim and Witness Intimidation.* Washington, DC: National Institute of Justice, Bureau of Justice Programs.

Henggeler, S. W., G. B. Melton, and L. A. Smith. 1992. Family Preservation Using Multi-Systemic Therapy: An Effective Alternative to Incarcerating Serious Juvenile Offenders. *Journal of Consulting Clinical Psychology* 60: 953–961.

Hoyert, D. L., K. D. Kochanek, and S. L. Murphy. 1999. Deaths: Final Data for 1997. *Vital Statistical Reports* 1999, Vol. 47.

Hubler, Shawn. 1996. ATM Crime Rate Is Low Compared to Anguish Level. *Los Angeles Times,* October 2, A-16.

Hunter, Ronald D., and C. R. Jeffrey. 1992. Preventing Convenience Store Robbery through Environmental Design. In *Situational Crime Prevention,* ed. Ronald V. Clarke. Albany, NY: Harrow and Heston.

Jacobs, J. 1961. *The Death and Life of Great American Cities.* New York: Random House.

Jeffrey, C. Ray. 1971. *Crime Prevention through Environmental Design.* Beverly Hills, CA: Sage.

Kansas v. Hendricks, 117 S.Ct. 2072 (1997).

Karmen, Andrew. 1995. Towards the Institutionalization of a New Kind of Justice Professional: The Victim Advocate. *Justice Professional,* Winter.

Kates, D. B. 1995. Gun Control: Epidemic of Violence or Pandemic of Propaganda. *University of Tennessee Law Review,* Spring.

Kleck, Gary. 1998a. *Point Blank: Guns and Violence in America.* New York: Aldine de Gruyter.

Kleck, Gary. 1998b. What Are the Risks and Benefits of Keeping a Gun in the Home? *Journal of the American Medical Association* 282(August): 135–136.

Kleck, Gary, and M. Gertz. 1995. Armed Resistance to Crime: The Prevalence and Nature of Self-Defense with a Gun. *Journal of Criminal Law and Criminology* 86.

Kleck, G., and M. Hogan. 1996. A National Case-Control Study of Homicide Offending and Gun Ownership. Paper presented at annual meeting of the American Society of Criminology, Chicago, IL, November.

Klein, M. W. 1995. *The American Street Gang.* New York: Oxford University Press.

Krikorian, Greg, and Rich Connell. 1997. Wide Injunction Sought against 18th Street Gang. *Los Angeles Times*, August 4, A-1.

Laird v. E-Z Mart, D-137,310 D.Ct. Jefferson County, Texas (1995).

Leape, L. L. 1994. Error in Medicine. *Journal of the American Medical Association* 272:23.

McDowell, David, C. Loftin, and B. Wiersema. 1991. General Deterrence through Civilian Gun Ownership: An Evaluation of the Quasi-Experimental Evidence. *Criminology* 29:167–171.

Meadows, Robert J. 1995. An Analysis of Jury Verdicts for Premises Liability Litigation in California. *Security Administration* 17:2.

Moffitt, T. E. 1997. Neuropsychology, Antisocial Behavior, and Neighborhood Context. In *Violence and Childhood in the Inner City*, ed. J. McCord. Cambridge, England: Cambridge University Press.

National Association of Crime Victim Compensation Boards. 1995. *Crime Victim Compensation Program Directory*. Alexandria, VA: National Association of Crime Victim Compensation Boards.

National Center for Victims of Crime. 2008. Washington, DC. www.ncvc.org.

National Institute of Corrections. 2005. Restorative Justice. Washington DC: U.S. Department of Justice. www.NICIC.org (Retrieved November 10, 2005).

National Victim Center. 1995. *Restitution Legislation*. Arlington, VA: National Victim Center. www.nvc.org/.

National Victim Center. 1996. *Community Notification of the Release of Sex Offenders*. Arlington, VA: National Victim Center. www.nvc.org/.

Newman, Oscar. 1972. *Defensible Space: Crime Prevention through Urban Design*. New York: Macmillan.

Newman, Oscar. 1992. *Improving the Viability of Two Dayton Communities: Five Oaks and Dunbar Manor*. Great Neck, NY: Institute for Community Design Analysis.

Office for Victims of Crime, U.S. Department of Justice Office of Justice Programs 2007.

O'Neil, Ann W. 1999. *Los Angeles Times*, May 28, B-2.

Padget, Kathy, William Bales, and Thomas G. Bloomberg, "Under Surveillance: An Empirical Test of the Effectiveness and Consequences of Electronic Monitoring," Criminology and Public Policy, Florida State University, February 2006.

Parent, Dale G., Barbara Auerbach, and Kenneth E. Carlson. 1992. *Compensating Crime Victims: A Summary of Policies and Practices*. Washington, DC: U.S. Department of Justice, National Institute of Justice.

Payne v. Tennessee, 501 U.S. 808 (1991).

People v. Grago, 24 Misc. 2d 739,741 204 N.Y.S. 2nd 774 (1960).

Reid, Sue Titus. 1997. *Crime and Criminology*. Madison, WI: Brown and Benchmark.

Roig-Franzia, Manuel. 2005. Florida gunlaw to Expand Leeway for Self-Defense. *Washington Post*, April 26, A-1.

Sampson, R. J., S. W. Raudenbush, and F. Earls. 1997. Neighborhoods and Violent Crime: A Multilevel Study of Collective Efficacy. *Science* 277:918–924.

Seper, Jerry. 2004. Border Patrol Hails New ID System. *Washington Times*, December 21.

Sessions, William S. 1990. *Crime in the United States: 1989 Annual Report*. Washington, DC: Federal Bureau of Investigation.

Sherman, Lawrence W., Denise Gottfredson, Doris MacKenzie, John Eck, Peter Reuter, and Shaw Bushway. 1996. *Preventing Crime: What Works, What Doesn't, What's*

Promising. A Report to the United States Congress. Washington, DC: National Institute of Justice.

Simon & Schuster, Inc. v. New York Crime Victims Board, 112 S.CT. 501 (1991).

Smith, Mary. 1996. Crime Prevention through Environmental Design in Parking Facilities. Washington, DC: National Institute of Justice.

Splawn v. Lextuj, 603 N.Y.S. 2nd (1995).

Stewart, Jill. 1996. The Next Eden. California Lawyer, November.

Stockfisch, Jerome. 2005. Jessica Lunsford Act Makes Florida Laws Even Tougher. Tampa Tribune, May 3.

Suter, E. A. 1995. Violence in America—Effective Solutions. Journal of the Medical Association of Georgia 85:253–263.

Taylor, Ralph, and Adele V. Harrell. 1996. Physical Environment and Crime. Washington, DC: U.S. Department of Justice, National Institute of Justice.

U.S. Department of Justice. 2000. Safe from the Start: Taking Action on Children Exposed to Violence. Washington, DC: U.S. Department of Justice, Office of Justice Programs, Office of Juvenile Justice and Delinquency Prevention. (NCJ 182789).

Vargara, Camilo. 1994. Dwellings, Safety, and Security Measures. New Statesman and Society 7.

VINE Bears Some Appealing Fruit for Crime Victims in Louisville Area. 1995. Law Enforcement News 21.

Weisel, D. L. 1994. Addressing Community Decay and Crime: Alternative Approaches and Explanations. Washington, DC: Urban Institute.

Wilson, James Q., and G. L. Kelling. 1982. Broken Windows. Atlantic Monthly, March.

Witkin, Gordon. 1994. Should You Own a Gun? U.S. News & World Report, August 15, 24.

Zappile, Richard A. 1991. Philadelphia Implements Security Watch. Police Chief, August.

FURTHER READINGS

Broader, John M. 1996. Clinton Calls for Victims' Rights in Constitution. Los Angeles Times, June 26, A-12.

Bureau of Justice Statistics. 1995. Civil Juries Award Punitive Damages in 6 Percent of Successful Suits. Washington, DC: U.S. Department of Justice.

Bureau of Justice Statistics. 1996. National Crime Victimization Survey. Washington, DC: U.S. Department of Justice.

Chaiken, Jan, Michael W. Lawless, and Keith A. Stevenson. 1974. The Impact of Police Activity on Crime: Robberies on the New York City Subway System. Santa Monica, CA: Rand Corporation.

Cottrol, R. J., and R. T. Diamond. 1991. The Second Amendment: Toward an Afro-American Reconsideration. Georgetown Law Journal 80.

Daily News. 1996. Sex-Offender Data Soon Will Be Keystroke Away. September 12, 4.

Cohen, M. A. 1994. The Costs and Consequences of Violent Behavior in the United States. In Understanding and Preventing Violence 4, eds. J. Roth and A. Reiss. Washington, DC: National Academy Press.

Gorman, Dave. 1996. Loss Prevention Racks Up Success. Security Management, February, 2.

Kirch, John. 1996. Strictly Speaking: Rx for Alarms. Security Management Magazine, July, 7.

McDaniel, Patricia. 1993. Self-Defense Training and Women's Fear of Crime. *Women's Studies International Forum* 16:1.

Miller, Ted. 1996. *Victim Costs and Consequences: A New Look*. Washington, DC: U.S. Department of Justice, National Institute of Justice.

Newman, Oscar. 1976. *Design Guidelines for Creating Defensible Space*. Washington, DC: National Institute of Law Enforcement and Criminal Justice.

Poyner, B. 1991. Situational Crime Prevention in Two Parking Facilities. *Security Journal* 2.

Project DOVE. 2000. Everett, WA. www.dove-wa.org/.

United States Code, 18 U.S.C. Section 1513 (1996).

United States Code, 42 U.S.C. Section 13942 (1996).

Ventura Star. 1996. Veteran Bank Robber Shares Tricks of Trade. October 6, 16.

Youth Gang Programs and Strategies. 2002. *Office of Juvenile Justice and Delinquency Prevention Summary*. Washington, DC: Office of Juvenile Justice and Delinquency Prevention. August.

Major Sources of Victimization Data and Information

1. *Uniform Crime Reports* (annual publication)

   Federal Bureau of Investigation
   U.S. Department of Justice
   J. Edgar Hoover Building
   935 Pennsylvania Avenue, NW
   Washington, DC 20535
   (202) 324-3000
   www.fbi.gov/

2. *Sourcebook of Criminal Justice Statistics* (annual publication)

   The Hindelang Criminal Justice Research Center
   University at Albany
   135 Western Avenue
   Draper 241
   Albany, New York 12222
   518-442-5608
   www.albany.edu/sourcebook/

   The *Sourcebook* is divided into the following six sections:

   1. Characteristics of the Criminal Justice Systems
   2. Public Attitudes Toward Crime and Criminal Justice-Related Topics
   3. Nature and Distribution of Known Offenses
   4. Characteristics and Distribution of Persons Arrested
   5. Judicial Processing of Defendants
   6. Persons under Correctional Supervision

3. *Criminal Victimization in the United States* (annual publication) *National Crime Victimization Survey Report*

   U.S. Department of Justice
   Bureau of Justice Statistics
   810 Seventh Street, NW
   Washington, DC 20531
   1-202-307-0765
   www.ojp.usdoj.gov/bjs/abstract/cvusst.htm

   To obtain databases contact:

   National Archive of Criminal Justice Data
   ICPSR
   Institute for Social Research
   P.O. Box 1248
   Ann Arbor, MI 48106
   USA
   1-800-999-0960
   1-734-998-9825

4. The National Center for Victims of Crime

   2000 M Street NW Suite 480
   Washington, DC 20036
   www.ncvc.org/

INTERNET SOURCES FOR VICTIMIZATION RESEARCH

1. Bureau of Justice Statistics. www.ojp.usdoj.gov/bjs/
2. Crime Statistics Page. www.crime.org/
3. National Archive of Criminal Justice Data. www.icpsr.umich.edu/NACJD/
4. National Criminal Justice Association. www.ncja.org/
5. National Criminal Justice Reference Service. www.ncjrs.org
6. Sourcebook of Criminal Justice. www.albany.edu/sourcebook/
7. Vera Institute of Justice. www.vera.org/
8. The World-Wide Web Virtual Library: Statistics. www.stat.ufl.edu/vlib/statistics.html
9. Victim Offender Mediation Association. www.igc.org/voma
10. Crime Prevention (NCJRS). http://virlib.ncjrs.org/more.asp?category=51&subcategory=131
11. Crime Prevention Unit. www.geocities.com/CapitolHill/1591/
12. National Crime Victims' Research and Treatment Center. www.musc.edu/cvc/
13. National organization for Victim Assistance. www.trynova.org/
14. New York Missing and Exploited Children Clearinghouse. http://criminaljustice.state.ny.us/missing/

15. Office for Victims of Crime. www.ojp.usdoj.gov/ovc/

16. OVC Victim Assistants. http://www.ojp.usdoj.gov/ovc/help/links.htm

17. Victims (NCJRS). http://virlib.ncjrs.org/VictimsOfCrime.asp

18. Federal Bureau of Investigation. www.fbi.gov/

Note: Addresses subject to change.

INFORMATION AND REFERRALS ON VICTIMS' RIGHTS AND SERVICES

1. Childhelp USA/Forrester National Child Abuse Hotline. 800-4A-CHILD. www.childhelpusa.org/

2. Family Violence Prevention Fund/Health Resource Center. 415-252-8900 endabuse.org/programs/healthcare/

3. Justice Statistics Clearinghouse. 800-732-3277.

4. Juvenile Justice Clearinghouse. 800-638-8736. www.criminology.fsu.edu/jjclearinghouse/internet%20links.htm

5. Mothers Against Drunk Driving. 800-438-MADD. www.madd.org/home/

6. National Center for Missing and Exploited Children. 800-843-5678. www.missingkids.com/

7. National Domestic Violence Hotline. 800-799-7233; 800/787-3224 for the hearing impaired. www.ndvh.org/

8. National Institute of Justice. 800-851-3420. www.ojp.usdoj.gov/nij/

9. National Resource Center on Domestic Violence. 800-537-2238. http://endabuse.org/programs/healthcare/

10. National Victim Center. 800-FYI-CALL. www.ncvc.org/links/Sl.htm

11. Office for Victims of Crime Resource Center. 800-627-6872. www.ojp.usdoj.gov/ovc/ovcres/welcome.html (a good statistics resource)

12. Rape, Abuse and Incest National Network. 800-656-4673. www.rainn.org/

B

Resource Guide

The following organizations are sources of information on violence in the workplace:

American Management Association
135 West 50th Street
New York, NY 10020-1201
212-586-8100
www.amanet.org/index.htm

American Psychological Association
750 First Street, NE, Washington, DC 20002-4242
(800) 374-2721
(202) 336-5500
www.apa.org/

American Society for Industrial Security
O.P. Norton Information Resource Center
1625 Prince Street
Alexandria, Virginia 22314
703-519-6200
http://www.asisonline.org/

Center on National Labor Policy
5211 Port Royal Road, Suite 103
North Springfield, VA 22151
703-321-9180

Employee Benefit Research Institute
1100 13th St. NW, Suite 878
Washington, DC 20005
(202) 659-0670
www.ebri.org/

National Mental Health Information Center
P.O. Box 42557
Washington, DC 20015
1-800-789-2647
www.mentalhealth.samhsa.gov/.asp

International Foundation of Employee Benefit Plans
P.O. Box 69
Brookfield, WI 53008
www.ifebp.org/

International Public Management Association for the Human Resources
1617 Duke Street
Arlington, VA 22314
703-549-7100
www.ipma-hr.org/

National Crime Prevention Council
2345 Crystal Drive, Suite 500
Arlington, VA 22202-4801
Tel: 202-466-6272
www.ncpc.org/

National Crime Prevention Institute
134 Burhans Hall
Shelby Campus
University of Louisville
Louisville, KY 40292
800-334-8635
http://louisville.edu/a-s/ja/icsps/

National Institute for Mental Health
5600 Fishers Lane
Rockville, MD 20857
301-443-4513
www.nimh.nih.gov/

National Institute for Occupational Safety & Health (NIOSH) Centers
for Disease Control
1600 Clifton Rd
Atlanta, GA 30333, USA
404-639-3311
www.cdc.gov/niosh/homepage.html

National Research Council
Panel on the Understanding and Control of Violent Behavior
500 Fifth St. N.W.,
Washington, DC 20001
202-334-2000
www.nas.edu/nrc/

National Safety Management Society
P.O. Box 4460
Walnut Creek CA 94596-0460
800-321-2910
www.nsms.us/

Index

A

abductions, 126–127
abuse
  animal abuse, 77, 125
  child abuse (*See* child abuse and neglect)
  definitions, 91–92
  elder abuse (*See* elder abuse and neglect)
  partner abuse, 73, 88 (*See also* intimate partner
    violence (IPV))
  substance abuse (*See* substance abuse)
*Ackridge v. Philadelphia Department of Human
    Resource*, 167
acquired immune deficiency syndrome
    (AIDS), 102
acquisitiveness, in Hentig's victim typology, 40
active precipitation, 45
active victims, 45
advocacy groups, 291–297
age (*See also* child abuse and neglect; elder
    abuse and neglect)
  carjackings, 115
  as a demographic, 3
  fear of crime, 4
  Hentig's victim typology, 40
  home invasion robbery, 112, 115
  homicides, 10
  intimate violence, 58
  school violence, 174
  victims of serial killers, 124–125
aggression, early childhood, 186
agroterrorism, 233
AIDS (acquired immune deficiency
    syndrome), 102
Aimee's Law, 289
alcohol abuse (*See* substance abuse)

ALF (Animal Liberation Front), 232, 240
Al-Qaeda, 234, 235
American Civil Liberties Union, 218
Americans with Disabilities Act (ADA), 167
anger, school violence and, 175
animal abuse, 77, 125
Animal Liberation Front (ALF), 232, 240
anonymous victimization, 118
anorexia, 72
anthrax, 244
anti-abortionists, as domestic terrorists, 230
anti-stalking legislation (*See* legal issues, stalking)
Antiterrorism and Effective Death Penalty Act
    of 1996, 235
Arm of the Lord, 128
Armstrong, Joie, 2–3
arrest policies, 79
arson, 144
Aryan Brotherhood, 128
assault, 4 (*See also* rape and sexual assault)
ATM crime, 263, 267
Attention Deficit Hyperactivity Disorder
    (ADHD), 16, 17, 185, 186, 191
Automated Fingerprint Identification System, 261
auto theft, 15

B

Bailey, Christopher, 87
Baker v. United States, 67
Bakker, Jim, 43
Baron, Anthony, 145
Bartley-Fox law, 218
battered women's syndrome, 37
battering (*See* intimate partner violence (IPV))
behaviors (*See* traits and behaviors)

Beirut bombing, 243
Bianchi, Kenneth, 125, 126
bias and hate crimes
   domestic terrorists and, 128
   hate groups, 127
   legislation, 131
   passive precipitation and, 46
   terrorist groups and, 228
Bin Laden, Osama, 234, 245
biological and chemical weapons, 243–244
Black, Laura, 61
black nationalists, 230
blaming the victim, 70
Boyer, Amy Lynn, 66
Brady Act, 260
broken windows theory, 49
brown nationalists, 230
Bryant v. Livigni, 162
BTK killer (See Rader, Dennis)
bullying, 157, 159, 189–190, 191
bump and rob, 116–117
Bundy, Ted, 125
Buono, Anthony, 125
Bureau of Justice Statistics, 4
burglary, prevalence of, 5 (See also robbery)
Bush, George W., 243, 244, 246
business risk predictors, 156
Buss, David, 118

C

California anti-stalking laws, 60, 65
California Corporate Criminal Liability Act, 163
California Penal Code, §, 646, 9, 65
Campus Sex Crimes Prevention Act, 289
Carjacking, 115–117
celebrities, stalking and, 59, 61
celebrity acquittals, 209
Centers for Disease Control and Prevention, 136
character risks, youth deviance and, 184
chat rooms, 52, 53
chemical dependency (See substance abuse)
child abuse and neglect, 91–96
Child Abuse Prevention and Enforcement
      Act, 289
children and youth
child abuse and neglect, 91
      gender, 71
      health issues, 79
      homicide, 11, 93

McMartin case, 210–213
      race, 96
      reporting, 94
      victims, 92–93
   child sex offenders, 126
   cyberspace issues, 51
Christian Identity, 229
Church Arson Prevention Act (1996), 131
civil justice system, 294–295
Civil Rights Act of 1964, 163
clearance rates, 9
Clinton, Bill, 131
closed-circuit television (CCTV), 261, 262, 296
coercive parenting style, 186
collateral damage, 240
color of law, 207
Columbine High School, 175
Commonwealth v. Berkowitz, 101
community policing, 270, 294
community violence, 24–26, 187, 254–257
compensation (See restorative justice)
computer technology, 51, 245
constitutional issues, 65
Convenience Store Act, 268
corporate downsizing, 142
correction system, 86
costs of victimization, 12, 13, 16, 220
counterculture groups, 188 (See also bias
      and hate crimes)
court orders, 64, 66
courtship violence (See intimate partner
      violence (IPV))
"coyotes", 41
crime control legislation, 216–217
crime data
   community influences, 24–26
   determination of crime rates, formula, 6
   explaining violence
      Gilmore, Gary, 15
      Wuornos, Aileen, 14
   familial influences, 21–24
   individual influences, 15–21
   influences of violence, 13
   The National Crime Victimization Survey
         (NCVS), 9–10
   percentage of reasons for not reporting victim-
         izations to the police, by type of crime, 7–8
   sources of data on victimization, 5–10
   statistics on violent crime, 10–12

understanding violence, 12–15
The Uniform Crime Reports (UCR), 5–9
Violent Criminal Apprehension Program
(VICAP), 10–12
Wuornos, Aileen(explaining violence), 14
crime prevention through environmental design
(CPTED), 266–271
crime rates, determination of, 6
criminal justice system
Brandon Hein, 218–219
corrections, 221–223
crime legislation, 216–221
deliberate victimization, 204
Donald Scott, 206
inadvertent, 186, 204
McMartin Ritual Abuse Cases: Guilt
by Association, 210–213
police, 204–208
The Rape of Larry, 223
What Did They Really See? Problems of
Eyewitness Identification: The Case
of Steve Titus, 214
zero tolerance, 196–197
criminology, 1–2
Cruz, Rolando, 215
cultural influences, school violence, 188
cultural trappings theory, 44–45
cyber crime, 51–52, 60
cyber terrorism, 51, 241, 245–246
cycle of violence, 17, 74–75, 94

D

Dahmer, Jeffrey, 125
dark figure of crime, 5–6, 9
Data sources (*See* National Crime
Victimization Survey (NCVS);
Uniform Crime Reports (UCR))
date rape and violence, 98–102
Davis, Richard Allen, 221–222
Death Penalty Information Center (DPIC), 251
defensible space theory, 49, 264–266
deliberate victimization, 204
demographics, definition of, 5
Department of Homeland Security
(DHS), 246–247
Department of Justice (DOJ), 208
depression, in Hentig's victim typology, 40
Dignity of Victims Everywhere (DOVE)
program, 292

dirty bombs, 245
Doe v. First Gibraltar Bank, 160
Doe v. System Parking, Inc, 296
domestic terrorism (*See* intimate
partnerviolence (IPV))
drive-by shootings, 123
"driving while black", 218
drug abuse (*See* substance abuse)
Duffy v. City of Oceanside, 160
dull normals, in Hentig's victim
typology, 42

E

early childhood aggression, 186
early childhood learning, 73
Earth Liberation Front (ELF), 232–234
economic issues
cost of incarceration, 220
economic abuse, 73
financial abuse, 88
school violence and income level, 176
unemployment, 26, 69, 74, 179
eco-terrorism, 230
elder abuse and neglect, 3, 4, 14, 87–91
electronic communication, 51–52, 60
electronic surveillance devices, 256, 261
ELF (Earth Liberation Front), 232–233
e-mail, 60, 67
embassy bombing, 241
*Emergency Response to Terrorism Self-Study
Manual,* 241
emotional abuse, 73, 88
employee assistance plans (EAPs), 138, 167
employment/unemployment (*See also*
economic issues; workplace violence
and harassment)
environment
crime prevention through environmental
design, 266–267
environmental criminology,
264, 271
environmental toxicity, 185
terrorism and, 239–240
Equal Employment
Opportunity Commission
(EEOC), 163
erotomania, 61
excessive force, 203
eyewitness misidentification, 213

F

false victimization syndrome, 61–62
family relationships, 186, 254, 255
Fatal Attraction, 59
Fear of crime and violence, 3–4, 175, 176,
    177, 193, 253
    fear-victimization paradox, 4
    terrorism and, 3, 227, 228, 229, 233–235
fear–victimization paradox, 4, 5
Federal Bureau of Investigation (FBI), 5, 52,
    192, 229
federal code, stalking, 67
Federal Hate Crime Statistics Act (1990), 127
Federal Interstate Stalking and Prevention
    Act of 1996, 87
Federal Violent Crime Control and Law
    Enforcement Act (1994), 86–87
felony murder, 123, 218
Ferrell, Rod, 186
focused governmental agency, 292
focused independent nonprofit groups, 291
foreseeability, 159, 160
Frances, Connie, 297
fraud doctrine, 161
freeway murder, 123
Furrow, Buford, 127

G

Gacy, John Wayne, 125
gamma hydroxybutyric acid (GHB), 99
gang and youth violence
    community policing and, 270
    as domestic terrorism, 228–229
    fear of, 3
    homicide and, 118, 119
    legislation and, 287–288
    robbery and, 112
    routine activities theory and, 49
    school violence and, 175, 176, 177, 186, 191, 193
Ganor, Boaz, 227
gender
    bias crimes, 127
    carjacking, 115–116
    chat rooms and teenage girls, 53
    child abuse, 71, 91
    child murder, 71
    as a demographic, 31
    fear of crime, 3
    in Hentig's victim typology, 40

home invasion robbery, 112
homicides, 11
    intimate partner violence (IPV), 69–72
    intimate violence, 59
    rape and sexual violence, 96–97, 101
    school violence, 175, 177, 179, 184
    sexual harassment, 163
    stalking, 59–64
    victims of serial killers, 126
    workplace violence, 136, 137, 141–144
genocide, 240
GHB (gamma hydroxybutyric acid), 99
"going postal", 141
Goldman, Ronald, 43, 61
*Gonzales v. Southwest Security and Protection
    Agency, Inc*, 162
Gonzalez, Jose, Jr, 216
Gott, Patrick, 118
Greenfield v. Spectrum Investment Corp, 162
Green, Kevin Lee, 214–215
Griffin, Michael, 144
guardianship, 165, 272
gun control (*See* weapons)
Gun-Free Schools Act of 1994, 196–197
Gunn, David, 144

H

handguns (*See* weapons)
Hansen, Robert, 124
harassment, 52, 62 (*See also* workplace violence
    and harassment)
Harding, Richard, 184
Hate Crimes Prevention Act (1999), 131
hate crimes (*See* bias and hate crimes)
Hate Crimes Sentencing Enhancement
    Act (1999), 131
health issues
    access to health care, 255
    child abuse, 79
    cost of victimization, 32
    intimate partner abuse (IPV) and, 79
        rape and sexual violence, 102, 103
    victims of abuse and, 71–72
    violence in health care settings, 140, 144
hedonistic killers, 127
Hein, Brandon, 218–219
Hernandez, Alejandro, 215
Hern, Warren, 144
high-crime areas (*See* spatial relations)

Higher Education Act (HEA) of 1965, 284–285
Hillside Stranglers, 125
hitchhiking, 118
HIV (human immunodeficiency virus),
        72, 102–103
Holloway, Natalee, 50
home invasion robbery, 112–115
homeland security, 246–247
homelessness, 71, 290–291
homicide
    A Day Shooting, 119
    bias and hate crimes, 127–131
        child abuse and neglect, 93
    intimate partner violence (IPV) and, 69
    intimate violence, 71
    justifiable, 117
    prevalence, 3
    primary and secondary, 118
    race/ethnicity, 11
    recovery of losses, 278
    school violence, 183
    serial killers, 124–127
    spontaneous murders, 118–123
    spousal, 71
    in the workplace, 136, 137, 140
hostile work environment, 164
housing projects, 266
human immunodeficiency virus (HIV),
        72, 102–103

I

immigrants, in Hentig's victim typology, 41
inadvertent injustice, 204
incarceration (*See* prisons)
injustice (*See* criminal justice system)
inmate victimization, 223
Innocent Images National Initiative, 51
insurance, 7, 35, 221
Interface Children and Family Services
        Program, 292–293
international terrorism (*See* terrorism)
Internet, 51–52, 60
Interpersonal violence, 1
Interstate Domestic Violence Law, 87
Interstate Stalking Punishment and Protection
        Act of 1996, 87, 285
intimate partner violence (IPV)
    cycle of violence, 74–75
    factors and methods, 73–76

legal issues, 78–86
    Mary's Story, 75
    risk factors, 77–78
    victim retaliation, 76
    victims, 68–71
    warning signs of abusers, 76–78
    in the workplace, 142–143
intimate violence (*See* child abuse and neglect;
        elder abuse and neglect; intimate partner
        violence (IPV); rape and sexual violence;
        stalking)
Israel, terrorism and, 233

J

Jack the Ripper, 124
Jackson, Michael, 209
Jacobs, Sonia, 215
Jacobs v. Singletary, 215
Janjaweed, 207–237
Jemaah Islamiya (JI), 236
Jennifer's Law, 289
Jessica Lunsford Act, 290
jihad movement, 234–235
job stress, 137, 143, 207
Jordan, James, 124
Jordan, Michael, 124
juror misconduct, 215–216
justice (*See* criminal justice system)

K

Kanka, Megan, 286
Kansas Sexual Predator Act, 287
Kansas v. Hendricks, 287
Kemper, Edmund, 125
Kennedy, Anthony M., 216
ketamine (ketamine
        hydrochloride), 99
Killen, Edgar Ray, 209
Kim Jong-il, 237
King, Martin Luther, Jr, 203
King, Rodney, 205
Kinkel, Kip, 19
Klaas, Polly, 221
Kristen's Act, 289–290
Ku Klux Klan, 128

L

Laird v. E-Z Mart, 296
Lao-tzu, 257

law enforcement
  date rape cases, 98–99
  injustices, 204–208
  police officers as targets of workplace
      violence, 141
  school violence, 193
  stalking, 62, 64–66
lead poisoning, 185
legal issues
  intimate partner violence (IPV), 68–76
  legal abuse, 74
  legal duty, 160
  liability, 160–166, 268, 295–298
  nursing home negligence, 89–90
  rape and sexual violence, 96–102
  respondeat superior doctrine, 161
  sexual harassment, 163–169
  stalking, 59–60, 64–66
  teachers and school violence, 183–184
  victim's rights, 275–284, 288–291
  workplace violence, 159–163, 166, 168
legal issues (*See also* criminal justice system;
      individual legal cases)
  battered women's syndrome, 37–38
  bias and hate crimes, 129–130
  bullying, 157–159
  carjacking, 115
  child abuse and neglect, 91–93
  civil litigation, 297
  combating terrorism, 246–247
  cyberstalking, 60
  fraud doctrine, 161
  HIV/AIDS transmission, 102–103
Letterman, David, 61
liability (*See* legal issues)
lighting, 261
London bombings, 240–241, 242, 247
loneliness, in cvictim typology, 42
Long-Term Care Ombudsman programs, 90
Lopez v. Crouse, 160
love obsession, 61
Lunsford, Jessica, 290
Lyons v. Penn Hill School District, 198

M

McMartin case, 210–212
McVeigh, Timothy, 228, 229
magnetic resonance imaging (MRI), 18
mandatory arrest, 79

mandatory minimum sentences, 217
MAOA gene, 18
marital rape, 97–98
Mary M. v. City of Los Angeles, 161
media influence, 3–4, 188–189
mediation (*See* restorative justice)
medical issues (*See* health issues)
Megan's Law, 286
Mendelshon's typology, 42–43
mental health issues (*See also* post-traumatic
      stress disorder (PTSD))
  battered women's syndrome, 37
  correctional system, 222
  costs of victimization, 32, 35
  in Hentig's victim typology, 41
  psychological abuse, 73
  rape trauma syndrome, 38
  stalking, 61, 67–68
  victim precipitation, 46
  victims of abuse, 71–72, 94
  workplace violence, 136, 141
mission-oriented killers, 127
monoamine oxidase A (MAOA) gene, 18
motives, 61–62, 111 (*See also* traits
    and behaviors)
MS-13 street gang, 231
Muhammad, Dennis, 196
multiagency cooperation, 11

N

National Crime Victimization Survey (NCVS),
    5–9, 97
National Institute of Education, 176
National Organization for Victim
    Assistance, 291
National School Safety Center, 194–195
National Victim Center (NVC), 278, 286
neglect, active and passive, 88, 89 (*See also*
    child abuse and neglect; elder abuse
    and neglect)
negligence, 89–90, 162
Neo-Nazis, 128
Newman, Oscar, 49
Norman, Jonathan, 60
Northern Ireland, terrorism and, 239
North Korea, 237
nuclear or radiological terrorism, 244–245
nursing home negligence, 89–90
Nursing Home Reform Act, 91

O

obsession, 61, 144, 146
obsessiveness, intimate partner abuse (IPV)
    and, 77
Office for Victims of Crimes, 285–286
Oklahoma City bombing, 128, 229
ombudsmen, 91
Open Campus Police Logs Act of 1995, 284
Oppositional Defiant Disorder (ODD), 185
Order, 103

P

pagers, stalking and, 60
Palestine, terrorism and, 235
panic buttons, 261
parenting, 18, 26, 256
Parker, Gerald, 215
passive precipitation, 46
passive victims, 46–47
Patriot Act (See USA Patriot Act)
Patterns of Global Terrorism, 235
Payne v. Tennessee, 285
pedophiles, 126, 286–287
peer mediation, 256
penalty enhancements, 287
People v. Grago, 276
People v. Humphrey, 37
personal factors victim theory, 40
physical abuse, 69, 88
physical environment (See spatial relations)
police misconduct provision, 207–208
police (See law enforcement)
politics, terrorism and, 239
pornography, 51, 53
positron emission tomography (PET), 20
Posse Comitatus, 128
postal service workers, 127, 139, 141
post-traumatic stress disorder (PTSD),
    32, 35, 37, 39, 72
poverty (See socioeconomic issues)
power-oriented killers, 127
preferred arrest, 79
premises liability, 159–160, 268, 297
prevention and control
    proactive
        community violence prevention
            strategies, 254–257
        opportunity reduction strategies, 264–271
        personal defense measures, 257–260
        prevention detention, 286–287
        security measures, 260–264 (See also security)
    reactive
        advocacy groups, 291–294
        civil justice system, 294–295
        compensation programs, 275–283
        legislation, 283–286
        restorative responses, 271–275 (See also
            restorative justice)
prisons, 207, 217, 222
proactive response to crime (See prevention
    and control, proactive)
probable cause, 64
Profile of a Domestic Terrorism Group:
    Christian Identity, 229
Profile of a Domestic Terrorist: Eric Rudolph, 230
    Profile of an International Terrorist Group:
        Jemaah Islamiya (JI), 236
    suicide bombing, 242
        Profile of an International Terrorist: Osama
            bin Laden, 234
    Terrorism Risk Insurance Act of 2002, 239
    USA Patriot Act, 238, 247–248
profiles, 144–145, 183, 193, 209, 218
Project Bioshield Act, 244
property identification, 261
property offenses, 40, 262
prostitution, 14, 25, 44, 47, 73, 118, 232
protection orders, 64, 79
protective custody, 294
pseudomasochism, 44
psychological consequences (See mental
    health issues)
PTSD (post-traumatic stress disorder), 32, 35,
    37, 39, 72
public housing, 264–265

Q

quid pro quo sexual harassment, 164

R

race/ethnicity
    bias crimes, 128
    carjacking, 116–117
    child abuse and neglect, 93
    domestic terrorism, 229
    fear of crime, 3–4
    in Hentig's victim typology, 41

home invasion robbery, 114
homicides, 11
intimate partner violence (IPV), 69, 71
justice system, 209–210, 215–216
passive precipitation, 46
prevalence of violence, 3
racial profiling, 218
school violence, 174, 175, 184
spousal homicide, 71
victimization in general, 10
war on drugs, 217–218
workplace violence, 135
Rader, Dennis, 60, 62, 125–126
rage, 47, 74
random victimization, 130
rape and sexual assault
    consequences of, 75
    cost of victimization, 32
    dating and, 98–102
    definitions of, 96–97
    and intimate violence, 58
    marital, 97–98
    nonreporting of, 10
    prevalence of, 5
    rape trauma syndrome, 38, 102
    school violence and, 176
    victim precipitation and, 45–46
    victims of, 96–97
    and workplace violence, 139
Ray, Margaret M., 59–60
reactive response to crime (See prevention
        and control, reactive)
reasonable force, 258
recidivism, 221, 222
religion, 124, 127–129, 131, 239, 243
Remsburg v. Docusearch, 66, 67
reporting
    child abuse and neglect, 95–96
    dark figure of crime, 5–6, 9
    intimate partner violence (IPV), 70
    rape and sexual violence, 96–97, 98
respondeat superior doctrine, 161
restorative justice, 271–272,
        274–275
restraining orders, 64, 65, 66, 75
ricin, 244
right to privacy, 166–167, 168
risky behavior, 72 (See also victim
        precipitation theory)
road rage, 3, 111, 119

robbery
    carjacking and, 115–117
    crime prevention through environmental
        design (CPTED) and, 266–267
    during home invasions, 112–115
    and intimate violence, 88
    murders during, 118, 120
    prevalence of, 4
    school violence and, 176, 178
    workplace violence and, 136
Rockefeller Law, 217
rohypnol (flunitrazepam), 99
Roosevelt, Franklin, 2
Ross, Michael, 125
routine activities theory, 49
Rudolph, Eric, 230
Ruiz v. Johnson, 222–223
"rule of thumb", 69–70

S

Safe School Study, 176
Schaeffer, Rebecca, 59
Schlisinge, Steve, 111
school violence
    Case of Rod Ferrell, 187
    A Father's Mistake Penalizes Honor
        Student, 197
    prevalence of, 3
    research on, 175–183
    responding to, 193–198
    teachers at risk and, 183–184
    theories of, 184–189
    warning signs of, 189–193
Scott, Donald, 206
screening, 272
secular terrorists, 240
security
    Closed-Circuit Televison and Crime
        Control, 262
    community prevention, 3–4, 256, 260–264
    fortification, 274
    against home invasions, 114
    personnel, 262–264
    policies and procedures, 264
    pretrial and courtroom, 293–294
    protective custody, 294
    routine activities theory, 49–50
    school violence, 193–197
    self-esteem, 255–256
    against terrorism, 247

self-help groups, 291–292
self-mutilation, victims of abuse and, 72
self-protection, 4, 258
Sellin and Wolfgang's typology, 43–44
sentencing issues, 204, 208, 217
September 11 2001, 3, 31, 227, 233, 234, 242
serial killers
    characteristics of, 124–127
    Dennis Rader: The BTK Killer, 125
    sexually transmitted diseases (STDs), 102
    stalking and, 62, 125
    subtypes, 127
    typical victims of, 126–127
Sexually Violent Predator Act, 286–287
sexual offenses
    laws and, 286–287
    sex offenders, 62, 97, 103, 126
    sexual abuse (*See also* rape
        and sexual violence)
        of children, 95–96
        of the elderly, 88
        by intimate partners, 73, 98–99
    sexual assault, carjackings, 117, 127
    sexual harassment in the workplace,
        163–166
sexual orientation, 46–47, 128
shelters, 76, 86
Shoot the Carjacker Law, 117
*Simon & Schuster, Inc. v. New York Crime
    Victims Board*, 277
Simpson, Nicole, 61
Simpson, O. J., 43, 61, 208–209, 295
Sinatra, Frank, 277
Sinatra, Frank, Jr, 277
situational crime prevention, 264, 271
situational victimization, 40
skinheads, 127–128
sniper attacks, 3, 31
socialization, 186, 240
socioeconomic issues, 41, 45–47, 68–71, 78,
    112–115
Son of Sam law, 277
spatial relations
    high-crime areas, 48, 122–123, 257
    location as a demographic, 2, 6
    school violence and, 179, 183, 185–186
    theories of, 48–50, 266–271
special relationship, 160
Spielberg, Steven, 60–61
Splawn v. Lextaj, 296

spontaneous murder, 118–124
spouse abuse (*See* intimate partner
        violence (IPV))
Spunaugle v. State, 216
stalking
    anti-stalking legislation, 64–68
    motives and behaviors, 62
    perpetrators and victims, 61–62
    public cases, 59–64
    third-party liability, 66–67
    through cyber space, 60
    victimization, 67–68
Stanton, Harry Dean, 115
Stayner, Cary, 2
STDs (sexually transmitted diseases), 102
Stewart v. Federated Department Stores, 160
Stone v. Prosser, 198
store robberies, 268
stranger violence and victimization
        (*See* violence)
Street Terrorism, Enforcement, and Prevention
        (STEP) Act (1988), 287–288
stress, 136–137, 238 (*See also* post-traumatic
        stress disorder (PTSD))
structural violence, 44
substance abuse
    correctional system, 221–223
    date rape and violence, 102
    home invasion robbery, 112–115
    homicides, 12, 118, 122–123
    intimate partner abuse (IPV), 73–76
    post-traumatic stress disorder
        (PTSD), 32
    rape and sexual assault, 97
    school violence, 175, 176, 177, 191–192,
        195–196
    victim precipitation, 45–47
    victims of abuse, 71–73
    war on drugs, 217–218
    workplace violence, 145, 154, 166–167
Sudan, 237, 240
suicide
    intimate partner abuse (IPV) and, 76
    school violence and, 174
    self-esteem and, 255–256
    terrorism and, 233, 241, 242–243
    in the workplace, 136
Sunni Islamic extremists, 234
surveillance, 256, 261, 272–273
Sword, 128

T

Tafero, Jesse, 215
Targeted Human Resource Approach
        (THRA), 166–169
targeted murders, 124–127
target hardening, 272
target removal, 272
teachers, and school violence, 177
technology, 51–53 (*See also* cyber crime;
        cyber terrorism)
terrorism
    biological and chemical weapons, 243–244
    combating, 246
    cyber terrorism, 245–246
    domestic, 228–233, 240
    fear of, 3, 230, 237–238, 243–244
    history, 228–236
    Homeland Security, 246–247
    international, 233–236
    methods, 241
    motives, 239–241
    nuclear or radiological, 244–245
    objectives, 237–239
theft, prevalence of, 4
theories
    early
        Hans von Hentig, 40–42
        Mendelsohn, 40, 42–43
        Sellin and Wolfgang, 43–44
    modern
        cultural trappings, 44–45
        electronic technology, 51–53
        spatial relations, 48–50
        victim precipitation, 45–48
third-party lawsuits, 295–296
threat assessment program, 168
three-strikes law, 217–219, 221
Thurman v. City of Torrington, 78
Timmendequas, Jesse, 286
Titus, Steve, 213, 214
tormentors, in Hentig's victim typology, 42
Town of Castle Rock, Colorado v. Gonzales, 66
toxic culture, 188
traits and behaviors, 16, 77, 192–193
        (*See also* profiles)

U

Underwriters Ins. Co. v. Purdie, 161
unemployment (*See* economic issues)

Uniform Crime Reports (UCR), 5–8, 118
USA Patriot Act, 247, 248
U.S. Department of Education, 179, 190
U.S. Department of Justice, 229
U.S. v. Dixon, 64

V

vandalism, 128, 176
van der Kolk, Bessel, 71
vertical prosecution, 79
VICAP (Violent Criminal Apprehension
        Program), 10–11
Victim of Crime Act (VOCA), 276, 293
victim impact statements, 284–286
Victim Information and Notification Everyday
        (VINE) system, 286
victimless crimes, 44
victimology, 31, 39–40
victim precipitation theory, 45–47
Victim's Family Access to Justice Act of 1996, 285
victim's rights, 275–284, 288–291
Victims of Trafficking and Violence
        Protection, 288
victim typologies, 40–42
Victim and Witness Assistance, 283–284
Victim and Witness Protection Act of
        1982, 283
violence
    intimate (*See also* intimate partner violence
            (IPV); stalking)
        child abuse and neglect, 91–95
        date rape and dating violence, 98–102
        elder abuse and neglect, 87–89
        marital rape, 97–98
        rape and sexual assault, 96–97
    stranger violence and victimization
        bias and hate crimes, 127–131
        carjacking, 115–117
        homicide (*See* homicide)
        robbery, 111–115
    structural, 44
Violence Against Women Act (VAWA)
        Reauthorization, 290
Violent Crime Control Act (1994), 285
visionary killers, 127
Volpe, Justin, 206
von Hentig, Hans, 40–42
Vulnerable Elder Rights Protection
        Program, 91

W

war on drugs, 217–218
warrantless arrests, 64
Warren v. State, 98
weapons
    carjackings, 115–116
    gun debate, 257–260
    homicides, 12, 119
    intimate partner violence (IPV), 68, 70
    justice system, 218
    of mass destruction, 243–244
    school violence, 175, 176, 177, 191–192, 195–196
    victims of stalking, 59
    workplace violence, 139, 148
Weinstein, Kathleen, 117
white supremacists, 127–128, 230
Wilson, Mary Ellen, 91
witness protection, 293
workplace violence and harassment
    An Office Romance Gone Crazy, 149–153
    bullying, 157–159
    business risk predictors, 156–157
    categories of, 141–142
    common incidents, 138–139
    employee assistance plans (EAPs), 168
    employer liability, 159–163
    gender, 131, 137, 144, 145
    homicides, 137–140
    nonsexual harassment, 144
    Obsession with Laura, 146–149
    security issues, 159–163
    sexual harassment, 163–166
    sources of, 142–144
    Targeted Human Resource Approach (THRA) to, 166–169
    targets of, 138–139, 141–142
    warning signs, 76, 78, 144–146, 189–193
wrongful conviction, 213–216

X - Y - Z

Youens, Liam, 66
Yunker v. Honeywell, Inc, 162
zero tolerance, 196–198
Zeta-Jones, Catherine, 59